Best Wishes Phic!

Ross Bernstein

12/13/97

Fifty Years · Fifty Heroes

A Celebration of Minnesota Sports

by
Ross Bernstein

*For Sara,
my wife and best friend,
I love you.*

<u>**Fifty Years • Fifty Heroes**</u>
A Celebration of Minnesota Sports
by Ross Bernstein

Self-Published by Ross Bernstein
P.O. Box 5597
Hopkins, MN
55343-0492

Edited by George Rekela

ISBN#: 0-9634871-1-6

Library of Congress Catalog Card Number: 97-94618

Copyright© 1997, by Ross Bernstein. First edition. All rights reserved.
No part of this book may be used or reproduced in any manner whatsoever
without written permission unless properly attributed, except in case of brief quotations,
articles or passages in newspaper, magazine, radio and television reviews.

<u>**Printed by:**</u>
Banta ISG
7000 Washington Ave. South
Eden Prairie, MN 55344-7327
(800) 765-7327

<u>**Distributed by:**</u>
The Bookmen
525 North Third Street
Minneapolis, MN 55401
(612) 341-3333

Photo Credits:
The University of Minnesota: 12, 14, 15, 19, 20, 21, 22 , 23, 24, 26, 27, 30, 31, 36, 37, 38, 39, 40, 43, 52, 64, 65, 66, 67, 70, 71, 78, 82, 84, 85, 88, 89, 90, 92, 96, 97, 98, 99, 106, 107, 108, 109, 114, 116, 122, 123, 124, 125
The Pioneer Press: 8, 11, 25, 33, 35, 46, 50, 53, 56, 57, 58, 59, 63, 69, 74, 75, 77, 83, 86, 87, 100, 101, 104, 105, 110, 111, 112, 113, 117, 118, 120, 121
Minnesota Historical Society: 9, 10, 16, 17, 28, 34, 72
Courtesy of the Minnesota Vikings: 41, 62, 68, 73, 93
Major League Baseball Hall of Fame Library: 32, 47, 48, 49, 51, 60, 61, 76
© Rick A. Kolodziej: 119
Courtesy of the University of Minnesota Duluth: 94, 95
Courtesy of St. John's University: 44, 45
Courtesy of Patty Berg: 29
Courtesy of Canturbury Park: 42
Courtesy of John Beargrease Sled Dog Marathon: 54
Courtesy of Ann Bancroft: 55
Courtesy of Janet Karvonen: 80, 81
Courtesy of Babe Winkelman: 91
Courtesy of Jill Trenary: 91

Acknowledgements

Cover Photos by
Tony Martin Photography

420 North Fifth Street
Suite 498
Minneapolis, MN 55401
(612) 305-0992

Cover Memorabilia Courtesy of Dick Jonckowski, "The Polish Eagle."
Dick is the voice of the Gophers, and coined the now infamous phrase *"This is Golden,*
Gopher Basketball!" With a lifetime of sports radio broadcasting, and color commentating
experience, "Joncko" is a walking encyclopedia of sports information. (He puts Cliff Claven to
shame!) Dick's personal sports memorabilia collection is without question the best in the state.
His "basement museum" is a regular fire hazard, because it is crammed so full of
wonderful Minnesota sports treasures. Thanks, Dick.

A Special Thanks to the Following Individuals Who Helped Make this Project Possible:

Joe Burns
Erik Dyste
Stew Thornley
George Rekela
Randy Johnson
Mike Roslansky
Marc Ryan
Megan Bouche
Karen Zwach
Rich Marshall
Todd Rendahl
Ted Hathaway
H.J. Pieser*

Table of Contents

6.		Foreword by Bud Grant	
8.	1948	George Mikan	The Lakers Dynasty Begins
10.	1949	Jim Pollard	The Lakers Repeat
12.	1950	John Kundla	The Lakers Make it Three in a Row
14.	1951	John Mayasich	The Eveleth High School Hockey Dynasty
16.	1952	Vern Mikkelsen	The Lakers Keep on Rolling
20.	1953	Paul Giel	The Winona Phantom is the Heisman Runner Up
22.	1954	John Mariucci	The Gophers Make a Run at the Title
24.	1955	Chuck Mencel	The Gophers Battle Iowa for the Big Ten Title
26.	1956	Dick Siebert	The Gophers Win the National Championship
28.	1957	Patty Berg	Another Incredible Year for Golf's Grand Dame
32.	1958	Gene Mauch	The Millers Win the Junior World Series
34.	1959	Elgin Baylor	The Lakers Make Another Run at the Title
36.	1960	Sandy Stephens	The Gophers Win the National Championship
38.	1961	Bobby Bell	The Gophers Win the Rose Bowl
40.	1962	Carl Eller	Madness at Camp Randall
44.	1963	John Gagliardi	St. John's University Wins its First National Championship
46.	1964	Harmon Killebrew	Killer Wins the Home Run Crown
48.	1965	Zoilo Versalles	The Twins Make it to the World Series
50.	1966	Jim Kaat	Kitty Wins 25 for the Twins
52.	1967	Lou Nanne	The Stars Hit the Ice
56.	1968	Jim Marshall	The Vikings Win Their First Central Division Crown
58.	1969	Joe Kapp	The Vikings Make it to the Super Bowl
60.	1970	Tony Oliva	The Twins Win the West
62.	1971	Alan Page	The Vikings Star is Named as the League's MVP
64.	1972	Bill Musselman	The Gopher Basketball "Iron Five"
68.	1973	Chuck Foreman	The Vikings Make a Run at the Super Bowl
70.	1974	Herb Brooks	The Gophers Win the National Championship
72.	1975	Fran Tarkenton	The Infamous "Hail Mary"
74.	1976	Ahmad Rashad	The Vikings' Final Run at the Big Prize
76.	1977	Rod Carew	The Incredible Year of Rod Carew
80.	1978	Janet Karvonen	The New York Mills High School Girls Basketball Dynasty
82.	1979	Neal Broten	The Gophers are National Champions
84.	1980	Kevin McHale	The Gophers Make a Run at the NIT Title
86.	1981	Bobby Smith	The North Stars Take a Shot at the Cup
88.	1982	Trent Tucker	The Gophers Win the Big Ten Championship
92.	1983	Bud Grant	The Vikings Coaching Legend Retires
94.	1984	Bill Watson & Tom Kurvers	UMD Plays One of the Greatest Finals in NCAA History
96.	1985	Rickey Foggie	The Gophers Win the Independence Bowl
98.	1986	Darrell Thompson	The Gophers Make it to the Liberty Bowl
100.	1987	Kent Hrbek	The Twins Win the World Series
104.	1988	Tom Kelly	The Twins Break the American League Attendance Record
106.	1989	Doug Woog	The Gophers Take Another Shot at the Title
108.	1990	Willie Burton	The Gophers Make it to the NCAA Elite Eight
10.	1991	Jack Morris	The Worst to First Twins Win the Pennant
12.	1992	Kirby Puckett	The Puck Inks a Deal that Makes Him a Twin for Life
16.	1993	Dave Winfield	Winny Hits Number 3,000
18.	1994	Cris Carter	CC Breaks the NFL's Single Season Receptions Record
20.	1995	Kevin Garnett	The Timberwolves Draft a High School Phenom
22.	1996	Paul Molitor	Molly Comes Home and Hits Number 3,000
24.	1997	Bobby Jackson & Clem Haskins	The Gophers Make it to the NCAA Final Four
26.		Afterword by Kent Hrbek	

Foreword by
BUD GRANT

Without question, Bud Grant is one of the greatest athletes and sports icons to ever play and coach in Minnesota. From his days as a three-sport star at the University of Minnesota -- where he lettered in football, basketball, and baseball -- to his two NBA championship seasons with the Minneapolis Lakers, to becoming an All-Pro NFL and CFL wide receiver, to coaching the Winnipeg Blue Bombers (at the age of 29) to four Grey Cup titles, to his 18 incredible years and four Super Bowls behind the bench with the Vikings. The NFL & CFL Hall of Famer even beat out Gopher Football legends Bronko Nagurski and Bruce Smith to be voted the top Minnesota athlete of the first half century way back in 1950. Modest as ever, Bud is a part of our fabric of life here and would have to be considered the patriarch of sports in our state. Bud is the quintessential All-American hero, and represents everything that is good about sports and athletic competition. Could there be anyone better suited to represent the past 50 years of Minnesota sports than Bud Grant?

When Ross Bernstein first called to interview me for a book he was writing about the history and heroes of Minnesota sports, I was skeptical "How could someone possibly do justice to so many people and events?" I wondered. But he has done a fine job. Anyone who is interested in Minnesota sports will undoubtedly relate to someone or something in it.

I am proud to have played a part in contributing to the wonderful history of Minnesota sports. Having been a member of the Gophers, Lakers, and Vikings, I have a unique perspective on sports in Minnesota. Sports has come a long way in this state. I remember always playing in front of capacity crowds at Williams Arena and Memorial Stadium at the University of Minnesota. But, today there is more competition for people's interests, especially with sports.

Like myself, people enjoy the outdoors here. Whether it's boating, fishing, hunting, camping, golfing, or anything else, outdoor activities are precious to Minnesotans. These people like to participate in sporting activities, but they still find time to watch them, as well. Sports fans here are knowledgeable and they appreciate good competition as well as good sportsmanship.

Fans in places like New York, Philadelphia, and Chicago are fanatics about their local teams, but it's a narrow band of people. Our state has a broader group of fans. Sports in Minnesota encompass more of the mainstream, from casual observers to the die-hards, who will check to see how the Twins, Vikings, Timberwolves, or Gophers did, even if they didn't watch or listen to the game. It doesn't matter if they're from International Falls or Pipestone: people love and follow our teams here because they're interested, and they genuinely care. Traveling throughout Minnesota over the years, it has always amazed me at just how insightful our fans are and how closely they follow Minnesota's athletes and teams. And, they are proud of their accomplishments and exploits.

In addition to following what's happening in Minnesota sports, it's nice to sit back and reflect on what's happened -- to reminisce about our past and allow it to conjure up fond memories. This book will help sports fans do just that. There's something for everyone in it. If you enjoy reading about sports, history, biographies and funny stories, then you'll love this book because it's all in there. This is history, and it's significant that it has finally been captured on paper for all to see.

We have a wonderful sports heritage to be proud of in Minnesota, and it's all brought to life in Fifty Years, Fifty Heroes

Introduction

After spending the last four years of my life living in both Chicago and New York City, it became apparent to me just how special our sports are to us here in Minnesota. Time and time again you'll hear Minnesota's native sons in the national media talking about how they are willing to take a lesser salary in order for them to come home again. The common denominator in almost all of those instances seems to be our amazing quality of life that we have here. I think that as Minnesotans we are proud of our own, and equally as proud of those who represent our entire state on the playing field. Something that I have always liked, is the fact that Minnesota's sports teams are all named after the state, and not after a particular city like most other teams are. I think we all enjoy when our teams do well, and we all whine when they don't. But win or lose, sports is an integral part of the fabric of our lives here.

This book was written with the intention of celebrating our local sports heroes and their teams' achievements. A hero is a very subjective word, and can mean a lot of different things to a lot of different people. In my opinion, sports heroes are people that we looked up to when we were very young. These relationships are fostered early on in life. As a kid growing up, my heroes were guys like Fran Tarkenton, Neal Broten, and Kirby Puckett. But, I think that at a certain age, people become aware of the fact that sports is a business, and at that point they no longer view athletes as heroes, but as businessmen or businesswomen. I think an appropriate analogy would be the fact that my mom loves 1950s music. It brings her back in time and reminds her of special, nostalgic moments in her life. Sports is the same way. I still get goosebumps every time I think about or see the replays of the two Twins' World Championships. I was in college for both of the series, and can still remember running through downtown Minneapolis in the middle of the night with all of my buddies heaving toilet paper rolls everywhere that we had confiscated from nearly every bathroom in our dorm. My hand hurt after both game seven's because of all the high fiving! It was awesome!

With that, I would hope that the readers of this book will be able to reflect back, reminisce, and remember a team, a player or even a special day at the ballpark that he or she spent just hanging out with their dad. Sports is changing, and I think it is important that we not only look to the future with optimism, but remember and celebrate our past, which is full of history and wonderful memories.

It is important to note that this book is not intended to be either the complete history of sports in Minnesota, or is it a list of the state's all-time top 50 athletes. Rather, it is a historical sampling of some of the many annual top sports stories that have happened over the past half century, tied into a home-town or home-grown sports hero. Because some of the years had several top stories to choose from (for instance, in 1976 the Vikings went to the Super Bowl, the Gopher hockey team won the national championship and the Kicks made it to the Soccer Bowl), it was difficult to choose one person tied into one event. Some chapters feature detailed accounts, extensive quotes and game summaries, while others focus on different aspects of that particular event or person. No two chapters are alike, and hopefully that will add to the uniqueness of the book.

I tried to have fun with it and pick interesting people and events to feature. Many times it was like trying to fit a square peg into a round hole, but overall I would like to think that it all worked out. There are hundreds of individuals who have either been born and raised in Minnesota, or have played here on either a professional or collegiate team that definitely could've been featured in this book. Obviously I couldn't accommodate all of those people, so I chose to celebrate a sampling of men and women who have made a difference in the world of Minnesota sports. Also I would like to add that undoubtedly some factual and historical errors may be found in the book. For that I apologize. There is a historical timeline that is featured across the bottom of each page. This too is a sampling of many of the events that happened for that particular year. It consists mainly of University National Champions, Minnesotans who medaled in the Olympics, and Division One All Americans in football, baseball, basketball, and hockey. There were so many things to include here, that I decided to just limit it to those things.

So, sit back, relax, and read a chapter or two. Then, whenever you're watching TV and hear another debate about a stadium or contract dispute, pick it up off of the coffee table, and grab a quick fix of Minnesota sports nostalgia.

GEORGE MIKAN
The Lakers Dynasty Begins

In 1946, a group of Twin Cities businessmen, including the likes of Ben Berger and Morris Chalfen, decided to bring major league professional basketball to Minneapolis. The group acquired the financially-strapped Detroit Gems of the National Basketball League (NBL), and moved them to Minnesota, where they would be renamed the Minneapolis Lakers. They hired John Kundla, who was coaching at St. Thomas, to be their coach and former fight manager and restauranteur Max Winter as their general manager.

The Lakers opened the first four games of their inaugural 1947-48 season with Jim Pollard at center. Pollard, an All-American at Stanford, was persuaded to come to Minneapolis instead of playing as a member of the 1948 Olympic team. Next, the fledgling Lakers made the most important acquisition in team history, a special kid from Chicago.

In the 1940s, professional basketball was struggling to find itself. New leagues came and went. Immediately after World War II, the NBA as we know it today, wasn't even in existence. Meanwhile, a rookie sensation out of DePaul University tore apart the National Basketball League (NBL) with his dominating play. In

1946-47, the Chicago Gears of the NBL, led by six-foot, nine-inch George Mikan, won the league championship. The next season, Gears ownership decided to leave the NBL for what they thought to be greener pastures, and they moved the franchise into the newly-formed League of America. After only a few weeks, the league folded, and the Gears, the reigning NBL champs, were disbanded. Gears' players, including Mikan, became subject to the NBL draft.

In their first season of existence, the Lakers, by virtue of having the worst league record (as the Gems) from the season before, were entitled to the first pick of the litter in the now defunct League. It came to no surprise to anyone when they selected Mikan.

Although the Lakers held Mikan's draft rights, he had several options which included accepting an offer from an independent team, as well as giving up basketball to fulfill his dream of becoming a lawyer. So, Winter flew the young center to Minneapolis with the hopes of hammering out a contract with him. George and the Lakers were unable to come to terms, so he decided to go home to Chicago. But, the young Minneapolis newspaper reporter, Sid Hartman, saved the day by mysteriously getting lost while driving big George to the airport. Mikan missed his flight and was forced to stay one more night. The next day, George sat down with Winter again, this time inking a deal.

Led by Pollard and Mikan, their new big man in the middle, the Lakers won 39 of 50 games to win the Western Division title by 13 games over the runner-up Tri-Cities Hawks. George was named the league MVP finishing the season with 1,195 points, nearly doubling the old league record, while averaging 21.3 points in 56 games. Pollard would also join Mikan at the league all-star game as well.

It was off to the playoffs for the Cinderella Lakers, and they defeated Oshkosh, and then Tri-Cities in the semi-finals to advance to the finals against the Rochester Royals. The Lakers kicked off the NBL Championship Series at the Minneapolis Armory by taking the first two of the best-of-five series against the Royals, despite being kicked out of their home court, in the Minneapolis Auditorium, because of the annual Sportmen's Show.

It was back to New York state for the final three games, and the pesky Royals stayed alive by taking game three, 74-60, despite a 32-point performance from big George.

The Lakers jumped out to an early lead in game four and never looked back. Mikan poured in 27 and Pollard added 19 to lead Minneapolis to a 75-65 victory, and their first-ever professional basketball title. A dynasty had begun.

"We were being judged on whether or not we could make it in the world of professional basketball," said Mikan, "and the excitement of winning that first Laker championship was just fantastic. It put us on the map, because at the time, big cities looked at Minneapolis as a tiny hick town. Well, we 'hicked' them all-right, we became league champions."

From the Windy City to the City of Lakes
George Mikan was born in 1924, in Joliet, Ill. Originally considering a life in the priesthood, George opted instead for college and basketball when he enrolled at DePaul University in Chicago. George worked hard with DePaul coach Ray Meyer on acquiring the skills that would eventually make him the most dominant player in professional basketball.

Meyer worked with Mikan on improving his coordination and quickness with drills that included shadow-boxing, jumping rope, and even ballet. (The Lakers went to Meyer years later for the team's playoff runs as a team consultant and assistant coach.) George developed and refined his soon-to-be famous signature hook shot, which coach Kundla later said looked more like a "shotput." It may not have been pretty, but it was good enough to make him a three-time All-American and become the nation's leading scorer in his junior and senior seasons. He went on to become DePaul's greatest star, also leading the Blue Demons to the 1945 NIT title.

Following his playing days at DePaul, George entered the uncertain world of professional basketball, first with his hometown Chicago Gears, and then with the Minneapolis Lakers, where he would lead his team to six championships in just seven seasons.

In a very "Jordanesque" way, George was the big draw for the new league. Fans came from all over the Upper Midwest to see the giant Laker center. One time, the Lakers were playing New York at Madison Square Garden, and the marquee in front of the Garden advertising that night's game read: "GEO. MIKAN vs. KNICKS." As game time neared, Mikan found himself to be the only player dressed for the game in the locker room. So, finally he said, "Come on, gentlemen. We have a ballgame to play." His teammates replied back: "No, George. You have a ballgame to play. We can't wait to see how you do against the Knicks!"

Revolutionary
Never before in the history of sports had someone come along and made such a lasting impact on professional basketball. The game's first dominant big man, George Mikan, was six-foot-nine when few else were. It was a game that had not yet evolved to account for a man of his sheer size and stature. There were several rules that were changed in basketball as a direct result of Mikan.

While in college, goaltending was essentially legal because it really hadn't ever been an issue up to that point.

TIMELINE								
The Gopher Men's Outdoor Track & Field team wins the NCAA National Championship	Minneapolis' Robert Fitzgerald wins an Olympic Silver medal in the 500M Speed-Skating competition	Gopher Gymnast Jim Peterson wins the NCAA Vault National Championship	Leonard's Ken Bartholomew wins an Olympic Silver medal in the 500M Speed-Skating competition	The states largest small-mouth bass is caught by Minneapolis' John Creighton on Battle Lake: 8 Lbs.	Gopher, Lloyd Lamois, wins the Outdoor track and field Triple Jump National Championship	The Saint Paul Saints, the Double-A farm-team of the Brooklyn Dodgers, win the Junior World Series with star players like Duke Snider, Roy Campanella, Spider Jorgenson, Eric Tipton, and Pat McGlothin.	Legendary Basketball coach John Wooden agrees in principle to accept the Gopher's head coaching position. But, due to a snowstorm the Gophers couldn't get through to Wooden over the phone lines. When no call came, the Wizard of Westwood went ahead and accepted the UCLA Bruins offer.

"We would set up a zone defense that had four men around the key and I guarded the basket," Mikan said. "When the other team took a shot, I'd just go up and tap it out." The pro game was no exception. George did most of his damage in the lane, which was only six feet wide. This allowed him to set up right in the low post right next to the basket, making him virtually impossible to stop. So, in 1951, the league doubled the width of the foul lane to 12 feet. This move was aimed at big men in general, but Mikan in particular. There was even talk after that of raising the basket, for fear that big George would completely ruin the game.

Opposing teams soon found out that the best way to beat Mikan and the Lakers was to simply try to keep the ball away from him. In 1950, the Fort Wayne Pistons refused to shoot the ball and dared not give up their possession, ultimately just sitting there and stalling out an unbelievable 19-18 victory. That was the lowest scoring game in NBA history and ultimately resulted in the creation of the 24-second clock. (Although it would be another four years until the 24-second shot-clock was implemented by the NBA. When it did happen, Winter reportedly said in disgust, "The 24-second clock discriminates against Mikan. It's like baseball legislating against Babe Ruth.")

On September 24, 1954, Mikan announced his plans to open his own law practice and retire as an active NBA player. Winter, wanting to focus his attention on landing an NFL franchise for Minnesota, sold his stock to George and announced that Mikan would succeed him as the team's general manager. He attempted a comeback in 1956, but struggled, eventually becoming team coach in 1957-58. But with a 9-30 record, coach Mikan once again left the game he loved.

He did return to basketball again in the next decade. When the American Basketball Association was formed in 1967, George became the first commissioner. With their trademark red, white, and blue ball, the new rebel league distinguished itself from the mighty, but conservative, NBA. Mikan was influential in creating many of the innovations that are commonplace in the game today such as the three-point shot as well as non-basketball halftime and on-court entertainment for the fans. When the ABA moved its headquarters to New York City in 1969, Mikan resigned.

Although Chamberlin, Russell, and Abdul-Jabbar would follow him, Mikan was the NBA's first truly dominant pivot man and the first big man capable of carrying his entire team. In 1950, Mikan was named the greatest basketball player for the first half of the 20th century; 46 years later, as part of the NBA's 50th anniversary celebration, George was named one of the 50 best players in league history. In 1959, he was a charter member of the Basketball Hall of Fame.

A Laker from 1948-54, and again from 1955-56, his statistics were incredible. Mikan became the first player in history to score 10,000 points, ultimately finishing with 11,764. A perennial seven-time all-star, four times he led the league in scoring. Amazingly, George missed only two games in his career with Minneapolis. He was the Lakers leading scorer 348 out of the possible 458 regular-season games that he played in, finishing with career averages of 22.9 points scoring and 13.4 rebounds per game.

He was unstoppable. They couldn't stop him with shot-clocks, wider lanes, double teams, or anything else. He was, in a word, awesome. There was one team that did a pretty good number on old George though. One time during a series in Syracuse, it was revealed in an interview that George was allergic to smoke. That next night at the game, nearly every Syracuse fan came in smoking a cigar. But even that didn't stop big George.

Who was your hero when you were growing up?
"Babe Ruth. I got to meet him when I was 10 years old, after winning the Will County Marble Championship. The reward for winning was tickets to a White Sox game against the Yankees. After the game I got to meet him and he gave me an autographed ball."

What did it mean to be a Laker:
"We played the Gophers when I was at DePaul in 1945 during the winter time, and I thought it was Siberia in Minneapolis. So, I didn't want to come here at first, but when I got up here the people of Minnesota received the Lakers with open arms. Living in Chicago, I didn't even know my neighbors, and out here I learned quick that this was a great place to raise a family. So it meant a great deal to me to be a Laker."

Laker tombstone? "Well, I would want to be remembered as Mr. Basketball. I earned that honor."

Where are they now? George and his wife live in the Twin Cities. They have six children and 12 grandchildren. He has retired from his law practice, as well as his Travel agency and is currently promoting his new book that he co-wrote with Joe Oberle called, "Unstoppable." George also played an influential role in landing the expansion Timberwolves, when he was appointed by then Governor Perpich to chair the committee that would bring pro ball back to Minnesota.

Tributes
"He was the greatest competitor and team player I ever had. He made the Minneapolis Lakers, and made this town a major-league city. I remember Wilt Chamberlain and Bill Russell telling George that he was their idol growing up, and the two said that he was partially responsible for much of their success in the NBA. He brought big league basketball to Minneapolis, and did so much for Minnesota. He is Mr. Basketball, and I owe all my success to him. He is the greatest." **-- John Kundla**

"He was in a class by himself. He never hazed the rookies, and when he went out for dinner and a movie, he invited everybody along. There was never any sign of him being a superstar around us. He would be on our backs something fierce when he needed to be, and he had an unbelievable faith in his ability to get the job done. He instilled an attitude in all of us that even if we were down, we weren't going to get beat. and that we could always win the game. He was a great player and is a great person." **-- Vern Mikkelsen**

"In my lifetime I have only seen two centers who could just take charge of a game, who could put so much fear in other players that they stayed away from him in the middle. One was Bill Russell, the other, and he was even more dominant, was George Mikan. Once he stationed himself under the basket, he was tough to push out. For rival players it must have been like trying to move the Statue of Liberty." **-- Jim Pollard**

"He was the greatest competitor that I ever played with in any sport. Although he was no gazelle, he could run the floor for a big man. The tougher the game, the more he wanted the ball." **-- Bud Grant**

"You had to be alive during Mikan's day to realize what a phenomenon he was. He was the big man of his era with remarkable tenacity and strength. He had the ability to pursue his own rebounds and no one could keep him off the boards." **-- Slater Martin**

"Pro basketball was ruled by George Mikan, at six-nine and with only a six-foot lane, he determined how the game was played. If you were going to win anything, you had to overcome Mikan. **-- Red Auerbach**

"George Mikan is the greatest all-around basketball player who ever lived as well as the greatest gate attraction. He's the Ruth, the Dempsey, the Hagen, and the Tilden of basketball." **-- Joe Lapchick**

| Gopher tackle Leo Nomellini is named to the All-American football team | Gopher center Jim McIntyre is named to the All-American Basketball team |

JIM POLLARD
The Lakers Repeat

In only their second year of existence, the Lakers began the 1948-49 season as reigning champions. They had won their first National Basketball League (NBL) title in the 1947-48 season, and, it would also be their last. Another professional basketball league had formed, known as The Basketball Association of America (BAA), and the Lakers had decided to break ranks and join the new league.

Led by their two star players, forward Jim Pollard and center George Mikan, the Lakers would kick off the BAA season in Baltimore. Led by guard Herm Schaefer with 23 points, the Lakers beat the Bullets, 84-72. They continued to roll, even on setting a single-game scoring mark when they defeated the Providence Steamrollers, 117-89.

Some of the drama that season would come from a scoring race that had developed between Mikan and Philadelphia's Joe Fulks. First George poured in 48 points during a game to break the league record for points in a game. Fulks then answered the big man's record by doing him 15-points better, shattering George's new record when he scored an unbelievable 63 just a few nights later. The two battled all season long, with Mikan scoring 40-plus points seven times throughout the season, and twice topping 50. He would go on to win the scoring crown with a 28.3 points per game average.

"The Greatest Show on Earth"
One of the highlights of the season for the Lakers was the annual series with the Harlem Globetrotters. Publicists ballyhooed it as the "Greatest Show on Earth." The Trotters had been feeling the pressure of basketball fans and needed to prove to the world that they were not only the most entertaining team in the game, but also the best. So, Laker general manager Max Winter and Trotters owner Abe Saperstein set up the series of games that proved to be a perennial fan favorite.

The first game was held at the Chicago Stadium. The Lakers played well despite the fact that they were without both Pollard and Swede Carlson, who were sidelined due to injuries. Behind the great ball-handling skills of Goose Tatum, "Sweetwater" Clifton, and Marques Haynes, who was regarded as the best dribbler in the world, the Globetrotters and their crowd-pleasing antics downed Minneapolis by 49-45.

For the rematch two-weeks later, a record 10,000-plus fans poured into the Minneapolis Auditorium. The highlight of the game came when the Lakers' Don Forman put on a crowd-pleasing dribbling act of his own. With Pollard and Carlson back, the Lakers easily beat the Trotters, 68-53.

At season's end, with a 44-16 record, Minneapolis would finish one game behind the Rochester Royals, good for second place in the Western Division. In March, the playoffs began for the defending champs and their first opponent would be Chicago in a best-of-three series. The Lakers rolled over the Stags, as big George hit for 75 points in the two-game sweep.

In the next round, Minneapolis would face the team they eliminated for the championship the year before, the Rochester Royals, in another best-of-three series. This time around, the Royals had their star center, Arnie Risen, who was injured during the finals of 1948.

Game one was held in Rochester. Despite building a 17-point lead, the Royals would come back and go ahead of the Lakers with less than a minute to go. With only 18 seconds on the clock, Tony Jaros nailed a jumper to tie it up. Rochester rallied, but the Lakers won it on the charity stripe, as Arnie Ferrin hit a free throw with only six seconds left, giving Minneapolis the 80-79 win. Mikan led the way with 32 for the defending champs.

Back at the St. Paul Auditorium, for game two, it was do-or-die for Rochester. The Royals were up by three after the third, but Mikan and Pollard were dominating in the inside, holding them scoreless from the field in the fourth. They went on to an easy 67-55 victory to win the West. The Lakers advanced to the league finals.

The Lakers faced the winners of the Eastern Division, the Washington Capitols, for the right to be named Basketball Association of America champions. The Capitols, who were led by legendary coach Red Auerbach, had a stellar six-foot-nine center, Bones McKinney, and a superb back-court which consisted of Bob Feerick and Fred Scolari.

Game one of the best-of-seven series came down to the wire as Carlson iced the victory for the Lakers by sinking a pair of free-throws with less than a minute to go. Big George led the way again, with 47, as the Lakers took the opener, 88-84. Minneapolis went on to take game two and then game three as well, behind the stellar play of Pollard and Mikan.

The Lakers won games two and three back in Washington, threatening a series sweep. However, the Caps fought back, winning game four by 83-71. Amazingly, despite suffering a broken hand in the first quarter, Mikan led Minneapolis with 27 points.

Game five was a real spectacle. Big George showed up to the contest wearing a big cast on his arm. The Caps took advantage of the big man's injury-caused limitations, and, despite Pollard picking up the slack, Washington took game five 74-65.

Dejected and concerned about Mikan, the Lakers went into game six at the St. Paul Auditorium with hopes of pulling off a miracle. But big George didn't concern himself with the fuss about his bulky arm cast. He played masterfully, despite being hacked at by the Caps throughout the game. "I can remember playing with my broken arm held up in the air during that game, and on one play in particular, the Washington players were going for my arm and not the ball - which was in my other hand!" Mikan and Pollard had done it again, rolling to an easy 77-56 victory, and their second straight title. This time they would be Basketball Association of America champions. For the season, Mikan averaged an incredible 28.3 points per game, while Pollard added nearly 15 as well.

There were still two major leagues battling for existence in the world of professional basketball, the NBL and the BAA. With both leagues struggling to make ends meet, a merger was agreed to for the next season. Finally, there would be one dominant league, and it was worthy of a new name, the National Basketball Association (NBA).

Problems soon occurred for the new 17-team league, and like its predecessors before, the NBA too would go through growing pains. Divisional alignment and playoff scenarios didn't always work out due to an odd

number of teams. Many fans found the entire mess confusing and opted to watch the college game instead. That year City College of New York went on to win both the NIT and NCAA tournaments, giving the fans even more reason to watch the college boys.

Through all this though, Minnesota still couldn't get enough of their new team, and they continued to support John Kundla's Lakers. The dynasty was well under way at this point and that summer, an already dominating team, got a whole lot better. Two new additions to the Minneapolis roster ensured success in the team's future for a long time to come. They were Slater Martin, an All-American guard out of the University of Texas, and a six-foot-seven center from Askov Minn., who led Hamline University to the NAIA national championship. His name was Vern Mikkelsen. The deck had been stacked for more NBA championships.

The Kangaroo Kid
The Lakers storied tradition begins with the team's first star center, Jim Pollard. (Remember, the Lakers didn't acquire Mikan until after the first few games of their inaugural season in 1947-48.) Pollard will always be remembered for the spring in his legs and his amazing jumping ability, hence the nickname, "Kangaroo Kid." They didn't measure the players' vertical leaping ability back then, but if they would have, Pollard's would've certainly been astonishing, even by today's standards. He was truly the Michael Jordan of his day.

Pollard's story of how he became a Laker is as interesting as the man himself. Just before the Lakers first season in 1947-48, Max Winter and associates were assembling the pieces to put together a winning team for their Minneapolis fans. Specifically, they were trying hard to land a young kid out of an Oakland Industrial league named Jim Pollard. (Companies used to sponsor pro ball teams back in that era and hire players, such as the Phillips 66 Petroleum Company.) In fact, a lot of pro teams had previously tried to sign the former Stanford star, who had been playing at the AAU level in hopes of his landing a spot on the coveted 1948 Olympic basketball team.

But somehow, someway, Minneapolis sportswriter Sid Hartman, one of Winter's associates, was able to persuade the young star to forego his Olympic dreams and move to the tundra. The news spread fast that somebody had finally talked him into signing. Oakland Mayor Joe Smith, even called Jim, and pleaded with him not to go. But Max signed him to a Laker contract, and the rest is basketball history.

At six-foot-five Pollard instantly became the tallest player on the Lakers roster. Amazingly, he was one of only a handful of basketball players in the country at the time who could dunk a basketball.

Born on July 9, 1922, Pollard's roots were formed in Oakland Calif., where he starred on the Oakland Technical High School basketball team. Full of promise and potential, the young Pollard took his talents to Stanford University, where he led the Indians to the 1942 NCAA championship. He joined the U.S. Coast Guard and played on service teams over the next three years. From there, he would play in the AAU

ranks, until he joined the Lakers in 1947.

In 1955, Jim Pollard announced his retirement from the Lakers to accept the head coaching position at LaSalle College in Philadelphia. Then on January 2, 1960, after a three-year stint in Philly, Pollard rejoined his beloved Lakers, this time as their coach. He would have his work cut out for him. Pollard took over the reigns in midseason from John Castellani, who had resigned. The Lakers were 11-25 at that point, and things were not looking good. Minneapolis would finish the season at 25-50, even upsetting Detroit in the playoffs, before ultimately losing to the St. Louis Hawks. That season would be Pollard's last, as well as the last for the Lakers in Minneapolis. In 1960 team owner Bob Short moved the Lakers to Los Angeles where the team's dynasty would continue for years to come.

An unscheduled stop in Iowa
Perhaps the highlight of Pollard's Laker coaching career happened in an Iowa corn field. On January 18, 1960, the Lakers took off in their team plane during a snowstorm after a game in St. Louis. Just after takeoff, the lights went out in the cabin. "I thought it was one of the guys joking around," Pollard said. "But when I got in the front, I saw the co-pilot shining a flashlight on the instrument panel, and all the instruments were dead." Flying by way of a magnetic compass and his knowledge of the stars, the pilot flew on.

Somewhere over western Iowa, and very low on fuel, the pilot began searching for a place to put the plane down. Finally, with the pilot sticking his head out of the window to see, and narrowly missing a grove of trees, they landed in a remote corn field. The people of nearby Carroll, Iowa, came to give the players rides to town. Pollard, who had brought his son along on the trip, got a ride to town from the local undertaker, who drove a hearse. "I had not been scared in the least while we were in the air or when we were landing," Pollard added. "But when I saw that stretcher in the back of the car, I realized how close we had come, and I got the shakes for a few minutes."

Pollard, the team's first captain, was the last of the original Lakers. A fabulous rebounder and all-around team player, he would finish his illustrious eight-year career with a 13.1 scoring average, averaging in double figures every year. Along with big George, he was the only Laker to be a member of all six championship teams. George Mikan had been named the Best Basketball Player of the First Half Century by the Associated Press, but two years later, the players who had been in the league since its inception, were given another poll. This time they chose Jim Pollard. The four-time All-Star was inducted into the Basketball Hall of Fame in 1977. Pollard died in 1993 at the age of 71.

Tributes

"We were very close friends and roommates for several years. He was probably the best athlete that I have

ever played with or against. He was a very moody player, but on the floor, he played way above his head. He was just a marvelous athlete and a great friend. I miss him."
    -- Vern Mikkelsen

"Jim Pollard was probably the most graceful ball-player that I ever had. He could do everything: run, pass, shoot, jump or whatever. He was the creator of the jump-shot. He was so graceful and smooth with everything. He could be playing today. When they put the press on, Jim would bring the ball down the court and nobody could guard him. We didn't keep track of assists back then, but he had a ton of them - most of them going to George! He was an excellent all-around ball-player with and without the ball." **-- John Kundla**

"The Kangaroo Kid, he was one fabulous ballplayer. He was just an extraordinarily fine basketball player who could do it all. He could run like a deer, and had a great ability to pass the ball. His pin-point passes were just amazing. What can I say, he was just a tremendous leaper, a great ballplayer and a fine person."
    -- George Mikan

"He was one of those guys that could do everything. Just like Julius Erving, he could take off at the top of the circle and glide into the basket and lay it in. He could hang in the air and shoot with different hands. He was special."
    -- Bud Grant

JOHN KUNDLA
The Lakers Make it Three in a Row

By 1950, the Lakers had won back-to-back-to-back league championships. They won their first in the National Basketball League (NBL) in 1948, the second in the Basketball Association of America (BAA) in 1949, and they won their third in the National Basketball Association (NBA) in 1950. Through attrition and mergers, the new NBA had taken over as the premier professional basketball league in the country, and, in only their third year of existence, the Lakers were champions again.

The Lakers finished the 1949-50 regular season on top of the NBA's Central Division with a 51-17 won-loss record. They then won six straight playoff games, sweeping Chicago, Fort Wayne, and Anderson to gain yet another shot at their third straight league title. They would faceoff against the Syracuse Nationals, who were led by player-coach fiery Al Cervi, and popular 6-7 star forward Dolph Schayes. The NBA finals that year featured two teams who had lost only one game apiece at home during the course of the regular season. Syracuse, winners of the Eastern Division championship, came into the series with a regular season record of 51 wins against only 13 losses.

26783

he best-of-seven series kicked off in Syracuse's State Fair Coliseum. In game one, behind big George Mikan's 37 points, the Lakers pushed the Nationals into overtime. Behind 66-64, with about a minute to go, coach Johnny Kundla called for a double pick with Jim Pollard taking the final shot. The ball swung around as designed, but when Pollard got the ball, instead of shooting, he threw it to Bud Grant. Said Grant: "I was the most surprised guy in the place, but I took a long shot and it went in to tie the game." Then in overtime, Bobby Harrison drained a 40-footer at the buzzer to win the thriller, 68-66.

The Nats went on to win game two, evening the series at one-apiece. The finals now headed back to the Twin Cities, but with the annual Sportmen's Show occupying the Minneapolis Auditorium, the Lakers suddenly found themselves homeless. They tried to book the Minneapolis Armory, but that, too, was occupied, so they looked to the University of Minnesota and the Gophers' home, Williams Arena. Nervous about the basketball competition, U of M athletic director Frank McCormick, pushed through a Big Ten rule that would prohibit pro teams from playing in conference facilities. Ultimately, the Lakers wound up winning games three and four over in the St. Paul Auditorium. The unfamiliar surroundings didn't seem to bother Minneapolis. The Lakers easily won games three and four.

Then it was off to upper New York state for game five, where Syracuse rebounded to defeat Minneapolis, narrowing their series lead three games to two. Back in Minnesota, they had cleared out the fishing rods and boats from the Minneapolis Auditorium just in time for game six. Feeling right at home, the Lakers engaged the Nats in a wild game that will go down as one of the most memorable in Lakers history.

Epitomizing the style of play which was commonplace of the era, the Lakers took it to the Nats. Fights broke out all over as Pollard squared off with Paul Seymour, and Slater Martin and Swede Carlson both went at it with Billy Gabor before the police came in and broke up the brawling. To make it more exciting, the volatile Cervi got tossed in the third quarter and four Lakers fouled out in the fourth. When it was all said and done, big Mikan had poured in 40, and Pollard, the Kangaroo Kid, added 16. Minneapolis then waltzed through game six and blew out Syracuse by the impressive score of 110-75. The term "dynasty" now officially preceded the word "Lakers."

"We had won a championship in all three different leagues at that point," said head coach Kundla following that 1950 season.

"That was really a wild series. I remember Harrison sinking that 40-footer to win the

first game at the fairgrounds. Then in the final game, I remember Seymour was guarding Mikan, and he was pinching George every time he got the ball. Finally George got so upset that when he went up for a shot, he gave him an elbow right to his forehead, giving Seymour a giant knot right on the noggin. George blew his top and I had to take him out of the game, but he did make the shot and the ref even called a foul on Seymour. Cervi, the player-coach, was really a mean competitor, and his teams would fight anybody. That series was a real brawl and at the time, because our teams didn't like each other very much. It was a great series, and it is always special winning a championship, particularly that one, because it was our first NBA title."

Pennsylvania born

Kundla was born on July 3, 1916, in Star Junction, Pa., and he grew up in Minneapolis, where he attended Central High School. After a great high school career, he went on to play basketball under coach Dave MacMillan at the University of Minnesota. John also played baseball at Minnesota, but his main sport was hoops. In basketball, he earned three varsity letters and led the Gophers to the Big Ten co-championship in 1937. He captained the Gophers in 1939 and also earned All-Big Ten Conference honors.

Following graduation, he played one season of professional baseball with Paducah in the Class C Kitty League. He would also play for the Rock Spring Sparklers, of Shakopee, and led them to the 1943 World Pro Tournament in Chicago.

Kundla returned to Minnesota and served as a basketball assistant to MacMillan and then accepted the head coaching job at DeLaSalle High School in downtown Minneapolis. He coached the Islanders to the Minnesota State Catholic Championship in 1944. Following a two-year stint in the Navy in World War II, Johnny decided to get back into coaching, this time at St. Thomas in St. Paul, where he coached the Tommies to a modest 11-11 record in 1947.

The youngest coach in the league

Then in 1946, the Minneapolis Lakers came to town. Originally, they had offered the head coaching position to a coaching legend, Joe Hutton, who had been Hamline's coach since 1931 and had built the Pipers into a national small-college power. Hutton politely declined, and the Lakers decided to hire the 31-year-old Kundla as their first coach. He thus left the security of St. Thomas and sign a three-year deal with Minnesota's fledgling professional basketball franchise.

In 11-plus years as the Laker head coach, Kundla compiled an impressive record of 466-319 for the Lakers. At the time, only the legendary Red Auerbach of the Boston Celtics had more professional coaching wins. Johnny won 60 playoff games while losing just 35, a record that translated into an amazing six world championships for the state of Minnesota.

TIMELINE

Gopher guard Whitey Skoog is named to the All-American basketball team	Legendary Gopher Football coach Bernie Bierman retires	Millers third baseman Ray Dandridge is named the league's MVP	The Minneapolis Millers finish first in the American Association	Minneapolis Miller's pitcher Dixie Howell throws a no hitter in a 6-0 win over Columbus	St. Paul's Francis "Moose" Goheen is named the Outstanding Midwestern Hockey Player of the first 50 years of the 20th century. The two-time Olympian starred for the St. Paul Saints and led them to two McNaughton Trophy's in 1916-17. He is one of only a handful of Americans to be enshrined in both the Hockey Hall of Fames in Toronto and Eveleth

12

In 1958, tired of the stress and travel demands, Kundla stepped down as coach of the "New Lakers," as they were now called, and with the blessings of management, became the teams' general manager. In his first move as G.M., he hired George Mikan to be his coaching predecessor.

Back to his alma mater

In 1960, the day after the Lakers lost to the Celtics in the NBA Finals, Kundla announced his resignation, in order to return to his alma matter as head basketball coach. After 11 seasons of coaching the Gophers, Ozzie Cowles decided to step down, and Kundla stepped in to take over. Johnny coached the Gophers from 1959 to 1968, earning 110 career wins against 105 losses in nine seasons with the maroon and gold. He also guided the U.S Nationals into international competition in 1964-65, and served on the NCAA Rules Committee. In 1968, University of North Dakota head coach Bill Fitch took over for the Gophers, and Kundla went over to the U's St. Paul campus, where he served as the University Physical Education Director. He subsequently was inducted into the NBA Hall of Fame.

Who was your hero when you were growing up?

"I was a great baseball fan back then and used to follow the Minneapolis Millers. Ernie Orsatti and Spencer Harris were my favorites, and I will always remember them. In basketball it was John Wooden. We played against each other in college when he played at Purdue, and I tried to imitate his scoop shot. I also looked up to Gopher basketball coach, Dave MacMillan, who was my mentor and got me interested in coaching."

What do you remember most about your playing days?

"When we won the Big Ten co-championship in 1937. Playing with guys like Gordy Addington, Gordy Spears, Paul Maki, Martin Rolick, and Butch Nash was just great. That was a fabulous season for University of Minnesota basketball."

What was your best Gopher team?

"The year I remember most was when we finished second in the Big Ten. I had a lot of great guys like Lou Hudson, Archie Clark, and Mel Northway. We had a good chance to go all the way that year, and it was so disappointing that we didn't win a Big Ten Championship with those guys."

What was your most memorable championship?

"I would have to say that winning in New York to beat the Knicks in three straight in 1953 was a title that stands out. They were all unique wins and each was special."

What did it mean for you to be a Gopher?

"It meant a lot to me. In those years, we weren't recruited to play basketball. I went out for the freshman team and made it. It was such a thrill just to play for the University of Minnesota. I was happy just to make the team and to be a Minnesota letter winner. Then, to be able to come back and coach my alma mater was something very special to me. It was a great honor to be a Gopher player and later their coach. I just wished that we could have won a championship for the U."

What did it mean for you to coach the Lakers?

"Sportswriter Sid Hartman actually talked me into becoming the Laker coach. Sid was really responsible for getting the franchise located in Minneapolis. He was the one who convinced Ben Berger into buying the Detroit Gems franchise. They gave me $6,000 a year, twice as much as I was making at St. Thomas. How lucky could I get? I mean the first player we got was Pollard, then we got Mikan, and then Mikkelson two years later! I didn't even have to coach them. They were so good that they did it all themselves. Those guys were just great players with great talent and so much character. I was very lucky to be a Laker, and there is no greater thrill than winning a world championship. The national recognition we got for the state of Minnesota was such a thrill for me to see."

Were you upset when the Lakers left for Los Angeles?

"I was coaching at the U at that point, and Bob Short offered me the head coaching position with the Lakers, but I didn't want to move to Los Angeles. I was very sad to see the Minneapolis Lakers die, and a part of me died too. I think their moving had a great deal to do with the fact that we didn't ever really have our own home court. Between the Minneapolis and St. Paul auditoriums, the Minneapolis Armory and even over at Hamline University, we never really had a facility to call our own."

What was your reaction to your Hall of Fame selection?

"I can remember Ray Meyer walking me down the aisle at Springfield, and it was such a thrill. My family was all there, and I don't think I will ever experience anything any better than that."

Laker and Gopher tombstone:

"As an active player with the Gophers, I was just happy to make the team. Professionally, I was very proud of our Laker teams and I owe it all to my players. I'm grateful to Mikan, Mikkelson, Martin, Pollard, Whitey Skoog, Bud Grant, and all the others. We had players with such character, team spirit, and a will to win. I was very lucky to be their head coach."

Where are they now? Johnny and his wife Marie live in Minneapolis. They have six children (Jack, Tom, Jimmy, Dave, Karen, Kathy) and six grandchildren. He is retired and still watches a lot of basketball!

Tributes

"John Kundla is one of the greatest coaches of all time. He's never been given the proper credit simply because everyone said that anyone could've coached our championship teams. I sort of look at John similarly today as I do with the Chicago Bulls head coach Phil Jackson. Like Jackson, John was wonderful at coaching each of us at our own individual levels, and that really motivated us to play for him and win. I am very grateful for the fact that he gave me the opportunity to play with the Lakers. He would always pick on George Mikan, for the sake of letting the rest of us know that there were no favorites on his teams."

-- **Vern Mikkelson**

"John is just an excellent guy. He had a great way about him, and he could keep the players focused on the game. He also had the ability to help you when things weren't going your way. He could critique your game and correct any problems that you had to get you back out there. He was great at analyzing team defenses and he was a master at setting up plays to would help us excel. He is a wonderful person and a great coach."   -- **George Mikan**

"John Kundla just got better and better, until he was one of the greatest coaches in basketball.

-- **Bud Grant**

Many will say that John Mayasich was Minnesota's greatest hockey player. To fully understand just how good of a hockey player he was, you need to go back to the hockey capital of the U.S. -- Eveleth, Minn.

Eveleth has often been referred to as the birthplace of hockey in the United States because of its wonderful puck traditions and roots that can be traced back to the sport's American beginnings. That's why the U.S. Hockey Hall of Fame situated in this relatively small town on Minnesota's Mesabi Iron Range, an hour's drive from Duluth. Many hockey greats came from this hockey Mecca, names that ooze with tradition: Mariucci, Brimsek, Karakas, LoPresti, Matchefts, Ikola, Finnegan, Dahlstrom, Romnes and Mayasich.

John Mayasich was taught by another Eveleth legend, Cliff Thompson. Thompson coached hockey at Eveleth High school in Minnesota from 1920 until 1958, finishing with an astounding 534-26-9 record. From 1947-1951, John Mayasich led Thompson's teams to four consecutive Minnesota State High School Hockey Tournament titles. When Mayasich had graduated from high school in 1951, his Eveleth

Golden Bears had amassed an unbelievable record of 69-0. This was a true dynasty, and one that is too easily forgotten.

That 1951 Eveleth hockey team had already come off of winning three consecutive state championships and were primed to win another. Competition can be fierce in northeastern Minnesota, but the Golden Bears breezed through their regular season undefeated en route to another State High School Hockey Tournament birth. Eveleth breezed through their first two tourney opponents and met St. Paul Johnson High School in the finals. The Golden Bears, led by Mayasich and teammate John Matchefts, went on to beat Johnson, 4-1, to win an unprecedented fourth consecutive state championship, securing their fame forever. In the state tournament, Johnny Mayasich scored 15 goals while amassing 18 points, both still tournament records. The title capped off a perfect 19-0 season, bringing Eveleth's four-year high school hockey record to 69-0.

"I remember that St. Paul Johnson game was a tough one," said Mayasich, "and there was a lot of pressure on us to keep the winning streak going through that fourth year. When it was all over we couldn't believe what we had done, it was very special."

On growing up in Eveleth
"We got our start learning hockey on the ponds and outdoor rinks in the city. The older kids would pick sides and the younger kids would learn from them. It went on from generation to generation. When the ice melted, we played street hockey and broomball. We had a lot of fun and we learned a lot playing those sports as well. Our coach, Cliff Thompson, had the advantage of having that type of kid who had already grown up in this environment coming into his programs. As far as the winning streak goes, every year we were expected to play better than the one before, so I looked at it that way and played that way myself. We were well conditioned athletes and we played a lot of different sports throughout the seasons. It was a wonderful experience, and we just had a lot of great players on those teams."

From one legendary coach to another
John Mayasich has long been regarded as one of the finest amateur hockey players ever produced in the United States, and his name has always been synonymous with hockey. After his incredible run with the Golden Bears under coach Cliff Thompson, John headed south, to the University of Minnesota, to learn more about the game from another Eveleth hockey legend, John Mariucci.

This was the dawn of modern hockey in Minnesota, and Johnny Mayasich was rewriting the record books as he went along. He

was described as a "velvety-smooth skater," with a keen, sixth sense into the psyche of the goalie's every move. He is credited as being the first college hockey player to develop the slap shot, a new weapon that instilled fear into an already perplexed group of goaltenders that tried to stop him. John was an artist with his stick and his stick-handling skills were legendary. On power-plays, he could kill penalties by toying with opposing defenses. He used to take the puck and simply weave around the rink without ever passing to a teammate until the penalty had been killed. With amazing ability like that, it's hard to believe that he was often criticized for passing too much.

Just like he had done in high school, he too would take his Gopher teammates to the promised land of college hockey, the NCAA Final Four, unfortunately, with not quite the same outcome. In 1953, his sophomore year at the U, the Gophers won the Midwest Conference championship, and went all the way to the NCAA finals in Colorado Springs. In the semifinal game, they knocked off R.P.I. 3-2 in a nail-biter to make it to the championship game before losing a heartbreaker to Michigan. That next season, they made it to the finals again, this time crushing Boston College 14-1 in the semis, only to lose to their old nemesis, R.P.I., in a 5-4 overtime heartbreaker for the title. "It's a loss that sticks with me still today," said Mayasich on the loss to R.P.I.. "To lose in overtime was bitter. It's not the ones you won that you remember, it's the ones you lost. To me, that was probably my biggest individual disappointment in all my years of hockey."

Before his career was over, he had tallied Gopher records of 298 career points and 144 goals. His totals worked out to an incredible 1.4 goals per game average with nearly three points per game. To put it into perspective, Pat Micheletti, the next Gopher player on the career goal-scoring list, has 24 fewer goals despite playing in 51 more games. In other words, in his 162 games, Micheletti would have had to amass 435 points just to match Mayasich's per-game average. That's an additional 166 more than his career total. Mayasich also holds the Minnesota records for most goals and most points in a single game. In his senior year, he had an incredible six-goal game against Winnipeg and also tallied eight points against Michigan that same season. At the end of his playing career with the Gophers, Mayasich fulfilled his military obligations and opted to suit up for the 1956 U.S. Olympic Hockey Team in Cortina, Italy.

The highlight of the tournament came against perennial power Canada, who had won seven of the eight Olympic gold medals since the games had begun. John played an incredible game, scoring a hat trick, en route to defeating the Canadians. The Americans would take home a Silver medal for their efforts.

Team of destiny
Mayasich also played a pivotal role on the 1960 U.S. Olympic "team of destiny," in Squaw Valley, Idaho The U.S. team beat the mighty Russians for the first time, and, in the process, won the first-ever U.S. gold

TIMELINE	Gopher fullback & tackle Bronko Nagurski is inducted into the College Football Hall of Fame	Gopher Neil Oftshun, wins the 125 lb. NCAA Boxing Championship	Hall of Famer Willie Mays plays 35 games for the Millers. He hit .477 with 8 homers and 30 RBI's.	Jimmie Foxx, a Minneapolis Miller coach in 1958, is inducted into the Baseball Hall of Fame	Gopher center Gordon Watters is named to the All-American hockey team	The Hamline Pipers win the National Association of Intercollegiate Athletics championship.	The NCAA Championship Basketball Tournament is played at Williams Arena as Kentucky beat Kansas State to win the title	Gopher goalie Larry Ross is named to the All-American hockey team	Gopher guard Whitey Skoog is named to the All-American basketball team

medal in hockey.

"At the time we were thinking it would be a great accomplishment if we could win a bronze, we had no idea we would win a gold," said Mayasich. "Beating the Russians was amazing and very similar to the 1980 team victory as well. I think for both teams, playing at home, in America, was a big factor, because it's nice having the fans there to support you. This was probably one of the biggest thrills of my life."

Simply amazing

Mayasich's list of achievements is mind-boggling. From 1952-1955, John was selected as an All-American. Following college, he went on to play with eight U.S. Olympic and National teams. Declining professional hockey opportunities in the six-team National Hockey League, Mayasich devoted his remaining hockey career to the Green Bay Bobcats. In 1969, he was named coach of the U.S. National team. Mayasich received numerous honors during his hockey days, including being the first Minnesotan to be voted into the National High School Athletic Hall of Fame. In 1976 he had a homecoming of sorts, being inducted into the U.S. Hockey Hall of Fame in his native Eveleth.

Things have changed in the world of hockey since Eveleth's incredible high school run. The attendance for the entire 1951 high school hockey tournament was 18,582. The attendance for the 1997 high school hockey tournament was nearly 120,000. However, in all those years, no one has come close to topping Mayasich's records, not to mention his legend. He was the best hockey player ever to wear a maroon and gold sweater, and one of the best players to lace them up anywhere. But as great an athlete as he was, so is his humility. Often in the limelight, he was always quick to share the credit and the glory with his teammates and coaches.

Who was your idol or hero growing up?
"John Matchefts"

What did it mean for you to be a Gopher?
"The camaraderie was the best, those friendships go back 40 years now. Playing with the players who I had played against throughout my high school career was really exciting. We had great Gopher players like Dick Meredith, Dick Dougherty, Gene Campbell, Ken Yackel, Wendy Anderson, and Stan Hubbard. I got to see the world through hockey, and the purity of the game is the bond that keeps these friendships together today. It was quite a time to be involved with the Gopher program as it was just taking off back then. It made me proud of the fact that I was there when all of this was happening. Now, to see what the program has grown into today, and to think that maybe, in a small way that I had something to do with it, is incredible. My time at the U of M was great."

Why did you pick Minnesota?
"I made a trip to Ann Arbor because Matchefts and Ikola were there, and we had played together in high school. At the time, it was understood that I would be going to Michigan. Everyone expected me to go there. I think the deciding issue was my girlfriend, who I am presently married to. She was a year behind me in school and that was the biggest factor. The new arena (Williams Arena) at the U was also a factor. Eveleth

came down to play a high school game there, and I was certainly impressed by the rink. Also, I had come from a large family of 11 and was not used to being far away from home. Eveleth is 200 miles from the U."

On not playing NHL hockey:
"I didn't try out for it, so I'll never know. I also had to go into military service right after college, and I was thinking of my family and financial security as well. However, I would have to say that meeting Stan Hubbard at the U and working for him since then, was even better than ever playing professional hockey. Stan had fun, worked hard, and was a contributor on the team. He didn't have the natural abilities that maybe some of us might have been blessed with, but he worked harder than most."

Will your records ever be broken?
"I would think so. They are playing 40-some games a year now, and most are getting four years of playing time as well. But with pro hockey tempting the better players with the money, I don't know."

Gopher tombstone:
"I was blessed with the opportunity of playing with and against some great hockey players. I was at the right place at the right time with the right people, and I made a contribution through a lot of hard work and effort."

Where are they now?
John and his wife Carol live in the Twin Cities. They have five children: Michael, Cheryl, Patrick, Mary, and Dan, as well as 12 grandchildren. John currently works as the director of public affairs at Hubbard Broadcasting in St. Paul.

Tributes

"John Mayasich brought college hockey to a new plateau. He was the Wayne Gretzky of his time, and if he were playing pro hockey today, he would simply be a bigger, stronger, back-checking Gretzky. The words to describe him haven't been invented. When I say he's the best, that's totally inadequate." -- **John Mariucci**

"Johnny was an excellent talent. He came along way back when hockey wasn't that popular and really changed the game. There weren't a lot of opportunities after he finished college. Although he did reach the ultimate in playing in the Olympics, it's unfortunate that he never took a chance on playing in the pros, because I think he would've been unbelievably successful. He was a terrific player and had a great amateur career." -- **Lou Nanne**

"John and I were roommates my freshman year in Pioneer Hall. He was the best athlete on campus at the University of Minnesota for all four years that I was there. We even ended up buying houses next door to each other in Brooklyn Center right out of college. We're still really good friends to this day." -- **Chuck Mencel**

"John was a quiet fox. He was the best player I ever saw play in Minnesota. Hockey made his life. What can I say, he is just such a wonderful guy."
-- **Doug Woog**

JOHN'S MINNESOTA STATE HIGH SCHOOL HOCKEY TOURNAMENT RECORDS

Most All Time Total Points:	46	(1948-1951)
Most All Time Total Goals:	36	(1948-1951)
Most Consec. Games Scoring:	12	(1948-1951)
Most All Time Hat-Tricks:	7	(1948-1951)
Most Points One Tournament:	18	(1951)
Most Goals One Tournament:	15	(1951)
Most Points One Game:	8	(1951)
Most Goals One Game:	7	(1951)
Most Points One Period:	5	(1951)
Most Goals One Period:	4	(1951)

*(Fittingly, his linemate, John Matchefts, holds the record for Most All-Time Assists, with 12.)

THE DYNASTY

YEAR	CHAMPION	RUNNER-UP	SCORE
1948	Eveleth (15-0)	Warroad	8-2
1949	Eveleth (13-0)	Williams	4-1
1950	Eveleth (22-0)	Williams	4-3
1951	Eveleth (19-0)	St. Paul Johnson	4-1

The Lakers win the Western Division Championship

VERN MIKKELSEN
The Lakers just Keep On Rolling

With a record of 40-26, the Minneapolis Lakers finished second in the NBA Western Conference, in 1952, one game behind the Rochester Royals. Minneapolis led by a dominant front line of George Mikan, Jim Pollard, and Vern Mikkelsen, while point guard Slater Martin dished out the assists.

The Lakers knocked of the Indianapolis Olympians in the first round of the playoffs, and then proceed to take on the defending NBA champion Royals in the semifinals. In game one, big Mikan scored 47 in a losing effort. Minneapolis won the next game in overtime to even the series up.

After returning to Minneapolis, the Lakers easily won game three, but made game four interesting. With the score tied and only two seconds on the clock, Pollard grabbed a rebound off a missed Mikan shot and put the ball in the hoop in to give the Lakers the victory at the buzzer. The Lakers were going to the finals. Was this a five-game series? There they met the New York Knicks who were anxious to avenge their championship loss to Rochester the year before.

The St. Paul Auditorium played host to the first game

of the series. Game one wasn't without its share of controversy, as the Knicks' Al McGuire made an apparent first-period basket that wasn't counted by the officials. Knick coach Joe Lapchick protested the game, but without success. Pollard led the Lakers with 34 points, as the Lakers took the opener 83-79 in overtime. The series went back and forth between Minnesota and the east coast, and, finally, in game seven, Minneapolis knocked off New York, 82-65. Led by the "Great Dane" Mikkelsen, who averaged an impressive 15.3 points per game, the Lakers were once again champions of the NBA, winning their fourth title in five years.

From Askov to the big city
Born the son of a Lutheran minister in the tiny town of Askov, a small community between the Twin Cities and Duluth, Vern Mikkelsen grew up to become a Minnesota basketball legend. Vern played his entire career in the Land of 10,000 Lakes, from high school to Hamline University to the Lakers.

"I was the fourth highest in my graduating class and still not in the upper third," chuckles Vern. "You see, we only had nine kids in my entire senior class. Back then, World War II was going on, and we needed warm bodies, so anybody that went out for the basketball team made it. No one was cut. Our superintendent was our coach, and I'm not sure he'd ever even seen a basketball before!" Despite this, Mikkelsen was recruited hard by University of Minnesota basketball coach Dave MacMillan and would have gone to play for him in the fall of 1945 had the Gophers not just signed highly-touted center Jim McIntyre, who had led Patrick Henry High School to two state championships. So, after being tracked him down in an Askov rutabaga field by a Hamline recruiter, the 16-year-old, 6'7" center decided to become a Piper.

Although Joe Hutton's Hamline Pipers were considered a small-college team, they played a big-time national schedule in those days. In 1949, as a senior, Mikkelsen led the Pipers to glory by beating Regis College of Colorado and winning the NAIA National Championship. He would later be inducted into the NAIA Hall of Fame.

"The NAIA championship at Hamline was very memorable for me because, for three years, we had been banging on the door and hadn't gotten through it," said Mikkelsen. "We finally made it in 1949 after being beaten by Louisville in the finals the year before. Losing in 1948 was especially disappointing, because, back then, the players from the NCAA and the NAIA championship teams got to go to the London Olympics. I was a year late."

In 1945, Hamline played in a Christmas tour-

nament at the Chicago Stadium. The tournament featured three of the nation's dominant big men at that time: Bob Kurland of Oklahoma A & M, Don Otten of Bowling Green and DePaul's Mikan. For the young Mikkelsen, the trip would be invaluable. "My first experience with big-time basketball came at an early age and I think that had a lot to do with helping me realize that these guys were just human beings," remarked Mikkelsen. "I was certainly in awe of them, but I learned to play at their level. I certainly didn't dominate anyone. I got a basket off Mikan and actually apologized to him."

The Minneapolis Lakers used a territorial draft choice (which allowed teams to select one local player from within 50 miles in the first round by substituting their regular draft position) to select the All-American Hamline star in 1949.

"I remember meeting with Max Winter to go over my first contract," said Mik, "and I told him that because I was a center, I was concerned about my playing time with big George Mikan around. Max went on to sell me on the notion that George was going to retire that next season. He was only off by five years!"

Mikkelsen's father came down to meet with Winter and help Vern sign his contract because Vern wasn't yet 21 years old. Now Max, wanting to reimburse Reverend Mikkelsen for his travel expenses, handed him some money as he was leaving. On the way home his dad looked at the money and realized that he had given him a $100 bill. He insisted on turning around and going back to Minneapolis so he could return the money, which he felt had to have been an oversight on Mr. Winter's part. Vern figured his dad had probably never seen a $100 bill before in his life. It was at that point Vern knew he was part of the big time of professional basketball. However, he saw little playing time as an understudy to big George in the beginning of his rookie campaign.

Then something happened that truly changed the game of basketball. In a game against Fort Wayne, Laker coach John Kundla decided to play both of his big men at the same time. Calling his creation the "double pivot offense," coach Kundla stationed both Mikan and Mikkelsen as his centers. Mik played the high post and George the low post. Thus, Minneapolis now had a "twin tower" lineup and the most formidable front line in all of basketball. But with both big men constantly crashing the middle, it simply became too crowded. Kundla's noble experiment didn't work. So he went go back to the drawing board, this time putting Mikkelsen out on the perimeter and facing him towards the basket. In doing so, the coach had inadvertently created the NBA's first true power forward. Mikkelsen's new role was not to score, but primarily to rebound, set picks, and pick up Mikan and Pollard's missed shots.

Vern later commented that his best scoring nights came when Mikan and Pollard weren't hitting anything. The league soon learned that the Minneapolis

TIMELINE

| Eveleth's Andre Gambucci wins a Silver medal as a member of the Olympic hockey team | Crookston's John Noah wins a Silver medal as a member of the Olympic hockey team | The state's largest bluegill is caught by Bemidji's Bob Parker on Alice Lake: 2 lbs., 13 oz | International Falls' Robert Rompre wins a Silver medal as a member of the Olympic hockey team | St. Paul's Ken Yackel wins a Silver medal as a member of the Olympic hockey team | Gopher Neil Oftshun wins the 125 lb. NCAA Boxing Championship | The state's largest carp is caught by Annandale's Frank Ledwein on Clearwater Lake: 55 lbs., 5 oz. | Roseau's Reuben Bjorkman wins a Silver medal as a member of the Olympic hockey team | Newport's Van Allen wins a Silver medal as a member of the Olympic hockey team |

16

Lakers had established a very powerful defensive and offensive rebounding front line. Although he would develop a great two-handed overhead set shot, Vern's new position was not an easy transition for him. The center spot had been the only position he knew, and now, as a professional, he was being asked to change and face the basket. "At first we tried to play a double pivot, but that didn't work, so Johnny moved me outside as a forward to face the basket," said Mik. "This was totally foreign territory for me because I had played my entire career with my back to the basket. It was scary! Guys my size just didn't do that back then. In the 1940s, they figured that if you were 6'7", you were big and clumsy, and you couldn't dribble or shoot, so you played center to rebound and get tip-ins. But, I learned how to do it, and it worked. This kept the defenses honest and really revolutionized the game of professional basketball as we know it today. Yet, I still can't believe guys like Penny Hardaway and Magic Johnson, who are 6'9" guards."

"We had the total team configuration back then that every NBA team strives for today: We had the big horse (Mikan) in the middle, the small forward on the left in Jim Pollard, who was one of the greatest pure athletes of all time, the brute strength guy, which was me on the right, and then Slater Martin at the point. We were very successful, and NBA teams today follow the same types of configurations."

The Iron Man
Known as the Lakers' "Iron Man," Mikkelsen played in 642 consecutive games. For 10 seasons the Great Dane had been a Laker fixture, ending his career with 10,063 career points while averaging 14.4 points per game. Vern didn't have to quit, and clearly he could've kept playing (just two months before he retired he hit for a career high 43 points). "The NBA wasn't as glamorous as people thought, with all the train travel and hotels, and after 10 years I had had enough." said Vern.

Laker owner Bob Short tried to convince him to stay on as a player/coach for the team, even offering him a $25,000 salary and 25 percent ownership of the team. Vern passed on the offer because he wanted to devote more time to his family and aspiring insurance business. Mikkelsen can still remember coming down to breakfast in 1965 and having his wife Jean show him the newspaper headline revealing the news that Short had sold the Lakers to Jack Kent Cooke in Los Angeles for a whopping $5 million. Vern would add, "She knew exactly what 25 percent of five million dollars was!"

Who was your hero when you were growing up?
"Growing up in the tiny town of Askov, the only contact we had with the outside world back then was the Duluth newspaper and the radio. I really didn't have any particular heroes as a youngster, although George Mikan was my idol when he was in college. I followed him very closely at DePaul, and later when he was with the Chicago Gears and the Lakers."

On his Hall of Fame induction: Vern is proud of the fact that he's the only Minnesotan in the Basketball Hall of Fame who played his entire career in Minnesota. He was escorted by fellow inductee, Bob Pettit, of the St. Louis Hawks. During Mik's speech he said of his former rival who he walked down the long carpet with, "That was the longest time I ever spent with Bob without having him score a point against me!"

Nine iron men:
"The Lakers played two full seasons with only nine guys. If you were injured, you would go anyway because you had to."

What did it mean for you to be a Laker?
"The Lakers had already established themselves as the premier team in the NBA by the time I got there. Mikan and Pollard were by far the outstanding players in the league. It was doubly fun in 1949 because there were three of us who made the team as rookies: Slater Martin, Bob Harrison, and me. We went on to win four championships over the next five years. We felt that we contributed to winning, and it was just a lot of fun back then. I could've made more money had I gone elsewhere, but I wanted to play here where it was my home. Being a Laker is who I am."

Train travel:
"One time we were playing a game in Rochester, and we had to take the train back to Minneapolis for a game that next night. The New York Central Railway came through Rochester at 10:30 p.m., and our game that night went into overtime. So we didn't even get a chance to shower, we just threw on our overcoats over our uniforms, and we ran to the train. Now to make it worse someone screwed up our advance reservations, and we couldn't get our usual roomettes. We had to spend the night in old-fashioned Pullman cars, which had the double bunks. By the time we got on board, all that was left were the coffin-like upper bunks, because the people on board who had already been sleeping for several hours took the lower ones. So here we are with our stinky uniforms that we had to air out for our game that next night. We had to hang our uniforms all over the car and in the morning, with that steam heat, the place stunk worse than anything I have ever been around! Those people sleeping below us got a good morning wake-up like you wouldn't believe! Our train got in at 6:00 p.m. that night, and we went straight to the Auditorium to play another game. It was brutal and not a very glamorous lifestyle for anyone to have."

Laker tombstone:
"He never gave up. I wasn't what you would call a gazelle. Everything I accomplished I did the hard way."

Where are they now?
Vern and his wife Jean live in the Twin Cities. They have two children, Tom and John. A one-time high school basketball coach at Breck, the semi-retired Mikkelsen is an independent broker, does fundraising work for his beloved Hamline University, and does some public speaking.

Tributes

"I can't say enough about him, he was my captain my last five years. He was a real competitor and such a hard working player. I never heard him swear or get mad at anybody. He was the most fundamentally sound player I ever coached, and he was just steady as could be. I couldn't find a better all-around player, he was just a great person."
-- John Kundla

"He was the first power forward. He was a fantastic guy and a fierce competitor on the court. He was a great rebounder, and he learned to shoot from the outside. He was a good friend and a very important part of our team."
-- George Mikan

"Vern was a great guy, and a great guy to play with. He was a very mature and professional person and basketball player. He went about his business and played hard every night. He had a great work ethic, and I enjoyed playing with a guy like Vern because of how hard he played."
-- Elgin Baylor

"Vern was the original power forward, and he was quite the basketball player. He was a great addition to the Lakers, and he complimented George really well. The two of them were the greatest."
-- Bud Grant

Minneapolis' Clarence "Biggie" Munn, a former All-American guard on the Gopher Football team, wins his second consecutive national championship as the head coach of the Michigan State Spartans. With a 54-9-2 career record in East Lansing, Munn is a member of the College Football Hall of Fame.

TIMELINE

WHEATIES: "THE BREAKFAST OF CHAMPIONS"

You know that you've it made as a star athlete if your face appears on a Wheaties box. It's even better than being on the cover of Sports Illustrated because it happens only occasionally, and is reserved for extremely special athletic achievements. That orange backdrop is some of the most coveted real estate in all of sports!

The story of Wheaties goes way back to 1921, when a health-conscious Minneapolis man accidentally spilled bran gruel on a hot stove. The result was a crispy flake that not only tasted great but was nutritious to boot. The man contacted Washburn-Crosby milling company, the forerunner of General Mills. In 1924, the creation was made into Gold Medal Wheat Flakes, and later the name became Wheaties. The breakfast cereal became an instant hit, and two years later a popular singing radio commercial that asked, "Have You Tried Wheaties?" made the product a household name.

Then, in 1933, its association with sports came to life when General Mills agreed to sponsor Minneapolis Millers baseball games on WCCO Radio broadcasts. As part of the promotion, a Minneapolis ad agency coined the phrase, "Wheaties, The Breakfast of Champions," for a giant billboard that was erected at the ballpark. They began doing national baseball broadcasts and became one of the first big-time sports marketers in the country.

It has even been said that if it weren't for those Wheaties baseball broadcasts, Ronald Reagan would never have been President of the United States. When "Dutch" Reagan, who was a baseball play-by-play broadcaster for the Chicago Cubs, was voted as the most popular Wheaties radio announcer, he won both a free trip to the Cubs' California training camp, and a Warner Brothers acting screen test. The rest is history.

The cereal became readily associated with athletic success, and Babe Ruth became one of the first big-time athletes to endorse it. In 1939, Wheaties even sponsored the first televised sports broadcast. From 1956-1970, gold medal pole-vaulting champion Bob Richards directed the Wheaties Sports Federation and also served as its spokesperson. Decathlon gold medalist Bruce Jenner took over the role in 1977 and began promoting physical fitness. In the mid-1980s, gold medal gymnast Mary Lou Retton became the first woman ever to appear on the Wheaties box. In 1985, when Pete Rose broke Ty Cobb's all-time hit record, he became the first major league baseball player to appear on the trademark orange box. Walter Payton, Chris Evert, and Michael Jordan are among the others who have graced its cover. And in 1987 our Cinderella Twins were immortalized forever when they made the box.

MINNESOTA: THE SNOWMOBILE CAPITAL OF THE WORLD

In 1954 three entrepreneurs from Roseau decided to go into business for themselves, constructing farm machinery. Edgar and Allan Heteen and David Johnson created a company named after the North Star, Polaris Industries, Inc. One day, Allan and Dave, tired of having to ski across the rough and snowy terrain whenever they wanted to get around to their favorite winter spots, decided to scrounge together various parts and pieces that were lying around and build a snow-contraption. The new machine would move them across the snow much quicker and a lot more efficiently than skiing. Edgar, upset at Allan and Dave for wasting their time and resources, sold the odd-looking machine to a local businessman in order to meet their payroll. Allan, unphazed by Edgar, built a new one, which he affectionately called "Number Two." This time, after Edgar sold it, they thought that they might be on to something. So, they started to build more Number Two's, which they renamed "Iron Dogs." In their first year, they sold a grand total of six "Iron Dogs" to the locals, who found them to be quite useful in getting around up in the north woods.

Forty-three years later, the Polaris plant in Roseau continues to mass-produce the finest snowmobiles in the world. Today it is one of the largest companies of its kind, and the publicly traded company's headquarters are located in Plymouth. Not only do they manufacture snowmobiles, they also make watercraft, all-terrain vehicles, and motorcycles. They went from a tiny farming operation of just three workers to a major multinational company which employs nearly 3,500 people world-wide, with annual sales of more than $1.3 billion.

Interestingly, in the mid 1960s, Edgar left Polaris and his brother behind to start his own snowmobile company, called Polar Manufacturing. That company evolved into Arctic Enterprises, or Arctic Cat Snowmobiles. He has since left that company and it has new ownership under the name of Arctic Cat, Inc. Based in Thief River Falls, Arctic Cat is one of the world's largest manufacturer of snowmobiles, Tiger Shark personal watercrafts and all-terrain vehicles. With some 2,000 employees, the company's annual sales are upwards of $500 million.

MINNESOTA FATS

Perhaps the most recognizable figure in the history of pool is Rudolph Wanderone, better known as "Minnesota Fats." Although he never actually won a designated "world championship," Wanderone, the game's leading comic, orator and publicity generator, probably did more for the game in terms of sheer exposure than any other player. Initially nicknamed "Brooklyn Fats," and "New York Fats," Wanderone dubbed himself "Minnesota Fats" after the film version of "The Hustler" hit movie screens around the country in the early 1960s. Since that time he has become known around the world as pool's foremost side show. "Fats," whose exact age was a mystery, hosted a national television show, "Celebrity Billiards," during the 1960s. He stopped playing in tournaments around that time. He was inducted into the Billiards Hall of Fame in 1994.

LEROY NEIMAN

St. Paul's LeRoy Neiman is one of the most famous artists of the modern era. Neiman, who started his career sketching nude women for Playboy, gained worldwide fame for his sports murals. He is especially well known for his quick-ly done renditions of sports scenes that feature his trademark brushing techniques with vivid color explosions that burst off the canvas. His works can be seen throughout the world, but perhaps his most celebrated pieces came during both the 1972 and 1976 Olympic Games when he was chosen as the official artist of the events. After that his paintings were seen by countless millions of people everywhere on television. He has taught his unique brand of artistry for many years at the Chicago Art Institute. Plans are currently in the works for creating a museum in his honor that would showcase his paintings in downtown St. Paul. Currently LeRoy lives in New York City.

CHRISTIAN BROTHERS HOCKEY STICKS

Billy and Roger Christian grew up as most kids did on Warroad's south side, playing hockey on the river. Today the pair make up the "brothers" part of Christian Brothers, Inc., one of the world's largest manufacturers of hockey sticks and equipment.

Today, the brothers only help add to the mystique of the tiny town of Warroad, otherwise known as: Hockey Town, USA. The tiny town which lies on the shores of Lake of the Woods on the Canadian border, is rich in hockey tradition, and the Christian brothers only add to that mystique.

Billy and Roger led the Warroad Lakers the 1953 State High School Hockey Tournament, where they finished runner's up to the St. Paul Johnson Governors. That team was coached by the legendary Cal Marvin, who guided the Lakers for nearly half a century.

Both graduated from high school in 1956, and both played for Warroad's Lakers amateur team. They then earned spots on the US National team, also coached by Marvin. That team was the first to play behind the iron curtain, playing both in Moscow and Prague, ultimately finishing fifth in the World Tournament, in Oslo. After that, the brothers returned to Warroad to work with their father as carpenters. The next year, Roger skated for the Warroad Lakers, while Bill played on the University of Minnesota freshman team.

Both brothers made the 1960 team that won a gold medal in the Winter Olympics in Squaw Valley. In that fabled event, Billy scored the tying and winning goals in the 3-2 pivotal win over the Russians. Roger and Duluth's Tommy Williams were his linemates. Roger also had a four-goal game against the Czech's, in what may have been the most memorable contest of the games. With the US down 4-3 going into the third, Roger scored a hat-trick in the final period to ice the game. The two brothers continued to play on US National teams and again made the 1964 Olympic squad in Innsbruck, Austria. The team didn't fare so well this time, but the Warroad Lakers did win the Hardy Cup, the championship of intermediate amateur hockey in Canada.

With the family's construction business prospering, Roger's brother-in-law, Hal Bakke (they're married to twin sisters), came up with a business proposition for the two brothers - manufacturing hockey sticks. The idea sounded good, so they dove right in. The three of them started their company at the old creamery in Warroad. With no money, they scraped and scrapped to get by, all the time working like dogs to get the company off the ground. Then, in the 1965 World Tournament in Finland, which was coached by former Gopher Ken Yackel, and managed by Cal Marvin, the brothers got to show-off their custom-made sticks to their teammates. They got a lot of great feedback, reinforcing the idea that their idea was a good one.

Back in Hockey Town, USA, they continued to work nights and weekends, with little or no pay for several years, hoping to catch a break. Then, in 1969, after deciding to raise capital by selling stock in their company, they constructed a new manufacturing facility along Highway 11, that allowed them to ramp-up and become a profitable corporation. When the company started in 1964, Northland Hockey Sticks represented their main US competitor. CCM in Canada, who also made sticks, got out of the stick business shortly after. "We were basically copying the Northland Stick," said Bakke. "We even toured their plant, and I think they were sorry they ever allowed us to do that. But little did we know then that we would end up owning Northland."

Today, with more than 60 loyal employees, and international and domestic sales of sticks and equipment reaching nearly 10 millions dollars annually, the company is on a roll. (They are still a distant second to the Marvin's, owners of Marvin Windows.) Not only are they one of the nation's top hockey equipment producers, they are also one of the most respected with regards to quality and innovation. There are more than 150 NHL players use Christian Brothers hockey sticks. The brothers still get a chuckle out of the fact that former UMD star, Brett Hull, who endorses Easton Aluminum Hockey Sticks, has refused to use it with anything other than a Christian Brothers replacement blade.

Billy and Roger, along with Cal Marvin, have all been inducted into the US Hockey Hall of Fame in Eveleth. The Christan's are synonymous with hockey in Minnesota, and there are already second and third generations that have come along to carry the torch. For example, Bill's son Dave, who skated two years at UND, played on the gold medal winning 1980 US Olympic Hockey team, and played for than 14 years in the NHL with the Jets, Capitals, Bruins, Blues and Blackhawks, before joining the IHL's Minnesota Moose in 1995, has the most goals of any Minnesotan in the NHL.

With their trademarked Diamond Design stick blades, Christian Brothers sticks are among the best in the world. And, more importantly, they are made right here in Minnesota.

THE HOBEY BAKER AWARD - A MINNESOTA TRADITION

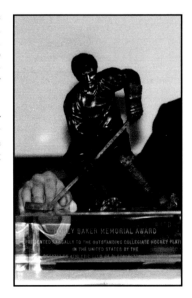

Each April the nation's best collegiate hockey player receives the Hobey Baker award, college hockey's equivalent to the Heisman Trophy. The recipient is the player who best exemplifies the qualities that Hobey Baker himself demonstrated as an athlete at Princeton University in the early 1900s. Baker was considered to be the ultimate sportsman who despised foul play, picking up only two penalties in his entire college hockey career. With his speed and superior stick handling, Baker opened up the game of hockey and set new standards for the way the game was played. A true gentleman, his habit of insisting upon visiting each opponent's locker room after every game to shake their hands became a model for today's players. A hero, Baker gave his life as an American pilot in World War I.

In 1981 Bloomington's Decathlon Club founded the Hobey Baker Memorial Award and each year presents the coveted honor to the nation's top skater. Fittingly, the nation's top hockey state hosts the top hockey player finalists from around the country for the gala event. The club also commissioned a Twin Cities sculptor, Bill Mack, to create the beautiful trophy. Since the awards' inception in 1981, three University of Minnesota Gopher players and three University of Minnesota Duluth Bulldog players have won it. All were first team All-Americans and all have gone on to play in the NHL. They are:

1981	**Neal Broten, Gopher center**
1984	**Tom Kurvers, Bulldog center**
1985	**Bill Watson, Bulldog defenseman**
1989	**Robb Stauber, Gopher goalie**
1994	**Chris Marinucci, Bulldog center**
1996	**Brian Bonnin, Gopher center**

PAUL GIEL
The Winona Phantom is the Heisman Runner-up

As a boy, Paul Giel grew up playing ball on the sand-lots of Winona during the Great Depression. Later, Giel tried to emulate the moves of his childhood hero, the University of Minnesota's only Heisman Trophy winner, Bruce Smith. Paul's imagination was refueled every Saturday as he religiously listened to the Gophers on the radio. Giel grew to be an amazing prep athlete, and people could see early on that he had a real athletic gift. In high school, Giel lettered in baseball, basketball, and football, earning all-state honors in the latter. He was heavily recruited in football and baseball, and even had several pro baseball offers right out of high school. But, luckily for us, his mind was made up early to attend the University of Minnesota.

Giel's dream of coming to the U came true in 1950, as he enrolled with the hopes of winning the same Heisman Trophy his idol Smith had done some nine years earlier. By the time Giel had finished his illustrious career in Minnesota, he had shattered most of Smith's records while single-handedly rewriting much of Gopher football's history. And, during the off-season to keep busy, he starred on Dick Siebert's Gopher Baseball teams.

Giel was a throwback, completely redefining the term "iron-man" football player. Not only was Paul an unbelievable halfback, but he was also an unbelievable quarterback, defensive back, punter, punt returner, kick returner, and sometimes even kicker for the Gophers. He hardly ever came off the field to catch his breath. Giel revolutionized the game and played simply because he loved the sport and the competition it presented to him. His tenure as "Mr. Everything" at Minnesota from 1951-1953 was just a springboard for other things in the world of Minnesota sports. He is truly a home-grown hero in more ways than one.

Because freshman couldn't participate in varsity sports at the U in 1950, Paul never got a chance to play under legendary coach Bernie Bierman, who retired at the end of that season. It was a tumultuous time for Gopher football, as Wes Fesler came from Ohio State to take the coaching reigns from Bierman, the legendary Gray Eagle, whose teams completely dominated college football in the Depression years. Bierman won seven Big Ten and five national championships, and had five undefeated seasons. But Fesler had one thing that Bernie didn't; Fesler had Paul Giel.

In 1951, Giel started out as a quarterback in Fesler's offensive scheme, but the coach later moved him to halfback. Even from deep in the backfield, he continued to call all of the team plays. From his first game, Giel became the Gophers new secret weapon, giving the team an added dimension to keep opposing defenses honest.

Giel's offensive regime is often credited for developing what was then called the "spread formation," which by today's NFL standards is called the "shotgun." It was that set-up that defenses feared most. Here Giel lined up five yards back from center. This is where he could do the most damage. Having the advantage of not having to take a seven-step drop to get set to throw, he could see the defense from the pocket, giving him valuable time to raise hell in the backfield. Often he would pass, lighting up the secondary. Other times he would follow his fullback up the middle or his halfback around the end. He could hand-off the ball to Gopher All-American Bob McNamara from Hastings, Minn., or split wide in the single wing formation to run the option. Sometimes he would line up at the running back position behind either quarterback Geno Cappelletti of Keewatin, or Hibbing's Don Swanson in the power-T formation and blast full speed ahead. Occasionally he would fool the defense and pull a quick kick or even punt the ball. Whenever he got into trouble, he would scramble - and boy could he scramble! On the other side of the ball Giel played corner-back, constantly making spectacular tackles, and with a quarterback's instincts, he could anticipate pass patterns to force timely interceptions.

Giel's storied career consisted of three fabulous seasons, but 1953 stands alone. The football gods blessed Paul for his senior campaign. It was the greatest individual season any Gopher has ever had in Gold Country.

The season didn't exactly start out well for Gophers, as they opened with back-to-back losses to USC, 17-7, and Michigan State, 21-0. They rebounded though, beating Northwestern 30-13, only to lose the following week to a very tough Illinois team, 27-7. A bleak season would all change, however, during the next game when Michigan came to town for the 50th anniversary of the Little Brown Jug.

In what many have called the greatest-ever single performance in Gopher history, Giel single-handedly crushed the Wolverines. Michigan, whom the Gophers hadn't beaten in more than 10 years, also held the Little Brown Jug for that same amount of time. Then ranked one of the top teams in the country, Michigan came to Memorial Stadium to spoil the Gophers' Homecoming festivities. That's when an absolutely possessed Paul Giel decided to take the game into his own hands. The Gopher captain rushed the ball 35 times for 112 yards, completed 13 of 18 passes for 169 yards as the quarterback, returned a punt 41 yards and even picked-off two passes on defense. The Gophers, anxious for revenge, spanked the Wolverines 22-0 for a spectacular shut-out. It was an unbelievable performance that proved to be Giel's most memorable of all games. "My top thrill of all-time was the Michigan game my senior year," said Giel. "They had kicked us around pretty good in those previous years and I really wanted to beat them badly. From a personal standpoint, I would have to say that it was my best all-around game ever."

The Gophers rode the momentum of that inspired performance for the rest of the season. They beat Pittsburgh the following week, 35-14, then held off Indiana, 28-20. They endured a shutout by Iowa in week eight, only to rebound and salvage a 21-21 tie against hated rival Wisconsin. The Gophers finished a respectable fifth in the Big Ten that season with a 3-3-1 record, as Fesler resigned and was replaced at season's end by Murray Warmath. Fesler apparently didn't want to face the future without the Winona Phantom.

So successful was Giel as a football and baseball player, as well as academically, that he was awarded the prestigious Big Ten Medal of Honor in 1954. In football he was a two-time All-American halfback, the first-ever two-time Big Ten MVP, and in 1953 was named UPI Player of the Year, and AP Back of the Year. He was second to Notre Dame's Johnny Lattner in the Heisman Trophy race that same year in what remains the closest balloting ever recorded. There is no question that Giel was robbed in the balloting, but he was up against Notre Dame and tradition that dated back to Knute Rockne.

TIMELINE

Ken Bartlett, a Gopher Gymnast, wins both the NCAA Still Rings and Rope Climb National Championships

The Gopher Hockey team loses to Michigan, 7-3, in the NCAA Finals

Gopher Wrestler Dick Mueller wins the 123 lb. National Championship

Brainerd's Charles Albert (Chief) Bender, a Chippewa Indian, is inducted into the Major League Baseball Hall of Fame. Called by legendary owner Connie Mack as "the man I would pick to pitch the one game I had to win," the Chief won 210 games and threw a no-hitter in 1910. The first player ever to win six World Series games, he played for 16 years, mostly with Philadelphia, in the big-leagues and retired in 1925 with a 2.45 ERA.

The Lakers win the NBA Championship

The Heisman disappointment could not overshadow Paul's other accomplishments. He was the first in Big Ten Conference history to be named MVP two years in a row. The all-purpose back passed or ran for 35 touchdowns and 4,110 yards, accounted for 212 of Minnesota's 443 points during his career, and also tallied seven career interceptions. He also led the team in punting from 1951-53 with a 36-yard average. He still ranks sixth all-time for career rushing at the U of M. His number 10 was officially retired on Sept. 24, 1991, in a half-time ceremony during Minnesota's game with the University of Pittsburgh, and in 1975, Giel was named to the National Football Foundation's College Hall of Fame

Gopher baseball coach Siebert said "Pitching Paulie" Giel was the hardest-throwing pitcher he had ever coached. From 1952-54, the pitcher was named to the All-American and All-Big Ten teams. On the mound, he earned 21 wins, and had the same number of complete games. He still holds the Gopher record for the most career strikeouts with 243, and remains number three all-time for the most single season strikeouts, with 92. He finished is brilliant career with a 2.16 ERA.

So, with a resume like that, what was Paul to do after graduation? "I knew in my heart that I wanted to play baseball over football, and I was trying to be realistic about myself," said Giel. "I wondered where in the heck I would play in pro football. I mean I wasn't fast enough to be a halfback in the pros, and I couldn't have made it as a pure drop-back quarterback. So, I thought I still had a shot to make it in baseball."

Giel turned down the opportunity to play professional football for George Halas' Chicago Bears and opted instead to play professional baseball for the New York Giants. The Minneapolis Millers were then the Giants' top farm club. From 1954-1960, Paul played in the big leagues with the New York and then San Francisco Giants and the Pittsburgh Pirates. He also served for two years in the Army in between those playing stints.

Then, in 1960, the Pirates sent him down to the minors. At the time he was going to graduate school at San Francisco State College and considered hanging it up. Suddenly, he was given an opportunity to come home to Minnesota. "Calvin Griffith called me and told me that the Minnesota Twins had purchased my contract from Pittsburgh and he'd like me to report to spring training," said Giel. "I thought I would give it another try in my own backyard, but I didn't do very well and they traded me to the Athletics that June. I went to Kansas City, played one game, said 'this is enough,' and retired."

"Luckily, the way it worked out, after playing with all those teams for all those years, combined with my two years in the service, I qualified for the Major League Baseball pension plan," added Giel. "I started collecting that at 59, and I must say, after all these years it's very nice!"

After his retirement from Organized Baseball in 1961, Giel moved back to his native Minnesota to work as a business manager with the expansion Vikings. From there he got into radio, where he worked for eight years as the sports director at WCCO.

Then he was presented with the opportunity to return to his alma mater, this time in an administrative capacity. In 1971, then University President, Dr. Malcom Moos named the native son as the school's new athletic director. In Giel's 18 years of running the athletic department, he described some of his biggest thrills as: retiring Bruce Smith and Bronko Nagurski's numbers, and renaming the baseball stadium, hockey arena and golf course as "Siebert Field," "Mariucci Arena," and "The Les Bolstad Golf Course," respectively.

Giel is also proud of the fact that his administration erased a $500,000 deficit that was bequeathed to him when he arrived, and left the program with a nice surplus when he departed. No sports were cut in his tenure, and overall he felt that the athletic department and all of its sports teams were stronger when he left than when he had arrived. He said that he doesn't miss the eleven Saturday's during football season, nor does he miss all the "hypocritical second guessing."

Paul Giel is a legend at the University of Minnesota. He was one of those players that comes around once in a millennium. He played the game like no one will again, and did it with an unpretentious demeanor, earning the respect of his teammates and his opponents alike. It has been 44 years since he first lived out his dream of playing football for the Golden Gophers at Memorial Stadium. The old brick stadium is gone, but memories of Paul Giel live on forever.

Perhaps Big Ten Commissioner Kenneth "Tug" Wilson said it best when he described Giel as being a great ambassador for collegiate athletics: "He was not only an inspiration to his teammates, he was an inspiration to anyone who was privileged to watch him play. A modest unassuming individual off the field, once on the gridiron, Giel seemed to be inspired."

Who was your hero when you were growing up?
"The great Bruce Smith. When I was kid, around eight or nine years old, Bruce Smith was my hero. When we would play football in the backyard, I pretended to be Bruce Smith. It was a thrill to meet him later on in life. He was an All-American in every sense of the word."

What did it mean for you to be a Gopher?
"Coming out of high school in Winona, I was really steeped in the tradition of the Gophers, and because of guys like Bruce Smith, I wanted to be a Gopher. Also, because I could play both football and baseball there, it was even better. It meant everything for me to be a Gopher."

Gopher tombstone:
"I owe everything I have to the University of Minnesota. It gave me a chance academically, athletically, and because of my visibility as a Gopher, it got me a chance to work with the Vikings and later WCCO where my name meant something. I might have been angry with a few individuals at the time I left the position of athletic director, but not the University itself,

and certainly not the Athletic Department. It was a great experience for me."

Where are they now?
Paul and his wife Nancy live in the Twin Cites. They have three children. Currently Paul works in fundraising for the Minneapolis Heart Institute Foundation.

Tributes

"As a kid I tried to copy Paul Giel, he was like a ghost. I used to emulate his style. He was so smooth."
-- Sandy Stephens

"If it wasn't for Paul Giel giving me a break and hiring me, I don't know what would've become of my career. I was very grateful for what he did for me."
-- Herb Brooks

JOHN MARIUCCI
The Gophers Make a Run for the NCAA Championship

The University of Minnesota's John Mariucci was the godfather of American amateur hockey and the patriarch of the puck sport in our state.

What John did for the sport was immeasurable. With his passion for competing, teaching, and spreading the gospel about the sport he loved, Mariucci went on to become the country's most important figure in the development of amateur hockey in America. After a storied career in the NHL, Maroosh came home to his alma mater to coach the Gophers. Although he never won the NCAA championship during his 14-year tenure at the U of M, he came pretty darn close in 1954 with the best line ever to play college hockey.

Bridesmaids again
When the 1953-54 collegiate hockey season started, the U was on a mission to avenge their NCAA Finals loss to Michigan the season before. After losing the first two games of the new season, the Gophers got back on track and lost only one of the next dozen games. After splitting with Michigan, Minnesota then swept Michigan State twice, Michigan Tech, North Dakota, and Denver, only to get beat twice by Michigan at season's end. The Gophers finished the

season with a 24-6-1 record, the best in the nation, and won their second straight WIHL title.

Hockey fans were anticipating a rematch in the NCAA Finals in Colorado Springs between Minnesota and Michigan. But the maroon and gold had to first get by Boston College in the semifinals. Minnesota pummeled outmanned BC, 14-1, behind an amazing effort from the best line in college hockey. John Mayasich scored three goals and added four assists. Dick Dougherty scored four goals and added two assists, and Gene Campbell added three goals and two assists. Then, to the Gophers' disappointment, they found out that the Michigan Wolverines had been knocked off by unheralded Rennselaer Polytechnic Institute (RPI) in the semifinals.

Minnesota was clearly favored (by five goals) in most spreads. Colorado Springs' Broadmoor Arena was packed with puck fanatics as the game got underway with the Engineers striking first at 17:07 of the first, on an Abbey Moore back-hander that beat Gopher goalie Jim Mattson. Then RPI scored on a Gopher power-play to make it two-zip. Then at 2:45 of the second, the Fighting Engineers threatened to run away with it, when they scored again to make it 3-0. The Gophers were stunned, but, 24 seconds later, Minnesota got on the board with a Kenny Yackel blast, followed by a Dougherty shot from team captain Campbell that made it 3-2. Then, after peppering the Engineer goalie, Mayasich put in a back-hander to even it up at three-apiece in the third. Four minutes later Mayasich set up Dougherty on a pretty "five-hole" goal to finally take the lead. But, at 16:10 the men from Troy, N.Y., evened things up one more time, as Moore scored again to send the game into overtime.

At 1:54 of the extra session, after a mix-up out in front of the net, RPI's Gordie Peterson, found a loose puck in front of Mattson and promptly drilled it home to win the game by 5-4. It was a devastating defeat and a big blow to coach Maroosh, who wanted so badly to win the big one for Minnesota. After the game, the players huddled around their coach to shield him from the press and their cameras. It was the first and only time Minnesota hockey players would ever see this giant of a man cry openly. Despite the loss, Yackel, Mattson, Dougherty, and Mayasich were all named to the All-American team.

Growing up in Hockey Central
John Mariucci was born the son of Italian immigrants on May 8, 1916, in the birthplace of hockey in the United States, Eveleth, Minn., on the great Mesabi Iron Range. He grew up on Hay Street, also referred to by locals as "Incubator Street" because it was said that there were so many nationalities living there, and every house had eight or nine kids inside. Many of the kids of the immi-

grants would play outdoor hockey to stay out of trouble. Some kids didn't even have skates, so they wore overshoes, and others used tree branches for sticks. John found his first pair of skates in a garbage can and, because he didn't have money to buy equipment, wrapped old magazines around his shins for pads.

Even though it was a mid-sized Minnesota Iron Range town, Eveleth was as sophisticated as New York City when it came to hockey. Eveleth was once a member of a big league hockey circuit that competed with cities such as Toronto and Chicago. Eveleth kids would try to emulate the many Canadians who were imported to the city to play hockey as one of the forms of entertainment provided for iron-ore miners. John learned the game from legendary hall of fame coach Cliff Thompson whose tenure as the Eveleth High School hockey coach lasted nearly 40 years.

Going south
In 1936, Maroosh left Eveleth and the Range and headed 200 miles south to the University of Minnesota. There he starred as a defenseman for Larry Armstrong's hockey team and also played offensive and defensive end alongside of Butch Nash under the Gophers' legendary football coach Bernie Bierman. Unfortunately, Mariucci played in between two bookend National Championship teams in 1936 and 1940. However, Minnesota did win the Big Ten football title in 1938. "I believe I have the only lineman in America who can extract people's teeth with his fists on the line of scrimmage," said Bernie about his star end Mariucci.

In 1940, led by Bud Wilkinson, the future football coaching legend at the University of Oklahoma in the nets, Mariucci captained the National AAU Championship team (at the time it was the only championship available in college hockey). After that season, Maroosh, who had been named to the All-American team, was offered the head coaching position at the U, but turned it down to play in the pros.

A yank in the NHL
After a brief stint with Providence in the American Hockey League, Maroosh joined the Chicago Blackhawks to finish out the 1940 season. At that time the NHL employed few Americans and not many college-bred players. (To put this into perspective, by 1968, only six Americans and five collegians had played in the NHL.) Johnny played there until 1942, when he was summoned to join the United States Coast Guard. There he played for the Coast Guard team in the Eastern Amateur League during the second world war. After turning down another offer to return to the U of M, he returned to the Hawks for the 1945 season. In 1947, Maroosh became the first American-developed player ever to captain an NHL team.

The rugged Maroosh was one of the biggest celebrities in Chicago during his playing days there. He became famous among Windy City hockey fans for his brawls, one in particular with Detroit's Black Jack Stewart, which remains the NHL's longest ever, lasting more

TIMELINE

Gopher defenseman Ken Yackel, Sr. is named to the All-American hockey team	Gopher halfback Bob McNamara is named to the All-American football team	Gopher goalie Jim Mattson is named to the All-American hockey team	Gopher end Bert Baston is inducted into the College Football Hall of Fame	Gopher fullback Herb Joesting is inducted into the College Football Hall of Fame	Gopher coach Fritz Crisler is inducted into the College Football Hall of Fame	Gopher tackle Ed Widseth is inducted into the College Football Hall of Fame	Gopher tackle Dick Wildung is inducted into the College Football Hall of Fame	Gopher winger Dick Dougherty is named to the All-American hockey team	Gopher tackle Leo Nomellini is inducted into the College Football Hall of Fame

than a half an hour. In 1948, Maroosh called it quits in Chicago. For his career in the NHL, he scored 11 goals and 34 assists for 45 points over 223 games. He also played in two Stanley Cup playoffs. More importantly, he led the team in penalty minutes, racking up more than 300 over his career. He was a role-playing hatchet man who protected and defended his teammates. That's why they loved and appreciated him.

Mariucci went on to play for St. Louis of the American League, St. Paul and Minneapolis of the U.S. League, and again with a Coast Guard team before hanging up his skates as an active player in 1951. He then turned to coaching, when he was named the head coach of Minneapolis Millers hockey team of the A.A.L.

Back to the U
After a year with the Millers, Maroosh finally came home to coach his Gophers, replacing former Blackhawk Doc Romnes. It was only a part-time job for him, as he continued to also work as a salesman for the Martin Falk Paper Company. "It's a good thing for me not to have to depend upon the hockey job for my livelihood," said Mariucci. "Financial independence removes me from the absolute necessity of producing a winning team, and the worry and pressure connected with it which might make me resort to some actions which -- well, you know, which are not quite above the board." In his first season he was awarded Coach of the Year honors. It was the first of many.

He got Minneapolis residents excited about college hockey, and they responded by coming out in droves to see his Gophers. The U even had to add an upper tier of seats to the Williams Arena rink to accommodate them all. Maroosh was always trying new things to keep the fans interested and was always looking for new recruits. One time while watching the giant Bill Simonovich, from Gilbert, Minn., play with the varsity basketball team, John said: "Man, what a goalie he'd make! Give him a couple of mattresses and a pair of skis and nobody would ever score on him."

In a sport dominated by Canadians, Maroosh championed the American boys and in particular, Minnesotans. After watching an NCAA Final one time, he said: "It's asinine that the only two Americans on the ice for the NCAA championship game were the referees." Maroosh was a visionary and saw the potential growth of the sport.

"College could be a developmental program for our own country, for the Olympics and for the pros," he said. "College hockey is a state institution and should be represented by Minnesota boys," said Maroosh. "If they're not quite as good as some Canadians, we'll just have to work a little harder, that's all." It became political for Mariucci as he battled to stop the importation of the older Canadian players and give the American kids an equal playing field. In the late 1950s, the U's athletic director, Marsh Ryman, refused to play Denver's Canadian-filled teams. This ultimately led to the end of the WIHL and the creation of the WCHA in 1959.

"What I was against was the junior player who played in Canada until he was 21, then, if the pros didn't sign him, he would come to this country to play college hockey as a 22-year-old freshman against our 18-year-olds," said Mariucci. "It wasn't fair to our kids, who were finishing college at the same age Canadians were freshmen."

Mariucci left the University in 1966 with a record of 207-142-15, including conference championships in 1953 and 1954 and three NCAA playoff appearances (including another Final Four appearance in 1961). Included in his tenure was an Italian homecoming of sorts, when he was led the Americans to a silver medal in the 1956 Olympics in Cortina. There were 11 Minnesota natives on the team that stunned heavily favored Canada before falling to the Soviet Union. Mariucci's successor at the U was Glen Sonmor, a former teammate with the Minneapolis Millers.

Back to the NHL
In 1966, another chapter of Mariucci's storied life unfolded as he became chief scout and special assistant to Wren Blair, GM of the NHL's expansion North Stars. There Maroosh applied his vast knowledge of recruiting, coaching, and scouting. In 1977, Mariucci coached the U.S. National team. He later rejoined the North Stars, this time as Assistant G.M. under his former player, Lou Nanne. "One word of advice to all you coaches," said Maroosh. "Be good to your players; you never know which one might someday be your boss."

The Noble Roman
John's accomplishments and honors are far too great to list here. Some of his more notable honors include: Being inducted as a charter member of the U.S. Hockey Hall of Fame in his hometown of Eveleth; being inducted into the NHL Hockey Hall of Fame in Toronto; and receiving the NHL's coveted Lester Patrick Award for his contributions to U.S. hockey. He also made a difference by giving to others. He devoted much of his life to Brainerd's Camp Confidence, for the mentally-retarded.

On March 2, 1985, in an emotional ceremony to give thanks and immortalize the man forever, the U of M renamed the hockey half of Williams Arena as Mariucci Arena, in his honor. It was also declared John Mariucci Day in Minnesota by Governor Perpich. During the ceremony, long-time Maroosh friend Robert Ridder said: "During the 1980 Olympics, a U.S. Destroyer passed a Russian ship and signaled to it: 'U.S.A. 4, Russia 3.' Probably nobody on that boat ever heard of John Mariucci, but it wouldn't have been possible without John Mariucci." Two years later, in 1987, Maroosh died at 70 after a long bout with cancer. He had seven children and several grandchildren.

The gentleman brawler
Maroosh was a legend, on and off the ice. Although he was tough as nails, his wit, intelligence, and personality were one-of-a-kind. John was one of the toughest Italians who ever lived. His face has often been referred to as a "blocked punt," because it was so beat up. But what separated him from the goons was that he wouldn't just knock his opponents down, he'd pick them up and then make them laugh at his jokes.

Perhaps Herb Brooks said it best: "In all social caus-

es to better an institution, there's always got to be a rallying force, a catalyst, a glue, and a magnet, and that's what John was, for American hockey. The rest of us just filled in after him."

Full of wit, he was described as a newspaperman's dream-come-true. From his famous brawls, which included once breaking thumb-wrestling champion Murray Warmath's thumb, Mariucci gained a lot of mileage. Local reporters found themselves having a lot of dinners that turned into breakfasts while listening to his endless stories. The sports community was in awe of him, and he made journalists who hated the sport want to cover hockey.

He was also the pioneer in the development of hockey in Minnesota. Because of that, his legacy will live on forever. Every kid that laces up his or her skates needs to give thanks to the man that started it all. He started grassroots youth programs, put on coaching clinics, attended new arena openings in countless cities across the state, helped former players find coaching positions, and even encouraged hockey moms to write to city councils to build rinks and develop recreation programs. Because of him, hockey in Minnesota carries the same pedigree as basketball in Indiana or football in Texas. Described best by his friends and players as father-like, magical, and even super-human, he was simply the greatest.

Thanks Maroosh.

Chuck Mencel could flat-out shoot, and that's why he was one of the greatest guards ever to play for the University of Minnesota basketball Gophers. Mencel had poise, court-savvy, tremendous ball-handling skills, and was extremely accurate from the field as well as the line. He worked hard at the fundamentals and optimized the cliché, "lead by example." In 1955, Chuck was honored as the first Minnesota player ever to be named as the Big Ten MVP. But, he would have traded it all to knock off the powerful Iowa Hawkeyes that year for the conference title.

Minnesota was coming off a respectable third place finish in the Big Ten in 1954, with a 10-4 conference record. The outlook was cautiously optimistic for the 1954-55 season. Although the Gophers were young, they had returning All-Big Ten players Mencel and Dick Garmaker, both of whom were named as the upcoming seasons co-captains. The other three Gopher starters were forward David Tucker, big Bill Simonovich at center, and Gerald "Buck" Lindsley at guard.

The season opened in the Windy City, where Ray Meyers' DePaul Blue Demons knocked off the

Gophers by 94-93 in an overtime thriller. Minnesota rebounded a week later when the Blue Demons came to Minneapolis as part of a home-and-home series to kick off the season. This time, the Gophers prevailed, 94-84. From there the Gophs were beaten by Oklahoma A&M, but rallied to win their next four games. The first two victories came at Williams Arena against SMU and Notre Dame. The maroon and gold then flew south to play in the Dixie Classic in Raleigh, N.C. There they defeated Wake Forest and Duke, but lost to North Carolina State for the championship.

It was back to Chicago for the U, as they headed north to take on Northwestern and open the Big Ten Conference schedule. In a heart-breaker, the Wildcats beat the Gophers 72-74. Next stop, Iowa, where the Gophers, led by Mencel and Garmaker, beat the arch-rival Hawkeyes, 81-80. That would prove to be a pivotal game for the squad as they sent a clear message to the Hawks that the Gophers meant business. The U of M went on to win their next two over Indiana and Purdue before losing to Michigan State, 75-87. From there the team rattled off seven straight wins, including triumphs over Northwestern, Purdue, Ohio State, Illinois, Indiana, Michigan, and Wisconsin.

In the game against the Badgers, Mencel poured in 23, and Garmaker had 28 to lead the way. Wisconsin, led by Dick Miller, who scored 31 in the game, rallied to go up by seven at the half. In the second, Hibbing's Garmaker took over, scoring 12 points in first five minutes to get the score to 49-48. The Badgers held the lead until Garmaker's tip-in made it 63-63. It went back and forth with less then two minutes left as Mencel stripped the ball from Miller. He passed it up to Garmaker, who put it in to make it 69-apiece. Now, with only 15 seconds to go, Mencel took the ball upcourt and got fouled. With only six ticks left on the clock, Mencel nailed both free throws to ice the game, 71-69.

The stage was set for the Big Ten title game as hated and feared Iowa came to town for the much-anticipated rematch of the titans. An record crowd, of 20,176 fans, showed up at Williams Arena in anticipation of the dynamic duo of Mencel and Garmaker bringing down the vaunted Hawkeyes. Williams Arena had never held so many spectators for a basketball game, and it will never again as fire codes now prevent such an occurrence. The contest went back and forth as Minnesota shot 43 percent in the first half to take a 35-33 halftime lead.

The Hawks were led by their big man, Bill Logan, who had 15 of his 25 points in the first half. In the second half, the battle continued as both teams sparred like heavyweight champions. With just over four minutes to play, Mencel scored six straight of his team-high 27 points to give the Gophers a 70-67

lead. But at 2:23, Iowa's guard play brought the Hawks back on top, 71-70. With two minutes to go, Mencel missed a key shot, followed by Buck Lindsley, who had a chance to get the Gophers back into it, but missed a free throw at the end of the game. It was Iowa's night, as they shot an incredible 67 percent in the second and held on to beat the Gophers, 72-70. It was an incredibly crushing loss for Minnesota and somewhat ironic in that Iowa, the league's worst from the stripe, won the game on the line, beating Minnesota, the league's best free throw shooting team.

The last game of the year featured a rematch with the Badgers. The Gophers not only needed to win the game, but also had to have some help from Lady Luck to have any chance to win the conference title. It was the great Mencel's farewell to Williams Arena. Appropriately enough, his last game was against his home-state Badgers. Minnesota, its backs to the wall, hung it all out on the line that night. Coach Ozzie Cowles' boys held the lead at the half, 32-31, after Mencel popped a deuce from the post.

Then, the Badgers went ahead, but the Gophers rallied with 12 minutes to go, narrowing the gap to 50-48 off a pair from Lindsley, who had 17 points. At the four-minute mark, the Gophers were still in it at 72-67, but that would be as close as they would come in the season finale. Cowles removed Mencel and Garmaker with a minute left and the crowd responded with a thunderous roar of appreciation for all their hard work over the years. Minnesota lost by the final of 78-72, and sent Iowa to the NCAA Tournament.

How good was Iowa that year? Led by Logan, Carl Cain, and Sharm Scheuerman, the Hawkeyes waltzed past Penn State and Marquette before losing to All-American sensation Tom Gola and LaSalle in the NCAA Final Four by 76-73.

"It was a letdown for me at the time, but also became the springboard to a much more expanded view of opportunity, both in an athletic and business sense," says Mencel today. "I'm not going to say we should have won the Iowa game, but we could have easily won it. I've got a video tape of the game, and I still bring it out and watch it every now and then. It was a great, great game - a disappointment - but definitely my most memorable as a Gopher. The thing that stands out for me most, was that it was probably my best game as a Gopher, but we still lost. And then losing to Wisconsin in the next game was a tough way for me to bow out."

The Gophers led the Big Ten in defense that season, and finished the year with a 10-4 record in the Big Ten, 15-7 overall. But because of the Wisconsin disappointment on the last day of the season, they wound up as the conference bridesmaids. Mencel was named as the team's MVP that year and was also named to the All-Big Ten and All-American squads. For his efforts he was awarded with the Chicago Tribune's Silver Basketball Award, signifying the Big Ten's most valuable player.

TIMELINE

Gopher forward Dick Garmaker is named to the All-American basketball team	"The Buffalo Rodeo" is started. Today, 43 years later, it is the state's oldest and largest continuous rodeo event.	The state's largest lake trout is caught by G.H. Nelson on Lake Superior, near Hovland; 43 lbs., 8 oz.	Gopher coach Bernie Bierman is inducted into the College Football Hall of Fame	The Minneapolis Millers host the American Association's All-Star Game	The Millers beat the Rochester Red Wings for the Little World Series Championship	The Hibbing Curling Club host's its first annual "Last Chance Bonspiel." Today, 42 years later, the invitational affair features 128 men's teams from both the US and Canada, which compete in five events over a five day period. A total of 13 sheets of ice are put into place at the Hibbing Memorial Arena for the event, therefore making it the largest bonspiel of its kind under one roof. The Hibbing Curling Club, rich in tradition, has won an amazing 14 National Championships since its inception in 1913.

The golden touch

Averaging 16 points per game, Mencel held five Gopher scoring records during his tenure at the U, and he still ranks eighth all-time in career scoring, with 1,391 points. He held the school's scoring record for nearly a quarter of a century, until Mychal Thompson broke it in the late 1970s. He also still holds the record for the most field goals attempted, with 1,635. During his sophomore, junior, and senior seasons in the Big Ten, he scored 766 points, then a school record. An outstanding student, he graduated that same year with a bachelor's degree in Business Administration. What's even more impressive is that he did it all while taking care of his family. You see, Chuck married his high school sweet-heart when he was a sophomore at the U, and before he graduated, he had two children.

Mencel's partner in crime during the mid-50s was fellow All-American Garmaker, a transfer student from Hibbing Junior College on the Mesabi Iron Range. Garmaker was a tremendous rebounder, defender, free-throw shooter and could do a lot of damage with his jump shot. Over his career at Minnesota, Garmaker set eight scoring records. He and Mencel went on to play together for a couple of years with the Lakers, and Garmaker went on to finish his career with the New York Knicks.

"Dick Garmaker and I were the two seniors on an otherwise underclass team," said Mencel. "We had a great time playing together for the Gophers and, later, the Lakers. He was certainly my closest friend on the team and he was a great ball player. We're still close today."

Chuck had the golden shooting touch and was acknowledged as one of Minnesota's greatest team players. He was widely regarded as the premier pure shooter of his day and, because of his quickness and shooting ability, revolutionized many aspects of the game. There's no telling just how good Mencel would have been if he had played in the NBA after the dawn of the three-point line. Although he didn't bring home the hardware for Minnesota in 1955, he made Minnesota proud of the U's basketball program and got people all over the state excited about college hoops.

From the Badger State

Chuck Mencel was born in Phillips, Wis., the oldest of three children. He grew up spending much of his time playing basketball at the local YMCA. "When my parents got divorced while I was in the seventh grade, the basketball gymnasium became my safe haven," said Mencel. He went on to play basketball at Eau Claire High School, becoming the only non-senior to make the squad. His team made it all the way to the Wisconsin State Basketball Tournament but lost in the championship game to St. Croix Falls. During that season, he broke his school's single-game and season scoring records. After his senior year he was selected to the national high school All-American team.

After a stellar prep career, Mencel accepted a scholarship to attend Bradley University in Peoria, Ill. But when allegations of a basketball betting scandal broke out that summer, Mencel elected to attend Minnesota. "The scandal was a big red flag for me, so I immediately decided to attend the U of M," said Mencel. Because of the Korean War, freshmen were allowed to participate in intercollegiate sports, and Mencel took every advantage of his playing time. While at the U, Chuck wound up living in possibly the most athletic dorm room of all time. That's because his roommate was Gopher hockey star John Mayasich.

After his illustrious career at Minnesota, Mencel was drafted by the Lakers. But, that summer before his first season, he was invited to play on the traveling team that played the Harlem Globetrotters. It was a 24-city tour and he was paid $100 per game. This was a real team Mencel played for. They played to win and weren't stooges like the Trotter opponents are today.

Chuck then started as point guard for the Lakers and averaged seven points and led the team in assists with three per game. His career was cut short after only two years in the NBA, due to the fact that he was required to fulfill his military obligation, which he had deferred out of college. So he joined the Army as a second lieutenant in the Transportation Corps and was stationed in Fort Eustis, Va. After that, Chuck decided to abandon the NBA and enter the world of business, where he applied that same zealous attitude of hard work and success that he had on the court.

Who was your hero when you were growing up?
"Clayton Anderson, the executive director of the YMCA in Eau Claire. He was a strong leader who believed in discipline and was able to motivate his young players. He was my inspiration to excel in athletics."

What did it mean for you to be a Gopher?
"In hindsight, it really set the table for a lifestyle that was unparalleled in my expectations as a young person. To have played and been successful at a major institution like the U of M and in a conference such as the Big Ten was just incredible. As an athlete, it was wonderful stepping stone to the business world that gave me the ability to raise my family and live a standard of life that I never dreamed would be possible. If I had not come to Minnesota - who knows? I can't imagine that it would have been any better for me anywhere else. It was a wonderful experience."

Gopher tombstone:
"I see myself as a very fierce competitor, never giving up hope of a victory. I hope that I demonstrated that during my playing time. I felt like I always expected victory, but I was never discouraged by defeat."

Where are they now?
Chuck and his wife Ann live in Minnetonka. They have three children: Vicki, Debra, and Mike, and seven grandchildren. "They all live within 20 miles, and that's one of the best things in our lives," said Chuck. As of 1994, Mencel retired as the president and chief executive officer of Caterpillar Paving Products, Brooklyn Park, Minn. He also remains active with his alma mater and was very involved in the capital campaign that helped finance the renovation and construction of various on-campus sports facilities.

Tributes

"Chuck was such a good, sound ballplayer. He was solid with the fundamentals and, not only that, he had such a great shot. He had his jumpshot of his down pat! He was a super guy and a great player. He had a great career at the University and he was a great addition to our Laker teams."
-- John Kundla

"He had a nice career here with both the Gophers and the Lakers and was just a real good player."
-- George Mikan

"I met Chuck as a freshman in Pioneer Hall, and we became roommates and best friends. I really admired him as an individual. He had such a wonderful personality. We were like brothers. We helped each other socially, athletically, and academically. He was a great athlete, student, and friend. He exhibits the same traits today, and we're still the best of friends. Now we see each other quite frequently on the golf course."
-- John Mayasich

There were plenty of reasons for optimism with University of Minnesota baseball heading into the 1956 season under head coach Dick Siebert. The Gophers were coming off a respectable 19-9 campaign that previous spring and had all the necessary confidence to make a legitimate run for the Big Ten title.

The maroon and gold did finish the regular season with an incredible 33-9 overall record, as well as finishing 11-2 in the conference. They captured the Big Ten title, but didn't stop there. They went on and become the first Golden Gopher baseball team to win the NCAA championship in the College World Series in Omaha.

Siebert's team met the Fighting Irish in the first round of the NCAA playoffs, beating Notre Dame in the best of three in Minneapolis. The Gophers then went on to sweep Ohio University in the Mideast Region finals in Athens, Ohio. Now it was onto Omaha for the College World Series. In the first round, they beat Wyoming, 4-0, then Arizona 3-1, followed by a win over Mississippi by the score of 12-5.

Minnesota was then beaten by Arizona, 10-4, but the

Gophers rallied back to beat Bradley University, 8-3, to earn a spot in the finals. There, they faced Arizona one more time, only this time it was for all the marbles.

The Gophers jumped out to a quick 1-0 lead when Gopher captain, Bill Horning, from Watertown, S.D., led off the first inning with a single, stole second, and then scored on a Doug Lindblom double. Minnesota never relinquished the lead after that. Doug Gillen followed with another double and, before you knew it, coach Siebert's boys were up by 3-0. It became 4-0 in the fourth after two walks, plus another Horning single, and 10-0 after a six-run fifth inning where the Gopher bats really came alive. With the score 10-1 in the seventh, Horning belted his second homer of the game to put the final nail in the Wildcat coffin. Along with Horning's four hits, other Gophers who had hits in the game included Gillen, McNeeley and David Lindblom, who each had a pair, and Jack McCartan, Jerry Kindall, R. Anderson and Gene Martin, who each added one.

Gopher pitcher Jerry Thomas pitched masterfully, giving up only five hits en route to mowing down four Wildcats, and walking only one. Amazingly, Thomas retired the side 1-2-3 for six of the nine innings and, at the plate, even added two hits for the cause. It was only after an error and a questionable wild pitch that Arizona even got on the board. For his efforts, Thomas, who earlier had also beaten Arizona, 3-1, was selected as the MVP of the College World Series. After the final out, Siebert rushed out to the mound to give his star pitcher a hero's ride on his a shoulders back to the dugout. With the convincing final score of 12-1, the Gophers won their first ever NCAA baseball championship.

In 1956, Minnesota featured a superb blend of intimidating hitting, dominating pitching, and smooth fielding. Led on the mound by All-American Thomas, who won 12 games that season while going 5-0 in conference games, the Gophers started a string of what would be 11 Big Ten championships and three NCAA titles over coach Siebert's brilliant 31-year career. Leading the way offensively was slugger McCartan, who was not only an All-American (1958) third baseman on the baseball team, but was also an All-American goalie on the hockey team. In addition McCartan went on to lead the USA Hockey team to gold in the 1960 Olympics where he was named the "All-World" goaltender.

Also, Kindall, the Big Ten batting champion and All-American, played a mean shortstop for the Gophers. Both men went on to successful pro careers, Kindall with the Cubs and Twins and McCartan in the NHL. The Gophers hit .320 as a team and boasted an amazing .976 fielding percentage. The con-

ference championship ended an 18-year drought for the Gophers, who are typically at an arctic disadvantage geographically against the southern schools who have the luxury of having longer and more temperate practicing weather.

On winning his first NCAA crown, said Coach Siebert afterward: "You're always prejudiced about your own kids, but I think this was the greatest team that ever played in the College World Series." He went on to add, "This was my greatest thrill, barring none!"

The Chief
A native of Fall River, Mass., Siebert began his baseball days at St. Paul Concordia High School and he later attended Concordia Junior College. From there he moved to the Concordia Seminary in St. Louis with full intentions of becoming a Lutheran minister. But the lure of baseball was too much for the calling of the pulpit, and so Dick started his pro baseball career in 1932. Originally a pitcher, Siebert switched over to first base when he developed some arm problems.

He went on to play for Ohio, Pennsylvania, and New York minor league teams, and, in 1935, he joined Buffalo in the International League. Siebert became a member of the Brooklyn Dodgers system, and later the Chicago Cubs and St. Louis Cardinals systems until 1938, when he became a regular first baseman for the Philadelphia Athletics under the legendary Connie Mack.

Siebert played for the A's through 1945 and appeared in the 1942 All Star game. He was chosen as an all star again in 1945 only to see the game canceled due to wartime restrictions. Siebert later recalled his greatest day in the big leagues was when he broke up a no hit attempt by Cleveland great Bob Feller. Siebert played in 1,035 games over his big league career and finished with a respectable .282 lifetime batting average.

Hanging up his cleats
Siebert's pro career came to an abrupt end in 1946 due to some unfortunate contract problems with management. He simply traded in his first-baseman's mitt for a microphone when he accepted the position of sportscaster with WTCN radio in Minneapolis. But, only one year later, Siebert would get the baseball itch one more time. This time it was to take over as head coach of the Golden Gophers. (Later he would do radio and television work with WCCO as well.)

Rookie coach
Dick took the reigns as the University of Minnesota head coach in 1947 from then-head coach David MacMillan. No one in the University's athletic department could've known it at the time, but they were creating a living legend when they hired him as head baseball coach. The "Chief" was one of the greatest coaches in college baseball history.

Siebert helped develop baseball at all levels in Minnesota. He was a pioneer and was credited with

introducing the aluminum bat and designated hitter to college baseball. As a coach, he emulated many of the mannerisms of his long-time mentor, Connie Mack.

A president of the American College Baseball Coaches Association, college baseball's Coach of the Year in 1956 & 1960, and three-time winner of the NCAA Championship, Siebert would later refer to the trouncing of Arizona in the 1956 College World Series and the amazing come-from-behind win over USC in the 1960 Series as his most memorable moments in baseball. He compiled one of the most incredible records in college baseball history. The winningest coach in Gopher history, his final record reads 754 wins against 361 losses, with a .676 winning percentage.

He is one of only a few coaches at major universities to have coached a team to more than 700 wins. He sent five different teams to the College World Series and of course, he brought home three titles. His teams also captured 11 Big Ten titles as well. Amazingly, he endured only three losing seasons. He is a member of the College Baseball Hall of Fame and was a recipient of college baseball's highest award, the Lefty Gomez Trophy, which recognizes the individual who has given the most outstanding contribution and service to the development of college baseball.

After 31 years of coaching in Gold Country, Siebert retired at the end of the 1978 season. Sadly, on December 9, of that same year, the Chief died, succumbing to numerous respiratory and cardiac illnesses. Dick was survived by his wife Marie and their children: Marilyn, Beverly, Richard, and Paul - who went on to play ball in the major leagues with the Mets and Cardinals.

In his last year of life, Siebert was quoted as saying: "I actually expected my coaching job at the U to last a few years and then I would go into business. No one in the world could have convinced me then I would still be here 31 years later. But I loved it, working with great young men and staying active in the best form of baseball I knew, the college game."

Immortalized
On Saturday, April 21, 1979, the University of Minnesota Baseball Stadium was officially renamed "Siebert Field," in honor of the greatest Gopher baseball coach. The entire baseball world mourned his passing, and tributes to the coach came from every corner of the baseball world.

For more than three decades, the Chief brought honor and respect to the University of Minnesota baseball program. Dick was a true ballplayer and a real throwback to another era. A tireless worker, his life was consumed with Gopher baseball. The cold weather was no match for the Chief, because he worked at his craft all-year long. Whether it was from his old Cooke Hall office, or from the fieldhouse, he was always trying to improve and help his teams to win.

He was a man who learned virtually every aspect of the game of baseball throughout his life and chose to teach others what he had to learn mostly on his own. He was a teacher, a coach, a mentor, and a friend. We appreciate coach Siebert for all these things, but also, maybe especially, for the fact that he did so much of it with local home-grown talent. He will be forever

thought of as the standard to which all other coaches will be measured against.

Tributes

"He was a tremendous teacher. I think baseball at the University of Minnesota was successful under him because of the fact that he knew how to teach college players to be fundamentally sound. He taught us how to execute and gave us a chance to be competitive with any college team in the nation. That's why we could go from the fieldhouse to the ball field at the University of Texas and be competitive, because we were always the type of teams that wouldn't beat ourselves. We did the little things that would give us the chance to compete on a day to day basis. Personally, he was great to me and is one of the people who helped me get to where I am today. When you played for the Chief, you were playing for a man with a national reputation. He felt he never had to go out of the state to get his players, and he competed on a national scale. The Chief put a lot of pride in that Minnesota uniform for us."   **-- Paul Molitor**

"Dick Siebert was a great coach, and I really enjoyed my playing days at the University of Minnesota working with him. I felt that I was as good a hitter as I was a pitcher in college, but they wouldn't let me hit, insisting instead that I become specialized. My friends would come to the games and yell at him, 'Put in Winfield and let him hit, because he's the best hitter you've got!' But it didn't matter how good or bad you were, you had to get out there and work when you played for the Chief. You could be a star on his team, but he played no favorites and treated everyone alike. I learned a lot playing for him."   **-- Dave Winfield**

"Dick Siebert was just a heck of an all-around guy. He was a very fine coach, and I had so much respect for him as a man. He knew the fundamentals of the game so well, but he had a sense of humor and made it fun for you. I learned the game from Dick, and even while I was in the majors, I still felt like he was better than

most of the managers that I had. Every person on the team respected him and he got a lot out of his kids."
                    -- Paul Giel

"He was one of the finest coaches I ever had. He was a great baseball teacher."   **-- Bud Grant**

"Obviously, he was one of the great college coaches of all time. But I remember Dick Siebert best as a great baseball player with the Philadelphia Athletics. He was a damn good first baseman. He had a style of hitting with a distinct open stance. And he could field as well as anyone who ever put a mitt on. He was fantastic in the field."   **-- Calvin Griffith**

"When you think about Dick, you don't just think about his record at Minnesota, which is distinction enough in itself. But I don't think people realize what he did for college baseball in general. Dick was one of the leaders in restoring good relations with major league baseball. There was a time when there was an antagonistic, very tense, relationship between the colleges and the pros. He overcame that. And he was the most expert of all college baseball coaches on the rules of the game. He served on virtually every committee that college baseball has instituted. I think it's safe to say - and I don't think I'm stretching it at all - that Dick was the most highly respected and honored coach in collegiate baseball."   **-- Jerry Kindall**

"The Chief started it all for me. He gave me a shot my freshman year and it's been straight ahead for me since. He recommended me to a Texas scout when nobody else wanted me."   **-- Steve Comer**

Gopher tackle Bob Hobert is named to the All-American football team	Gopher shortstop Jerry Kindall is named to the All-American baseball team	Gopher pitcher Jerry Thomas is named to the All-American baseball team	The St. Paul Saints beat the Minneapolis Millers 4-0 in the last ever game played at Lexington Park Stadium	Duluth's Walter Hoover, considered one of the great oarsmen of his time, coaches the Olympic Rowing team to five medals.	Gopher track & field star, Ron Backes, wins the NCAA National Indoor shot-put Championship

TIMELINE

27

PATTY BERG

1957
An Incredible Year for Golf's Grand Dame

The greatest woman golfer ever to hail from Minnesota has to be Patty Berg. Born in Minneapolis in 1918, Berg's storied career as a golfer began in 1933, when at the age of 15 she entered her first tournament. It wasn't exactly an auspicious beginning, but since she has accomplished more than any other woman in the history of the game. She is today without question the matriarch of women's golf, as witness having been a founder of the LPGA (Ladies Professional Golf Association) in 1949 and having served three years as it's first president.

Berg's career resume is a Who's Who and What's What of women's golf; her list of tournament victories, lifetime achievement awards, honors, and tributes rendered her by organizations within and without the sports world borders on the incredible. She is indeed a living legend.

In 1940, having won 28 amateur titles, and having decided she wanted to make a career in golf, Berg turned professional. Apart from whatever else her decision may have resulted in, from 1941 through 1962 she won 57 professional tournaments, 15 of which were deemed majors. In all, throughout her

career as both an amateur and a professional, she won 85 tournaments.

A standout year for Minnesota's Patty was 1957. Named Woman Athlete of the Year by the Associated Press, she won five tournaments, two of them majors - the Titleholders Championship and the Western Open. Her other victories included the World Championship, the All-America Open, and the Havana Open. With earnings of $16,272, she was that years leading LPGA money-winner. (By way of contrast, today's LPGA leading money-winner earns over $1million.) In recognition of her outstanding year she received Golf Digest's Performance Average Award.

Early on Berg showed signs of being a natural athlete. She played baseball, took part in track and field events, and as a member of the Minneapolis Powderhorn Club won several national medals as a speed skater. She even played quarterback on her 50th Street and Colfax neighborhood football team, called the "50th Street Tigers." Patty was the quarterback because, as she puts it "I was the only one who could remember the plays!" Another famous Minnesota athlete, Bud Wilkinson, was a tackle on the team. Wilkinson, of course, went on to the University of Minnesota where he became an All-American football player and also played hockey for the Gophers. (From there, Bud went on to become one of the greatest college football coaches ever. During one stretch, his University of Oklahoma Sooners compiled five consecutive undefeated seasons.) According to Patty, it was only after Wilkinson suggested she "was too short and too slow, and that there was no future in football for me that I gave it up." Furthermore, her parents wanted her to specialize in a less violent sport, one that didn't tear her clothes. So the freckled-faced tomboy swapped her sneakers for golf shoes.

Patty's father came home one day in 1931 only to find his daughter digging up the back yard with one of his golf clubs. So, Herman Berg, a successful grain merchant, took his 13-year-old daughter to play at the prestigious Interlachen Country Club. It wasn't too long before she was outplaying her father.

Ready to test her new-found skills. patty entered her first ever tournament - the 1933 Minneapolis City Ladies Championship. "I qualified for the last flight with a 122," she recalls. "Then the woman I played in the first round beat me like a drum!"

A self-proclaimed perfectionist, Berg vowed to learn from that experience by going home and practicing for an entire year. "I said I'm going to work, and I'm going to work, and I'm going to see if I can't do better," says Berg. "And I worked. I concentrated and took my lessons, and finally, a year later, I came back

and I won that same Minneapolis City Ladies Championship!"

It was this relentless determination and pride that made her the premier player she was to become.

Patty won the Minnesota state title in 1935, then finished as runner-up to one of her golfing idols, Glenna Collett Vare (the woman for whom the LPGA's low annual scoring average honor is named) in the U.S. Women's Amateur, which was played at Interlachen. In between stints at the University of Minnesota, three years later she won the U.S. Women's Amateur title and was named the Associated Press' Woman Athlete of the Year.

Patty's father had a big influence on her as she grew up. In many ways her persona as a gallery favorite was shaped by him as he encouraged her both as a player as well as an entertainer. "I had played nine years of amateur golf, and during that time, when I wasn't in a tournament, my father had me play in a clinic and exhibition every weekend around the state of Minnesota to promote golf," says Patty.

"I'd take a popular football player or amateur golfer with me. The local club pro would put it (a clinic) on and we'd hit shots. Dad said that I had to do something for the game, and he felt this was a great idea." On train rides between exhibitions, Patty recalls reciting her favorite poems, particularly "Casey at the Bat."

In 1940, after winning 28 amateur titles, including three Titleholders Championships, which then were majors, Patty signed a contract with the Wilson Sporting Goods Company. Wilson took advantage of her outstanding communication skills as a motivator and educator by having her give clinics and exhibitions at universities throughout the country. An already famous woman and only in her early 20s, her name appeared on several different lines of Wilson clubs for women.

In 1941, after winning the Western Open, the Asheville Open, and the Lake Champlain Invitational, Patty was involved in an automobile accident that seriously injured her knee. As a result, she was sidelined for a year and a half. Then in 1943, the nation at war, Patty enlisted in the Marine Corps, serving as a first lieutenant, and doing what she did best -- recruiting, public relations, and promotions.

Over the next six years Patty won 15 tournaments including the first-ever Women's National Open Golf Championship, two Westerns, and one Titleholders Championships -- all considered major wins. As the first half-century ended, women's golf was gaining momentum, and there were new LPGA tour stops being created across the nation, with the prize money increasing annually.

Absolutely amazing
Throughout the ensuing years Patty was a vital, driving force behind the growing and struggling women'

28

rofessional golf tour. From 1950 to 1962 she won 41 tournaments, seven of them majors including four Western and three Titleholder Championships. She also received her third AP Woman Athlete of the Year award in 1955. In 1959 at Churchill Valley Country Club in Pittsburgh for the U.S. Women's Open she made a hole-in-one, becoming the first woman ever to do so in the event. Her 57 tour victories rank third all-time for women, only behind Kathy Whitworth's 88 and Mickey Wright's 82.

It must be remembered that Minnesota's Berg once literally dominated women's golf. Accordingly she has received nearly every major golf award known to the sport. Other accomplishments include setting a world record for a par 72 golf course by shooting a 64 (which stood for 12 years); becoming the LPGA top money winner in 1954, 1955, and 1957; and winning the Vare Trophy for the lowest tour scoring average three times. As an amateur, she also was a two-time member of the U.S. Curtis Cup Team.

Along with being inducted into the LPGA, American, Minnesota, Florida, and PGA halls of fame, Patty was formally inducted into the World Golf Hall of Fame at Pinehurst, N.C. in 1974. Her fellow inductees included Jack Nicklaus, Ben Hogan, Arnold Palmer, Sam Snead, Gary Player, Byron Nelson, and Gene Sarazen.

The LPGA named one of its top awards after Patty in recognition of attributes that include sportsmanship, diplomacy, goodwill, and overall contributions to the game.

In 1995 Patty became the first woman ever to receive the PGA's coveted Distinguished Service Award. It placed her in some fast company - Gerald Ford, Gene Sarazen, Byron Nelson, Arnold Palmer, and Bob Hope.

The showstopper

Patty has won nearly every major award for sports achievement and humanitarianism. What she did for, and gave to, golf is immeasurable. In great demand throughout the U.S. as a speaker, she once was described as having the delivery of Winston Churchill and FDR rolled into one. And she was sure to give everybody goosebumps at the end of her talks when she said, "God be with you and God Bless America!"

One of Patty's former golf students, fellow LPGA Hall of Fame member Kathy Whitworth, recalled, "We all accused Patty of being a frustrated actress. Her clinic was really a staged production. It ran like clockwork. Even though we all knew each line of Patty's, we'd still laugh and get tickled every time we heard her."

In a business relationship that has stretched nearly six decades, the Wilson company eventually rewarded Patty with a lifetime contract. What started as a speaking job for the company evolved into the clinic and exhibition routine she now calls her "golf show." It has been estimated that she alone has entertained several million golfers worldwide at her humorous yet informative instructional clinics and exhibitions. "She has done more to promote golf than any person in the history of the game," said LPGA great Betsy Rawls.

Golf's Grande Dame

Known for her shot-making ability as well as her showmanship, she will be remembered as one of the game's all-time best. Much of her marvelous iron play and pin-point accuracy can be traced back to the teachings of former University of Minnesota golf coach, Les Bolstad, who advised her for more than 40 years.

"I learned so much from Les over the years," said Patty. "He always told me that I had to learn the golf swing so that I could always teach myself how to conquer my flaws. He also taught me that all the clubs were equal, and one was no more important than another."

"Patty was a colorful performer and drew big crowds," said Bolstad. "She had it right from the start. Champions are a breed apart. They have a little extra stamina, talent, and coordination...plus a will to win. They can do things ordinary mortals can't do. They just stand out. Patty Berg was one of them, and she was a scrapper. She made clutch putt after clutch putt from above the hole to win tournaments."

Goodwill ambassador

Patty's name is synonymous with golf in that she has transcended gender and age to become one of the game's great goodwill ambassadors. Undoubtedly she's the best female promoter golf has ever had. And she truly made a difference in the world. One of its most admired and highly respected women, she is a sports role model kids can look up to. She was a pioneer, a good friend to all who knew her, and she devoted her entire life to the game she loves. And there's a generous and humanitarian side to her as well as she continues to give of herself, evidenced by her name on the cancer wing of the Southwest Medical Center in Fort Myers, Florida.

Who was your hero when you were growing up?
"When I was a young girl, I read about every athlete and tried to learn from them. Babe Zaharias was one of my idols, though. She was a great, great friend. She had a wonderful sense of humor. She got a charge out of everything."

Golf tombstone:
"I always tried to do the very best that I could, and that way if I ever lost I could always go home and put my head on my pillow still feeling satisfied. I remembered my mistakes and I learned from them. I always kept a journal of my mistakes so that in the off-season I could practice on my flaws. That was part of my will to win -- practicing the things that I needed to work on to improve my game every year."

On giving back to the game
"Golf has been so wonderful to me. In return, I enjoy doing something for it. If I can help somebody play a little better it makes me happy. If I feel that through showing them different shots, and making them laugh a little bit, and putting a few smiles on peoples' faces, well, that makes me happy, too."

What would you change?
"I wouldn't change anything. I couldn't be this lucky twice."

Any advice for golfers?
"Too many people have the wish to win when what they really need is the will to win."

On Minnesota
"I still have a lot of friends and family that live here. I love Minnesota, and I love the four seasons."

Where are they now?
Today, Patty is just "seven-over-par" at the tender age of 79. She is still as active as ever and keeps her game sharp by regularly hitting balls at the practice range. As enthusiastic as ever, she continues to be involved wherever there's a need. She makes speeches, meets with groups of her devoted fans, receives new awards and honors annually, and continues to give her time to junior programs to youngsters who seek her guidance and wisdom. She lends her name and support to two annual charity tournaments - one for women, the other for men - that raise funds for the American Cancer Society. She also supports and is active in the staging of an annual tournament known as the Nolan Henke/Patty Berg Junior Masters. An unofficial junior event, it's played on her home course (Cypress Lake Country Club in Fort Myers, Florida) and is entered by 18-and-under boys and girls from around the world.

THE LITTLE BROWN JUG

The Little Brown Jug is arguably the most famous and celebrated college football rivalry trophy in the country. Its lore goes all the way back to the turn of the century - and head coach Fielding Yost's fabled "Point-a-Minute" football teams from the University of Michigan. In 1903, Yost's Wolverines charged into Minnesota with a 28-game winning streak. More than 20,000 crazed Gopher fans packed into the stadium to see the highly anticipated contest. They poured out of streetcars and into the bleachers, as well as atop trees and telephone poles.

When the Gophers tied the score at 6-6 on a second-half touch-down, the crowd went nuts and stormed the field in celebration. The chaos was so wild that the officials called the game with two minutes left on the clock. After the dust had settled that next morning, a University of Minnesota custodian found an earthenware water jug on the field, so he brought it in to L.J. Cooke, head of the athletics department. Still excited, they decided not only to keep their captured prize, they even painted the score on it and kept it as a souvenir of their tie. Shortly after, Yost sent Cooke a letter asking for the prompt return of his team's mis-placed jug. Cooke kindly responded, "If you want it back, you'll have to win it."

It would be six years before the two teams would meet again, and this time, when Michigan won, Minnesota respectfully returned the jug. That next year the Wolverines left the conference, so the Gophers would have to wait nearly a decade to win it back. But, in 1919 they did just that, on a 34-7 trouncing in Ann Arbor. Soon after, the two schools decided to give the old piece of crockery a paint-job and display the scores on its side. In the 78 meetings since the jugs' inception, Michigan has had the bragging rights 55 times, compared to the Gophers 21, while their have been two ties.

FLOYD OF ROSEDALE

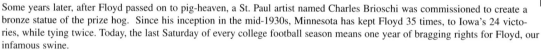

In the world of celebrity swine, only Arnold, Babe, and Porky are more famous than Floyd of Rosedale. Floyd's story is an interesting one that goes all the way back to 1935. The annual Minnesota - Iowa game is one of the fiercest rivalries in all of college football, and that year was no exception. Emotions were running high for Bernie Bierman's Gophers, who were 5-0 going into the big game on Iowa's home field. The Hawkeyes had only recently regained their eligibility following a suspension for slush-fund violations, and the Iowa fans were still upset from the year before, when the Gophers knocked their star, Ozzie Simmons, out of the game. In a diplomatic attempt to ease the pre-game tension that had turned into a border war, Minnesota Governor Floyd Olson sent Iowa Governor Clyde Herring a telegram that read: "I will bet you a Minnesota prize hog against an Iowa prize hog that Minnesota wins." The Gophers went on to beat the Hawkeyes, 13-6, in a cleanly played game. As a result of their victory, the Gophers became the proud owners of an award-winning prize pig which was donated by the owner of Rosedale Farms, near Fort Dodge, Iowa. So, our governor's namesake was immortalized forever as "Floyd of Rosedale."

Some years later, after Floyd passed on to pig-heaven, a St. Paul artist named Charles Brioschi was commissioned to create a bronze statue of the prize hog. Since his inception in the mid-1930s, Minnesota has kept Floyd 35 times, to Iowa's 24 victories, while tying twice. Today, the last Saturday of every college football season means one year of bragging rights for Floyd, our infamous swine.

PAUL BUNYAN'S AXE & THE BACON SLAB

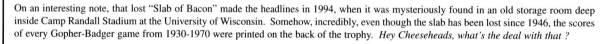

The legend of Paul Bunyan's Axe, which wasn't actually created until 1946, encompasses more than a century of football between Minnesota and Wisconsin, a rivalry that goes back to 1890 when the Gophers pummeled the Badgers 63-0. After four decades of one of the fiercest bor-der-battles in football, the schools decided to create a traveling trophy that was symbolic of their competitive traditions. So, in 1930, a "Slab of Bacon" was carved out of a block of black walnut wood to do just that. It featured a big football on one end that was inscribed with an "M" or "W", depending on which way it was held. The concept was that the winners would "bring home the bacon." The two schools were set to have a symbolic presentation of the trophy after that first game, but, in typical fashion of the type of football that was played during that era, a post-game melee spilled onto the field following the Gophers' victory. In the mess, the slab was lost forever. Sixteen years later the schools tried again, this time creating "Paul Bunyan's Axe," honoring the Midwest's greatest lumberjack. The Gophers took that first game in 1946, 16-0, and the rest is history. Today the six-foot long handle proudly displays the scores of all 105 games, the longest rivalry in the history of Division 1-A football.

On an interesting note, that lost "Slab of Bacon" made the headlines in 1994, when it was mysteriously found in an old storage room deep inside Camp Randall Stadium at the University of Wisconsin. Somehow, incredibly, even though the slab has been lost since 1946, the scores of every Gopher-Badger game from 1930-1970 were printed on the back of the trophy. *Hey Cheeseheads, what's the deal with that ?*

"BADGER" BOB JOHNSON

Minneapolis native Bob Johnson, a graduate of Minneapolis Central High School, played left wing for the Gopher Hockey team from 1954 to 1955. Following high school coaching careers at Warroad and Minneapolis Roosevelt, he took over the reins at Colorado College in 1963. After several years at C.C., he moved to the University of Wisconsin, where, in a period of 11 years, he led the Badgers to seven NCAA tournaments, winning three championships and one second-place finish. It was there where the 1977 NCAA Coach of the Year recipient was given the nickname, "Badger Bob." He led the 1976 U.S. Olympic team to a fourth-place finish at Innsbruck, Austria, and coached the 1981,1984, and 1987 U.S. teams in the Canada Cup. He also coached the 1973, 1974, 1975, and 1981 U.S. National Teams. Beginning in 1982 Johnson coached the NHL's Calgary Flames for five seasons. In 1990 he took over as coach of the Pittsburgh Penguins, where in his first season, he led the team to the Stanley Cup over the North Stars. He also served as Executive Director of USA Hockey for a three-year period. In the fall of 1991 Johnson died of brain cancer at the age of 60. Bob Johnson's memory lives on from his now-famous phrase which epitomized his love for the game: "It's a great day for hock-ey." Described as driven, compulsive and even hyperactive, Badger Bob was one of the greatest hockey coaches ever to hail from Minnesota.

BERNIE BIERMAN

ernie Bierman was born in 1894 in Springfield, Minnesota. His boyhood home was Litchfield, and he grew up in Detroit Lakes. s evidence of his stature as a local legend, all three communities claim him as their home-town hero. He decided to attend the niversity of Minnesota, where he starred as an All-Conference halfback in 1915. Bierman captained the team that won a share the Big Ten title that year. In 1932 Bierman was named coach of his alma mater, where he coached and perfected the single-ing attack and buck-lateral play series.

nown as "The Silver Fox" or "The Grey Eagle" for his prematurely grey hair, Bernie became one of the greatest college foot-ll coaches in the history of the sport. During his first ten years as head coach (1932-41), better known as the "Bierman ecade," the Gophers not only won seven Big Ten titles, they went undefeated for five of those seasons winning as many nation-championships. During that amazing span, the Maroon and Gold went three straight seasons and half way through the fourth ithout a defeat. They lost only eight conference games during that unbelievable decade. In 1942, Bierman rejoined the mili-ry for a three-year stint. He came back to the University of Minnesota for six more seasons before finally retiring from coach-g in 1950. With a 93-35-6 coaching record, Bernie was without question the greatest college football coach in Gopher histo-. Having coached 13 All-Americans at the U, Bierman is a member of the Helms and National Foot-ball Halls of Fame.

TOM BROWN

s a kid growing up, aside from doing my paper route and mowing lawns, my obsession was sports," said Gopher)otball great, Tom Brown. Tom went on to star in football, track, and swimming at Minneapolis Central High :hool. There, individually he won the state championship in the shot put and discuss. It's safe to say that he car-:d the team on his back, considering the fact that his team won the high school track and field title three times ith only six people on the squad. The heavily recruited prep football and track star decided to attend the niversity of Minnesota, where he not only threw the shot put on the track team but also played offensive and *fensive tackle on the Gopher football team.

1960, Tom's senior year, the Gophers tied for the Big Ten title, were voted national champions and went to the)se Bowl -- where they ultimately lost to Washington. The defensive unit allowed only 88 points that entire sea-n. One of the stars of that team was the "Rock of Gibraltar," Tom Brown. Considered by many to be the great-t interior lineman in Gopher history, he was also called the "rolling boulder" for his ability to blast holes in)posing defensive lines. His Herculean strength was legendary.

uring that season, a play occurred against the top-ranked Iowa Hawkeyes that forever secured his lore as a giant. 3rownie" had been stuffing the Hawkeye linemen all day and was just dominating both sides of the line. Then, a a third-down play with the ball on the Gopher five-yard line, Tom fired through the line just as the ball was apped, and knocked the center into the quarterback and then into the fullback, pancaking all three of them on eir butts on one play for a five-yard loss. After that game Brown proudly hoisted Floyd of Rosedale over his head r all to see. "The year before we finished near the bottom of the Big Ten, but we were actually very close to inning a lot of close games that we lost," said Brown. "So, Murray Warmath got us all together and told us that e needed that extra little effort to cross that thin line between winning and losing. Beating the number two ranked ebraska Cornhuskers in a preseason game really built our confidence, and from then on we felt like we could do me real good things that season. The Big Ten at that time was very dominant on the national football scene."

'hen Brown graduated he received a truck-load full of honors and awards. The tackle/guard was awarded the utland Trophy, recognizing him as the best lineman in the country. He was named as the Big Ten MVP, a first am All-American, and runner-up in the Heisman Trophy voting. The team MVP was named to the 1960 All-Big en team and played in the Coache's All-America Game and the Hula Bowl in 1961.

fter his collegiate career, Tom was drafted by the NFL's Baltimore Colts as well as the British Columbia Lions in the Canadian Football League. "I didn't want to move to altimore," said Brown. "I thought that the Great Northwest would fit my outdoor lifestyle much better." So he headed north of the border. In 1964 he was named the Lions' VP, the same year the team won the Grey Cup. He would win one more Cup during his tenure in B.C. before having to retire prematurely due to a neck injury in 1967.

'hat did it mean to be a Gopher? "It's a super school and being a Gopher was a very prominent part of my life. Growing up there, I used to follow everything at the niversity even though there wasn't a lot of TV at the time. When I saw all of the other kids not only from Minnesota, but from other states trying to get into the University play sports, it made me want to go there even more."

'here are they now? Today Tom and his wife, Marnie, live in Bellingham, Washington, in a cabin overlooking the Pacific Ocean. "I love the outdoors, the ocean, the rca's, the mountains, river rafting -- it's so beautiful up here," he said. He has three children from a previous marriage; Steven, Tracy and Susan, as well as five grandchil-en. Years ago he ran a river rafting company, but now he works in Vancouver and runs the sales and marketing for a plastics fabrication company.

Brownie was one of the greatest linemen ever to wear the maroon and gold, and his teammates and coaches had nothing but praise for him.
    "He was one of the strongest, most agile players that I ever witnessed playing on the football field." said Sandy Stephens. "I remember the game against Iowa hen he knocked down the All-American center, the quarterback, and the fullback -- all on the same play. I'll never forget that play as long as I live!"
    "He was a great athlete and a great lineman," said Carl Eller. "He was a great lineman in the sense that he was built like a lineman. He was so strong and had big)per-body and trunk strength, with so much quickness. He was the picture offensive and defensive lineman. He was so quick and tough, he would just come at you with a reat charge. He was a really great player."
    "Tom was originally recruited as a running back," said Bobby Bell. " Coach Warmath decided to take this strong, quick guy with good speed and move him into e line. He was a quick, very quiet, content, strong, solid football player. If you wanted somebody on your football team, that was the guy you wanted. He didn't say too uch, but he got the job done."
    "He was the most amazing lineman that I have ever seen, bar none," said Bill Munsey.
    "Tom Brown scared more people on a football field than any player in Minnesota history," said Murray Warmath. "He was a one-man interior line."

The remarkable baseball history of the minor league Minneapolis Millers goes way back to the good old days at Athletic Park in the late 1880s, on to Nicollet Park, and ends at Metropolitan Stadium until 1960.

The Millers accumulated a storied past throughout Minnesota's history and played a vital role in the development of American baseball. The following is a little history about this wonderful baseball team, leading up to a fabulous Junior World Series, and a baseball great who played with the Millers and also managed them, Gene Mauch:

In the 1950s, the Millers were the triple-A farm club of the New York Giants. The late 50s were the golden years for the Millers, highlighted by two Junior World Series championships in 1955 and 1958, as well as their involvement with Fidel Castro in the series of 1959.

No good story would be complete without a rival, and the Millers' crosstown counterparts were the St. Paul Saints, who were the Brooklyn Dodgers' triple-A farm club. The Millers-Saints rivalry was an exciting one that often featured doubleheaders at each stadium.

Fans would take the trolley between the games form Nicollet Park in Minneapolis to Lexington Park in St. Paul. A lot of Hall of Fame players came up through the Millers over the years on their way to the big leagues like the Say-Hey Kid, Yaz, and the great Teddy Ballgame.

1955 was special

In 1955, the Minneapolis Millers celebrated their ninth American Association pennant en route to win their first ever Junior World Series title against the International League champion, Rochester Red Wings. They were led by the Association's MVP, shortstop Rance Pless, and wins leader, pitcher Al Worthington. The 1955 Junior World Series saw the last game ever played at old Nicollet Park near Lake Street and Nicollet Avenue, as the Millers moved outside the city to the newly-constructed Metropolitan Stadium in Bloomington the next year.

Red Sox take over

Although the Millers were enjoying a 1950s "golden era," it seemed to fans that the Millers and Saints might not be enough for them. Milwaukee got major league baseball in 1953, and tour-bus business flourished between the Twin Cities and Sudsville. Minnesotans wanted to see major-league ball. Minneapolitans, too, wanted to be in the big-time, and Metropolitan Stadium renewed their hopes. It had been widely speculated that the New York Giants were going to move to Minnesota. The rumors intensified when Giants' president Horace Stoneham announced that 1957 would be the last year for the Giants in New York. The Giants eventually moved, all the way to San Francisco.

With the Giants now in San Francisco, it seemed the Minneapolis Millers were no longer needed as a farm club. The resultant void was filled in Minneapolis by the Boston Red Sox, who named the Millers as their triple-A farm club.

In 1958, the "new" Millers hired a young ballplayer to manage their team as well as play second base. His name was Gene Mauch. Mauch would be joined on the bench by Hall of Famer and Red Sox great Jimmie Foxx. The Millers finished third in the American Association that year with a record of 82-71. Even so, things looked promising for the young club as they headed into the playoffs, where they would face a tired Wichita club.

The Millers knocked off Wichita and then proceeded to upset Denver in the next round, to find themselves back in the Junior World Series. They opponent would be the mighty Montreal Royals. The Millers first opponent in game one was a young pitcher named Tommy Lasorda. They went on to win game one, and just kept on winning until they had

swept the Royals in four straight, winning their second Junior Series Championship in three years.

"I remember sweeping Montreal four in a row and winning it all in 1958," said Mauch. "I was still playing and managing at that point, and it was a pretty special championship for me. That year was great, and even still have the giant pennant from when we won that series."

In 1959, the Millers finished second in their division with an impressive 95-57 record. They opened the playoffs against Omaha, and the series went back and forth until both teams had split two games apiece. Then, back home at the Met for the fifth game of the series, the Millers new second baseman, who had just been activated before game time, scored the game winning run in the bottom of the tenth. His name was Carl Yastrzemski. (Like Ted Williams had done 22 years earlier, "Yaz" spent a season in Minneapolis playing triple-A ball, before heading to Boston, where ironically, the Hall of Famer would succeed Teddy Ballgame in the outfield.)

The game was officially protested by Omaha, who challenged Yaz's series eligibility. The Omaha officials were proved to be right, and the league president ordered the game replayed. So, even without the services of Yaztrzemski, the Millers went out and still won the next game, to take the series. Led by feisty manager Mauch, they went on to beat the Fort Worth Cats for the league championship, earning a trip to the Junior World Series against the Havana Sugar Kings

No tropical paradise

This Junior World Series proved to be one of the most amazing spectacles in sports history. The first two games were played at Metropolitan Stadium. There were supposed to be three games at the Met, but because of freezing weather, game three was moved to sunny Havana. During the first two games of the series, the Sugar Kings, not quite used to Minnesota's balmy climate, could be seen in their dugout huddling around a fire they had lit in a wastebasket to stay warm. A series highlight was a two-run-homer hit by Mauch's brother-in-law, Roy Smalley, Sr., in game two. (Smalley's son subsequently played a key role in Minnesota Twins' history.)

The five games played in the Cuban capital drew more than 100,000 fans, not counting the thousands of Castro's gun-toting soldiers, who had stationed themselves throughout the dugouts. Down three games to one, the Millers rallied in the series and won games five and six. With the series tied at three-apiece, the stage was set for the much anticipated game seven. As Fidel, a former pitcher himself, made his entrance to the game, he walked by the Millers' bullpen with his hand on his revolver and said to the Minneapolis pitchers, "Tonight we win." It was looking great for the Millers as they built a two-run lead going into the eighth. But Havana came back. They evened it up in the eighth, and then in the bottom of the ninth Havana's Don Morejon's knocked in the game-winner

Williams Arena hosts the first NCAA Hockey Championship ever played outside of Colorado Springs	Gopher goalie Jack McCartan is named to the All-American hockey team	Gopher third baseman Jack McCartan is named to the All-American baseball team	Gopher center Mike Pearson is named to the All-American hockey team	Gopher winger Dick Burg is named to the All-American hockey team	Gopher halfback Francis "Pug" Lund is inducted into the College Football Hall of Fame	St. Paul's Michael Gibbons, known as the Phantom, is inducted into the Boxing Hall of Fame. The uncrowned king of the welter weights and middleweights, was named the greatest Minnesota boxer for the first 50 years of the 20th century.

o take the Junior World Series.

I imagine it was about as gripping a time as I had ever experienced," said Mauch, who first met Castro when the two played together in the Cuban winter league in 1951 and knows him personally to this day.

It was standing room only every night. Fifteen minutes before game time, Castro would come walking in through center field with his entourage. Every fan rose and waved a white handkerchief and yelled 'Fidel,' 'Fidel!' Then he would come sit down behind home-plate. No baseball player in history was ever greeted the way he was greeted down there. About half of my players were afraid to win the championship game because there were Cuban soldiers on the bench with loaded rifles and bayonets. In fact you couldn't get from the batters box to the dugout without wading through 50 to 100 soldiers. A lot of my players were fearful, and wanted to get the hell out of there, I know that. The whole thing was quite an experience."

On October 27, 1960, at 2:15 p.m., it was announced that Calvin Griffith was moving his Washington Senators to Minnesota. Major league baseball would also mean the end of the Millers and Saints. One golden era of baseball was over, but the Twins would start another.

The most fun there is in the world
Gene Mauch was born in Salina Kan., on November 18, 1925. At the age of 13, his family moved to Los Angeles. Gene grew up playing sports and, in high school, played football, baseball, and basketball. He had the opportunity to attend USC or Stanford on football and baseball scholarships, but went into the service instead where he became an air cadet.

Mauch played 16 seasons in the majors. He started out playing ball in Durham, in 1943, and from there the list of cities is long: Montreal, Brooklyn, St. Paul, Pittsburgh, Indianapolis, Chicago (AL&NL), Boston (AL&NL), St. Louis, Milwaukee, Atlanta, Los Angeles, and finally the Minneapolis Millers, where he retired as an active player. He had a career .239 batting average, nothing to write home about.

Mauch started managing at the age of 27 with the Atlanta Crackers in the Southern Association. He continued to manage with the Millers and got his big break in 1960 when he went to manage the Phillies. He stayed in Philadelphia until 1968, when he left to take over the expansion Montreal Expos.

Mauch managed the Twins from 1976-1980. His career record as the Twins skipper was 378-394. He is among a select fraternity of big-league skippers on the all-time seniority list, having managed for more than three decades. In 1987, when Mauch retired as manager of the Angels. He holds the dubious distinction of managing the most years (26) without winning a pennant.

Mauch is an intense competitor, and a great ambassador of baseball. He played baseball when it was still a game and was a true throw-back to another era. He will be forever remembered as an integral thread in the fabric of Minnesota's baseball history.

Who was your hero when you were growing up?
"The first major league ballplayer I ever saw was Charlie Gehringer. Right then I said I want to be just like him."

On managing the Twins:
It was a wonderful experience. I worked with some great, great people, including Calvin Griffith, Rod Carew, Tony Oliva, Larry Hisle, Danny Bostock, Butch Wynegar, and my nephew Roy Smalley."

Any regrets when you were with the Millers?
"Originally, when I came to Minneapolis, I thought that I would eventually go on to become the manager of the Red Sox, because we were their triple-A farm club. One of the biggest disappointments of my life came in 1959, when Boston didn't name me to be their manager. Bucky Harris, the Red Sox G.M., said I was too young and didn't think that I would be able to handle guys like Ted Williams, who, at the time, was older than I was. Not being able to manage some of those kids like Carl Yastrzemski, who played for me up in Minneapolis, was a real disappointment."

What did it mean for you to manage the Twins?
"Being able to have the opportunity to manage guys like Rod Carew and Tony Oliva, I felt like my time in Minnesota wasn't a job, it was a privilege."

On the people of Minnesota
"I loved the people up there, they were just outstanding, super people, and were just wonderful to me. Hell, they even gave me a new car! I was just so intrigued by Minnesota and was really thinking of moving there. I still maintain close relationships with a lot of people from that area."

Millers and Twins tombstones:
"There were guys in baseball, such as Casey Stengel and Joe Cronin, whom I thought so much of and had so much respect for. But now when you mention their names, no one even knows who the hell you're talking about. So it seems like kind of a superfluous thought. Why should you even worry about being remembered?"

Where are they now?
Gene and his wife Nina retired to Palm Springs, Calif.. They had one daughter, Leanne. Mauch admits that with his new satellite dish, he watches up to four games a day.

Tributes

"We went through some tough times together in 1977 and 1978, when the fans were on us about nepotism. It was a difficult situation, but it was also a great situation to be in, at the same time, because we were able to be together. I learned that being successful takes care of everything, and once I realized that, everything took care of itself. We have a lot of love and respect for each other. He was one of my heroes growing up.

I've played for 15 managers throughout my career, and there was nobody that could hold a candle to him. He was just the best. I learned more baseball in my time with him than with all the rest combined. He was the best prepared, best tactical, and best teaching manager I've ever been around. I can't imagine a better manager in the game, ever."   **-- Roy Smalley, Jr.**

"Gene was one of the best managers that I ever played for. He could really get the best out of his players and teach them the correct way to play the game. We both had tremendous respect for each other, even to this day. I knew that if I ever had any problems on or off the field, I felt comfortable enough that I could always go in and talk with him, and he would always help me through it. He was a great person."   **-- Rod Carew**

"He managed a long, long time, and he was a great manager. He was very serious about his job, and he wanted to win no matter what. He knew a lot about the game and was just a great person to be around."
-- Tony Oliva

"I liked Gene very much. I thought he was a very good manager and certainly an intense guy. When he was managing the Twins, he asked me to come back to the club to help out as a hitting instructor, and I was grateful for that."   **-- Harmon Killebrew**

Sometimes being the worst team in the NBA isn't necessarily a bad thing, especially when your prize for futility is a superstar. In 1958, the Minneapolis Lakers got to choose first in the annual college draft as the result of their appalling losing performance in the 1957-58 season. The Laker selection was Elgin Baylor, and he did not disappoint the Minneapolis fans. In his first year Elgin became the NBA Rookie of the Year, the all-star Game MVP, and first team All-Pro. More importantly, Baylor led his team to the NBA Finals.

Although the top-rated senior in college basketball was Indiana's Archie Dees, Seattle University's Baylor was the player every team wanted. Elgin, who led the nation in rebounding in 1957, had taken his Seattle Chieftains to the 1958 NCAA finals before eventually losing to Kentucky.

Born in Washington, D.C., Baylor opted to first attend the College of Idaho in 1954. There he led the school's basketball team to a 23-4 win-loss record and averaged 31 points and 20 rebounds per game. The following season, Elgin transferred to Seattle University and sat out the year because of the NCAA transfer rule. In

1956-57, Seattle had 22 wins against only three losses with Elgin pulling down 508 rebounds and averaging 30 points per game. During his junior year at Seattle, he averaged 32.5 points per game and grabbed 559 boards. During the NCAA tournament, Baylor averaged 27 points and 18 rebounds in five tourney games against the best college basketball teams in the land.

Baylor had publicly stated his intention to complete his senior year at Seattle and not enter the NBA draft. But with draft day nearing, and the Minneapolis franchise's future in doubt, team owner Bob Short opted to gamble and drafted Baylor with his first pick, eventually signing him after month of negotiating. Short was later quoted as saying that if Baylor had turned him down, the club would have "gone out of business" and declared bankruptcy. The NBA had put the Lakers on financial probation and specified that if the club didn't average at least $6,600 in gate receipts for home games, the league could take over the team. All that changed, however, as the fans poured into the Minneapolis Auditorium to see the Lakers new phenom.

On the rebound

Coming off the worst Minneapolis Laker seasons ever, the team came back in 1958-59 to finish second to the St. Louis Hawks in the West, with the modest record of 33 wins against 39 losses. In addition to Baylor, the team was consisted of an aging Vern Mikkelsen, Hibbing's Dick Garmaker, "Hot" Rod Hundley, veteran center Larry Foust, inexperienced Jim Krebs, Bob "Slick" Leonard, and guard Ed Fleming. Baylor was also joined by new teammates Alex "Boo" Ellis and the 6'8" Steve Hamilton who would later go on pitch for the New York Yankees as their ace-lefty out of the bullpen.

The 1959 NBA finals were supposed to feature the two best teams in the NBA that year, Boston and St. Louis, in what would've been their third-straight meeting for the championship. However, in the West, the Baylor-led Lakers knocked off the defending world champs from St. Louis. The Hawks had won two of three to start the series against the Lakers, but Minneapolis won the final three, and the stage was set for the new-look Lakers to take on the mighty Celtics. It wouldn't be easy though, as the Lakers had lost 18 straight against the Celtics, and, to make matters worse, Elgin was nursing a badly bruised knee.

Owner Short sought to motivate his players by offering them presents such as new sets of tires and sports coats if they won the Championship. That might have spared Laker coach Johnny Kundla from any Knute Rockne-like motivational speeches that he had to deliver to get his players ready to play the mighty Celtics.

Even though they kept the margins of victory to within in less than five points for three of the games, the Celtics went on to sweep the Championship Series four games to none. It was the first time ever that a finals would end in a sweep, and for the Celtics, the Minneapolis Lakers thus became their first victims en route to winning eight straight championships. The day after the fourth loss, coach Kundla announced his retirement and accepted the newly-vacated head basketball coach position with the University of Minnesota Golden Gophers replacing Ozzie Cowles.

Rookie of the Year

Elgin won the Rookie of the Year Award in 1959, averaging nearly 25 points, 15 rebounds, and four assists per game while placing fourth in league scoring behind Bob Pettit, Jack Twyman, and Paul Arizin. He also finished third, behind Bill Russell and Bob Pettit in the Player of the Year voting..

When asked about the 1959 season, Elgin said, "My rookie year with the Minneapolis Lakers was a great one for me. Being the number one player chosen in the draft, playing on the NBA all-star team, and just to be playing in the NBA was wonderful. The reception by my teammates in Minneapolis was great, and I was accepted and treated like one of them right away. The year before the team had finished in last place, so it was a thrill because no one thought we would get close to the finals. We beat the defending world champion St. Louis Hawks to win the West, and we were all very proud of our accomplishments that season Minneapolis had a good year, made a great run, and a lot of wonderful things happened that season, but the Celtics had a better team, and they beat us."

Big things were expected from the Lakers for the next season. Bob Short would raise the ticket prices which had ranged from $.90 to $2.40, to the gaudy price range of $1.50 to $4.50. And, after nearly a dozen years at the Minneapolis Auditorium, along with several playing stints at the Minneapolis Armory, St. Paul Auditorium, and even Hamline's Norton Fieldhouse Short did some interior decorating to the Lakers' official new homecourt, the Armory, by spending to add a new floor and new seats.

Replacing Kundla as the new head coach was John Castellani, who had been Baylor's coach at Seattle University. Regarding the speculation in Minneapolis that Castellani's hiring was a move to keep Baylor happy, Elgin said, "John was a great person, and I had a great relationship with him. When they hired him, I was happy, but no one came to me and asked me what I thought about it, because at the time I was in San Antonio, in military service."

Bringing practice to Elgin

In 1959, Baylor fulfilled his military commitment by joining the Army Reserve Medical Corps training program at Fort Sam Houston, in San Antonio, Texas. Because Short didn't want him to fall behind in practice, he moved the entire team's training camp to San Antonio to be with their All-Pro.

Elgin said, "I had no place to play down there, and, fortunately, the Lakers came down to Texas so we could have training camp together. It was tough, but when I got out of the service I went right into the line-up. I remember that during the first game, I developed some unbelievable blisters on my feet."

"Elg" was an incredible player, and he had a great second season for the Lakers. In the season opener against the Detroit Pistons, he scored 52 points. Against the Celtics, Baylor scored an NBA single-game record of 64 points, breaking Joe Fulks' 10-year old record by one point.

The savior

While Baylor may have saved the Minneapolis Laker franchise from going out of business in 1959, in the process, ironically, he also helped the team become good enough to become marketable. Short moved the franchise moved to Los Angeles in 1960. Minnesota wouldn't see NBA action again for another 29 years, until the Timberwolves franchise was organized.

Baylor may be best remembered most for his unbelievable driving, twisting, lay-ups which featured spectacular mid-air antics. The terms "hang time" and "body control" became synonymous with him. He was also known for following his own shot, and it has been said that if that statistic would have been kept, he may very well hold the NBA record for scoring the most points off of his own put-backs. Often, during the course of a tight game, when the Lakers really needed him, he would switch from the forward to the center or guard position when the situation warranted. When the opposition was engaged in full-court pressing situations, Baylor was the only one trusted to bring the ball upcourt.

Elgin has been called the father of the modern aerodynamic game. Boston Celtic great Bob Cousy remembers: "Elgin was the first one who would go up for the jump shot, hang up there for 15 seconds, have some lunch and a cup of coffee, and [then] decide to shoot the thing. Elgin was that spectacular. He was the first guy who literally couldn't be stopped."

Baylor was more than the first of the great skywalkers, he was an explosive scorer; whose career scoring average is exceeded only by Wilt Chamberlain and Michael Jordan. Baylor used his body control and unbelievable creativity like no other before him. His Laker career stats from 1958-1972 include averaging: 27.4 PPG, 13.5 RPG, 4.3 APG, and he was a 10-time All-NBA first teamer.

He is considered among the greatest rebounders for his size the NBA has ever known, posting-up any big man. He could pass and dribble with the best guards in the league, and his amazing speed made him a stellar defender. He was truly the complete package.

During his career, he appeared in 11 All-Star games and was named the co-MVP in 1959. He holds the NBA All-Star game record for most career free throws attempted (98) and made (78). Baylor was named to the NBA 35th anniversary all-time team and is enshrined in the Basketball Hall of Fame.

Elgin was undoubtedly the greatest NBA player never to win a championship. Ironically, the Los Angeles Lakers won their first championship the season after Baylor retired as an active player. His Los Angeles teams lost in the finals seven times in 11 years; three of those finals were decided in seventh games with the Celtics, which the Lakers lost by a combined total of seven points. Of all the battles against Bill Russell and the Celtics, Baylor said, "It was fun. It was disappointing to lose. But it was the ultimate challenge. They were a proud team. I enjoyed playing against them. They were the best."

Who was your hero when you were growing up?
"As a kid living in Washington D.C., we couldn't afford to have any television, so I never really watched the game, and, as a result, I never really had a basketball idol growing up. I got turned on to the game when I was 13 years old, by tagging along with my two older brothers to play pick-up games at the park."

What did it mean for you to be a Minneapolis Laker?
"It was really exciting for me. In college I never thought about playing professionally. The only thing I thought about was being able to go to college. Growing up, I knew my family could not afford to send me to college, so I really hoped that I could just get a scholarship either in football or basketball. Then, to be able to play for the Minneapolis Lakers was very special to me. The honor, the pride, and the glory of just being a professional in the sport of basketball was great. Playing with and against the best players in the world was tremendous. All the traveling, meeting people, and making friends was all very special to me. I loved the city of Minneapolis. It still is a great city, and the people there were great to me."

Laker tombstone:
"That I was person who cared about other people and cared about my profession. I felt like I gave it all that I had, and I played as hard as I could."

Where are they now?
The former Clippers and Jazz head coach is serving as the general manager of the Los Angeles Clippers. Elgin and his wife Elaine have two daughters and a son and reside in the Los Angeles area.

Tributes

"I can't say enough about Elgin. He could play an entire game without getting a little tired because he had more stamina than any player I ever saw. He was a tremendous all-around ballplayer. He could just hang up in the air and he could do it all -- passing, shooting, dribbling, jumping, and defending. He was just great. His first year with us was so terrific, and right away I knew he was one of the best all-around athletes I ever saw play the game of basketball. Elgin took us to our last championship against Boston in 1959, and he became even greater after the team moved out west. One time, he scored 50 points in a game off of only two field goals he shot from the out-

side. His other points came off of rebounds and put-backs."
-- John Kundla

"My last year with the Minneapolis Lakers was Elgin's first, and we were kind of a rag-tag bunch when he came in as a rookie. Coach Kundla wanted me, as team captain, to teach Elgin about how to play the pro game. He didn't need any teaching. Elgin had a pocket full of press clippings, and he was the best there was to came out of college at that time. I could tell he was in a class by himself. He had all the ability in the world and became such a fabulous player. But, at first, he was also kind of a loner, and we couldn't really get him into being a part of our bunch. Later he joined the poker-playing group of players called the 'dead-enders,' which consisted of Dick Garmaker, Hot Rod Hundley, Slick Leonard, and I. Garmaker used to say that he would pick Elgin up at his house and bring him to the airport for the road games because he didn't want any chance of him missing the plane. Dick also said that he made more money off Elgin in poker than he made in salary. Eventually, Elgin turned out to be quite a talker out on the court. In fact, he became a real magpie. He had a wonderful career with the Lakers, both in Minneapolis and Los Angeles, and he is a great person."
-- Vern Mikkelsen

SANDY STEPHENS
The Gophers Win the
National Championship

After losing eight of nine football games the year before, the 1960 University of Minnesota Gophers were on the rebound. In fact, the only regular season loss the team would have that year was against Purdue. The Gophers went to Madison for the final game of the season, with the Big Ten title and a possible Rose Bowl invitation hedged on the outcome. With the top-ranked defense in the nation, they pounded the Badgers, 26-7, scoring two touchdowns early and two late.

For the first time since the invasion at Pearl Harbor, the Gophers were national champs, although they shared the Big Ten title with Iowa because each team finished the season with conference records of 5-1. Minnesota could have won the Big Ten title outright with a 6-1 record, had the team's Indiana win been counted, but the Hoosiers were on probation for recruiting violations. Both major polls ranked the Gophers number one in the land, handing them the official national championship. Things were coming up roses for the Gophers, and they were off to the historic old Rose Bowl in Pasadena, Calif.

On Jan. 2, 1961, nearly 100,000 fans invaded

Pasadena, to see the national champion Gophers play the Washington Huskies in the Rose Bowl. Many described it as a tale of two halves. The Huskies winning the first 17-0, and the Gophers taking the second 7-0. Unfortunately, the Gophers came up short, and Washington held on to win by the score of 17-7. In the first half, Huskies one-eyed quarterback Bob Schloredt rushed for 46 yards and a touchdown, while throwing for another 16 yards. Gopher sophomore quarterback Sandy Stephens went 0-4 and also threw for two interceptions.

After an inspiring half-time speech by head coach Murray Warmath, the Gophers started the second half by returning the opening kick-off 23 yards. Two plays later they proceeded to get a first down, and in less than six minutes, the Gophers' Bill Munsey ran 18 yards for a touchdown. Minnesota threatened again in the third, but each drive was killed by penalties. The third quarter ended with the score at 17-7.

Midway through the fourth, on the Washington six-yard line, Stephens was trapped for a 13 yard loss. Minnesota went for a field goal. As Sandy set up to hold the kick, he called for the fake, but unfortunately his intended pass to Tom Hall was intercepted. The maroon and gold threat died, and the Huskies were Rose Bowl champions. Sandy would finish the game rushing for 51 yards and throwing for another 21.

"We made some stupid mistakes in that Rose Bowl game, but we knew we had a good team," said Stephens. "After the game, I recall that I had never felt so bad after losing. However, it was a fantastic experience for me. The Rose Bowl was everything I thought it would be and more. The whole first half we were sort of awe struck, but the second half we were ready to play. I think they only got one first down in the entire second half, and that was off a long quarterback sneak. We just couldn't get any offensive momentum going at that point, and we couldn't overcome Washington. I don't want to take anything away from the Huskies. They were a fine team. But they were just a better football team on that day. We lost the game, but were still national champions, and they can't take that away from us."

The 1960 turnaround was one of the most dramatic in Gopher history. There were many great athletes on that team besides Stephens, among them were Tom Brown, Munsey, Bobby Bell, Judge Dickson, Greg Larson, Joe Salem, Larry Johnson, Bill Kauth, Frank Brixius, Hall, Jack Mulvena, Bob Deegan, Dick Larson, Dave Mulholland, and Julian Hook.

After all he had been through, perhaps vindication was the word that best described the feelings Murray Warmath had after the sea-

son, and he was rewarded by being named national Coach of the Year. Bud Wilkinson, former Gopher football and hockey great who went on to even more fame as the football coach at Oklahoma, said: "What he (Warmath) did under that pressure was one of the greatest things to happen to college coaching in a long, long time."

Growing up in football country

Sandy grew up in Uniontown, Pa. Sandy's parents encouraged him in his academic and athletic endeavors, and upon high school graduation, more than 50 colleges and universities, eight from the Big Ten alone, recruited him. Sandy felt pretty strong about his football roots, and he later said: "We always felt that those of us who lived in Western Pennsylvania had the best high school football in the country, bar none - including Ohio and Texas too!"

Stephens was a tremendously gifted all-around athlete, earning nine letters in football, basketball, and track . He garnered high school All-American honors in football, was an All-State basketball player, and, although he never played high school baseball, was a good enough pitcher and centerfielder to be romanced by several major league baseball teams, including his home state Philadelphia Phillies, who drafted him out of high school.

With assurances that he would be given a shot at quarterback, as well as the opportunity to play baseball, Stephens enrolled at University of Minnesota in the fall of 1958. So did an old friend and high school rival from Clairton, Pa., who would be his roommate for the next four years, Judge Dickson. Even though Ohio State and Penn State were close to home, the Pennsylvania pair wanted to start their own traditions somewhere else.

"We felt the University of Minnesota was interested in us as men and not just as football players," Stephens said, "so Judge and I signed Minnesota tenders in my house. There were other reasons I decided on Minnesota though. Our high school league in Pennsylvania was considered one of the best in the nation, and I wanted to measure how good I could be playing in the best college conference in the nation. Also, being black, I knew there were other many other top colleges then that would never allow me to play the quarterback position."

Still considered by many to be one of the top five all-time greatest players ever to wear the maroon and gold, Sandy is a football legend in Gold Country. From 1959-1961, he threw for nearly 1,500 yards. For his career his still remains fifth on the all-time career rushing touchdowns list with 20, and twice he led the team in punting. In 1961, Sandy led the team in rushing with 534 yards while throwing for nine touchdown passes, as well. For his efforts in leading the conference with 1,151 yards of total offense that year, he was named the Big Ten MVP, an All-American (first-ever black man to be so honored), College Back of the Year and the Los Angeles Times Back of the Year. He also

Freeborn County's Burdette Haldorson wins a gold medal on the Olympic Basketball team	Gopher Dick Meredith wins a gold medal on the Olympic Hockey team	Minneapolis' Edwyn Owen wins a gold medal on the Olympic Hockey team	St. Paul's Jack McCartan wins a gold medal on the Olympic Hockey team	St. Paul's Paul Johnson wins a gold medal on the Olympic Hockey team	Warroad's Billy and Roger Christian win gold medals on the Olympic Hockey team	The Gopher Baseball team beats USC, 2-1, for the National Championship	The St. Paul Saints hockey team win the IHL's Turner Cup championship	Gopher center Ron Johnson is named to the All-American basketball team	Gopher pitcher Larry Bertelsen is named to the All-American baseball team

finished fourth in the balloting for the Heisman Trophy. Additional accolades included: being inducted into the Columbus Touchdown Club, and being named as the University of Oregon's Outstanding Opponent. (Honoring the individual who represented the toughest competition for all sporting categories that the University faced that season.)

After college, Sandy was drafted in the first round by the New York Titans of the American Football League. "At the time," Sandy says, "the Titans didn't want a black man playing quarterback. Cleveland had my NFL rights, but the NFL still wasn't ready for a black quarterback. So, I was forced to play in Canada." With the promise that he would be given a chance to play quarterback, Sandy went north of the border and the Montreal Alouettes. Montreal had finished last in the Canadian Football League the year before, but rookie quarterback Stephens led the Als to the CFL finals.

After three years in Canada, Sandy's life was abruptly changed when he was involved in a nearly fatal car accident. The doctors said that he wasn't supposed to ever walk again, but Sandy was determined. In 1964, Sandy's old teammate, Bobby Bell, asked his Chiefs coach, Hank Stram, to give his old friend a shot at a comeback. Sandy overcame the odds and went on to play with Kansas City for two seasons, both as a defensive halfback as well as a quarterback. He retired from the game in 1970. Eventually, Sandy's family relocated to the Twin Cities, and his younger brother, Ray, followed his older brother's footsteps to the U where he would star in both football and basketball.

In 1997, Sandy was inducted into the Rose Bowl Hall of Fame. "Getting this honor now, after all these years, is thrilling and definitely a high point in my life," said Stephens.

Sandy was the greatest quarterback to ever wear the maroon and gold. He blessed the University of Minnesota football program with his talents and leadership like no other, before or since.

Who was your hero growing up?
"Jackie Robinson and Willie Mays. It was always a dream of mine to play major league baseball."

What did it mean for you to be a Gopher?
" The main reason I came to Minnesota was because of coach Warmath. He guaranteed me a chance to play quarterback. I loved everything about being a member of the University of Minnesota football team. In fact, the only negative thing that I remembered about coming to Minnesota, was the fact that a gopher was their mascot. I almost didn't come to Minnesota because of that nickname. In Pennsylvania, being a gopher didn't mean anything good. It meant you'd 'go-fer' anything!"

Gopher tombstone:
"I hope that they'll remember the championship teams that we had. That's my biggest thing. I have always been a team player. The only reason that you achieve accolades is because of the teammates that you have, and I had great teammates all the way through. We were all champions."

On racism and football:
"There was racism towards black quarterbacks in the early 1960s. And there is still racism today - very much so! It's a shame that we even have to distinguish the term 'black quarterback.' When I played, you just didn't see blacks playing quarterback, center, or middle linebacker. Back then we would have to go to Canada to play. That's what happened to Warren Moon, and a whole lot of other black quarterbacks. The only reason Warren ever had a chance in the NFL was because his Canadian Football League coach got the head coaching position with the Houston Oilers. I never thought I would ever see the Vikings have both a black coach (Dennis Green) and a black quarterback (Moon) - that was beyond any comprehension I could ever have imagined. I was proud to be the first black All-American quarterback. Doug Williams was the second, and he played 17 years after me."

Where are they now?
Sandy is single and lives in Bloomington. He works for the State of Minnesota, Department of Employee Relations in the office of Diversity and Equal Opportunity.

Tributes

"Sandy was a great quarterback. If they would've given Sandy the opportunity to have played in the NFL, he would have been the first black quarterback in league; that's how good he was. He was a player that just wanted to win. He had the quickness, the speed, the arm, and the agility. Defenses couldn't pin him down and contain him because he was so fast and so smart. He could beat you in a lot of ways, but especially one-on-one. He was so versatile; he would punt, pass, run, and do just about anything for the team. He hated to lose. I don't care if you were playing ping-pong, he wanted to beat you. He drove us to win and to be national champions. He was an all-around fun guy to play with and a tremendous competitor."
-- **Bobby Bell**

"He was a great leader and commanded a lot of respect from everybody. His teammates really liked him and always played hard for him."
-- **Tom Brown**

"He was the field general, in the truest sense of the word. He was in command out on the field, and there was no question about it. We had total confidence in him. and we knew that he could get it done. He would tell us in the huddle that we were going to either run over my side or over Bobby Bell's side, and we would do it. He had a lot of confidence in us. He was just a fabulous football player."
-- **Carl Eller**

"I grew up only a block away from Sandy, and we grew up together playing sports. After my senior year, I had received 58 full scholarship offers, but I chose to go to Minnesota because my best friend Sandy was there. I saw those big Swedes and Norwegians on the line and thought about the possibility of playing with Sandy in the backfield. He was stubborn, and there is probably no cockier person in the world than Sandy,

but to play quarterback you have to have those ingredients. He had so much ability and was just a great natural athlete."
-- **Bill Munsey**

"He was a hell of a great football player, but he was never given the publicity and acclaim he deserved. He was one of the greatest football players I ever saw. He was a great running back, a good passer and an excellent defensive player. He could do everything and do it well."
-- **Murray Warmath**

Gopher pitcher Ron Causton is named to the All-American baseball team

Gopher first baseman Wayne Knapp is named to the All-American baseball team

The Minneapolis Lakers move to Los Angeles

The national champion University of Minnesota Golden Gophers weren't going to sneak up on anyone in 1961, although several key members of the 1960 squad had graduated and moved on. The Gophers still had Bobby Bell, Sandy Stephens, Bill Munsey, Judge Dickson, and a new sophomore tackle that would make a fine compliment to Bell, Carl Eller, who stood 6'5" and weighed 240 pounds. The tandem bookend tackles from North Carolina anchored the Gopher defense, and eventually lead Minnesota back to Pasadena.

The team's season opener against Missouri attracted a lot of national interest because the Tigers were the team that Minnesota had climbed over to earn the number one ranking in the polls after the last week of the 1960 season. The playing conditions that day were less than desirable, to say the least. Gopher quarterback Sandy Stephens described the game as, "the worst game in terms of weather conditions that I ever played in. It was just awful, and it was so cold that I couldn't feel the ball when it was centered." Amidst constant rain and wind, the Tigers from Columbia, Mo., won the game by the score of 6-0.

Minnesota won six in a row after the sorry Missouri opener, starting with Oregon, and the Gophers had to rally to beat to beat the Ducks, 14-7. At Champaign, quarterback Stephens beat the Fighting Illini all by himself, passing four four touchdowns and scored a fifth. In the 23-20 win over Michigan, Stephens played one of his best games ever, racking up over 300 yards running and passing another the come-from-behind win.

Then there was the 13-0 shutout over the then top-ranked Michigan State Spartans at Memorial Stadium. Munsey, who recovered from an injury that sidelined him from the Wolverine game the week before, scored both touchdowns for the Gophers.

After winning over Iowa and Purdue, only the Wisconsin Badgers stood in the way of the Gophers' first perfect Big Ten record since 1941. Wisconsin coach Milt Bruhn, an ex-Gopher, watched his quarterback, Ron Miller, connect with Pat Richter for two touchdowns as Wisconsin surprised Minnesota by 28-21.

Normally a 6-1 Big Ten record might be good enough to win the title, but, in 1961, the undefeated Ohio State Buckeyes claimed that honor. Then something bizarre happened. Ohio State, invited to play UCLA in the Rose Bowl, declined the invitation. If an official Big Ten-West Coast agreement been in effect at that time, Minnesota would have been ineligible to play in the big game two years in a row, but there was no such agreement in 1961. The Rose Bowl didn't even have to invite a Big Ten team. But the Rose Bowl committee did, and the grateful Gophers were off to Pasadena for the second year in a row, knowing full well that they had a chance to avenge their loss the year before to the Washington Huskies.

The Rose Bowl

Reminiscent of the 1961 Rose Bowl, when Washington scored a field goal on the opening drive, UCLA would also strike first in 1962. After being held deep in Gopher territory, the Bruins settled for a 28-yard field goal by Bob Smith just seven minutes into the game. The 98,214 fans that had poured into Pasadena to see the game could sense early on that Minnesota wasn't just happy to be there. That would be all the scoring the Bruins would do that day against the stingy Minnesota defense. The Gophers, haunted by the previous year's shame, bounced back on a one-yard touchdown plunge by Stephens resulting from a Dickson fumble recovery, just before the second quarter. Coach Murray Warmath had decided early that he wasn't going to play as conservatively on this go-round, and his Gophers went for it on several pivotal fourth down plays, picking up a first down on one, and scoring on another. Just

before the half, Stephens marched the Gophers 75 yards for a second touchdown with Munsey scoring on a reverse.

Dominating the game with their amazing defense, Stephens led the Gophers to one more scoring drive, going 84 yards, and scoring his second touchdown of the game from two yards out, late in the final period. The 19-play drive ate up 11 minutes off the clock, leaving little time for UCLA to do anything but wonder what could have been. The Gophers dominated the game, compiling 21 first downs while holding UCLA to eight. Led by the outstanding defensive play of Bell and Eller, Minnesota held the Bruins to a paltry 107 yards of total offense and a mere field goal. Minnesota would not be denied in their second run for the roses, winning the game, 21-3, for the team's first and only Rose Bowl victory. As coach Warmath was carried off the field, it was said that his smile could be seen all the way back in Minnesota.

"We went out the year before and lost to Washington, so this year we were going to win the Rose Bowl, no matter what." said Bobby Bell. "We beat UCLA pretty bad, and I have to say it was amazing. It was one of the greatest things that ever happened to me in college. I was playing with cracked ribs during the game, but at the time I didn't care because I wanted to win so badly. I can remember our defensive coach was saying to us, 'hey, if you let these guys run three or four yards up the middle, then we are not players at all, we might as well pack up, put our dresses back on, and go home.' Their running back, All-American, Charlie Smith, was a great player, but every time he got close to that line, we were all over him. We shut him down completely. It was great, and when it was over, we were sitting on top of the world."

"It wouldn't have mattered who we would have played this go around," said Big Ten MVP, Sandy Stephens. "I would have died before I lost that game, even if I had to win it all by myself. We just completely dominated UCLA from the point after they made that opening field goal. The game started out similar to the Rose Bowl of the year before, and that shocked us and woke us up pretty quick. That was the first and last time UCLA would score on us that day."

"I don't know if this is something that is very well known," said Carl Eller, "but I think that a lot of the senior players weren't sure if they even wanted to go back to the Rose Bowl in 1961. We actually had a team meeting on whether or not we should even go. Many of the players didn't want to go if Coach Warmath, who was a task-master, was going to lock them up in a retreat again when they were right down the street from Hollywood. Now, I was only a sophomore at the time, so I didn't have a voice on the team like the juniors and seniors did, but I felt like there was a mutiny going on. So, I stepped up and said, 'Hey guys, I don't want you to rob me of my chance to go to the Rose Bowl.' I didn't care at what hotel we stayed, I just wanted to go to the Rose Bowl! I think in retrospect, he (Warmath) probably did relax a little

| The St. Paul Saints hockey team wins the IHL's Turner Cup Championship | Gopher swimmer Steven Jackman wins the 100 yd Freestyle National Championship | Tommy Mason, a running back from Tulane, is the first overall pick by the Vikings in the NFL draft | George Keogan, a Detroit Lakes native who coached the Notre Dame Basketball team for 20 years, is inducted into the Basketball Hall of Fame | Gopher Football coach Murray Warmath is named the College Coach of the Year | Gopher first baseman Wayne Knapp is named to the All-American baseball team | The Minnesota Vikings, an NFL expansion team, beat the Bears in their first-ever game | Hall of Famer Lou Brock steals 38 bases for St. Cloud of the Northern League | The Washington Senators baseball team moves to Minnesota where they become the Minnesota Twins |

bit on us out there, and we had a great time that year. We had a very strong team in 1962, and we just overpowered UCLA, physically dominating them. It was a tremendous experience."

A high school quarterback
Growing up in Shelby, N.C., Bobby Bell played quarterback for his high school six-man football team, until his senior year when he finally piloted an 11-man team. Bobby originally came to Minnesota with every intention of playing quarterback for the Golden Gophers. As a sophomore, he could run as fast and throw farther than all the quarterbacks in practice. But Coach Warmath had already begun to mold the great Sandy Stephens as his quarterback, and since the talented Bell was too good to keep on the bench as Stephens' replacement, the coach put him in the lineup as an offensive and defensive tackle. Bobby, who just wanted the chance to play, accepted the role and eventually became one of the greatest tackles in Big Ten history.

The 6-4, 220-pounder's transition from signal-caller to tackle was hailed by sportswriters of the day as one of the modern wonders of college football. He led Minnesota to a 22-6-1 record during his stay with the Gophers, including a national championship and only Rose Bowl victory. There aren't many All-American tackles today that could boast to have the same sized 28 inch waist as Bobby did.

Bell is one of only eight Minnesota football players to earn All-America honors in two different seasons, 1961 and 1962. He was awarded the prestigious Outland Trophy his senior year by a landslide vote, recognizing him as the nation's top interior lineman. During his career at Minnesota, Bell won the conference MVP in 1962 and was All-Big Ten in both 1961 and 1962. He was elected to the College Football Hall of Fame in 1991.

The amazing athlete was recruited by several other U of M teams including the gymnastics team and basketball team. Wanting to do more in the winter, he became the first African-American to play a varsity game for the Gopher basketball team. One time, Gopher Hockey coach, John Mariucci tried to talk him to playing goalie for the team. "He told me that I had the quickest reflexes that he'd ever seen and that I was going to be the first black hockey player in the country," said Bell. "Now, coming from North Carolina I had never even seen hockey before. So, when we got out on the ice and someone nearly took my head off with a puck, I told him that the only way I'd get out there is if he turned the net around in the other direction!"

As a pro in the NFL, Bell made another transition, this time to linebacker, and guided the Kansas City Chiefs to two Super Bowls. Bell was one of the stars of the team that stopped the Minnesota Vikings and his old teammate and friend Carl Eller in the 1970 Super Bowl. He played 13 seasons, was an all-pro for eight consecutive years, and became the Chiefs' first inductee into the Pro Football Hall of Fame in 1983. Bobby was undoubtedly the greatest lineman and probably the greatest athlete ever to wear the maroon and gold.

Who was your hero when you were growing up? "Jackie Robinson."

What other sports did you play at the U?
"I ate and slept baseball. Coach Warmath told me coming in that I could play baseball as well as football for the University. But I never got a chance to play because he always insisted on me playing spring football instead. I did get to play varsity basketball, but I would have to say that my number one favorite sport was baseball, followed by basketball, and, last, football."

What did it mean for you to be a Gopher?
"I thought I had died and gone to heaven when I arrived at the University of Minnesota. Coming from North Carolina, I remember the first time I ever saw snow, it was so exciting. Being on campus as a Gopher was one of the most exciting things in my life. Playing in those Saturday football games was just so great. The fans and everybody were just really involved in the game.

The night before the football game, we would stay at a hotel in St. Paul. Then, on Saturday, we would drive down University Avenue with a police escort, and it was just wall-to-wall people everywhere yelling and screaming for us. My heart started to pound like crazy. I was so excited, and my stomach was churning. I couldn't wait to get my uniform on. Getting off that bus and seeing all the people hanging out of the frat house windows was incredible. Seeing all that excitement in one place was fantastic. Everybody was so into it! Tickets to our games were no where to be found. I had so much fun there, and to this day I have a real love for the University of Minnesota."

What do you want on your tombstone? "He gave it his all."

Where are they now?
Bobby is currently retired and travels all over the world as a motivational speaker. He plays in celebrity golf tournaments and spends time with his family. Bell lives in Lee's Summit, Mo., and has two sons and a daughter.

Tributes

"He had great ability and range on the football field. He had so much tenacity, and he was just an incredible ball player." -- **Tom Brown**

"Bobby was probably the most versatile player that I ever had the pleasure of playing with. I don't know of anyone else who could have gone from quarterback to tackle. When he came in, the only place we had open was at left tackle, and coach Warmath realized that since he was such a good athlete, he had to play him somewhere. Bobby said that he just came here to play and didn't care where it was that he played. He was one of the only guys that could throw the ball five yards further than me, and I could throw 80 yards." -- **Sandy Stephens**

"He was one of the most naturally-talented athletes that I ever saw. He was a person who really worked hard, but he had a lot of stuff to start with. He had speed and stamina, and he was a person that really enjoyed the game. Bobby made it look like fun, because he was so talented. He probably had talents that were maybe never really totally challenged, and that was the kind of guy that he was - just a tremendous player." -- **Carl Eller**

"Bobby was my roommate, so I know for a fact he had more natural ability than any football player his size. I never met anyone with a build like his. For a 6'4" - 240 pound converted quarterback with a 28-inch waist to be playing tackle was just amazing. He was just a neat guy and a very smart player." -- **Bill Munsey**

"Bobby Bell was the best football player we've ever had at the University of Minnesota." -- **Butch Nash**

Hibbing's Roger Maris hits homer no. 61, breaking Babe Ruth's long-standing single-season home-run record of 60, in the last game of the regular season. The two-time league MVP's record still stands today as one of the greatest records in all of sports.

TIMELINE

CARL ELLER
Madness at Camp Randall Stadium

In 1962, Carl Eller and Bobby Bell stood like two giant oak trees in a forest of great college football defensive players. The two anchored perhaps the greatest defensive unit in Gold Country history. In seven games, the Gophers' Big Ten opponents averaged less than 60 yards rushing per game, allowed just 61 points in nine games -- 34 alone in a freak loss to Northwestern. Five of the nine opponents were held scoreless (Michigan had negative 46 yards rushing). In an era of high scoring, wide-open play, this was truly amazing.

Joined by their new signal caller, Duane Blaska, who had taken over for the graduated Sandy Stephens, the Golden Gophers set off on the road to winning another Big Ten Title. After an opening 0-0 standoff with the stubborn Missouri Tigers, Minnesota shutout Navy, Illinois, Michigan, and Iowa, a feat that probably will never be equaled. They went on to beat Michigan State, 28-7, and knocked off Purdue by 7-6. The only blemish to an otherwise fabulous season was the loss to Northwestern early in the year. It all came down to this: Minnesota needed to beat Wisconsin at Camp Randall Stadium in Madison in their final game to win the Big Ten title. Both teams were 5-1 in the conference, and the winner would be smelling roses.

Unfortunately, what ensued was one of the most bizarre college football games ever played. The officials, not the players, played the pivotal role, in a game that will long be remembered in Gold Country.

Minnesota scored first in the second quarter, with Blaska connecting with Jim Cairns on a 15 yard scoring strike. Quarterback Ron VanderKelen rallied his Badgers back with a 65-yard scoring drive to take the lead at 7-6.

In the second half, the game started to turn into an penalty-filled sideshow, capped by the Gophers being penalized 15 yards for illegally aiding the advance of a

runner. Minnesota settled for a Collin Versich 32-yard field goal. The scoreboard read: Minnesota 9, Wisconsin 7.

The Gophers later punted, and the coverage team, seeing the ball hit a Badger player, jumped on the loose ball rolling in the end zone, and claimed a touchdown. The officials didn't see it that way, however, and returned the ball to Wisconsin.

Then it happened -- an event that will live in infamy. On the Gopher 43 yard-line, VanderKelen dropped back to pass and he was sacked hard by Bell. The ball flew into the awaiting arms of Gopher John Perkovich, but referee Dr. Robert Jones nullified the interception. Incredibly, he called Bell for roughing the passer. At this point, head coach Murray Warmath could no longer contain himself. The 15-yard roughing penalty suddenly turned into 30 when Dr. Jones slapped the Gopher bench with an additional unsportsmanlike conduct call. So, instead of Minnesota having the ball at midfield, the Badgers now had a first down on the Minnesota 13-yard line with less than two minutes to go. Three plays later Wisconsin scored, taking the lead by 14-9.

Then, amazingly, the officials decided to even things up and let the Gophers back into the contest by calling the Badgers for a personal foul on the ensuing kickoff, and, then, slapped them with two pass interference calls. Suddenly, with a minute to go in the game, the Gophers found themselves with a first down on the Wisconsin 14. Now it gets weird. Mysteriously, all communications from the press box to the Gopher bench disappeared, and the assistant coaches who had the bird's eye views were silenced. So, on first down, Blaska went for it all. But, his floater was picked off in the end zone. Wisconsin had won the Big Ten championship.

"I was called for roughing the Badger quarterback,"

said Bell, "but you could see on the film that he still had the ball in his hands, so it couldn't have been roughing. It was a blown call. It was a mess, and they ended up getting about 45 yards out of the whole thing, which ultimately led to them winning the game. It was the craziest game I ever played in. I bet that I've received hundreds of letters and newspaper clippings from around the country about that one play, and people still want to talk to me about it. The referee's name was Robert Jones. I will never forget that guy."

The run was over. For three seasons in the early 1960s, Minnesota had earned 22 wins, suffered only six losses, and had one game end in a tie. They won a national championship, a Big Ten title, and a Rose Bowl game. Their accomplishments had quieted the critics, but then Murray Warmath, like Bernie Bierman before him, and Fritz Crisler before him, and Bill Spaulding before him, and Dr. Henry Williams before him, would eventually feel the wrath of the Monday morning quarterbacks.

From Winston-Salem to Minneapolis
Carl Eller grew up in Winston Salem, N.C. He was both an offensive and defensive tackle for the Golden Gophers from 1961-63 and was twice named All-American and All-Big Ten. In 1964 Eller was drafted by the Minnesota Vikings with the sixth overall pick of the first round of the NFL draft. He went on to play 15 years for the Vikings and one year for the Seattle Seahawks. He was named All Pro six times, was the NFL's Most Valuable Defensive lineman two times, and played in six Pro Bowl games. Eller is the Vikings all-time sack leader, credited with 130 quarterback sacks, 44 in one three-season period. Overall in Eller's career, he recovered 23 fumbles (fourth best in NFL history) and is often given the credit for leading the Vikings to 11 wining division titles and three NFC crowns. He retired after 16 professional football seasons in 1979.

Eller is very much a part of our fabric of life here in the Upper Midwest. He is synonymous with football in Minnesota and will always be remembered not only for his big smile, but as a fierce competitor as well. All his life, he just wanted to play football. In his first season at the University of Minnesota, he played, despite suffering a broken bone in his hand. Carl wore a cast in practice but tossed it aside come game day. He once played MacBeth at the Guthrie Theater and was voted one of Esquire magazine's Best Dressed Jocks in 1972. He has been through a lot in as a resident of Minnesota but will always be a state legend.

Who was your hero when you were growing up?
"Joe Louis"

What did it mean for you to be a Gopher?
"Being a Golden Gopher was great. Going to the U was one of the better choices that I made in my life. Being on a metropolitan campus and being a part of the Saturday football scene at Memorial Stadium were wonderful experiences for me. Sure, it was a culture shock for me because I had come from a segregated

Steven Jackman, a Gopher swimmer, wins both the 50 yd and 100 yd Freestyle National Championships	Virgil Luken, a Gopher swimmer, wins the 200-Yard Breaststroke National Championship	Twins pitcher Jack Kralick throws the only nine inning no-hitter at the Met	Bill McKechnie, a Minneapolis Miller in 1921, is inducted into the Baseball Hall of Fame

town in North Carolina. Everything at the U was a new and wonderful experience for me, and it was my first exposure to big-time football. Since freshman couldn't play at the time, during my first year I was like the average fan watching the Gopher games. To watch the games and to know that the next season I was going to be a part of all the excitement was just a great experience. Yes, it means a lot for me to be a Gopher."

What did it mean to be a Viking?

"It still means a lot. But, truthfully, I felt I was totally misunderstood by the media. You see, when I played, I felt like I was an artist. I could have easily been the equivalent of a violinist, or a painter, or whatever. Football is a mental game, and I was a craftsman who had great skill and technique. The culmination of all those things made me a great player. Professional football was a real test of all my skills, and I looked at playing as a performance. In other words, when I would do things like putting on a pass rush, or stopping a double-team, or making a tackle behind the play, I had to push and test myself to the limit to do those kinds of things that were just barely humanly possible. I had to be quick off the ball, and I had to beat the the opponent to the ball. Sometimes I had to beat two guys, and sometimes I would have to like hold one guy off with one arm and try to grab the quarterback with the other, all while trying to maintain my leverage, and all while watching out for the back who was coming to cut me at my knees. You have to do all that in a split second, and I took great pride in being able to do it well. I really felt like playing professional football was an art."

What about the Purple People Eaters?

"The nickname was special because we were in it together. There was compassion among us, because we knew what each other guy was going through. If a guy was holding Jim or Alan or Lars or me, we knew what that meant, and we took care of each other. We all had to step up when the game was tight, and we stuck together. It was special."

Does never winning a Super Bowl still hurt?

"Well, we had four shots at winning the big one. People can look at it whatever way they want to, but the four losses never came off as a negative to me. I can say that we were champions of the National Football Conference three times and NFL once, we went to four Super Bowls, defeated some great teams, and lost to some of the best football teams ever in Miami, Oakland, Pittsburgh, and Kansas City. It wasn't like we took a dive in our Super Bowls, or anything like that. I have nothing to be ashamed of. I have nothing to regret. We lost four games fair and square. But we didn't lose because we didn't put our best effort out there. We didn't lose because we weren't the best team to make it there. Regardless of what anybody says, those were my greatest moments. Those games were great Vikings moments and a unforgettable part of the great Vikings' history. We never quit. It takes a lot of strength and character to come back time and time again. I think that says a lot more about the Vikings than perhaps some of the teams that actually won the Super Bowl."

What was your most memorable game?

"In the 1969 playoffs, tackling the Rams' Roman Gabriel in the end zone for a safety."

Gopher & Viking tombstone:

"He loved both life and the game of football."

Where are they now?

Carl works for the State of Minnesota and also operates a satellite communications company. He has three children and lives in the Minneapolis area.

Tributes

"Carl was a very talented football player. He was strong, quick and agile, and he was a very intense football player."   -- **Alan Page**

"Moose was a great talent. He got a lot of sacks and knocked down a lot of balls back then, he was just a dominant player. He played his best against the best players, and would dominate each team's top players that they put up against him."   -- **Bud Grant**

"He was one of the biggest, strongest, toughest guys to come down the pike. When he wanted to destroy an opponent, I don't think there was anyone who could stop him. He was a great, great football player and I have so much respect for him. We played throughout our entire careers together, he was my roommate and one of my closest friends."
    -- **Jim Marshall**

"These guys, 'the Purple People Eaters' were household names when I grew up. It was so great to play on the same team with them, because if we scored 7 points - it was a blowout. We would win because the other team wasn't going to score on them. I used to love watching Carl battle. I couldn't wait for the offense to get off the field so I could watch him go up against those huge 300 pound linemen. It was a massive battle of the titans watching them go at it out there, and Carl would usually win."
    -- **Ahmad Rashad**

"He was the enforcer. Carl wasn't just a great football player, he was a great athlete. He was also a very bright guy. He was probably the greatest defensive end that ever played the game." -- **Chuck Foreman**

"As great a player as Carl was, I always admired the confidence that he added to our team each time we went onto the football field. He was like a chieftain out there. He was as big, as fast and as tough as anybody in the league, and yet he had such a will and spirit to win. Confidence is what separates losing teams from winning teams and Carl passed that quality onto our team."   -- **Joe Kapp**

"We named him the moose, because he was a so big and strong. Being from North Carolina, he hated the cold, so we had to indoctrinate him to the balmy Minnesota weather! He had so much enthusiasm and was just a great player." -- **Sandy Stephens**

"He was an all-around athlete. I got recruited with Carl from Winston Salem. He was so tough and strong, that's why we named him the 'Moose'. He was a happy-go-lucky fun guy, and he was a guy you could

coach. I remember playing that great Michigan State team where they had the number one offense in the country and we had the number one defense in the country. I think they were averaging something like 550 yards of offense per game, and at half-time they had like 26 yards - we shut them down, and Carl was just unstoppable. We unbalanced the line that game so he could come down to my side and double down. Carl would drive their guy into the ground every play and our offense took over. He was the greatest."
    -- **Bobby Bell**

"Carl was extremely quick. With he and Bobby Bell on the ends, it was quite a sight. He was a super player."
    -- **Bill Munsey**

DON'T "SHOW ME THE MONEY"

In an interesting phenomenon during the 1990's, a string of native Minnesotans completed a pleasant reverse migration and either came home or stayed home in their beloved Minnesota. In all cases, the baseball stars took less money for the opportunity to either have the opportunity to play with, or finish their careers as Twins. The common denominator for all of the players: quality of life. Despite the Arctic winters, the players love Minnesota and think it is a great place to live and raise a family.

The latest in the parade of prodigal sons was New Ulm's all-star catcher, Terry Steinbach, who turned down a four-year $18.75 million bid from the Toronto Blue Jays. "What's happiness, though?" asked Steinbach. "There's more to baseball, and more to life, than money. Sure, it's a factor, but it's just one part of a whole equation."

Many of Steinbach's fellow major league Minnesota brethren seemed to agree, including Jack Morris, Dave Winfield, Paul Molitor, and Kent Hrbek, all of whom were free agents who either signed or re-signed with Minnesota, despite the fact that they could've gotten a lot more money somewhere else.

Here is a list of the big-name free agent Minnesotans, including Californian Rick Aguilera and Chicagoan Kirby Puckett, who also decided that money isn't everything.

Player	Season	Twins Contract	Best Offer Passed Up
Kent Hrbek	1990	5 Years, $14 Million	5 Years, $15.5 Million
Jack Morris	1991	1 Years, $1 Million	3 Years, $9.3 Million
Kirby Puckett	1992	5 Years, $30 Million	5 Years, $38 Million
Dave Winfield	1993	2 Years, $5.2 Million	Didn't Wait For Offers
Rick Aguilera	1996	3 Years, $9 Million	3 Years, $12 Million
Paul Molitor	1996	1 Year, $2 Million	Took $1.5 Million Pay Cut
Terry Steinbach	1997	3 Years, $8 Million	4 Years, $18.15 Million

Source: Sports Illustrated

THREE OF THE MOST FAMOUS MINNESOTA BRED HORSES THAT HAVE RACED AT CANTERBURY PARK: BLAIR'S COVE, PRINCESS ELAINE, AND TIMELESS PRINCE

BLAIR'S COVE

The all-time leading Minnesota-bred money winner, Blair's Cove traveled to 14 race tracks during his career. With 14 starts and seven wins at Canterbury Blair's Cove became Canterbury Horse of the Year in 1988 and Champion Grass Horse in 1989. His last start and victory came at Canterbury in the inaugural Festival of Championship Classic in 1992. Blair retired with 57 lifetime starts, 17 wins, 10 seconds, and 4 thirds. Total earnings were $533,528 with $197,500 coming from turf victories. Blair's Cove was the first Minnesota-bred horse to win a graded stakes in winning the Bashford Manor Stakes at Churchill Downs in 1987. Competing against the tough-est horses of his generation, he competed in major stakes races at Keeneland, Gulfstream Park, Colder Arlington, the Meadowlands, Golden Gate, and Bay Meadows.

PRINCESS ELAINE

The all-time leading money-earning Minnesota-bred filly or mare, Princess Elaine was loved by every Minnesota racing fan, many of whom even traveled to the other race courses she visited. With 27 lifetime starts, nine wins, five seconds and 2 thirds, Princess Elaine earned $232,240. She won nine races at Canterbury from 15 starts, including victories in the USA Handicap, Red Wing Stakes, Lady Slipper Stakes, and Minnesota Breeders' Oaks. As Canterbury Champion Older Filly or Mare in 1989 and Champion 3-year-old Filly in 1988, Princess Elaine never ducked the "big" mares. Most notably, she ran sixth in the Very Subtle Stakes on the Breeders' Cup undercard in 1989, after receiving an extremely troubling trip, and was assigned 127 pounds to Blair's Cove's 122 pounds in the 1990 Jim Binger Handicap (where she lost by a head). Her rider, Chris Valovich, says Princess Elaine is the best horse he has ridden. When Princess Elaine suffered a life-ending injury during a race at Hawthorne Race Course, Steve Davidowitz of the Star Tribune wrote an obituary - likely the only equine obituary to appear in a major newspaper.

TIMELESS PRINCE

Canterbury Champion Timeless Prince had many owners throughout his career. Currently he is owned by the St. Paul Police Department where he serves as a mounted police horse. It is "Lester's" (Lester Partners) breeder, Mr. Coss of Cannon River Farms, who deserves the credit for finding a new career for Lester. A winner of $327,403 in his racing career, Lester became Champion Two-Year-Old in 1990 and Champion Three-Year-Old colt in 1991. He started 21 times at Canterbury with 10 wins (stringing together five consecutive victories in 1991). He traveled to 11 race tracks during his career and was claimed by Hall of Fame nominee Steven Herold in 1995. During his prime, conditioner Joey Ruhsam and his owners, Lester Partners, brought Lester out loaded for bear in each of his races, and fans were never disappointed in his courageous efforts.

TERRY STEINBACH

Terry Steinbach was born on March 2, 1962 in New Ulm. He went on to star as an infielder at New Ulm High School and in American Legion ball. He learned the game under the tutelage of Jim Senske, Minnesota's all-time winningest high school baseball coach. He also played on the frozen pond and remains the school's all-time leading scorer in hockey. He then followed in his big brother Tom's footsteps and came to the University of Minnesota in 1980 on a baseball scholarship. (His brother Tim also played in Gold Country in 1981).

Today he remains tied for third in career hitting for the U of M baseball team with a .375 average. He is fourth in home-runs (behind his brother, Tom, who is the Gophers all-time career leader), and in the top ten in most other career offensive categories. The two-time All-Big Ten slugger led his Gopher teams to a Big Ten championship and two NCAA regional appearances.

From there Terry was drafted by the Oakland Athletics. While playing in Double-A ball, the A's converted the third baseman into a catcher. He took to it like a duck to water and has been referred to as not a hitter who catches, but as a catcher who hits. After 14 years in the A's organization, he hit .275 with 132 homers, 205 doubles, 595 RBI, and 1,144 hits. Considered by many to be one of the games' premier defensive catchers, he's gunned-down 37 percent of the runners who have tried to steal on him. He led the A's to four Western Division titles, three American League pennants, and a World Championship in 1989, where he led the team with 7 RBIs in nine post-season games. He's also played in three All-Star games, even earning MVP honors in the 1988 mid-season classic. And, in typical Steinbach fashion, he donated the van that he won for being named as the MVP to the New Ulm United Way. He also finances a college scholarship every year for a student-athlete from one of New Ulm's three high schools.

A Minnesota homecoming
In 1996, after a career-year in Oakland, where he set a number of career batting highs --including his AL-record 34 homers as a catcher (35 total) and 100 RBI (33 more than any previous season) -- Terry exercised his free-agent status and came home to sign a three-year contract with the Twins. For Steinbach, even though it meant taking a several million dollar pay cut, it was worth it. He could now be closer to his family and be able to do what he loves most, enjoy the outdoors.

The avid angler and hunter wanted to see his first Minnesota spring in over 14 years, something very important to him. He even bought his very own outdoor paradise: a 110-acre plot of land, which borders half of an 80-acre lake, near his Plymouth home. Sometimes during hunting season, he and Simon, his Brittany spaniel, come to the oasis two or three times a day to check up on things. To say he loves the outdoors might be an understatement. In 1989, after winning the World Series, Terry balked at the opportunity to visit the White House and meet President Bush because it conflicted with the opening of deer season. His wife, Mary, was none too pleased to say the least.

Terry is one of the best baseball players ever to come from Minnesota. He is best described as a pro's pro who respects the game, plays hard, and has fun. "He's one of the most respected players in the league because of his knowledge and how he calls a game," said teammate and fellow Gopher, Paul Molitor. The Twins were lucky to get him, and have him groom in their young pitching staff, something he takes great pride in. He may be one of the most-liked players in the league because he is genuine and an overall nice guy.

Who was your idol or hero growing up? "Killebrew, Oliva and Carew. Those were the guys growing up in Minnesota that we looked up to. You'd see them do something incredible and the next day at the park, you would try to do it like they did. But also I looked up to Cesare Maniago, Bill Goldsworthy, Gump Worsley as well as Fran Tarkenton and the Purple People Eaters."

On moving home: "For my particular situation, the timing was right for me to come home. With my kids at the age that they are, it is nice for them to go to just one school, live in just one house, and keep up with their friends. It's great to be back and to be playing with the Twins. We love it here."

On catching: "Pitching is hard, so a catcher has to do anything he can to reduce the burden. Your number-one job is to make your pitcher comfortable so he can have the best possible game he can. It's what I enjoy doing most."

On the game: "What I love most are those nine innings. When you're between the white lines, it's like there's a barrier nobody else can penetrate, nobody can touch. When the umpire says 'Play ball!', for two or three hours there are no interviews, no contracts, no distractions. It's just ball."

What did it mean for you to be a Gopher? "It was pretty special, especially having my brother Tom there before me. He set the way for me there and it was a pretty neat experience. Once you get there and realize the baseball talent that they have put out over the years there, it was amazing. John Anderson was a great coach and I had a lot of great memories playing there."

What does it mean to be a Twin? "Playing against the Twins while in Oakland, we had a tremendous rivalry throughout the late 80's and into the early 90's. It was always fun to come back home and play and see all of my family. I'm 35 now and I would love to finish here with the Twins. It's great to be home now, I can see all my family throughout the season and get in plenty of hunting as well."

Gopher/Twins tombstone: "I would like my character to be thought of more than my accomplishments. I would like to be remembered as a hard worker and willing to work with everybody. I would like to thought of as someone who was always approachable and not hung up on himself, and as a guy who was respected by his peers."

Where are they now? Currently Terry and his wife, Mary, reside in Plymouth. They have three children: Jill, Lucas, and Lake. Terry continues to catch for the Twins, where, in 1997, he is having a respectable year at the plate.

JOHN GAGLIARDI
St. Johns Wins its First
National Championship

In 1963, a dynasty of sorts officially began. This was the year that football coach John Gagliardi, of St. Johns University, in Collegeville, Minn., won his first national championship, barely beating Prairie View A&M.

You must remember that football in Minnesota was gaining popularity in the early years of the 1960s. The University of Minnesota Golden Gophers were coming off of two Rose Bowl appearances, and the fledgling Minnesota Vikings were gaining fan support at Metropolitan Stadium in Bloomington. But, quietly, another team was making some noise about 90 minutes north of the Twin Cities.

The 1963 Minnesota Intercollegiate Athletic Conference (MIAC) season was very successful for the St. Johns Johnnies of Collegeville, Minn. Gagliardi's team was led by halfback Bob Spinner, who won his second straight MIAC scoring championship in the season finale against St. Thomas. The Johnnies trounced their arch-rival Tommies by 32-6.

Next, it was off to the small-college playoffs for St. Johns, where they met the College of Emporia of Kansas. It wasn't even close as the Johnnies crushed them, 54-0, en route to waltzing through the playoffs and advancing to the title game. The match was held in Sacramento and labeled Camellia Bowl. The opponent was, NAIA's Prairie View A&M of Texas.

Prairie View A&M was the dominant black college team in America at the time. They played a big-time schedule against teams like Grambling State and Florida A&M and dominated them all. Prairie View had some great players on that team who would go on to become stars in the NFL, such as Hall of Famer Otis Taylor, and Jim Carnie, their quarterback, who would later become an all-pro defensive back for the Chiefs.

The Johnnies were decisive underdogs going into the contest. Prairie View had 40 "free-ride" football scholarships for their players. St. John's had none. The only thing the Johnnies did have in their favor was the atypical California weather on that day, which was a chilly 39 degrees - freezing to a Texan.

Prairie View scored first on a 29 yard roll-out by quarterback Jimmy Hall. The Johnnies answered though, on Bob Spinner's 41 yard punt return in the second, making it 7-6. But the Panthers came back on Jimmy Kearney's 61-yard pass to Otis Taylor, going up by 14-6.

St. Johns' defensive back John McCormick then returned an interception 44 yards, and Johnnie quarterback Craig Muyres hooked up with halfback Bernie Beckman to make it 14-13 at the half.

Then, in the third, the Johnnies took the lead for good on Muyres' 23-yard pass to Hardy Reyerson. Muyres hit Ken Roering for the extra point and St. Johns led 20-14. Late in the same period Beckman, off a double re-verse, connected with Roering on an 18-yard touchdown.

The Panthers rallied back in the fourth as Kearney threw a 14 yard TD pass to halfback Doug Broadus cutting the margin to 26-21. But the Johnies answered, this time on a 19-yard Muyres to Reyerson aerial, followed by a Spinner extra point catch. Prairie View scored on an Ezell Seals one yard plunge, with only 2:15 to go on the game block. But it was too little too late, as Roering recovered the Prairie View on-side kick to run out the clock. The Johnnies had done it, beating the Panthers 33-27, as the 12,220 fans, many of whom had make the trek from Minnesota, went wild.

Beckman, the smallest man on the field, ran for 52 yards, caught three passes for 43 passes including a conversion and played brilliant defense. He was named the game's MVP.

"It was a tremendous win for us," said Gagliardi. "Prairie View is the best team we played all year. Believe me, we knew we weren't going to be playing St. Catherine's! I mean it, it was like coming back after two nine-count knockdowns. And the second knockdown really had us hanging on the ropes. I give credit to the team. They managed to come through with the big play when it was needed all season, especially Craig Muyres, who I believe is the best clutch quarterback in the United States."

The legendary Gagliardi

John Gagliardi was born in 1927, the son of an Italian-born body shop owner in Trinidad, Colo. To fully understand this man's life-long calling of coaching, you have to go way back to Trinidad Catholic High School. Gagliardi's storied coaching career ironically began when his high school coach was drafted into World War II. Without a coach, the school was just going to drop the football program until "Gags" talked the administration into letting him do the coaching. Gagliardi, the teams' captain, took over the reins at the age of 16. Even at that young age people could see the man had a gift for teaching, working with young people, and instilling in them a winning attitude. His teams won four conference titles over the next six years. Upon graduating, he put himself through school at Colorado College, where he coached the high school team for two more seasons and then took over as Colorado College's head coach for his junior and senior seasons.

After graduation from C.C. in 1949, the 22-year-old Gags accepted his first college coaching position at Carroll College, a small Catholic liberal arts school in Helena, Mont. He coached not only the football program, but also the basketball and baseball programs as well. Inheriting a Carroll College athletic program in utter disarray, he turned things around in a hurry, leading the football and basketball teams to three straight championships.

His success drew the attention of another small Catholic college - St. Johns University of Collegeville, Minn. St. Johns needed a coach to succeed the mythical Johnny "Blood" McNally, former Green Bay Packer great and a charter member of the Pro Football Hall of Fame. SJU had not won a conference title in 15 years, and Johnny Blood, their departing head coach, offered these inspiring words to the new coach: "Nobody can ever win at St. Johns."

In 1953, all John Gagliardi was given was a mandate to turn the program around and nothing else that was tangible. Amazingly, he immediately quieted the skeptics by winning the MIAC title that fall with the help of his first great halfback, Jim Lehman, the father of Minnesota golf great Tom Lehman, who led the country in scoring. Gags also went on to turn around the Johnnies' track and hockey teams, proving his unique coaching methods and motivational skills could make any team a winner.

TIMELINE	Gopher swimmer, Steven Jackman, wins the 50yd Freestyle National Championship	Former St. Johns University football player and coach, and Duluth Eskimos player Johnny Blood, is inducted into the Pro Football Hall of Fame.	Gopher swimmer Wally Richardson, wins the 100 yd Butterfly National Championship	International Falls native Bronko Nagurski, a Gopher football and Chicago Bears legend, is inducted into the Pro Football Hall of Fame.	Paul Flatley, a Vikings wide receiver, is named as the NFL's Rookie of the Year	Gopher second baseman Jon Andresen is named to the All-American baseball team	Gopher swimmers Alfred Ericksen, Virgil Luken, Wally Richardson, and Steve Jackman, win the 400 Yard Medley Relay national championship	The Minneapolis Millers hockey team, led by player/coach Ken Yackel, who was a former three-sport star at the U of M, loses to Fort Wayne in the International League championship game

Simply unbelievable

There have been more than 25,000 head coaches in college football history. Only five have won more than 300 games. They are (ranked by most wins): Eddie Robinson, John Gagliardi, Bear Bryant, Amos Alonzo Stagg, and Pop Warner. Of them, only Robinson and Gagliardi are still coaching. Robinson, the head coach at Grambling State University, has the most career wins of all-time with 405, while Gagliardi remains number two on the all-time list with 336 at the start of the 1997 MIAC season.

One of his biggest moments in coaching and perhaps in life happened in 1993, when his Johnnies pulverized Bethel, 77-12, for Gags' 300th win. After that historic event the eyes of the world of sports were suddenly on Gagliardi. The national media invaded Collegeville for words of wisdom from the man who was became known nationwide as a coaching genius.

Another milestone happened two years later when the Johnnies beat Carleton, 35-24, to give the coach his 324th career victory, topping the famed Bear Bryant of the University of Alabama by one.

More Gagliardi tidbits:

Gagliardi has built one of the nation's top NCAA Division III programs. The attitude and winning tradition he instills in his players is unprecedented. Among this seven-time national coach of the year's many achievements are his three small college championship teams. First, in 1963, then two years later, when they crushed Linfield College of Oregon, 35-0 (amazingly the Johnnies allowed only 27 points to be scored against them that entire season), and, in 1976, when they beat Towson State of Maryland, 31-28. In addition he has won 18 conference titles and his teams have been nationally ranked 32 of the past 35 years. SJU has not suffered through a losing season since the Lyndon Baines Johnson Administration. Also, from 1962-1964 the Johnnies owned the nation's longest winning streak (20 wins). In more than four decades at Collegeville, Gagliardi has posted 79 career shutouts and has coached five national player of the year winners.

Gags

Among his numerous awards and achievements, Gagliardi has been inducted into the Minnesota and Montana halls of fame and is a member of the College Football Hall of Fame. He has been the subject of a Sports Illustrated cover story and was awarded the Football Writers of America Citation of Honor. Perhaps his greatest honor will live on forever though. The NCAA honored the coach by naming the Division III equivalent of the Heisman Trophy after him. The Gagliardi Trophy is given annually to the outstanding NCAA Division III football player.

No sign of slowing down

After 54 years of coaching, 49 of them in college, and 44 with St. Johns, Gagliardi's teams are still setting the standard for MIAC competitors. In 1993, SJU became the first NCAA team since the 1904 Gophers to score more than 700 points in a season, when the Johnies put up an amazing 702 points in 13 games. Then, in 1994, St. Johns was within one game of making the Division III championship game before losing in the final-four to Albion.

Gagliardi's success is attributable to more than mere football strategy and tactics. He is an astute judge of talent. He creates an environment of fun and high expectations, and he concentrates on methods and practices that truly focus on winning football games. John Gagliardi has built a legacy that is unrivaled in college football, and what's frightening for all the other MIAC schools, he may just be getting his second wind.

Who was your idol or hero growing up? "Frank Leahy, the legendary Notre Dame Football Coach."

On joining the 300-wins fraternity:

"It was just a big relief and I was glad to get it over with. We were in the middle of the season and there was so much build-up towards it. I never had so much attention in my life, it was hard to get anything done that week! I'm sure the big-time coaches were used to all the attention, but I didn't really like it. As far as being in the fraternity, those people are so great. Never in my wildest dreams did I ever think that I would be mentioned in the same sentence with them. But remember, you couldn't win all those games without a lot of great players through the years."

Will you go after Eddie Robinson to be the number one of all-time?

"He's played a lot more games than we have over the years in that sunny weather. There were a lot of seasons that we could only play seven games because of the cold weather up here. So who knows what could've been if all things were equal? If I'm healthy and we're winning, maybe I'll go for his all-time record. Eddie's quitting after this year and I guess there's around 50-60 wins to go, so you never know. Hey, I'm only 70!"

St. John's tombstone:

"I dared to do a lot of things that no one else dared to do - like the way we practice. We've never gone 'full-go' in practice I am proud of the fact that I saved a lot of guys from permanent injuries because of that. I've been a lucky guy and I've always had great athletes to make me look good along the way."

Where are they now?

John and his wife Peggy live in Collegeville and have four children: Johnny, Nancy, Gina and Jim - who is an assistant coach at SJU. It's business as usual for the coach, as he enters his 45th season and prepares for his long journey to catch Eddie Robinson, maybe sometime around the year 2008. We'll see you all at the festivities, but remember, NO Gatorade shower!

His unorthodox coaching methods have been distilled into a series of: "WINNING WITH NO'S"

THE OVERALL PROGRAM
- No athletic scholarships.
- No big staff, just four assistant coaches.
- No coordinators.
- No freshmen or junior-varsity program.
- No discipline problems.
- No insisting on being called "Coach."
- No players cut.
- No pampering athletes.
- No one persuaded to come out or stay out.
- No hazing tolerated

THE SEASON
- No staff meetings.
- No player meetings.
- No film sessions after Monday
- No grading films.
- No special diet.
- No training table - team eats with other students.
- No special dormitory.
- No signs in dressing rooms.
- No slogans.
- No superstitions.
- No play-books.
- No statistics posted.
- No newspaper clippings posted.

THE PRACTICES
- No practice pants - shorts or sweats worn at practice.
- No agility drills.
- No lengthy calisthenics (about three minutes.)
- No pre-practice drills
- No practice apparatus or gadgets.
- No blocking sleds.
- No blocking or tackling dummies.
- No tackling.
- No laps.
- No wind sprints.
- No special coaching clothes worn.
- No use of the words "hit," "kill," etc...
- No clip boards.
- No whistles.
- No practice on Sundays.
- No practice on Mondays.
- No drills.
- No spring practice.
- No practice in rain, extreme heat or cold.
- No practice if mosquitoes, gnats, etc... are bad.
- No long practices - varies from 30 to 90 minutes.
- No practice under the lights.
- No water or rest denied when players want it.
- No practice modules.
- No underclassmen carry equipment other than their own.

THE GAMES
- No big deal when we score - we expect to score.
- No Gatorade celebrations.
- No trying to "kill" opponent.
- No trash talk tolerated.
- No tendency charts.
- No use of headphones.
- No coaches in press-box.
- No player NOT played in rout (as many as 143 have played in one game)
- No spearing allowed.
- No cheap-shots or foul play tolerated.
- No belief that aggressive teams get penalties.
- No counting tackles.
- No precision pre-game drills.
- No precision huddles.
- No big games pointed to.
- No special pre-game meals.
- No special post-game meals.
- No computer analysis.
- No cheerleaders.

THE OFF-SEASON
- No meetings.
- No between season practices or conditioning.
- No captains' practice.
- No study or tutoring program necessary.
- No weightlifting program

THE RESULTS
- No player has not graduated.
- No discipline problems.
- No player lost through ineligibility.
- No class has NOT had at least one prospective pro player.
- No small college has larger crowd support.
- No wider point margin in national playoff history.
- No team has fewer injuries.
- No team has fewer penalties.

TIMELINE

Minneapolis' Bud Wilkinson retires as head football coach at the University of Oklahoma. The former Gopher guard earned All-American honors in football, where he played on three national championship teams and also captained the 1935 hockey team. At one point, his Sooners won 47 consecutive games, enroute to three national championships.

Lake City's Ralph Samuelson was given credit by the American Water Ski Association as the "Father of Water Skiing." Forty-four years after his first "ride" in 1922, around Lake Pepin, Ralph's invention is finally given its due. He took two pine boards, held them over a tea kettle, put them in a vice to curve them upward, and fastened the ski's to his feet. Behind his brother's clamming boat, he reached speeds of more than 80 mph.

St. Paul's Tommy Gibbons, known as the Phantom, is inducted into the Boxing Hall of Fame. The light-heavyweight champion once went 15 rounds with Jack Dempsey in 1923.

Minneapolis' Dr. Emmet Swanson wins the Service Bolt division in the National Rifle Championships. One of the greatest marksmen in US history, Swanson competed on four Olympic teams (1948, 1952, 1956 and 1960)

Willow River native Ernie Nevers, a former football player for the Duluth Eskimos, is inducted into the Pro Football Hall of Fame. He once scored 40 points in a game, still an NFL record

HARMON KILLEBREW
Killer Wins the Home Run Crown

Coming off a promising third-place finish the year before, the Twins would sink deep into the cellar of the American League basement in 1964, finishing in sixth place with a modest record of 79-83. But there was some good news. The season was just a warmup to the fabulous World Series run in 1965.

The highlight of the 1964 season was when Twins legend Harmon Killebrew earned the title of Major League Baseball's sultan of swat, easily winning the home run title. Not bad for a guy who had just come off of a serious knee operation during the off-season.

Killebrew would belt out 49 circuit clouts in 1964, the highest total of his career, and enough to win the home run crown for the third straight year. That accomplishment would put Harm in a very select class. Only seven players had ever led their leagues in home runs for three or more consecutive years up to that point. The Pittsburgh Pirates' Ralph Kiner holds the all-time record of seven straight years, and Babe Ruth had two streaks, four in a row from 1918 to 1921, and six in a row from 1926 to 1931. Killebrew finished the 1964 season with some other very impressive stats. He hit a modest .270 in 1964, but scored 95 runs and accumu-

lated 111 RBIs. With the addition of teammate Bob Allison's 32 homers, the two combined for 81, the most prolific homer-twosome ever for the Twins.

At a sports banquet in Baltimore, he was officially honored as the 1964 Sultan of Swat. He was presented with a crown of jewels, symbolic of the major league home run championship. Killebrew would join a select fraternity of prior winners, which included Mickey Mantle, Ted Williams, Ernie Banks, Eddie Mathews, Hank Aaron, Willie Mays. and Roger Maris.

"Over my career I led the league six times in home runs", said Killebrew, "but that year was special because it was the first time I hit 49 homers. That was probably one of my best years ever as an individual, but we didn't win anything as a team. So 1964 doesn't stick out to me as much as the next year, when we went to the World Series, or in 1969, when we won our first division championship under Billy Martin."

Growing up in Idaho

Harm grew up playing baseball on the vacant lots of Payette, Ida. The neighbor kids would emulate the late Hall of Famer Walter Johnson, who had played semi-pro ball just 15 miles away. What set Killebrew apart from other kids was his intense dedication to the game and his desire to improve himself. While many boys were content simply to play the game, Harmon would practice for hours in the backyard of his home at 726 North Seventh Street, swinging his bat at imaginary pitches. He would become an Idaho high school football, basketball, and baseball sensation. Upon earning 12 high school letters, he decided to accept a scholarship from the University of Oregon to play both football and baseball.

But, after being heavily recruited by both colleges as well as major league baseball scouts, Harmon suddenly was presented with another interesting option. At the time, Idaho Senator Herman Welker was a close friend of Washington Senators owner Clark Griffith, and one of Welker's favorite subjects was talking about a certain local star playing baseball back in his home-state of Idaho. Welker persuaded the Old Fox to check out the kid Killebrew, and Griffith immediately dispatched employee Ossie Bluege to Idaho. As the story goes, the first time Bluege saw him play, the 17-year-old Killebrew hit a 400-foot shot out of the park, prompting Bluege to shout, "sign him up!"

Harmon truly wanted to go to college that fall, but when Griffith flashed a $30,000 signing bonus in front of him, he just couldn't refuse. So, Harm became the Senators first bonus baby. (The bonus-baby rule meant that players were forced to spend at least two seasons in the big leagues before being sent

down to the minors. The rule was notorious for damaging young ballplayers by depriving them of necessary minor-league teaching and experience, and it would nearly ruin Killebrew's career.)

Harmon spent the required two seasons riding the pines in Washington, D.C., before spending several more years in the Senators' farm system. He received a "last look" in 1959 when he was placed on the team's major league roster. Three major league managers had expressed doubt that he would ever make it as a big league ballplayer. They saw his potential as a power hitter, but needed to be sold on Harmon the fielder, runner, and thrower.

That's when Calvin Griffith, who had succeeded his uncle as president of the Senators, decided to see what the family money had bought and insisted that Harmon be given an extended shot with the Senators. The new Washington third baseman surprised everybody in 1959 by becoming one of the most feared sluggers in the American League. Harmon led the usually dormant Senators, finishing the season with a surprising 42 homers and driving in 105 runs. Killebrew tied Cleveland's Rocky Colavito for the home run title in Harmon's first full year in the bigs.

When the Senators moved to the Twin Cities in 1961, Killebrew continued his torrid home run hitting pace, winning three successive home run titles from 1962-64. He rose to Hall of Fame stardom in the early 60s in Minnesota, becoming the primary attraction at old Metropolitan Stadium. On the field, Harmon assumed the position of Twins' team leader. His hustle and tenacity made him the complete player that had eluded him earlier on in his career. He became known as a fierce competitor, a solid fielder, and a true gentleman off the diamond.

"The Killer " went on to win the American League MVP in 1969, when he hit 49 dingers with 140 RBIs and 145 walks, all team records that still stand. In 1974, sensing that the end was near for his aging veteran, Calvin encouraged Harmon to retire and manage in the Twins farm system. Griffith was grooming Killebrew to be an eventual Twins manager. But the old Killer wanted to play just one more season. So he declined Calvin's suggestion and signed on as a designated hitter with the Kansas City Royals. Killebrew's playing career in Minnesota was over.

On May 4, 1975, Harmon returned to Met Stadium, this time as a member of the opposition. His No. 3 was officially retired in a pre-game ceremony, and to top it all off, he smacked a homer to left field in his first at-bat. Minnesota fans went crazy as he rounded the bases in what some have said was the loudest ovation Twins fans have ever have given an opposing player.

Harmon Clayton Killebrew, Jr., will be remembered as one of the greatest home run hitters in history with 573 career roundtrippers. He was second only to Babe Ruth in the history of the American League to hit more

TIMELINE

| St. Olaf wrestler Dave Schmidt wins the 177 lbs. Division III National Championship | The Gopher baseball team Beats Missouri, 5-1, for the National Championship | Mankato State wrestler Howard Gangestad wins the 123 lb. Division II National Championship | Gopher swimmer Walt Richardson wins the 100 yd Butterfly National Championship | Urban (Red) Faber, a Minneapolis Miller in 1911, is inducted into the Baseball Hall of Fame | Gopher winger Craig Falkman is named to the All-American hockey team | Gopher catcher Ron Wojciak is named to the All-American baseball team |

46

than 40 home runs, (eight times), 30-or-more home runs, (10 times), all while driving in 100-plus RBIs (nine times). Killebrew was the consummate team player, always more interested in the team's achievements rather than his own, "You know, it's fine to hit homers, but it's RBIs that mean the most," he said. Over his career he tallied 1,584 RBIs, while garnering 2,435 hits and playing in 10 All-Star games.

Because of his tremendous contributions to the game of baseball, on January 10, 1984, Killebrew became the first Twin ever to be elected to the Baseball Hall of Fame. At the induction ceremony, he went on to tell the gathering that he attributed much of his success to his father, who had once explained to someone who had commented on the families' sports-worn front lawn, by saying that he was "raising children, not grass."

Harmon was more than just a slugger. He overcame his early fielding problems and emerged as a solid all-around baseball player. Twins manager Sam Mele recognized him as a genuine team leader whose presence in the lineup in-spired the other players to do their best. Quiet and unassuming, Harmon was always more interested in his team rather than personal accolades, and he is the first to deny his greatness. He is quick to give thanks and appreciation to the game of baseball for everything it has done for him and his family.

Just outside the town of Payette, there is a sign that says, "Home of Harmon Killebrew." There also is a street named for him, and his No.12 football jersey still hangs prominently in the halls of his high school for all the kids to see. His hometown didn't forget him - nor will baseball. Killebrew ranks as one of the greatest right-handed sluggers of all time. "One of the quietest team leaders of all time," remarked a sportswriter, "but a leader nevertheless."

Did was your hero when you were growing up in Idaho? "Ted Williams"

On the 1965 World Series:
"It was an unusual year for me, missing much of the season due to a dislocated elbow, but a great year nonetheless. After winning the first two, we thought we had a chance to sweep the series. Sandy Koufax had such a great game on only two days rest, throwing mostly fastballs to us. I'll always remember getting the last hit of the Series off of Koufax and that we still had a chance to win it right up to the final out."

On coming to Minnesota:
"I was really apprehensive about moving to tell you the truth. I liked playing in Washington, I thought it was a great place to play, and I really enjoyed the excitement of seeing and meeting all the presidents, congressmen, senators, and other famous people who would attend our games. Although I didn't like playing in the cold Minnesota weather, the warm hearts of the people made it warm up in a hurry. They were great. I really enjoyed the years I spent playing in the Twin Cities. The fans were just wonderful to me. The 1960s were an exciting time for sports in Minnesota with the Vikings' success as well."

What did it mean for you to be a Twin?
"I think it meant that I had an opportunity to play on a lot of great ballclubs, and play with some great players over the years. Just putting on that uniform and walking on that Met Stadium field to represent the Twins was about as big a thrill as anything for me. Of course playing in the World Series is every ball player's dream, and playing the Los Angeles Dodgers in 1965 was a the biggest thrill for me."

Twins tombstone:
"I guess that I'd always like to be remembered as being a member of the Minnesota Twins."

Most memorable home run
"There were two: the one off Don Drysdale in the 1965 World Series and the other one was at the All-Star game that same year, at the Met, for the home town fans."

Where are they now?
Harmon and his wife Nita live in Scottsdale, Ariz. He currently works for a hospital foundation for terminally ill people, plays a lot of golf, and has created the first annual "Harmon Killebrew Golf Invitational." Harm continues to make appearances for the Twins and also enjoys sitting in on Twins telecasts as a commentator. Killebrew has five children and 12 grandchildren. The children are: Cam, Shawn, Kathy, Erin, and Kenny. The latter operates the Killebrew Root Beer business.

TRIBUTES

"He was a steadying influence on our teams. The greatest thing that I learned from Harmon was here was a man who would hit two or three home runs in a ball game one day, and then maybe strike out four times the next night. But, I never once saw him get upset or gesture to the fans even when people booed him. His whole career was one of dignity. I watched him day in and day out and saw that here was a future Hall of Famer who could handle harassment from the people in the stands and not let if affect him as a player. I knew that if he could do that, then I could, as well.

Harmon was a great hitter and a great ballplayer."
-- Rod Carew

"Harmon was just what you would expect. He was the perfect poster-boy for the Minnesota Twins. He was this big, hulking power hitter, very soft-spoken, a gentleman in every sense of the word, and he was the perfect person to be identified and associated with the Twins. I respect what he did on and off the field, and it was a great pleasure playing with him. Just the way he carried himself during good times and bad times was a great influence on all of us." **-- Jim Kaat**

"You couldn't have played with a better person than Harmon. I think he was almost too nice to be a major league ballplayer. He is just a wonderful person, and I considered it to be an honor to be able to play baseball with Harmon." **-- Tony Oliva**

"I had the dream of being a major-leaguer as a kid and, of course, being from St. Paul and following the Twins, I regarded Harmon Killebrew as the one player who I tried to emulate when I was playing out in my backyard. I was always fascinated by his home-run power and by just what he had meant to the Twins. Harmon is a tremendous gentleman. You know, sometimes you get deflated if and when you are finally lucky enough to get to meet your childhood hero. This was by no means the case when I met him. If anything, my respect for Harmon has grown by getting to know him well. " **-- Paul Molitor**

"Harmon is just so loved here in Minnesota. He was an idol of mine when I was growing up in Bloomington. He was just a fantastic player. He is probably the best right-handed home run hitter of all time." **-- Kent Hrbek**

On September 26, 1965, after battling Chicago and Baltimore for the right to represent the American League in the World Series, the Twins clinched the honor when they beat the Washington Senators on their home field, 2-1. Minnesota finished in first place during that magical year, seven games ahead of the pack with a club-record 102 wins. They would go on to face the mighty Dodgers of Los Angeles in that fabled October get-together.

In 1965, the attention of the baseball world was focused on Minnesota. American League MVP Zoilo Versalles led the league in at-bats, runs scored, doubles, and triples. Outfielder Tony Oliva batted .321 and won his second batting title. Mudcat Grant won 21 games to lead the league. Jim Kaat who won 18 games. The Twins had four 20-plus home run hitters: Jimmie Hall, Bob Allison, Don Mincher, and Harmon Killebrew.

There was also the bullpen of Al Worthington, Johnny Klippstein, Jim Perry, and Bill Pleis who were, at times, untouchable. The Twins won with smart pitching, a solid defense, and clutch hitting. Minnesota even hosted the All-Star game that year, highlighted by

Killebrew hitting a dinger for the home-town crowd.

World Series bound, the Twins now were presented with the monumental challenge of facing the heavily-favored Los Angeles Dodgers and their ace pitchers Sandy Koufax and Don Drysdale, who had won 26 and 23 games, respectively. "The Twins are game, but they are not in the same class as the Dodgers, they'll be lucky if the Series goes to five games," one national sportswriter noted.

Game one
On October 6, at the old Met, Mudcat Grant threw the first pitch of the first World Series ever to take place in Minnesota. He would be driven by the familiar chatter of his shortstop Versalles, as he chanted, "Hubba-Hubba-Hubba--Cat!" Dodger ace Koufax missed the opener to attend Yom Kippur services, His place was taken by the fearsome Drysdale. The Dodgers struck first with a Ron Fairly home run in the second, but Minnesota answered with a homer of their own, this one from Mincher. Minnesota scored six unanswered runs in the third, highlighted by a Versalles three-run tater. The 47,797 fans watched their Twins take game one, 8-2.

Game two
The next game featured a pitcher's duel between two of the greatest baseball has ever seen, Koufax and Kaat. The game was scoreless until the sixth, when Oliva doubled to score Zoilo, with Killebrew coming in on the next play. In the bottom of the seventh, MVP Versalles tripled and scampered home on a Perranoski wild pitch. To add some salt to the wound, Twins pitcher Kaat knocked in Allison and Mincher with an eighth-inning liner. Minnesota was shocking the baseball world, winning, 5-1, and threatening to sweep Los Angeles.

Game three
Back at the Chavez Ravine, reality bit as Dodger lefty Claude Osteen faced Camilo Pascual for the third game of the series. The Twins threatened early in the game with Killebrew and Zoilo on the corners, but that would be as close as the Twins got that day, as they were both thrown out in run-downs. The Dodgers' John Roseboro singled in the fourth knocking in Fairly and Jim Lefebvre. The Dodgers added two more runs, as the Minnesota bats remained quiet. L.A. took game three by 4-0.

Game four
In a replay of game one, Grant and Drysdale were rematched for game four. Errors and miscues were the story of the day for the Twins, as the Dodgers got two easy runs early. Killebrew and Oliva smacked solo taters to make it 3-2, but errors by Hall, Oliva, and Frank Quilici in the sixth, accompanied by a Lou Johnson solo homer in the eighth,

opened the flood gates. Los Angeles went on to win the game, 7-2, tying the series at two games apiece.

Game five
October 11 featured a rematch of the titans, Kaat and Koufax. This time, Sandy would have the last laugh as he would blank the Twins 7-0, striking out ten for the World Series shutout victory. Maury Wills led the Dodgers with a four-hit performance that equaled the entire Twins' hitting attack. The Dodgers had gone ahead three games to two with the series headed back to Bloomington.

Game six
The Twins were now 0-for-Osteen in their last seven tries under Mele. But the Mudcat, despite not feeling well, had the performance of his life. With Earl Battey aboard, Allison started off the festivities in the fourth by slamming an Osteen offering over the fence. Then, in the fifth, Grant masterfully pitched his way out of a bases -loaded, no-outs jam. Then, Mudcat amazed the Metropolitan Stadium crowd by going deep for a home run with Allison and Quilici on board to make it 5-1 in the sixth. Fairly homered for the Dodgers in the seventh, but it was way too little, way too late for Los Angeles. The Mudcat had pitched a six-hit, complete-game gem to tie the series at three games apiece. It would all come down to game seven.

Game seven
For their third World Series go-around, it was Koufax vs. Kaat one last time. No one could believe that Koufax was going to pitch on only two days rest. In the third, Zoilo singled off Sandy, and then stole second as the hometown fans cheered, only to have the home plate umpire wave him back to first. Dodger announcer Vin Scully, explained the call to the millions of radio and TV listeners across the nation: "Umpire Ed Hurley has just ruled that batter Joe Nossek interfered with catcher Roseboro's throw. Versalles is going back to first, and manager Sam Mele is coming out of the dugout." Mele protested, but the call stood. The next batter, Oliva, struck out, ending the potential rally.

In the top of the fourth, Kaat served up a dinger to Johnson, then was abused for a double and then a single, good enough for another run. That would be all for "Kitty," as relief pitcher Worthington was sent in with the Twins down by the score of 2-0. In the fifth , Twins second baseman Quilici doubled off the left field wall. Then Rich Rollins, batting for Worthington, walked, setting the table for Versalles. Zoilo ripped the Koufax offering down the line, only to have L.A.'s Jim Gilliam make the catch of his life, robbing Versalles and the Twins of the World Series crown. Koufax then retired 12 Twin batters in a row before Killebrew could manage a single off him in the ninth. With the tying runner at the plate, Koufax stuck out Battey on three straight. Allison was the last hope. With the count 2-2, the Twins leftfielder whiffed. The game ended 2-0, and the Dodgers were the new world champions.

TIMELINE

Mankato State wrestler Howard Gangestad, wins the 123 lb. Division II National Championship	The St. John's University Football team wins the national Division III Championship	Joe Hutton, Hamline University's legendary basketball of 34 years, retires. Hutton led the Pipers into a small-college power nationally, winning three National Association of Intercollegiate Basketball (NAIB) championships, compiling a record of 591-208.	Mankato State University wins the Division II National Wrestling Championship	Gopher forward Lou Hudson is named to the All-American basketball team	Twins pitcher Mudcat Grant is named as the American League Pitcher of the Year	Gopher end Aaron Brown is named to the All-American football team	Twins manager Sam Mele is named the American League Manager of the Year	The Sporting News names Twins owner Calvin Griffith as Baseball's Executive of the Year

48

Koufax had pitched his second shutout of the 1965 World Series while striking out 10 batters. For the Series, he would finish with an astonishing ERA of 0.38 in 24 innings pitched. He had held the Twins, the American League champs, to a measly team batting average of .195. Minnesota was simply no match for possibly the greatest pitcher of all time.

Zoilo the MVP

There had been some question as to whether or not Versalles would be named the AL MVP. The 1965 candidates for the honor were a regular who's who of baseball: Yankees pitcher Mel Stottlemyre; Tiger shortstop Dick McAuliffe; Oriole third baseman Brooks Robinson; and Red Sox outfielder Carl Yastrzemski. There also were three Twins in the running: Tony Oliva, who had won the batting title for the second straight year; Mudcat Grant, who had won 21 games; and "Zippy-Zee" Versalles.

At the annual team dinner, Twins owner Calvin Griffith gave Zoilo the good news. "My next announcement should wipe away any last doubts as to why the Minnesota Twins won the pennant this year. I've just received word from the commissioner's office of the choice for the Most Valuable Player in the American League for 1965. The choice is Zoilo Versalles of the Minnesota Twins!"

"That year," said Minneapolis Star sportswriter Max Nichols, "Zoilo became the senior shortstop in the American League. He carried the Twins on his strong, if not broad, shoulders when Harmon Killebrew was injured. This was the year that the Minnesota Twins have a champion among many champions."

Then Billy Martin joked, "And this was the year that Zippy-Zee made me the smartest coach in the American League."

It had been a great season for Zoilo. His achievements that year included: most total bases with 308, most runs scored with 126, and most times at bat with 660. He tied for the lead in doubles with 45 and hit 12 triples. He hit 19 homers, batted-in 77 RBIs, and his batting average was a respectable .273, in spite of a mid-season slump.

Upon receiving the honor, Zoilo was asked to say a few words. He stood silent for a moment, as a hush fell over the audience. Perhaps he was thinking, just then, of growing up on the dusty streets of Marianao, Cuba, and all he had gone through in his life to get to where he was at that moment. As he stood next to the trophy, he said: "I am just lucky. Lucky to get a base hit, lucky to get a home run, lucky to steal a base, and lucky to be here!"

At that point, manager Mele responded: "And we are the luckiest of all, because we have a player like Zoilo Versalles!" Yet, Zoilo would insist that the honor should be given to his best friend Oliva. "Tony's hitting brought us the pennant," he added. "He was the most valuable to our team."

The kid from Cuba

Versalles was one of the greatest players ever to play for the Twins. From 1961-1967, his Twins career batting average was .252, while he had 1,046 hits, scored 564 runs, belted 86 homers, knocked in 401 RBI's,

and stole 84 bases in a total of 1,065 games. On November 28, 1967, he was traded to the Dodgers for pitcher Ron Perranoski and catcher John Roseboro.

Brought into this world on December 15, 1940, in a one-room straw hut in Marianao, Cuba, Zoilo was born to baseball and poverty. Although he was still small, at the age of 12, he was fast enough to play sandlot baseball. Not being able to afford a glove of his own, he shared a glove from an opposing player when the teams switched sides.

The young shortstop's favorite player was Willie Miranda, then a great star in the Cuban National League who would later play for the Yankees and Orioles. At 14, he had all the tools that made up a great shortstop: an arm, the hands, the eyes, and speed. As he grew older, Versalles taught himself to read by slowly sounding out the players names on the rosters and in the sports pages of the local paper. Baseball had become his life, and would eventually be his ticket out of poverty.

He was discovered by "Papa Joe" Cambria, the Washington Senators scout who found him in Cuba. He helped him come to America where he would become a hero to his native Cubans. Cambria's advice to the young Zoilo: "Eat, sleep, and think baseball." Cookie Lavagetto, manager of the Washington Senators, had a simple formula for his team's success: "Tight pitching and a healthy Zoilo Versalles at short."

Where are they now?
Sadly, Zoilo is no longer with us. Survived by his wife, Maria, who still resides in the Twin Cites area, the couple had five children.

Tributes

"Zoilo had a real fine year in 1965. He played a great shortstop, and he hit real well too. He was kind of erratic at times as a young player, but he certainly learned to play the game. He was a big reason we won the pennant that year."   **-- Harmon Killebrew**

"We had played together in the minors as well, and he was a great talent. He had as good a year as any ballplayer could have in 1965. I don't know how he did it all, because mentally there was so much additional pressure on him because he was taking care of his family responsibilities on top of everything else. Coming out of Cuba from a situation that we all would consider poverty, and then all of a sudden becoming a star in the major leagues, it was very difficult for him to handle and his career fizzled out a lot quicker than it should have."   **-- Jim Kaat**

"Zoilo was the best Twins shortstop ever. And, there was nobody better in the league than Zoilo in 1965. He could hit and could catch everything. He covered a lot of ground at shortstop, so nothing got by him. He was a great friend and was like my brother. It was comforting for me to have someone to talk Spanish to,

because I spoke very little English."   **-- Tony Oliva**

"He was a hero of mine as a kid, so I really looked up to him. He had a unique style and flare and was just a great ballplayer. I once got a chance to meet him, and it was a genuine thrill for me."   **-- Dave Winfield**

JIM KAAT
Kitty Wins 25 Games for the Twins

The Minnesota Twins, coming back to earth after their phenomenal World Series run of 1965, encountered some rough luck and caught a few bad breaks in 1966. Led by their ace, Jim Kaat, who had the season of his career with a 25-13 record, they finished in a respectable second place in the American League with a record of 89-73.

Injuries kept Bob Allison out for most of the season, and skipper Sam Mele was none too pleased when his overweight catcher Earl Battey who after an apparent single, was thrown out at first base from right field by Boston's Lu Clinton, Battey's performance prompted the wry sportscaster Halsey Hall to recall some years later that watching him round second base "looked like he was pushing a safe."

That season, Mele juggled the lineup to shake things up. Harmon Killebrew was moved to third, Don Mincher went to first, and Bernie Allen was posted at second. Ted Uhlaender filled in for the injured Allison, and Jimmie Hall and Tony Oliva rounded out the outfield. Zoilo Versalles, coming off his incredible MVP season, seemed to be only a shadow of his 1965 self, leading the American League in errors at short-

stop. One of the bright spots for Minnesota that season was the effort of Mr. Versatility, Cesar "Pepe" Tovar. The Twins' sparkplug hit in the leadoff spot, while playing short, second, and in the outfield.

The pitching staff was strong in 1966. Along with Kaat's 25 wins, Jim Merritt and Mudcat Grant each added 13, Dave Boswell came up with 12, and Jim Perry, who would win the Cy Young four years later, won 11. Camilo Pascual sat out most of the season with a sore arm, but did win eight games. Al Worthington was steady in the bullpen, adding six wins, combined with 16 saves.

With a phenomenal 25-13 record, "Kitty" Kaat had an impressive 2.74 ERA, striking out 205 hitters. In 41 outings he pitched 304 innings, completing 19 games.

"For a pitcher, and all pitchers realize this, sometimes it's not always how you pitch, but when you pitch," said Kaat. "Sometimes you have those years when you pitch mediocre, your team scores a lot of runs, and then when you pitch well, you win 2-1. That's the kind of year I had in 1966. I won a lot of games by blowouts, but I also won the close ones. I think maybe my best year personally, was probably 1971, when my record was 13-14. But in 1966, it all just came together for me and I just happened to pitch on the right day a lot that year."

Kitty-Kaat
Born in Zeeland, Mich., Kaat was the model of baseball consistency. From 1959 to 1983, the red-headed southpaw become the first pitcher in major league history to ply his trade for 25 years. Winning 20 games several times throughout his career, he was more than just a good pitcher; he ranks up there with the likes of Bob Gibson and Bob Lemon as among the best at all aspects of the game. Though he only had a lifetime .185 batting average,

Kaat was nevertheless highly respected as a hitter, understandable since he belted out 16 home runs over his career. What might be most amazing, however, was the fact that Jim was awarded 16 consecutive gold gloves for his spectacular fielding, a record unlikely to ever be matched by another pitcher.

After a remarkable 25 seasons in the major leagues, he had appeared in 898 games, placing him fifth in history in the category, and he won 283 of them. With a lifetime ERA of 3.45, Kaat fanned 2,461 batters, had 31 career shutouts, 180 complete games, and 18 career saves. He went on to win the Sporting News American League Pitcher of the Year Award in 1966.

As a member of the Minnesota Twins from 1961-1973, Kaat won 189 games, posted a 3.30 ERA, struck out 1,824 batters, and was

selected for an appearance in the All-Star game in 1962 and 1966. 1961 was the first year that Jim pitched more than 200 innings for the Twins. For 10 out of 11 succeeding Twins seasons, he appeared in more than 200 innings for the club. In 1966, he pitched in 304 and two-thirds innings. During his stint with the Twins, he pitched 23 shutouts. He led the team in pitching in 1964 with a 17-11 record and an ERA of 3.22. Two years later, his 25 wins against only 13 losses led the major leagues. He was the Twins opening-day pitcher in 1965 and 1967. Kaat was the recipient of the Twins Joseph W. Haynes Pitcher of the Year Award in 1966 and 1972.

On August 15, 1973, Kaat was unceremoniously sent packing for the Windy City to join his new team, the White Sox.

"I would have liked to have played my entire career in Minnesota," said Kaat. "I was heartbroken when I heard Calvin Griffith had put me on waivers. Yet, in the back of my mind, I knew what was going on because the Twins had gradually phased me out of being a regular starter and made me into a long reliever. In 1973, I was coming back from a wrist injury that had happened the year before while I was sliding into second base. It took me a while that year to get my stuff back together, and I knew that I was getting stronger and healthier, but could sense the end was near."

"I remember getting a phone call from Calvin while I was golfing at the Minnetonka Country Club, and he told me that the White Sox had picked me up on waivers. That night I went in to clean out my locker and to personally thank Calvin for the years I had in Minnesota. Calvin said 'You know, I really would have liked to have kept you, but my manager told me that he didn't think you could pitch in the big leagues anymore.'

"Then, when I went down to the locker room to pack my bags, I saw Frank Quilici, the manager, and said to him, 'Thanks a lot, good luck, and I appreciated the opportunity.' Frank's words were, 'You know, I would have liked to have kept you, but Calvin didn't think you could pitch in the big leagues anymore.'

"I remember driving to Chicago that day, and it was a very difficult trip for me, reminiscing on my days in the Twin Cities. I really enjoyed it in Minnesota and would have loved to have finished my career there. Looking back, in retrospect, it was a great break for me. Going to Chicago was a stepping stone for me to play another 10 years in the majors, and I got to experience a World Series win with St. Louis in 1982."

After his days as an active player ended, Kaat returned to the Twin Cities as a broadcaster. He teamed with Ted Robinson to do Twins KMSP-TV broadcasts in 1988. The following year, he and Robinson joined WCCO-TV and Midwest Sports Channel on Twins games. He served as a Twins broadcaster until 1993. Kaat was known for his pithy and insightful observations, particularly of pitchers. He currently serves as one of the New York Yankees broadcast team. Kitty will be undoubtedly be remembered as one of the best pitchers ever to throw for the Twins.

Who was your hero when you were growing Up?
"Bobby Shantz, a great left-handed pitcher for the Philadelphia Athletics."

Most memorable game as a Twin
"Winning game two of the 1965 World Series to clinch the pennant on the way to the World Series. That was really special."

On playing in the 1965 World Series
"We had such a good team that year. When you're in your mid-twenties, it was so exciting just being there, and I don't think you ever realized how difficult it was just to get there. My feeling at the time was that we were good and going to the Series was going to happen to us more than once. So, maybe I didn't think there was enough sense of urgency. We were enjoying all the festivities, and that may have taken a little of the focus off our winning as well.

From an individual standpoint, I can remember sitting on the bench next to pitching coach Johnny Sain in game two. I had never seen Sandy Koufax in person, and I had heard a lot about him. After seeing him pitch for a few innings, I remember telling Johnny that if we gave up just one run, this game would be over.

What stands out in my mind is just thinking that there was no way we could win against him, because he looked completely unbeatable. I remember what a dominant pitcher Sandy was. I mean we had a really good hitting ball club that year, and we couldn't touch him at all. Well, it turned out that we scratched out a couple of runs that day off of him, and then they pinch hit for him later on in the game."

Did you always want to play ball?
"Growing up as a kid in Michigan, my first exposure to baseball was the 1945 World Series between the Cubs and the Tigers. From that point on, I just always knew that I wanted to play baseball. It was my dream."

What were your happiest days?
"I was happiest very early on in my career. I can remember a former Twins minor league manager of mine, Del Wilbur, who said to me 'Kid, when you get to the big leagues don't be content to just live there, accomplish something while you're there.' I enjoyed getting there but was driven to make my mark. After you win 20 games, make an all-star team, and play in a World Series, your career kind of settles in from there."

What was it like to win a World Series?
"Winning the world series with the Cardinals in 1982 was unbelievable. I was 44 years old, and it had been 17 years since I had been in a World Series. I had been given up on a couple of times up to that point, and here I was contributing to a team that won the World Series. I think that was probably as satisfying a year as I ever had."

Twins tombstone:
"I think after 25 seasons in baseball, I can look back and honestly say that I never gave less than a maximum effort. Throughout my career, I never had to turn the ball down and was ready to play every day. I take pride in the fact that I never missed a start because of a sore arm, and I felt that I gave the Twins their best days work for their money.

I'll never go down as one of the all-time greats, but in my mind I feel good about the fact that I got the most out of my abilities. It meant a lot to me that my teammates had confidence in me, and that I was the guy that they wanted on the mound when we had a big game to win."

Were Twins pitchers forgotten heroes?
"The Minnesota Twins have always been known as the lumberjacks, with all those great home-run hitters through the years, but you have to have pitching to win too. I don't think the pitchers who have gone through that organization have gotten the same high recognition that the Twins hitters have. I'm speaking of pitchers like Frank Viola, Bert Blyleven, Mudcat Grant, Camilo Pasqual, Jim Perry, and I. That's not sour grapes on my part; it's a matter of fact."

Who today reminds you of you?
"Yankees pitcher Andy Pettitte. I enjoy watching him, and when I see him both personally and the way he conducts himself on the mound with his competitive nature, I think I see a lot of him in me, and me in him. There are some similarities; we're both tall lefties. Although, back then, I wish I could have had the poise that he shows now in his early 20s, as well as his unbelievable pick-off move."

Where are they now?
Jim is currently a television broadcaster for the New York Yankees. He lives in the New York City area with his wife Mary Ann. They have four children: Jim, Drew, Jill, and Stacy.

Tributes:

"Jim was a great pitcher and was always a great competitor. He was one of the finest fielding pitchers that I have ever seen. I mean, he won 16 gold gloves as a pitcher -- that's just incredible. He should be in the Hall of Fame."
-- **Harmon Killebrew**

"Jim was great to be around. He was one of the best hitting pitchers in baseball and one of the top left-handers in the game. Being around Jim and watching him perform day in and day out was an inspiration to me as a young player coming up. He is a very classy person."
-- **Rod Carew**

"He is a very nice guy and was a good teammate. He was a pitcher that was great to play behind because if you ever made an error, he would never say anything bad to you about it. He would just say 'come on, let's go!' He was a pleasure to play with, and I really like him."
-- **Tony Oliva**

"I really like Kitty. He was a great pitcher. He does a super job broadcasting and is just a super guy."
-- **Jack Morris**

"He is a great guy and a great announcer. I saw Kitty play at the old Met many times. He had a very unorthodox pitching style, and he would just come right at you with whatever he had. He would tell you to your face that his pitches probably couldn't even break a pane of glass, but, nonetheless, he knew how to pitch and was just a great pitcher. He is a super great guy who can play golf from both sides."
-- **Kent Hrbek**

Mahnomen native Joe Guyon, a former NFL halfback, is inducted into the Pro Football Hall of Fame

On March 11, 1965, National Hockey League President Clarence Campbell announced that the six-team league would expand, creating six new teams for the NHL's Western Division. A group of nine Twin City businessmen led by Gordon Ritz, Bob McNulty, and Walter Bush, Jr., joined in a partnership to control the new franchise.

Plans were swiftly put into motion and the ground in Bloomington was broken for the new $7-million Metropolitan Sports Center. The structure was erected the next year, just in time for the North Stars' maiden season in the league. At the time, Met Center was considered one of the finest sporting arenas in the world. In 1967, the Stars hit the ice. Later that season, a rookie sensation out of the University of Minnesota, Lou Nanne, was to make the hockey world take notice.

Putting all the pieces together
Wren Blair, a hockey veteran of junior and minor league coaching, scouting, player personnel, and managing, was named the team's first general manager and later the first coach. He masterminded the expansion draft selection of the 20 new North Stars at a whopping cost of $2 million dollars.

In the first expansion draft, the North Stars selected goalie Cesare Maniago from the New York Rangers. They also selected Wayne Connelly and Bill Goldsworthy from the Boston Bruins. Goldsworthy, a 23-year-old right wing, from Kitchener, Ont., took full advantage of his chance with the new team. He would emerge as the team's first major star and fan favorite with his famous "Goldie Shuffle," ultimately having his number retired at the end of his career in Minnesota. The Stars also acquired J.P. Parise, a 26-year-old from the Toronto Maple Leafs who would also turn into a solid player, and later become the team's general manager.

The first season
On October 11, 1967, the Stars played their first game, at St. Louis, tying the Blues, 2-2. The Stars would go on that season to earn a modest record of 27 wins, 32 losses, and 15 ties, finishing fourth in the Western Division. They then upset the second-place L.A. Kings in the opening playoff round and advanced to the division finals against the St. Louis Blues.

Like any expansion team, the Stars weren't yet exactly commanding respect in the Twin Cities. Five of the seven second-round playoff games had to be played in St. Louis because the Ice Capades were in the Twin Cities, removing the Stars from their own ice. They thus suffered the same fate as the Minneapolis Lakers, who often were supplanted at the Minneapolis Auditorium by ice shows and sportsmen's conventions.

Although they would take the series to seven games, the North Stars came up short. That final game had it all. In what had been the longest game in playoff history, there were two overtimes, a breakaway mugging of Wayne Connelly that got no penalty-shot call, and, after nearly 83 minutes, the Blues' Ron Shock scored to win the game, 2-1.

Al Shaver, the veteran Stars play-by-play man, said: "We came home on Braniff Airlines, and they had to pull the plane away from the gate area because thousands of people had come out to welcome the team. Everyone was quite amazed by this the reception because we didn't win the series."

They had lost the series, but had jelled as a team. They were a huge success at the gate as well, playing to one record crowd after another throughout the season. "We were just thankful to have a job. We were a bunch of guys who just wanted to prove something and sell the game of hockey," said Bill Goldsworthy.

"It was just a phenomenal experience," said Nanne, who joined the team after the Olympics. "To be able to have NHL hockey right in your own back yard and see it every

week was something that I really was excited about. Playing was just a thrill for me and that the first season we had a pretty good year, making a great playoff run. For the first time, the Stars got some credibility after that playoff series with the Blues."

Tragedy changes the game
In their first season, the Stars would encounter a tragedy that was to influence hockey players of all ages for years to come. Near midseason, on what seemed to be a normal play, North Star Bill Masterton was fatally injured after falling and striking his head on the ice. Masterton, a popular player, was a long-time minor leaguer who was enjoying his first NHL season with the Stars when the accident occurred. Today every player in the NHL is required to wear a helmet because of that incident some 30 years ago.

The NHL Writers' Association, pays homage to Masterton each season by presenting the Bill Masterton Memorial Award to the player who they feel best exemplifies the qualities of perseverance, sportsmanship, and dedication to hockey. Although there is only one overall winner, each franchise nominates a player for the award as well, as a way of extending the value of the trophy and keeping Masterton's memory alive. Claude Provost of the Montreal Canadians, was the initial honoree. (The North Stars', Al MacAdam won the award in 1980.)

"Sweet Lou from the Soo"
Nanne has become synonymous with game of hockey in Minnesota. A native of Sault Saint Marie, Ont., Louie played Junior hockey with Phil and Tony Esposito. He went on to become a member of John Mariucci's Golden Gopher Hockey teams from 1961-1963. Nanne referred to Mariucci as his "second father." They would become great friends through the years, and later Nanne even got his old coach a position in the North Stars' front office as his assistant general manager.

Earning Gopher captain and All-American honors in his senior year, defenseman Nanne, known as Minnesota's "Ice God," tallied a career total of 74 points, becoming the first defenseman to win a WCHA scoring title. For his efforts he was named the league's MVP. Upon graduating from the University, Lou was drafted by Chicago into the NHL. However, Nanne got into a contract dispute with the Blackhawks, ultimately refusing to play for them, which led to a five year lay-off from hockey.

While he sat out, he worked for Minneapolis business-man Harvey Mackay's envelope company. He also coached the Gopher freshman hockey team for four years. During that time, he played on and off with the USHL's Rochester Mustangs, and then went on to captain the 1968 Olympic hockey team, coached by former Gopher All-American Murray Williamson. When the NHL expanded, Chicago couldn't "freeze" him anymore because of the new reserve list, so Nanne became a free agent. He decided to play for Minnesota's new expansion team, the North Stars.

TIMELINE									
Mankato State wrestler Bob Soulek wins the 130 lb. Division II National Championship	Mankato State Wrestler Bob Wendel wins the 145 lb. Division II National Championship	Gopher center Tom Kondla is named to the All-American basketball team	Gopher end Bob Stein is named to the All-American football team	Gopher first baseman Dennis Zacho is named to the All-American baseball team	UMD center Keith Christianson is named to the All-American hockey team	The Gopher football team earns a three-way tie for the Big Ten title	George Mikan founds and serves as president of the new American Basketball Association, headquartered in Minneapolis	The ABA's Muskies, coached by former Laker Jim Pollard, play in Minnesota for one season	Harmon Killebrew hits the longest homerun ever in Metropolitan Stadium: 520 feet

"I was playing on the Olympic team when the Stars made a hell of an offer to me," said Nanne. "I used to practice daily with the Stars, and on the weekends I would play with the Olympic team. Since I was an Olympian that year, and was ineligible to play professionally, I became the Stars' television analyst, co-hosting a show with Frank Beutel. When the Olympics were over I joined the Stars fulltime. That first year, while I was negotiating my contract, I actually bought season tickets so I could watch the games. I think I might be the only guy to ever go from being a season ticket holder to a starting player."

Louie would go on to play defense and winger for the North Stars through 1978, becoming the only player to play with the Stars in all of the first 11 years of the team's existence. For his career, including playoffs, he tallied 72 goals and 167 assists for 239 points. He went from player to coach in 1978, and then was appointed general manager by Glen Sonmor from 1978-1988. He finished his 24-year career with the Stars as the team president from 1988-1990. Bobby Smith was his first pick and Mike Modano would be his last. Of the players on the 1981 Stanley Cup team, only five were left from the team that Nanne took over in 1978.

Although Canadian by birth, Nanne became a well-known advocate of the Americanization of the NHL. He was one of the first to scout U.S. colleges for American talent and to take an active role in the support of player-development programs, which also included Olympic and international competition.

Possibly the most recognized hockey figure in the state, Lou is well liked and respected by his peers. He had been a fixture with the club from start to finish and is the authority on hockey in Minnesota today.

Who was your hero when you were growing up?
"Gordie Howe. He was the best."

What did it mean to be a Gopher?
"I loved playing hockey at the University of Minnesota. It was tremendous fun all the way through, and it was just a great experience. It was really neat for me, coming from Canada, and not knowing anything about college sports - it was such a privilege to play for the U. It was totally different than anything I had experienced before, and there was a tremendous amount of satisfaction playing for the university. I really enjoyed the atmosphere, and it was something I will always cherish. When it was over, it actually hurt me to think that I would not be going to be an active part of the program anymore. Thinking back on those four years, it seems to me that the time went by like the speed of light."

What did it mean for you to be a North Star?
"Growing up in Canada, it's every kids' goal to be a professional in the NHL. As my college career went along, I thought I might have a chance, and when it happened, it was tremendous. From my first season playing defense with Moose Vasco, to later in the early 70s, when I played on one of the top scoring lines in the league with Murray Oliver and Dean Premis, it was an amazing experience."

Most memorable game:
"Playing against Montreal in the 1972 playoffs. In one

game, I had a hat-trick and had five points, and we won 6-5. In the playoffs, I got the winning goal in the first game, and it was the first time that an expansion team had ever beaten one of the original six established clubs."

Which was more satisfying, being a player or the GM?
"I found satisfaction at both ends. It was a lot of fun as a manager, making very important day-to-day decisions, but there is not a better job in the world than actually playing the game on the ice. Whenever you can play something that you loved as a kid and then they pay you for it, well it doesn't get any better than that."

On the Stars moving to Dallas:
"It was like losing a relative. It was just a really disheartening experience for me."

On the difference between being a collegian, Olympian and pro? "College is the most enthusiastic experience of the three. It's really different because it's school against school, and there is so much enthusiasm. The Olympics is really special because you are playing for your country. It's a feeling you can't achieve in anything else, and one that I wouldn't trade for anything. But playing professionally is the ultimate. Playing the pro sport that you were able to play well as a kid is the best of all, because the NHL is the top rung of the hockey ladder. The three each have individual characteristics that are unique and satisfying, and along with being a coach and manager, I was very fortunate to have experienced them all."

On high school hockey in Minnesota:
"I've worked as a broadcaster at the state tournament since 1964. It's really fun to watch the evolution of the high school game in Minnesota. In the early 1960s, there might be one good player on the team, and the teams played with only two lines. Now, teams have four lines and they play at a faster pace with more good players. The evolution of the American hockey player over the years has been dramatic. I'm not a fan at all of the two-class tournament; I like to see one winner. I know everyone likes to experience the tournament, but it's like achieving success in anything -- you can only have one winner, and that's what you should play for. I've enjoyed my state high school hockey experience. It's been a lot of fun."

Final thoughts: "I have been very fortunate in achieving the kind of goals that you set for yourself as a kid. First and foremost, I have a wonderful wife and family. I was able to play the sport that I loved professionally, see the world, and go into a very successful business. The only other thing you can ask for is good health, and I have had that."

Gopher / North Star tombstone: "He always played with the philosophy of never letting anybody beat you because they outworked you."

Where are they now? Lou and his wife Francine live in Edina. He is as a senior vice president at Voyager

Assets Management in Minneapolis, and is a TV commentator for the high school hockey tournament. The Nannes have four children: Michelle, Michael, Marc and Marty as well as 11 grandchildren.

Tributes
"Lou is such a dynamic, dominating personality who has overcome whatever had been in his way - and I mean that very respectfully. He is an achiever in life. He has achieved so much, and he was never given a thing along the way except for an opportunity to succeed. He has emotion and the will to try things, and because of that, he succeeds."   **-- Doug Woog**

"Louie is a great hockey man. He was a lot of fun to work with, and I have a lot of respect for him. He is a classy guy, and I enjoyed my time with the North Stars under Lou. I remember he was always superstitious. If we won or lost he might not change his shirt or socks or something until we got it right. It was hilarious! He has done a lot for Minnesota hockey and is a really good guy."   **-- Neal Broten**

"Lou is a very good hockey man. He was the first general manager I ever had. I remember that he was very hands-on in building a Stanley Cup winner. It was unfortunate that he wasn't able to do it, but was always his goal, and I respect him for that. I really enjoyed playing for the teams that he operated."
-- Bobby Smith

Twins pitcher Dean Chance throws two no-hitters in the month of August (2-0 over Boston and 2-1 over Cleveland) [One was a five-inning perfect game]

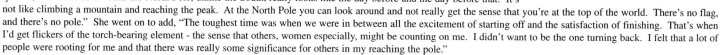

ANN BANCROFT

St. Paul's Ann Bancroft is one of the worlds pre-eminent polar explorers, having become the first woman ever to cross the ice to both the North and South Poles. Growing up in Minnesota, Ann loved the outdoors and never seemed to mind the icy cold winters. After receiving her Bachelor of Science degree in Physical Education from the University of Oregon, she went into teaching. Aside from her amazing polar expeditions, Ann has taught physical and special education in Minneapolis schools. She has also coached sports, at various age levels, such as softball, basketball, track and field, volleyball, tennis, cross-country skiing, backpacking, and canoeing.

Following her successful ascent of Mt. McKinley in 1983, Ann became the first woman to travel across the ice to the North Pole, when she accomplished the feat in 1986 with fellow Minnesotan Will Steger. Ann, then a 30-year-old schoolteacher from Sunfish Lake, made history when she joined the seven-person team that crossed the Arctic ice pack with Steger's International Polar Expedition. They averaged 20 miles a day on the 500 mile trek, living primarily on pemmican, butter, cheese, peanut butter, and oats. The team wasn't totally primitive though. With the aid of homing devices that talked to satellites, they arranged to have some of their 49 sled dogs airlifted out as their load lightened. Bancroft even documented the dogsled journey as a photographer and cinematographer for National Geographic.

"Reaching the North Pole was almost anticlimactic, mainly because we'd just put in a series of 14-hour days and were pretty tired," said Bancroft. "And the North Pole, unlike the South, really looks like the day before and the day before that. It's not like climbing a mountain and reaching the peak. At the North Pole you can look around and not really get the sense that you're at the top of the world. There's no flag, and there's no pole." She went on to add, "The toughest time was when we were in between all the excitement of starting off and the satisfaction of finishing. That's when I'd get flickers of the torch-bearing element - the sense that others, women especially, might be counting on me. I didn't want to be the one turning back. I felt that a lot of people were rooting for me and that there was really some significance for others in my reaching the pole."

The pole leader
Then, in 1993, after more than four years of training, which included an Antarctic trip to Great Slave Lake in the Northwest Territories and a traverse of the Greenland ice cap, Ann went to the South Pole. This time she served as team leader for the American Women's Expedition (AWE), a group of four courageous women who skied over 660 miles (averaging 10 miles per day for 67 days), pulling 200-pound sleds through the ice and snow across Antarctica to reach the pole. The group set off from Hercules Inlet and skied into headwinds of up to 50 miles per hour during the constant daylight of the Antarctic summer, in sub-zero temperatures. In so doing, the team became the first all American women's team to ski from the edge of Antarctica to the South Pole as well as the first all women's team to traverse Greenland. They also became the first women to travel to the South Pole without dogs or motorized vehicles

The group's achievements included highlighting the strengths of women as well as providing an educational program for thousands of young people on the environmental challenges in Antarctica. They also conducted physiological and psychological research pertaining to women under extreme conditions and heightened awareness surrounding environmental issues facing Antarctica and their global impact. Ann has brought a much needed awareness to the continent, which represents 70 percent of the world's fresh water supply and is a vital resource for further understanding global warming on our planet.

She has truly made a difference in this world
Today Ann resides in the Twin Cities. Now a busy entrepreneur with interests in film and education as well as outdoor adventures, Ann is popular on the lecture circuit as a speaker and seminar leader for corporations, schools, and non-profit organizations. Her presentations cover a variety of topics ranging from polar exploration to women's issues. She has also been an active citizen diplomat -- working with American/Soviet exchange programs, such as the "Ski for Peace" program, which are designed to foster communication and understanding between people of different nations. Today she can frequently be found in the woods of northern Minnesota, doing what she loves most: exploring and learning. Ann is an active participant in a number of non-profit and volunteer organizations. A recipient of countless awards and honors, including Ms. Magazine's Outstanding Woman of the Year in 1987, as well as being inducted into the National Women's Hall of Fame, she continues to give of herself and set a positive example for young women everywhere. She is a true Minnesota treasure.

WILL STEGER

Ely's Will Steger is one of the greatest explorers of the modern era. Steger grew up outside Minneapolis but spent his summers in the Yukon region of Canada as well as in Alaska. A science teacher who also runs wilderness programs in the Boundary Waters Canoe Wilderness Area in Northern Minnesota, he is also an avid solo Arctic traveler.

In 1986, Steger put together a team of seven men, and one woman - fellow Minnesota explorer Ann Bancroft -- that journeyed to the North Pole on foot, something that hadn't been done since 1909, when Admiral Robert Peary accomplished the feat. The unsupported mission was a success and launched both of the Minnesota explorers into the national spotlight. Then, in 1990, Steger raised the bar and aimed at the Antarctic. But he wanted to do more than just reach the South Pole, so he decided to go from the Pacific Ocean to the Atlantic and cross the entire 4,000 mile continent. There were six men and 36 dogs that comprised the International Trans-Antarctic Team. The 220-day journey ended when they crossed a finish line created by the awaiting Soviet welcoming party.

After an Arctic Ocean crossing in 1995, Steger was at it again in 1997. This time, in an effort to increase the awareness of the Arctic region, the 53-year-old explorer set out on an unsupported solo-trek from the North Pole across the Arctic Ocean to Ellesmere Island. With enough food for 50 days, he paddled and pulled a 275-pound, 13-foot canoe alone across 500 miles of ice and water between the Pole to the Canadian Island. To train for the trip, Steger took two 10-day expeditions through the Boundary Waters, where he hauled his loaded canoe through the spring ice. He also spent months training at his Northern Minnesota cabin, where he built his strength and endurance by hauling logs through the snow. After months of vigorous preparation, he set out to boldly go where no man had gone before. When he disembarked at the pole from the Russian icebreaker, the Sovetskiy Soyuz, he was attempting what no other explorer before him had ever dared to begin, a major expedition on the Arctic Ocean during the summer. The ocean is deadly during that time of the year because it is covered with thick fog, cracked ice, and large gaps of open water. Surrounded by a perpetual blanket of thick fog, Will camped on an ice island surrounded by blue ice, water, slush and magnificent pressure ridges. Burning as many as 900 calories per hour hauling the canoe-sled, every day he ate approximately 4,000 calories, or about two-and-a-half pounds of food, to keep up his strength in the bitter cold environment. He drifted an average of three miles per day due to the constant movement of the sea-ice. "The conditions are sobering," he said. "There is always moisture and an eternal silence that I have never heard."

Unfortunately, because of the extreme weather conditions, Will was forced to abort his expedition. He was plucked from his ice island near the North Pole by a helicopter that he called in. Although he didn't complete the journey, he was able to communicate his thoughts and pictures through a unique program called Solo From The Pole. The expedition combined exploration and adventure with technology to create an educational project which allowed him to regularly communicate via a digital camera through the internet to millions of interested people around the world.

Today the Minnesota explorer is a motivational speaker, teacher, and lecturer. Stay tuned to find out just where the exotic adventure enthusiast winds up next!

MINNESOTA'S MUSHER EXTRAORDINAIRE -- JAMIE NELSON
AND THE LEGEND OF JOHN BEARGREASE

Coming in just 30 minutes shy of 100 hours, Togo's Jamie Nelson won her third John Beargrease Sled Dog Marathon in 1997. The state's premier musher averaged 8.11miles per hour over the four-day-long trek. Her other two victories came in both 1988 and 1995. The 49-year-old has competed in 10 such Marathons since the Northern Minnesota race's inception in 1982 and has finished as a bridesmaid three other times as well. It's obvious that she loves her dogs, as evidence of her Best Cared for Team Awards in 1993, 1994, and 1995. Jamie also participated in the Upper Peninsula 200 race, coming in first in both 1992 and 1993, and receiving the Best Cared for Team Award both years. In 1989 Nelson finished the grand-daddy of all sled-dog races, Alaska's world famous Iditarod, where she won the coveted Sportsmanship Award. She admits, "I can't give up. I'm addicted to running dogs."

The pride of Minnesota
In an annual Northern Minnesota right of passage, each January thousands of eager spectators gather on the shores of Lake Superior to cheer on more than a thousand sled dogs and their mushers as they pay homage to the legend of the North Shore's most infamous mail carrier, John Beargrease.

Each year more than 30 sled dog teams follow the beautiful North Star Trail from Duluth through Two Harbors to Grand Marais and back, for the $10,000 first-prize of what's commonly referred to as "The Beargrease." The route, precariously nestled in between the rugged Sawtooth Mountains and treacherous Lake Superior, makes for a spectacular backdrop. For 500 grueling miles the competitors run around the clock, taking 13 six-hour mandatory layovers over the four-to-five day trek, finishing at Duluth's Lester Park.

Though most dogs are Alaskan Huskies, there are a few Greyhounds, Coonhounds, and Foxhounds thrown into the mix. On a typical sled dog team, there is either a lead dog or a pair of point dogs out in front. Then there are a pair of swing dogs, followed by the pair just before the sled -- the wheel dogs, who are responsible for pulling the sled around tight corners.

As race time approaches and the festivities heighten at Duluth's Ordean Field, the mushers make last-minute adjustments to make sure everything is just right. They untangle their harnesses and ropes, fit their dogs with protective booties, and even pamper their pooches with canine pedicures.

Each team begins the race pulling two sleds, complete with two drivers and a passenger. When the race starts there are two people on the sled. The second passenger, who pays a hefty sum for the privilege of the bumpy ride, serves a purpose. They ride along for the first six miles and then get off at the first check-point. As one of the mushers explained: "These dogs don't have a low gear. It's full speed ahead regardless of the terrain, time, or temperature." With only foot-brakes that drive metal spikes into the snow to slow them down, the mushers can't contain an anxious Husky. When the race starts, the dogs are hyper and excited, and unless there is a lot of weight to slow them down, they will take off and go like hell. The result could be deadly if they take a corner too fast and send the sled crashing into a tree.

Before the race is started, a "Scent team" of 16 Huskies is given a five-minute head start. Much like the pace-car, for the Indianapolis 500, the team lays down its' scent for the first team to follow. With their keen senses of smell, the dogs follow the scent, overriding any smells of humans, snowmobiles, or even a stray wolf or moose.

The dogs can't stand the wait, and it sometimes takes a dozen people just to contain the howling hounds. The mushers also have to be well-conditioned athletes, often having to run for miles at a time through the snow behind their sleds to ease the load.

With their sleds packed with gear, food, and plenty of dog chow, they take off. The snow flies as dozens of paws go for broke through the snow! Some sleds are old and others are fabricated out of space-age polymers, but they all take off to the roar of the crowd in hopes of not only winning, but finishing the grueling race. When the mushers take off from the starting chute, the first team wears number two. That's because number one is always reserved for the spirit of John Beargrease. In addition to basic survival gear, among the standard attire for each musher is a mail bag -- in memory of the race's namesake.

"It's great to be running at night when all you hear are the dogs breathing and the squeak of the snow beneath the runners . . . and you see all those stars through the pine tops. It's unreal!" said Chris Adkins, a Montana musher.

The legend
In 1858, John Beargrease was born the son of Chippewa Chief Moquabimentem, to the Grand Portage Band of Chippewa. John married Louisa Wishcob and together they had ten children. Beargrease was best known for his legendary mail delivery runs up and down the North Shore. From 1887 to 1900, he hiked, sailed, and rowed, and, in the winter months, traveled by dog sled, devotedly delivering the mail week after week. He was even known by some as "the renown pilot of Lake Superior," often times dangerously challenging its thin and shifting winter ice to get the mail through. Today's postal creed of "Nor rain, nor sleet, nor snow..." mentions nothing about Lake Superior ice, bears, wolves and frostbite -- all daily occurrences for John.

His round-trip, bi-weekly mail route went from Two Harbors to Grand Marais. Known for his dependability and predictability, he provided the only link of communication to the outside world for many of the North Shore's isolated inhabitants. As soon as they heard the familiar sound of the bells on the dogs' col-lars (worn to scare off wolves), they knew John was coming with good news. Each homestead and settlement depended greatly on him for news and messages from their loved ones.

His ability to drive a dog sled in Minnesota's extreme conditions remains legendary. Averaging 30 to 40 miles a day, he once made the trip from Two Harbors to Grand Marais in 20 hours. More impressive is the fact that he raced with a team of only four dogs, who, at times, were pulling a loaded mail sled that weighed up to 800 pounds. And, that was over ungroomed trails, all while navigating through streams and rocky terrain with only the stars as his guide. Sometimes Beargrease found it easier to trek across frozen Lake Superior to avoid the hilly landscape. Often times he broke through the treacherous ice and plunged into the lake's deadly winter waters.

In 1895 John was given a two year con-tract from the government to deliver the mail for the annual sum of $728. In 1897, with the population growing in the northwoods and the trails improving, he traded in his dogs for a team of horses named Red Charley and White Charley. Together they hauled the mail on a new steel sled that weighed 350 pounds. It was John's efficient use of his horses on those trails that convinced Lake County officials to finally upgrade them, eventually leading to the construction of Lake Shore Road. John Beargrease ended his postal duties in 1900 and retired to Grand Portage.

Beargrease lived a heroic life, and fittingly, he died while performing a heroic act. In 1910, as a result of rushing to the aid of another mail carrier whose boat was caught in the high seas off Tamarack Point in Grand Portage Bay, John contracted pneumonia and died. He was laid to rest in Beaver Bay's Chippewa Cemetery.

Today his lore lives on forever, and in some parts rivals that of Paul Bunyan. Through his memory, Northern Minnesota honors and celebrates the man through the annual John Beargrease Sled Dog Marathon. With participants that come to Duluth from all over the world to participate in the event, it has become the main long-distance dogsled race in the lower 48 states. Because of the race's popularity and success, there are also two shorter races from Duluth to Grand Marais (100 miles) and Duluth to Beaver Bay (190 miles).

JIM MARSHALL
The Vikings Win Their First
Central Division Title

In Bud Grant's second season as head coach, the Minnesota Vikings won their first Central Division Championship. The players were finally adapting to Grant's conservative style of coaching. After a 3-1 start, Minnesota lost three straight, won its next three, dropped two more, and then won the final two games of the season.

With the title hanging in the balance, the Vikings met Grant's former team, the Philadelphia Eagles, and they won 24-17.

"We had to win our last game against the Eagles to clinch it, and I remember it was snowing and icy," said Grant. "We ended up scoring a couple big play touchdowns on a bad field. Usually teams play conservatively on bad conditions, but I had played enough games on bad fields to know that you can make big plays on bad fields easier than on good fields. So we got a couple big plays and won the game. Then we sat in the locker room and listened to the outcome of the Packers - Bears game. The Bears won, and we had our first divisional title. Sid Hartman of the Minneapolis Tribune was relaying the information over the phone to us. It was a great feeling."

The Vikes finished the season with a modest record of 8-6, but went on to face the mighty Baltimore Colts in the playoffs. Led by coach Don Shula, the Colts defeated Minnesota, but the Purple played tough in the mud, eventually losing the game 24-14. Quarterback Joe Kapp was 26 of 44 and played like a hero, throwing for a pair of touchdown passes. But Earl Morrall, who had taken over for Johnny Unitas, was the top ranked quarterback in the NFL, and he also threw a couple of TD passes, while Mike Curtis returned a fumble 60 yards for a score to highlight the big win for the Colts.

"It was a rough game," said Vikings quarterback Joe Kapp. "The Colts blitzed us with everything they had,

sometimes with as many as a nine men at once, and it caused problems for us."

After the loss, the Vikings went on to play the loser of the Miami - Dallas game where they lost to the Cowboys, 17-13, in the NFL's "Runner-up Bowl." In that game, a young Bobby Bryant, in his first Vikings season, returned a punt 81 yards for a touchdown, and Fred Cox kicked two field goals to help Minnesota build a 13-0 lead. But the Cowboys, led by quarterbacks Don Meredith and Craig Morton, each tossed a touchdown pass to rally Dallas to victory. 1968 also saw another great addition to the Purple, offensive tackle Ron Yary, the NFL's No. 1 draft pick, as compensation from the Giants, for Fran Tarkenton, who was traded a year earlier.

The Vikings were a team on the rise and one of their emotional leaders, Jim Marshall, played an important role in taking them to the promised land the very next season. "Winning the divisional title in 1968 was very special." he said. "We worked very hard to get there, and we knew that we had a great core of guys that could go even further. Unfortunately, in our first Super Bowl, we were in a cloud. I think we felt that there was no way we could lose. We were very confident that we could go out, perform, give our best, and win it all. I was deeply saddened at the loss to Kansas City, but it was a wonderful experience just getting there.

"It was different from the 1968 season when we were sitting on a bus and waiting to see if we had made the playoffs. We needed help from other teams to get into the playoffs and to win the conference title. But, in 1969, we made our own destiny, and we went all the way on our own. Throughout the entire Super Bowl game, I felt that we were going to do something to pull it out, but it just didn't happen."

The Marshall plan
Marshall was born in 1937 in Danville, Ky., and went

to East High School, in Columbus, Ohio. He was an All-American at Ohio State, and was on the 1959 Rose Bowl championship team that beat Oregon 10-7. He was the ultimate Viking, anchoring the famous "Purple People Eater" defensive line as an end from 1961 - 1979, and the perennial all-pro was the Vikings defensive captain from 1966 - 1979. He also spent one year in the Canadian Football League and another with the NFL Cleveland Browns before coming to Minnesota. His records include playing a NFL record 282 consecutive regular season games, playing in a NFL record 302 consecutive regular season and post season games, and playing in a NFL record 270 consecutive regular season games with a single team. Jim played in every regular and post season game in the Vikings history until his retirement in 1979.

On his unbelievable durability and undoubtedly playing hurt, he modestly replied, "I played because I loved the game."

Jim was a warrior in the best sense of the word. Marshall legend and lore includes several incredible stories that exemplify the many obstacles he hurdled over the course of his career. For example, a few months before joining the Browns, while stationed at an army training camp, Marshall was stricken with encephalitis. Although he lost over 40 pounds, he still reported to camp and insisted on playing. In 1964, while cleaning his gun, Marshall accidentally shot himself in the side.

Once during training camp, he was hospitalized when a grape became lodged in his windpipe.

Another time, while visiting the troops during the Vietnam War, he underwent a tonsillectomy that resulted in severe hemorrhaging.

In 1971, Marshall almost died in a snowmobile accident on a trip throughout the Grand Teton Mountains in Wyoming. According to the official Vikings' publication "The First Fifteen Years," Marshall's snowmobile went over a cliff and nearly crushed him in the midst of a blizzard. Marshall later said, "It was the toughest thing I've ever encountered in my life, I thought we were all going to die." In fact, one member of the 16 person group didn't survive the trip.

Then, in 1980, Jim survived a near-fatal motorized hang-glider accident.

Perhaps Ahmad Rashad, a former Vikings receiver and teammate portrayed Jim best in his book "Rashad: Vikes, Mikes and Something on the Backside," when he described Marshall as "a Viking among men, and a giant among Vikings. He was thrilled by danger."

Marshall said, "Every one of us wants to he the baddest dude in the valley, and that's what it was all about," One of the initiation rituals for many Vikings rookies was to make the roadtrip to training camp in Mankato with Marshall at the wheel. For most humans that trip took two hours, but Jim usually made

TIMELINE

Duluth's John Clawson wins a gold medal on the Olympic Basketball team	Ron Yary, a tackle from USC, is the first overall pick selected in the first round by the Vikings in the NFL draft	Gopher center Gary Gambucci is named to the All-American hockey team	The Edina boy's High School basketball dynasty ends after winning three state championships	Gopher end Ed Rogers is inducted into the College Football Hall of Fame	The ABA's Minnesota Pipers finish second in the Eastern Division. They leave town the next year.	Twins utility player Cesar Tovar plays all nine positions in one game

56

it in about 45 minutes with the rookies screaming the entire distance.

Marshall describes life as "wonderful, with so many things to be enjoyed. I think too many times we restrict ourselves to a small box with a limited wish list on each wall. I like to raise my head above the walls and look out into the horizon and think about all the possibilities that are out there to better enjoy my life. That outlook makes life interesting. It gives you the opportunity to grow as a person. I want to enjoy everything as much as I can while I still occupy this physical body. Because, one day, when I no longer have this earthly vehicle, I want to feel as though I truly had an opportunity to enjoy everything that was available to me."

When Jim took a brokerage test, he was given a genius rating. He modeled men's clothes. He became a skydiver. He even sold wigs to women. There was nothing Jim Marshall couldn't do. He will always be remembered as a Vikings legend.

The wrong-way-play
In 1964, while playing in San Francisco against the 49ers, Marshall was involved in a play that will forever be a part of NFL film anthologies. During the game, he picked up a San Francisco fumble and ran for the end zone - only it was the wrong end zone! He motored 66 yards right into his own end zone, in the process handing the 49ers two points for a safety. Luckily though, to Marshall's considerable relief, the Vikings still beat the Niners 27-22.

When asked about the play Jim said, "It was very simple in my mind. It was one of those things where I just got all turned around. I picked up the ball and thought I was going the right way. Of course I wouldn't have run at all if I didn't think I was going the right way. So I crossed the goal-line and threw the ball out of bounds to celebrate, and then, Bruce Bosely, a 49er, ran up to me and said, 'Thanks Jim!' He was giving me the razz, and then it hit me...I had really done something bad. But, what nobody remembers, is, that during that game, I went back and caused the fumble that Carl Eller picked up to score the game-winning touchdown. They don't really talk about that now do they?"

Who was your hero when you were growing up?
"My first hero was my grand-dad, George Marshall, Sr. He was an extremely strong-willed person who made things happen. He had so much wisdom, common sense, and experience to make things happen, and he knew how to solve problems. When he passed on, my dad George Marshall, Jr., took over as my hero. I also thought of Bill Willis as a hero of mine. He grew up in my neighborhood in Columbus, and was one of the first black all-Americans at Ohio State. He later played for the Cleveland Browns. Willis inspired me to understand that you can accomplish anything that you want to, and there are no limits to what you want to do. I also looked up to Woody Hayes, my coach at Ohio State, because he was a great person."

What was your most memorable game?
"We were playing the Rams in the playoffs, and they were on the one-foot line ready to score the game-winning touchdown. But we dug in, held them, and eventually blocked a kick to win the game. It was an amazing experience."

When were you the happiest in your career?
"The early 1970s. Particularly 1970, when we lost to the Niners in the playoffs, 17-14. We had our best Viking football team that year, maybe of all time. It was unfortunate that one bad call by the referee changed everything. Overall, it was my happiest season and also the saddest season at the same time. I really felt like we were headed back to the Super Bowl."

Vikings tombstone:
"I would like to be thought of as a guy who gave everything he had to give on the football field and did whatever was necessary for his team to help win the game. I had fun doing it, and I tried to give the best that I could give to win."

Where are they now?
Presently Jim is divorced and works in the inner city with at-risk youth. He formed a social service agency along with Oscar Reed, a Viking teammate, called Professional Sports Linkage. Jim described it as, "a service that has programs to help everyone from young people, to senior citizens, to new immigrants, to adjudicated youth - while they are incarcerated, all to create positive, tax-paying, productive members of our society."

Tributes

"Jim Marshall was one of the finest athletes I have ever coached. He had durability, and that was the greatest ability you could have. He was one of the finest competitors the Vikings have ever had, period."
-- Bud Grant

"He was the best. He epitomized the term 'Viking.' I am still very good friends with Jim, and I cherish our friendship very dearly. Together we went through a lot out there and he was just a fabulous football player. He was so quick off the ball and was just fearless. I have a lot of respect for him as a player and as a person."
-- Carl Eller

"Jim was a phenomenal football player and a really good friend. He is somebody who was dedicated and committed to the game of football and to his franchise. I guess the best way to describe him would be when you look up the definition of professional football in the dictionary, you should find Jim Marshall's name."
-- Alan Page

"Jim Marshall was our leader. A guy that anybody would follow. He is a unique man in that he had the greatest mind control of anybody I've ever seen. He was the heart and soul of the Minnesota Vikings."
-- Chuck Foreman

"Captain Marshall! Man, he was fearless. He was the epitome of a football captain. He should definitely be in the Pro Football Hall of Fame. No, they should have a separate wing in the Hall of Fame just for him."
-- Ahmad Rashad

"To me, aside from being a magnificent player, Jim was the spirit of the Vikings. He represented the essence of spirit and leadership. There would be no player who would stand up more for basic, fundamental, consistent values in team sport than Jim Marshall. He was always there for his teammates on and off the field, and he is a wonderful person." **-- Joe Kapp**

1969

JOE KAPP
The Vikings Make it to Their First Super Bowl

After losing a tough season opener 24-23 to Fran Tarkenton's New York Giants, the 1969 version of the Minnesota Vikings put together a then league record of 12 consecutive victories. The winning streak was highlighted by the 52-14 tattooing of the Baltimore Colts in week two. Quarterback Joe Kapp tied an NFL record by throwing an amazing seven touchdown passes in that game. The Vikings were awesome that season, outscoring their opponents 379-133, while finishing with a 12-2 record atop the Western Conference.

In the first round of the playoffs, then called the Western Conference Championship series, the Vikings met the Los Angeles Rams in a game that ranks as one of the most exciting ever in team history. On December 27, in front of nearly 48,000 frozen fans at Metropolitan Stadium, Minnesota overcame a 10-point fourth quarter deficit to rally and beat the Rams 23-20. The highlight of the game happened when Carl Eller sacked quarterback Roman Gabriel in the end zone for a fourth quarter safety - clinching the win for the Purple.

One week later, the Vikings went go on to beat up on the Cleveland Browns, 27-7, in front of another 48,000

at the icy Met. The Vikings were NFL champions and would meet the American Football League champion Kansas City Chiefs for the fourth-ever Super Bowl in New Orleans.

Super Bowl IV
The Vikings were listed as a clear two-touchdown favorite over the Chiefs, who were making their second appearance in the NFL's football extravaganza. The pre-game controversy surrounding the game involved Chiefs quarterback Len Dawson, who subsequently was called to testify in a federal sports gambling investigation. A cloud of suspicion surrounded many players and coaches who were angered by the timing of it all. Although Dawson was later cleared of any wrong-doing, he was reportedly devastated by the accusations. Many thought the distraction had killed any chances the Chiefs had to upset the Vikings. They were wrong.

The Vikings weren't without controversy as well that week. Kapp, bothered at suggestions made by the media that he lacked a classic throwing style, was quoted as saying: "Classics are for Greeks. Who is a classic quarterback? I think I can play some ball."

Before the game, a hot-air balloon with the Vikings logo on it crashed into the stands, a dreadful omen of things to come. The Chiefs went on to give the AFL its second straight Super Bowl upset, tying the young series at two games each. Dawson's short, precision passing picked apart the famous Minnesota Purple People Eater defense. And, the Chiefs defense stuffed Minnesota's once powerful running game. Very methodically, and without flash, Kansas City dominated the game.

Perhaps the opening kickoff as an indication of things to come for Minnesota, as Charlie West bobbled and lost the wind-blown offering, giving the Chiefs the ball deep in Viking territory. Jan Stenerud kicked three field goals and running back Mike Garrett scored on a five-yard run in the second. The Chiefs used an elaborate trapping scheme to neutralize the Vikings great pass rusher Alan Page and went into the locker room at half-time up 16-0.

Dave Osborn scored on a four-yard run in the third-quarter to give the Minnesota faithful some hope, only to see Dawson hit wide receiver Otis Taylor on a six-yard out pattern, whereupon Taylor broke two tackles and raced 46 yards for the clincher. The final blow to the Purple came in the fourth, when quarterback Kapp, battered and injured, had to be helped off the Tulane Stadium field after being sacked, dramatizing the Vikings futility.

Adding insult to injury was Chiefs' bombastic coach, Hank Stram, who was wired with a

microphone during the game, said of the Vikings: "They can't figure us out. They don't know what they're doing. It's like a Chinese fire drill out there!"

Although the loss to the Chiefs stunned the Minnesota faithful and most of the NFL, it did not diminish the accomplishments of a brilliant season. This was the last season of the AFL and NFL as rival leagues, as they merged the next season, becoming the AFC and NFC, both unified as part of the NFL.

On the 1969 season:
"I remember I had hurt my knee just before that season," Kapp says, "and the doctors' remedy was to put it in a cast. Well, I did that for about 10 days, and finally I couldn't handle it anymore, so I went down to a tire store and cut the cast off to get ready to play football again.

"By the time I got ready to play, Gary Cuozzo had started the first game of the season. I thought Gary played well, but Bud (Grant) didn't. For the second game, we were matched against the Colts, and I got the chance to get the starting job back. We beat them, 52-14, and I threw seven touchdown passes. I had showed them what I could do and what we could do as a team. I was in my third season, and I had prepared myself -- I studied the films from the Colts game the year before. That was a memorable game for me, and it was just the start of that season."

On the Super Bowl: "Kansas City had some really great players. They definitely outweighed us, and they probably had more speed. They beat us on that day, but I'm not sure that they were a better team. We lost, but not convincingly.

"We did some things in that game that we hadn't done all season. For example, there had been a lot of shifting and using odd-man lines in the AFL. It was unusual to us, and we didn't really adjust well to their strategy. Also, we said 'ho-hum' to the whole Dawson gambling story that was going on, but I think they got some emotion out of that.

"The weather told our story that day. It was a cold, dreary day. Our only fire seemed to come when we were down and then marched 70-some yards for a touchdown. We were starting to come back. Then they connected on a hitch pass and were able to score an easy one on a long run. We started to have to play catch-up, and we weren't that kind of team. We were a team that needed to get out and play our game from the opening bell. In the Super Bowl, we didn't do that. We missed our opportunity to be champions of the world, or at least I did. The rest of those guys got to go three more times! Still, that season has its own special place for me."

Kapp grew up as a sports fanatic in southern California. "We played all sports growing up, whatever was available," he says. "We didn't have hockey, but I guess I would've played that as well had they offered it." He attended The University of California at Berkeley. There he played football and basketball for the Golden Bears. He went to a Rose Bowl, and under basketball head coach Pete Newell he would play on championship teams.

He then played professional football in Canada for eight years. He played in Calgary and then in British Columbia, where he won a Grey Cup with the Lions. He took the Vikings to the Super Bowl in 1970 and turned down the the team's MVP award for his own reasons. He finished his NFL career with the Boston Patriots.

He later became head football coach at his alma matter, Cal, staying there for five years. He later got the acting bug, did some commercials, (including one for Wheaties), and performed in a number Hollywood motion pictures.

Kapp was a throwback to when football was really a game and played because he loved it. He led the Vikings in passing all three years he was with the team, from 1967-1969. For his career with the Vikings, Joe threw for a total of 4,807 yards. Kapp passed for 37 touchdowns and had 47 interceptions. His Vikings career quarterback rating was a modest 64.9. He completed 351 of 699 pass attempts for a 50 percent completion rate.

He would eventually leave the game, not on his terms, but he will always be remembered by NFL fans for his achievements and fiery attitude. Joe will undoubtedly go down as the guttiest and toughest quarterback ever to wear the purple. When you think about the rich tradition and history of the Minnesota Vikings, you have to include the legacy of Joe Kapp as one of the all-time classics.

On leaving the Vikings for the Patriots
"I didn't want to go to Boston. I was 32 years old and I figured I was in my prime. I believe we would have won a Super Bowl in Minnesota if I could have stayed there. It didn't work out. That's a memory that I want to put out of my mind."

Who was your hero when you were growing up?
"I guess Joe Louis stands out in my mind because he was champion of the world. We used to listen to his fights on the radio. In those days, it was all radio. I grew up following the Niners and Rams, but it was unheard for us kids to actually go see a game in person."

On turning down the team MVP award:
"I didn't plan it or anything, it was just down deep in me. I just couldn't accept it. Hell, I was sitting at the same table as Jim Marshall. Tell me I was more valuable than Jim Marshall. Or Mick Tinglehoff. Tinglehoff was the most determined player I ever played with, and I thought so after seeing Dick Butkus finish the game with bite marks all over his body. Billy Brown? I mean is anybody tougher? I don't know, maybe Dave Osborn? What about Alan Page or Carl Eller or Gary Larsen? I turned down the MVP trophy with a very real belief that there wasn't any Vikings most valuable player."

What did it mean for you to be a Viking?
"Minnesota has the most wonderful, finest, beautiful people - even if they're all blonde. It was a great three

years, and we continued to improve and build the team every year. We showed the fans some spirit, and we didn't play the game with clean pants. We got down and rolled up our sleeves, and we had fun doing it."

On Forty for Sixty:
"Forty for sixty was the recipe that meant that every person counts, and it was unacceptable for anybody not to participate. I recognized the value of every person on the team. I started my college career on the bench as a substitute defensive end, and I learned to appreciate the guys that didn't get to play. So, I've always felt that as a team you are only as strong as your weakest player, not as strong as your star. I learned from my basketball coach, Pete Newell, that there is a value in not being the guy starting on the court or field. That's where the forty for sixty came up. It's the unsung guys that make you good. Our whole team attitude of forty for sixty was for real and we were a family."

Viking tombstone:
"When I played, the effort showed, and I think that's why people appreciated me as a player. You accept the responsibility of playing quarterback for a team and building excellence takes value points such as toughness, determination, persistence, and fortitude. All of the those are things that a player brings with him in addition to skill, and those are the things that make winners."

Where are they now?
Joe and his wife Jennifer reside in Los Gatos, Calif. They have four children. Joe is involved with a family restaurant called "Kapp's" in Mountain View and does motivational speaking work.

Tributes

"Joe was a football player who probably did not have a sense of what was good for Joe Kapp as an individual. In other words, what Joe was about was what was good for the team. It didn't really matter whether it was good for Joe or not, he was a true team player."
                                                                -- **Carl Eller**

"Joe was kind of a rebel, but maybe he over 'rebelized'. I watched him as a player in Canada, and I knew he could play, so we got him down here to play for us in Minnesota. He was a tough guy for a quarterback. He really overstepped what you could do in that era. He played here for a couple years and then something else came up, and so he ended up in New England. It was too bad that Joe didn't just settle down and make the most of it where he was. You can't hold a team hostage all the time. He ended up playing with different teams and did well with all of them, but it was too bad he just didn't stay with one - the Vikings. He would've been better off. But he challenged the NFL contract system, so we let him go."   -- **Bud Grant**

"Joe is a guy that you would want to be in an alley fight with. He would do anything that was necessary to get that ball down the field and to make something happen. He didn't throw the prettiest passes in the world, but, he threw winning passes. It didn't make any difference what his passes looked like, but they always got to his target. He made some great efforts in the short time he was with the Minnesota Vikings. He is one of my most dear friends, and I am so respectful of his ability and his qualifications. Most of all I'm respectful of the attitude and toughness that he brought to the team. No quarterback that I know of ever had that kind of toughness, period. I've seen him fight linebackers, and come out winning. I've seen him put guys like Jim Houston, one of the toughest all-pro defensive ends in the league, out of a game. He didn't care who you were, he was going to hit you as hard as you were going to hit him. As soon as that ball left his hand he was looking to deliver a blow to someone coming at him. You don't find that anymore. He was a genuine throwback to the earliest days of professional football."   -- **Jim Marshall**

"Joe Kapp was a great leader. He could make people do things in terms of their ability which they probably didn't think they were capable of. He brought out extraordinary qualities in people."   -- **Alan Page**

TONY OLIVA
The Twins Win the West Again

1970

Led by All-Star right fielder Tony Oliva, the Minnesota Twins won the wild, wild AL Western Division for the second year in a row in 1970. This was indeed a wild year for Minnesota baseball, and it all started out with a pre-season managerial change. The popular Billy Martin, who had led the Twins to an impressive 97-65 record and the American League West title only the year before was fired by owner Calvin Griffith and replaced with former Minneapolis Miller manager Bill "Captain Hook" Rigney. (Rigney earned his nickname "Captain Hook" by his tendency to yank his pitchers at the slightest sign of trouble.)

There was endless speculation as to why the fiery Martin was fired. Perhaps it was because he punched the Twins traveling secretary, or maybe it was his fight he got into outside a Detroit bar, or possibly it was because he publicly aired his grievances about the Twins front office management to the press. Regardless of the reason, the fact remained that Calvin canned Billy. The whole mess didn't bode well with the fans. "Bring Billy Back" bumper stickers were everywhere, and there was even a country-western song that uttered, "Are you leavin' Billy Martin? It's a shame, it's a shame."

But Rigney, the Twins new skipper, ignored the distractions and went on to guide his team to a 98-64 record and their second straight Western Division title. The season started off well for the Twins. But, midway through the season, pitcher Luis Tiant broke his shoulder, so the Twins brought up a 19-year-old rookie to replace him. His name was Bert Blyleven. Rigney also had a pet nickname for the rookie -- "The Baby." Despite this, Bert went on to have a pretty good year, winning 10 games for the Twins. One of the highlights that season came on May 20 against the Kansas City Royals, when Rod Carew became the first Twin ever to hit for the cycle.

The Twins pitching staff was led by Jim Perry, brother of future Hall of Famer Gaylord, who with 24 wins, a modest 3.03 ERA and 168 strikeout's, became the first Twin ever to win the Cy Young Award. And, whenever Perry needed help, closer Ron Perranoski came in to mop up. Ron's American League leading 34 saves, combined with Stan Williams' 15, made up the best bullpen in the league. Throw in Jim Kaat and Tom Hall, and statistically, the Twins had the second best pitching staff in the league that year.

The Twins bats were hot in 1970, Killebrew hit 41 dingers with 113 RBI's, and Carew, Tovar, and Oliva all hit .300 or better. As a team, the Twins would go on to lead the American League in batting. Tony-O had another of his fabulous seasons in 1970, cranking out the most hits in the American League for the fifth consecutive year, with 204, and once again leading his club to the post-season. He led the team in batting with a .325 average, while driving in 107 RBI's, scoring 96 runs, and hitting 23 homers. And don't forget his league-leading 36 doubles as well.

The Twins were champions of the American League West, and the 1970 playoffs were a rematch of the year before, with, unfortunately, the same results. Being swept by the Orioles the season before, observers might have thought that some sort of revenge factor would've been motivated the Twins. The observers were wrong.

On October 3, the Twins opened the American League Championship Series at the Met. Minnesota jumped out to an early one-run lead, but Perry got rocked as the O's went on to beat the Twins, 10-6.

In game two, it got a lot worse, believe it or not. Baltimore topped their Game One power surge by crushing the Twins 11-3, despite homers by Oliva and Killebrew.

Back in Baltimore for game three, Rigney sent Kaat up against Jim Palmer. It wasn't even close, and the Orioles went on to complete the sweep.

In the first two years of the ALCS, the Twins were 0-6, all six losses coming at the hands of mighty Baltimore.

"Losing two years in a row to the Orioles was tough," says Oliva, who batted .500 for the ALCS. "After the first game, I thought that we had a chance to beat Baltimore, but we lost a very tough playoff series to a really good team. That year was a lot of fun and winning the West for the second time was a real thrill. We had a great ball club back then, and it was too bad we just couldn't make it past that next round to make it to the World Series like we did in 1965. There were a lot of great players on that 1970 team, and we were like a family."

From Cuba to Minnesota

Pedro Oliva grew up in the western province of Cuba, on his father's farm in Pinar del Rio, about 100 miles from Havana. He went to school through the 8th grade in a two-room wooden schoolhouse. He grew up as one of 10 kids; five boys and five girls. (He told his father he was a lucky man because he had hit .500!) Baseball consumed the boys life, and it would be his ticket to prosperity.

"When I was a boy, we would help my father with the work on the farm after school, then play baseball," said Oliva. "We grew tobacco, oranges, mangos, potatoes, corn, and raised cows, pigs, chickens, and horses. My father loved the game and always found time for my brothers and me to play it. He helped all the kids play and enjoy the game by going to Havana and buying gloves, bats, and balls for us. Once he came back to the farm with nine gloves. We kept them in our house, and when the kids came to our farm to play baseball, they used them."

He got his big break when he was spotted by Cuban scout, "Papa" Joe Cambria, and came to the states for a tryout. His teammates on his Cuban team even chipped in to buy him some clothes for his trip. "Since I didn't have a passport, I had to use my brother Antonio's. So, everyone started calling me Tony," said Oliva. "I found I liked the name. In fact, I liked it better than Pedro, so I didn't ever tell anyone my real name."

The newly-christened Tony was invited to a rookie camp with the Twins, and in 1961, he led the league with a .410 average. After one-year stints in Class A and AAA, he made it to the majors in 1964. As a rookie with the Twins, Oliva led the American League with a .323 batting average, becoming the only rookie ever to win the batting title. He was named Rookie of the Year, earning every penny of his lavish $7,500 salary.

That same year, Tony got a new teammate from his native Cuba, Zoilo Versalles. Twins manager Sam Mele said simply, "Now I've got two kids from Cuba!" The two became instant friends. "Best roommate I ever had," said Versalles of Oliva. "He doesn't smoke, doesn't drink, and doesn't snore. All he does is eat, sleep, and breathe baseball."

Oh Tony-O

Oliva would go on to become one of the greatest players in Twins history. One of the highlights of his career was when he led his team to the World Series in his sophomore year, winning another batting crown en route to being named American League Player of the Year by the Sporting News. "It was a great series and something I will never forget," said Oliva. "I look at it this way, there were two champs -- one from the American League and one from the National League. But, only one team can win when you play seven games. Anything could've happened that last game, and we got beat by the Dodgers."

Tony won a Gold Glove in 1966 and captured a third batting crown in 1971. In 15 seasons, six of which were affected by a knee injury, Oliva would finish with 1,917 hits, 947 RBI's and had a career average of .304. His prowess as a hitter was demonstrated in the fact that he led the league in hits five times, and his 220 career home runs rank third all-time among Twins. An eight-time All-Star, his number six was officially retired on July 14, 1991.

From 1962-1976 Tony was a delight to see. He could hit for power and average as well as run, field, and throw. His versatility made him one of the most feared hitters of his day. If not for knee problems which cut short his career, Oliva would have been a certain choice for the Hall of Fame. He became a part time coach in 1976 and upon his retirement from the game that same year, Oliva began coaching for the Twins, where he has been ever since. Tony-O will forever be remembered as one of the Minnesota Twins all-time greats.

Who was your hero when you were growing up?
"When I was a kid in Cuba, Minnie Minoso was always my hero."

Most memorable moment:
"One time I hit a ball out of the old ballpark at Kansas City. and it went 517 feet out over the street and it hit the top of a house. Someone got the ball for me, and I still have it today. People couldn't believe that a little guy like me could hit the ball that far!"

On leaving his family in Cuba:
"It was always hard for me knowing that my family was back in Cuba. I wasn't happy without them, and I was very lonesome. It was very hard for me for many, many years."

Twins tombstone:
"I would like to be remembered as a ballplayer that gave 100 percent and also a person that was able to get along with everybody. I think the fans here in Minnesota are great, and it was a pleasure to play here for them. I have lived here for over half of my life and my family, and I am grateful to the good people of Minnesota."

On the Hall of Fame:
"Everybody thinks I should be in the Hall of Fame except for the people that vote. I feel a little bit disappointed. I think I should be in the Hall because I achieved so much. It was too bad that I got hurt, but there were people that did less in the same amount of time than I did that got in. A lot of pitchers now in the

Hall of Fame, who pitched against me, have told me over the years that when they were asked by baseball writers who they felt should be in the Hall that isn't, they said me. I had a lot of great accomplishments in my career, and I hope I can still make it in through the back door."

Where are they now?
Tony and his wife Gordette have four children, and live in Minneapolis. He is currently a hitting instructor with the Twins minor league system and is a scout for the club as well.

Tributes

"He was like a brother to me. He was the one who took me under his wing when I was a rookie. He even taught me how to tie my first necktie. He allowed me to be his roommate for nine years, and he taught me how to handle myself and how to handle people. He always had that great smile about him. He was never upset at people for anything, and that was one of the reasons that even today the people have a great love affair with this guy. He is a tremendous person aside from being a tremendous baseball player. We knew where we came from. We came from nothing -- countries where we wouldn't have been able to make the type of living that we were to make by playing professional baseball."
-- Rod Carew

"He didn't have any legs left when I got there. But I remember in 1976, it was Tony's birthday, and he beat Mark Fidrich all by himself that day, going four-for-four. He was one of the all-time greatest hitters. He's not recognized nearly as much as he should be."   **-- Gene Mauch**

"Here's a guy that deserves to be in the Hall of Fame. He was a Rod Carew - type hitter, with power. He was one of the finest hitters that I have ever seen. He could hit the ball all over the park and he was the best off-speed hitter that I ever saw. You could throw him 99 fast-balls and one change-up and he'd hit it out. He was such a great hitter."   **-- Harmon Killebrew**

"Tony is special to me. Tony has been short-changed with regards to the Hall of Fame. He was one of the greatest hitters and all-around players in all of baseball. If you were to ask catchers from the 1960s who they feared the most with the winning run on base: Killebrew, Carew, or Oliva, and they would say Tony was the guy pitchers feared most. Jim Palmer and I have talked about that at length and that's how he felt. Tony was a combination of average, power, speed, and he could drive the ball to produce runs. He was as good a pure hitter as there was."   **-- Jim Kaat**

"I think if you cut his head open, a bunch of baseballs would fall out. That's all he knows is baseball. Tony-O was one of my heroes growing up, and I even wore his number six on my first T-ball jersey."
-- Kent Hrbek

"Tony is just a really nice guy and a great human being. He was such a gifted player. When he used to hit, he could take a low and inside pitch down the right field line, and the next time he'd take the same pitch down the left field line. He could hit the ball anywhere he wanted. I was in awe watching that man play baseball."   **-- Tom Kelly**

"He was my guru as far as hitting goes. He and I were just so much alike, we were just apples-to-apples. We were the same kind of hitters - wild swingers who were able to do what we wanted to do with the bat. He was one of the greatest and without a doubt, he should be in the Hall of Fame."   **-- Kirby Puckett**

Twins pitcher Jim Perry wins 24 games and is named the American League Cy Young Award winner. Over 17 years in the big-league's, Jim won 215 games. His big brother and fellow pitcher, Gaylord Perry, also won a Cy Young, making them the only brother tandem in baseball history to have won the award.

TIMELINE

61

1971

ALAN PAGE
The Viking Great is Named as the NFL's MVP

In 1971, the Minnesota Vikings won their fourth straight NFC Central Division title with a record of 11-3. The purple entered the playoffs with high hopes of returning to the Super Bowl. But, unfortunately for the nearly 50,000 Minnesota faithful who spent a frigid Christmas day at old Metropolitan Stadium, they came up short, losing to the Dallas Cowboys by 20-12.

In 1971, coach Bud Grant decided to play musical chairs with his quarterbacks. In the first game of the season, Gary Cuozzo sparked the Vikings to a key 16-13 victory over the Lions. Then, after a 20-17 loss to the Bears, Norm Snead came off the bench to take over the helm. Snead led the Vikings to back-to-back shutouts over Buffalo and Philadelphia. Then Grant decided to shuffle the deck one more time, putting Cuozzo back in for the next five games. For four of the final five games of the season, Bobby Lee was the quarterback, until being benched in favor of Cuozzo during the Dallas playoff game. This marked the last time that Grant's Vikings had an unresolved quarterback problem, as Francis Tarkenton would return from the Big Apple to take over the next season.

Defensive tackle Alan Page, the first rookie ever to

start for Grant, made history in 1971, by becoming the first defensive player in NFL history of to win the league MVP. Page's presence in the middle gave ends Jim Marshall and Carl Eller much more freedom to rush the quarterback, and by season's end, everyone had heard of those now legendary "Purple People Eaters." In 14 games that season, they would allow their opponents a paltry 139 points.

After selection as an All-American and playing on the 1966 Notre Dame national championship team, Page was named by the Vikings as the number one pick of the 1967 draft. He played for the Vikings from 1967-78. Page was selected All-Pro six times and received nine Pro Bowl invitations. Almost never missing a game, he had 108 career sacks and 16 blocked kicks, third and second, respectively, on the Vikings all-time list.

Page was a nonconformist, often bucking heads with coach Grant. Grant let him skip training camp one year, but when he wanted to do it again, Bud refused, and that started some dissention between the two. Late in his career, Page had thinned down from 275 to 230 pounds, which was small for a NFL defensive tackle. When he went against the wishes of the coaching staff to keep his weight up, he was released on waivers by the Vikings for $100, essentially firing him. Page went on to play another three seasons before finishing his career with the Bears and retiring in 1981.

By 1979, Page had earned his law degree from the University of Minnesota. He would move from the gridiron to the attorney general's office. Page has always battled adversity, and his journey to become a Minnesota Supreme Court justice would be no exception. Typically, new judges are appointed temporarily and then elected without competition. When his opportunity to run kept being denied, he sued Governor Arne Carlson. A substitute Supreme Court ruled in Page's favor, allowing him to run successfully, with opposition, in 1992. He is the first African-American to sit on the state's highest court - or on any Minnesota state appellate court, for that matter.

With his spectacles and trademark bow-tie, Page hung up his NFL uniform for a well-earned black judge's robe. His left pinkie finger still sticks out at a 90 degree angle, brutally dislocated in a league game years ago. In his chambers, Justice Page is surrounded by momentos. His prized collection of pressed-steel toy trucks, a handwritten note from Ethel Kennedy, and several old signs from the days of segregation - one of the most disturbing reads, simply, "Colored Waiting Room."

What you won't find in Page's chambers, though, is a souvenir of his playing days with

the Vikings. There is not so much as a football card, photo, or ticket stub to be found. When a reporter visits, Page will tolerate questions about his days with the Vikings, but it will become obvious that it is the subject that seems to interest him the least.

Life after football
Immediately following the 1976 Super Bowl when the Oakland Raiders demolished the Vikings, in a locker room overcome with dejection, Page was quoted as calmly saying: "How on earth can otherwise sensible people get so involved in a football game? You could measure the lasting impact on the lives of the people who played in it, and those who watch it, as just about zero." Overzealous Viking fans, frustrated by the fourth-straight Super Bowl loss, were outraged.

"Football was a job," Page says, "and often a tedious one.

"There really isn't much to think about on a football field. Playing the game requires physical ability and a tremendous emotional commitment. Intellectually, it doesn't require much, There are a finite number of things that can take place on a football field. After 10 years, you probably have done most of them. Football to me became repetitious and boring."

Near the end of Alan's career with the Vikings, after he had graduated from the University of Minnesota Law School in the off-season, the Vikings were back in training camp, preparing for the upcoming football season. At a meeting of defensive linemen, one of the coaches asked some of the players to read aloud from the defensive playbook. "If you've ever read a playbook, it's not too exciting, and the toughest word is probably "tackle,'" Page reportedly said. Alan saw that many of his defensive linemen teammates couldn't read the playbook, and several others were struggling to get by. "In that moment, listening to my teammates unable to read a simple playbook, everything crystallized for me," Page said. "I don't know why it took me so long to realize, but at that moment it became clear that this wasn't a dumb-jock problem, or an athletic problem. These men were supposed to learn to read in first, second, or third grade, long before they were football players. You think about something, and you think about it again, but you can't point your finger at it. Well, that day, I realized the problem I wanted to try to address was education. Pure and simple."

The Hall of Fame
A native of Canton, Ohio, Page actually worked on the construction crew one summer that built the Hall of Fame in Canton during the late 1960s. So, in 1988, at his induction into the Pro Football Hall of Fame, declining the opportunity to swap gridiron gossip, as most of the football brethren do at their inductions, Alan shocked the pro football establishment by choosing Willarene Beasley as his presenter, principal at Minneapolis North High School. Never in the Hall of Fame's history had a person not in the football fraternity made an induction speech. Page selected her

TIMELINE

Garry Bjorklund, Gopher track and field legend wins the Six-Mile Run National Championship. A former collegiate record holder in the event, he broke 11 cross country and track records at the U, and still holds school records in the 3,000M and 5,000M runs. He won 10 Big Ten titles, and was a five-time All-American. He earned a spot on the 1976 Olympic team, he also competed on two US Pan-Am and 10 US National teams. Today the Grandma's half-marathon is named in his honor.	Mankato State wrestler Ken Stockdale wins the 134 lb. Division II National Championship	Vikings coach Norm Van Brocklin is inducted into the Pro Football Hall of Fame	Dave Bancroft, a Minneapolis Miller manager in 1933, is inducted into the Baseball Hall of Fame	The Gopher Hockey team loses to Boston University, 4-2, in the NCAA Finals	Gopher end Doug Kingsriter is named to the All-American football team	The Minnesota Fighting Saints begin play in the WHA's Western Division at the St. Paul Auditorium	UMD winger Walt Ledingham is named to the All-American hockey team

because of the fact that she was an educator and, as a black woman, represented minorities. Alan's speech was about the values of education, not football; about learning to tackle issues, not quarterbacks; about ABCs, not Xs and Os. "I wanted to take advantage of that recognition and use the day as a mechanism for something meaningful," Page said. Following her introduction, Alan launched the Page Education Foundation from the steps of the Hall of Fame.

Did you have a hero when you were growing up?
"Not really, other than looking up to my parents and other family members." After being asked if there were any African-Americans that he had looked up to, Page replied: "Thurgood Marshall, Roy Wilkins, and Martin Luther King Jr. were all individuals who helped develop my interest in the law. They sparked my interest because of their beliefs and actions in seeking equal justice and equal opportunity for all."

What did it mean for you to be a Viking?
"To be honest with you, I never really thought about it in that context. What I enjoyed and what I thought about, were the people that I worked with, being a part of a team, having great friends, and working with a lot of good people. That's really what was important to me. I suppose that I was fortunate to work with a number of talented people. Not only people like Jim Marshall, Carl Eller, Ahmad Rashad, and Chuck Foreman, but also Bobby Bryant, Charlie West, Clinton Jones, Gene Washington, and a whole host of others who were good friends, good people, and talented football players. I was very fortunate to be a part of all that."

On winning the MVP:
"The MVP award was by somebody else's measure. It's tough to say that any season was better than another. Certainly 1971 was a good one for me, but there were other good ones in there too. For me, it was trying to be the best that I could be. That was something that was constant for me, and it wasn't something that took place one year and not in others. When I look back, I look on a whole career, not any one particular season. I had a lot of success in a lot of successful seasons."

On Viking Super Bowl failure.
"To be quite honest with you, I don't look back. My perspective is to look into the future. The fact that we didn't win four particular football games is not terribly significant in the grand scheme of things."

Vikings tombstone:
"If I could choose a way to be remembered, it wouldn't be my association with football. Football is in the past - a good past, but nonetheless it is the past. I'd want to be remembered with children - with my children and other children."

On life:
"I saw a quote once that read that success is not a place where you arrive at, it's a manner of travel. The success and the joy is in working to get there, not getting there. Once you're there, what's interesting about that? I learned that lesson very early on as a football player. When I was selected as the league's MVP early on in my career, I felt that's about as good as it gets in professional football. It was at that point that I figured out

that the fun was in the journey, not arriving at the destination. The journey just never ends."

Where are they now?
Associate Justice Page is currently a member of the Minnesota Supreme Court. He is an avid runner, and he and his wife Diane live in the Twin Cities and have four children: Nina, Georgi, Justin, and Kamie.

Tributes

"As a football player, I feel very proud to have played with Alan Page. I think he was one of the guys that truly changed the game. They stopped calling holding because Alan was so quick and elusive, and he was so disruptive to the other teams. They intentionally allowed holding on him, because that was the only way anybody could block him. They gave more freedom to offensive lineman in the way they used their hands, and a lot of that was because of his elusive play. Never in the history of the game, and I have looked at films since the beginning of organized football, has there been any rule changes like they made in the 10 years that Alan was out there. Everything changed with the advent of television, and people wanted to see a more potent offensive representation on the field. That handcuffed the defensive teams. Today football is more of a form of entertainment, rather than the sport that it was back in those days. I think a lot of that had to do with the play of Alan Page." **--**
Jim Marshall

"Alan had a vision about his own personal life. To a great extent, within his greatness, he saw his own limitations. He felt that he really had to do something significant outside of football. I think that Alan felt consumed by his own greatness on the field, and it was probably too much for him. He's a torch-bearer right from the very beginning, and his being a Supreme Court Justice is just fabulous."
-- Carl Eller

"Alan was the consummate pro. Playing the game like no other, he always played 100 percent. He was very misunderstood as far as I'm concerned. He was a very

serious man who had a plan. When he came off the field and you said 'way to go,' to him, it was like, 'hey, I'm supposed to do this.' If you didn't know that about him, you might have thought he was aloof, but he wasn't. He was the kind of guy who came to play every down. He was the greatest defensive tackle to ever play the game - no question. He was way ahead of his time. He is a very brilliant man and a man of his word. He is his own man and played the game as it was supposed to be played. He is a man to respect. He's real - what you see is what you get - and I admire him greatly."
-- Chuck Foreman

"He probably had as much natural instinct for football as anybody who ever played the game. I would compare him to Charles Barkley in professional basketball. He was outstanding. He could make plays and play at a level that was right at the very top."
-- Bud Grant

"Alan was the greatest of players. As I look back on my career, I am so proud to have ever been on a team with him. He was one of the greatest who ever played the game. As great a player he was, he's a much greater person. He was one of the guys that I was drawn to when I got there. He played hard and worked hard in everything else." (In his book, "Rashad," Ahmad described Page as "the most professional ass-kicker in the business.")
-- Ahmad Rashad

"He was a great talent and was an extremely resourceful player. With his resourcefulness came a touch of madness. He would take risks that only he could evaluate, most often coming out on top. Alan used to take risks to succeed and, as a result, he was a tremendous football player."
-- Joe Kapp

"He's honest, he listens to people, he's fair and well respected. If anything, Alan is a gentle soul."
-- Hubert H. Humphrey III,
Minnesota attorney general

As a tribute to the town of Eveleth for all of its contributions to the sport of hockey, the U.S. Hockey Hall of Fame is constructed there on Hat Trick Avenue. More than 1/3 of its inductees are native Minnesotans

Central High School's Bobby Marshall, who played for the Colored Gophers professional Negro League baseball team as well as several professional football teams, is inducted into the College Football Hall of Fame.

Marshall, considered to be one of the greatest University of Minnesota athletes of all time, lettered in football, baseball and track. In 1903 he became the first African American to play football in the Big 9 Conference (now the Big 10), as an end for the Gophers.

Minneapolis' Joe Hutton, Hamline University's basketball coach of 34 years, is named the NAIA Tournament's all-time coach. His Piper squads won or shared 19 MIAC titles, 12 times qualified for the NCAA tournament, and won three NAIA national championships (1942, 1949 and 1951)

Kent, Minnesota's Jimmy Robinson is inducted into the Amateur Trapshooting Association Hall of Fame. Considered the nation's trap and skeet shooting authority for more than half a century, he was named as Minnesota's Outdoor Sportsman of the Year in 1955.

TIMELINE

BILL MUSSELMAN
The Gopher Basketball "Iron Five"

The University of Minnesota Golden Gopher basketball program has seen a lot of ups and downs over the course of its history, but one of the most colorful phases involves Bill Musselman and the unbelievable 1972 Big Ten championship run.

In 1971, at a ripe old age of 32, Musselman became the youngest head basketball coach in Minnesota's modern history. He was, in fact, the University's second choice for the job. Cal Luther, the head coach at Murray State in Kentucky, had originally accepted the position, but two days later changed his mind. So, Musselman, who was to be the Gophers third (Kundla, Hansen, Musselman) coach in as many years, would be the architect of a re-building program.

Musselman knew he needed to surround Jim Brewer, the best returning player from the previous regime, with talented new players. So, he went outside the system and brought in three junior college transfers: Ron Behagen, Clyde Turner, and Bob Nix

He now had the players, but he knew he still needed to fill Williams Arena with plenty of fans and excitement. So, he instituted one of the basketball's greatest pre-

game warm-up shows, maybe even the best, with the possible exception of the one originated by Harlem Globetrotters. "It was the greatest exhibition of ball-handling that a lot of people had ever seen," said Musselman. "It was precision ball handling to music like 'Sweet Georgia Brown.' We used to fill up the arena an hour before game time so people that could watch our warm-up."

The Gophers went into their Big Ten Conference schedule with a modest nonconference record of 6-3. They even picked up a new walk-on player part-way through the season, a man who would go on to become a pretty decent athlete in his day. In 1971, the University intramural basketball champs were a team called the "Soulful Strutters." The Strutters were led by a kid named Dave Winfield. When freshman coach Jimmy Williams saw Winfield play during a intramural ball, he couldn't believe his eyes. So he told Musselman that he better give the kid a look. Winfield, who was a star pitcher on the baseball team at the time, joined the team and suddenly become a two-sport star at the U.

Their first Big Ten opponent was against Indiana and Musselman's old childhood pal from Ohio, Bobby Knight. "I grew up just a few miles from Bobby, and as kids we used to shoot baskets by the hour together," said Musselman. "That game was one of the most competitive and intense games that I think I have ever been in, it was amazing!" Minnesota went on to win the game 52-51, on a blocked shot by Brewer and two last-second foul shots by Nix.

Minnesota added three more victories to make them 4-0 in conference play. There next opponent was Ohio State, a game that will forever be remembered in gold country.

The fight
With the Buckeyes leading 50-44 and 36 seconds left in the game, Ohio State's star center Luke Witte broke toward the basket. With Minnesota pressing, Witte outran the field and caught the inbound pass and, in the process, was fouled hard by both Clyde Turner and Corky Taylor. Turner was then called for a flagrant foul and immediately ejected. Then, amazingly and nearly simultaneously, Taylor reached out to help Witte, who was on the court, to his feet, but instead of helping him, proceeded to knee him in the groin. The crowd was stunned, and subsequent mayhem broke out. Ohio State's, Dave Merchant went to help Witte, pushing Taylor out of his way. Brewer and Taylor then ran after Merchant down the court, while Behagen, having already fouled out, came off the bench and attacked Witte.

For the next moment, complete pandemonium took over at Williams Arena. Some

18,000 fans went spontaneously crazy, and many started to pour on the court to partake in the festivities. Several Buckeye players were taken to the hospital, and a near riot ensued. Outside, they started to throw rocks at the police cars as they took the players to the hospital. When it was all over, a huge black eye was left on the University of Minnesota basketball program.

The opposing players had much different stories as to what really happened. "Witte was gong up to take the shot, and Clyde Turner and myself fouled him," said Taylor. "It was really how hard I fouled him that precipitated my helping him up. Basically, it was a situation where he had an easy two points, and we were trying to make sure he didn't score. When I went to help Luke up, he spit at me and I got pissed! It was a very tough game, and I kicked him. When I turned around, the entire floor had erupted. It was a scary situation."

To better understand the entire situation, you have to go back to the end of the first half where an incident took place that may have instigated the ensuing event. As the players ran off the court and into the locker rooms, Bobby Nix waived to the pumped-up crowd by raising his fists in the air towards the scoreboard. "Luke Witte, (who had been described as a rough, 'Bill Laimbeer-type player) crossed in front of me," said Nix. "There's no question in my mind or anybody's that saw it. It was a deliberate elbow to my face. He just threw it, and he damn near decked me. It was seen by a lot of people, except the officials."

The aftermath
That night, following the incident, replays of the fight were played on virtually every newscast in the country. Every paper ran a story about it, and the next week, Sports Illustrated featured the brawl as their main story. All fingers pointed at Musselman as the instigator. They tried to paint a picture that Musselman's "win at any cost" attitude had animalized his players into a fit of rage. National media had concentrated only on the game-ending fight, and they never mentioned the half-time incident that precluded the retaliation. Attempts were made to dramatize and polarize Musselman and the Buckeyes' Fred Taylor, the two coaches (both with roots to Ohio). Taylor was a coaching legend who built programs traditionally. Musselman was a rookie Big Ten coach, who they said took short-cuts to success by obtaining junior college players. Racism and even the Vietnam War were thrown into the stew. People were searching for a scapegoat, and the media had found one in Musselman.

Musselman on the aftermath:
"A lot of things were said in print that were wrong. I was blamed for the fight or for not stopping the fight, yet the fight was the last thing I wanted. My insides were torn up. My hopes and dreams were shattered that night. I couldn't believe life was like that. I believed if you were dedicated and outworked everyone, you'd be successful. That night it seemed like

The NHL's All-Star game is played at the Met Center in Bloomington	Minneapolis's Bruce McIntosh wins a silver medal on the Olympic hockey team	Minneapolis' Charles Brown wins a silver medal on the Olympic hockey team	Minneapolis's Craig Lincoln wins a Bronze medal in the 3M Springboard Diving competition	St. Paul's Franklyn Sanders wins a silver medal on the Olympic hockey team	Warroad's Henry Boucha wins a silver medal on the Olympic hockey team	St. Paul's James McElmury wins a silver medal on the Olympic hockey team	UMD's Keith "Huffer" Christianson wins a silver medal on the Olympic hockey team	Minneapolis' Larry Bader wins a silver medal on the Olympic hockey team	St. Paul's James McElmury wins a silver medal on the Olympic hockey team

everything I believed in was wrong. I went home and got down on my knees and prayed. And I thought then, 'Well, you asked for this; you wanted to coach in the big time.' Since then, my beliefs have been reaffirmed. But it was my background that got me through that situation. If I hadn't been mentally tough, I wouldn't have survived that incident."

Musselman 25 Years later:
"Obviously the fight was wrong, but I always felt that it was racially motivated. It was during the early 1970s, and there were a lot of racial overtones. The game got out of hand, and the officials let too much loose play go on. I took a lot of heat for it. It was ridiculous that people would insinuate that I wanted to have a fight. They tried to blame it on my pre-game warm-up routine, saying that it hyped the fans into a frenzy. It was too bad that it happened, but it was an intense heat of the battle thing. The sad part about it was the fact that all the players were good people. Now that I am back in college coaching, I see how many kids are getting in trouble off the court. Back then our kids never got into any trouble, they got their degrees, and they made a contribution to society."

The "Iron Five"
Following the game, Behagen and Taylor were suspended for the remainder of the season. The new squad used the suspension of teammates as a personal vendetta to salvage the season. So Musselman went almost exclusively with a five-man lineup: Turner and Winfield at the forwards, Brewer at center, and guards Nix and Keith Young.

They next game was at Iowa. There were plain-clothed police officers everywhere and the fans were skeptical. "The fans there were vicious," said Winfield. "One of them grabbed me. One of them threw beer on me. It was tense. That's the way it was every game, every week, always with the sense that a fight might break out." The Gophers won the Iowa game 61-50, and kept winning. With Ohio State in a tail-spin, Minnesota put it all on the line at Purdue, with a chance to win the Big Ten title.

"We had a one point lead and held them scoreless for the last 20-some seconds to win," said Musselman. "Our defensive effort was incredible because they didn't get a good shot off at all when they could've won it. Winfield grabbed the last rebound to seal it." They beat Purdue 49-48, and in the process became the first Gopher team in 53 years to win an undisputed Big Ten title.

In their first-ever NCAA Tournament appearance, the Gophers lost to Florida State 70-56, then came back to beat Marquette 77-72 in the Mideast Regional consolation game. With the top defense in the nation, they allowed just 58 points per game that season, finishing with an 18-7 record. Brewer was named the Big Ten MVP, and both he and Behagen were named to the All-American team. Amazingly, in 1973 Brewer, Behagen, Taylor, Turner, and Winfield were all drafted into the NBA.

Attendance nearly doubled at Williams Arena in his four-year career, and Musselman was the impetus, compiling a 69-32 record, for a .683 winning percentage, the best in school history. He rescued the program and for better or for worse got people excited about basketball again. He left in 1975 under the shadow of allegations and investigations by the NCAA, all of which were unfounded. Bill Musselman will always be remembered in Minnesota for a lot of reasons. Most importantly he will be remembered as a great coach.

Musselman's remarkable career
Musselman grew up in Wooster Ohio. He went on to Wooster High School where he was the captain of the basketball, football, and baseball teams. He also lettered in those same three sports at Wittenberg University in Ohio, and later earned his master's degree from Kent State.

His 24-year coaching career is remarkable. He has a (58.6%) 603-426 overall record in coaching at all levels. He started out coaching at Kent State High School. In 1963 he was coaching college basketball at Ashland College, where his top-ranked 1969 team allowed an NCAA season-low record 33.9 points per game, earning his players the nickname of "Musselman's Misers." From there it was off to the U of M, and then into the ABA, where he coached at San Diego and Virginia, as well as Reno of the WBA. Then he went to the CBA, where he skippered Sarasota, Tampa Bay, Rapid City, Albany and Rochester. He was named CBA Coach of the Year in 1987 and 1988, and in five years won four consecutive championships. In the NBA he has coached the Cleveland Cavaliers and the Minnesota Timberwolves, where he guided the expansion franchise to the best first-year record among first-year NBA teams.

Who was your hero when you were growing up? "I knew in the 8th grade that I wanted to be a basketball coach, so I looked up to a lot of my coaches along the way. I had a lot of respect and admiration for my college coach at Wittenberg, Ray Mears."

What did it mean for you to coach the Gophers?
"I was always impressed with the University of Minnesota. The thing that impressed me the most about coaching there was how loyal the fans are. I think they are the best basketball fans in the country. They were the most enthusiastic too, and the noise in Williams Arena was unbelievable. Every time I run into someone from Minnesota, they always make outstanding compliments about the time that I was there, and how much they appreciated the good basketball. I went to the Final Four in Indianapolis this year, and I just loved seeing all the Minnesota fans there. I was so happy when Clem won the Big Ten championship, because I felt that I was a part of the history of basketball in the state as well."

On being the Timberwolves' first coach: "When I coached the Timberwolves they broke every NBA attendance record. There aren't many places where you are going to get 40,000 people to come to a basketball game! The fans there were just incredible, where else can you find fans like that?"

Gophers / Timberwolves tombstone:
"I think my teams always played hard and played

together. I think that I have always had the ability as a coach to get the most out of players, and my teams have always played as hard as they could."

Where are they now?
In 1995 Musselman took over as the head coach of the University of South Alabama, and in 1997 he led the Jaguars to the conference championship and a trip to the NCAA's "Big Dance," where they lost to the eventual national champion Arizona Wildcats. (It was his seventh career trip to the Dance) "I have a 98 percent graduation rate in college coaching, and I even have a higher bonus in my contract for having my kids graduate than I do for getting into the NCAA Tournament." In October of 1997 he resigned from USB and accepted an assistant coaching position with the Portland Trail Blazers. Bill has two children, Nicole and Eric.

Tribute

"He was tough. He was a competitive guy and he loved coaching. People may question his style, but he was a very knowledgeable coach and he made us work very hard. I kind of likened the practices and games to boot-camp in the service. It was tough, and competed hard. I don't think I have ever been in that good of shape! I think that he liked me because I gave it my all, and I was a very aggressive rebounder. I really enjoyed playing for him, he's something else, and he's all-right with me!"
-- **Dave Winfield**

| International Falls' Mike Curran wins a silver medal on the Olympic hockey team | Minneapolis' Ron Naslund wins a silver medal on the Olympic hockey team | International Falls' Tim Sheehy wins a silver medal on the Olympic hockey team | Gopher diver Craig Lincoln wins the Three-Meter Diving National Championship | UMD winger Walt Ledingham is named to the All-American hockey team | Gopher halfback and Heisman winner Bruce Smith is inducted into the College Football Hall of Fame |

TIMELINE

THE ROETHLISBERGERS
A GYMNASTICS FAMILY DYNASTY

If you want to talk about the history of gymnastics in Minnesota, then you will undoubtedly spend a great deal of time discussing the Roethlisbergers. This family has completely rewritten the record books when it comes to the sport that they love. Father Fred, daughter Marie, and son John are all former Olympians, and each has made giant contributions to the sport of gymnastics. Each was a tremendous athlete, scholar, and competitor.

Marie

Marie is arguably the most decorated female athlete in Minnesota history. She became the first University of Minnesota gymnast ever to win an NCAA championship as well as the first to earn a spot on the US Olympic team. Incredibly, the four-time All-American did it all despite having to overcome a partial hearing loss she suffered as a young girl caused by spinal meningitis. In 1990, her senior year at gold country, she won the uneven bars title at the NCAA championships. The same year Marie earned the NCAA's highest accolade when she became the first Minnesota athlete to be named as an NCAA Top Six recipient, awarded to the country's top six athletes.

Marie was named as the Big Ten gymnast of the year from 1987 to 1989, earned All-Big Ten All-Academic honors for three straight years and also received the Big Ten Medal of Honor. In 1984 she earned a spot the US Olympic team set to compete in Los Angeles, but unfortunately an injury prevented her from competing. She did, however, compete on the 1985 US World Championship team. She graduated in 1990 and today is a Medical Doctor.

John

John is without question the greatest gymnast ever to hail from Minnesota. At the end of his four-year reign at the University of Minnesota, he shattered most every record and took no prisoners along the way. The four-time Big Ten athlete of the year is a five-time NCAA champion, 10-time conference champion, and 15-time All-American. He won three NCAA titles in the all-around competition, one on the parallel bars and another on the pommel horse. The first gymnast in Big Ten history to win four all-around championships, he is also a two-time All-Academic All-American.

In 1993, his senior year, he won the prestigious Nissen Award, presented to the nation's most outstanding senior gymnast based on athletic and academic achievement. A two-time Olympian, he competed in both the 1992 Summer Olympics in Barcelona, where he was a finalist in the all-around competition, and the 1996 games in Atlanta. Today John remains the nation's top-ranked men's gymnast. The 1993 graduate continues to train and compete internationally and is hopeful of earning a spot on the 2000 U.S. Olympic team.

Fred

Fred is the modern patriarch of men's gymnastic in Minnesota. For more than a quarter century, the head coach has been responsible for much of the success of the University of Minnesota men's gymnastics program. A former star at the University of Wisconsin, Fred won the school's Athlete of the Year Award. He earned his bachelor's degree in 1966 and his master's in 1970. At the 1968 Olympic Games in Mexico City, Fred was the second-highest scorer on the U.S. team. He also captained the 1967 Pan American team in Winnipeg, where he won gold medals in the all-around, horizontal bar and parallel bars.

During his coaching tenure over the past 26 years, the Gophers have won 11 Big Ten team titles. In addition, his teams have placed in the Top 10 in the nation a total of 16 times, finishing second, by a mere tenth of a point in 1990. He is a four-time Big Ten Coach of the Year, five-time Mideast Region Coach of the Year, and four-time United States Gymnastics Federation Coach of the Year. An assistant on the 1992 U.S. Olympic team, he coached the World Gymnastics Championship Team that participated in Dortmund, Germany in 1994.

In 1990, Roethlisberger was inducted into the U.S. Gymnastics Hall of Fame as a gymnast, coach, and contributor. Today he remains the head coach at the University of Minnesota while also serving as president of the Elite Coaches Association. Fred and his wife, Connie Foster, who is the women's athletic director at the University of Wisconsin-River Falls, have one son, Gus.

FORTUNE GORDIEN

Fortune Gordien was born in Minneapolis in 1922. He would go on to become arguably the state's premier track and field star.

He attended the University of Minnesota from 1942 to 1948, taking a two-year layoff for World War II. In 1948, he led the Gophers to their first-ever NCAA track and field championship, after the team had finished third the year before. That year the shot put and discus thrower won his third consecutive NCAA discus title. Gordien was a three-time Big Ten champion, six-time AAU national champion, and a three-time Olympian (1948, 1952, and 1956). He won a bronze medal in 1948 and added a silver in 1956.

In 1953, in Pasadena, California, he set a world record discus throw of 194 feet, six-inches that stood for more than a decade. In 1953, he was named to the Helms Hall of Fame. He retired from athletic competition in the early 1960s and later coached at the high school level. He died in 1990.

GOPHER WOMEN'S BASKETBALL STARS

Carol Ann Shudlick

Apple Valley's Carol Ann Shudlick is one of the greatest women's basketball player ever to hail from Minnesota. One of the most highly recruited prep stars in state history, luckily for us she opted to stay put at the University of Minnesota. By the time she finished her tenure in Gold Country, she owned eight school records and became the Gophers' all-time leading scorer with 2,097 points.

During her senior campaign in 1994, Shudlick became Minnesota's first-ever winner of the Wade Trophy, awarded to the nation's most outstanding senior basketball player. The three time all-academic Big Ten selection was also the first Gopher ever to be named as a first team Kodak All-American. To top it off she was named as the Big Ten's Player of the Year, the Sports Channel-Chicago Player of the Year, and the Chicago Tribune Silver Basketball Award winner. The Patty Berg Award honoree also received the Big Ten Medal of Honor Award and was also named to the every all-tournament team that she participated in that season.

After graduating with a journalism degree, Carol Ann played professional basketball overseas in Madrid, Spain. Currently she is playing for the Columbus franchise of the new American Basketball League and is still employed at the Missabe Group in Bloomington.

Laura Coenen

With 2,044 points, Laura Coenen was the all-time leading scorer among both men and women at the University of Minnesota. What's even more impressive is the fact she did it all while overcoming a thyroid problem that limited her to just 299 points during her junior season. Coenen still holds five Gopher single-game, season, or career records. She scored in double figures in 91 of 102 games and had 10 or more re-bounds in 53 games. She earned first team All-American honors in 1983 and 1985, and was also a District IV Kodak All-American. In 1983, as a sophomore, Laura was named the Big Ten MVP, and in 1985 she was named the Comeback Player of the Year by Women's Basketball News Service. She also was a Wade Trophy finalist as a senior. In 1986 the women's basketball program made her number 44 the first jersey ever to be officially retired. She was also inducted into the Minnesota Women's Athletics Hall of Fame in 1996. Upon graduation, Coenen played professionally in Germany. Then, wanting to try something different, she returned to the United States and competed on the gold medal winning U.S. handball team at the 1987 Pan Am Games and at the 1988 and 1996 Summer Olympics.

Linda Roberts

Linda Roberts was one of the best players ever to perform in Gold Country. She still holds 11 Gopher records, the most of any athlete to play for the Gophers. Linda, who played from 1977 to 1981, competed in 129 games during her career, starting 126 of them, the most of anyone in Gopher history. She also holds the career records for most free throws made (426) and most rebounds (1,413). In 1977-78, Roberts pulled down a team record 387 rebounds and also attempted a team record 254 free throws that same year. The next season, Linda sank 21 of 25 free throw attempts against Rhode Island, both team records. Roberts was twice nominated for the coveted Wade Trophy, was a three-time recipient of the team's MVP award, and three times won the Minnesota Gopher Award. In 1996 Roberts was rewarded for all of her accomplishment when she was inducted into the Minnesota Women's Athletics Hall of Fame. Currently she works in the Women's Athletics Department at the University of Minnesota as an administrative assistant.

Deb Hunter

Many consider Deb Hunter to be the greatest all-around player in Gopher women's basketball history. Known for her quickness, Deb was always quick to steal the ball and unselfishly dish it to her teammates for the bucket. She owns nine Minnesota records including most career assists and steals. She also holds the Minnesota record for most assists in a game (15), most assists in a season (241), most steals in a game (12), and most steals in a season (139). She holds the Minnesota records for best field goal percent-age in a season (.600), best career field goal percentage (.519), and best career free throw percentage (.829). The guard could also shoot the ball with great accuracy, as evidenced by her career-high 34 point outburst against Purdue in 1983. In 1983, the two-time team MVP received first-team All-Big Ten honors. In 1982 she received honorable mention All-American honors, and in 1983 she was named as a Kodak Region IV selection. Currently she owns a private business in Austin, Texas.

CINDY NELSON

Cindy Nelson grew up in Lutsen, Minnesota's premier skiing community. After a brilliant career on the slopes, she has long been considered to be the greatest skier ever to hail from Minnesota. In 1971, at the age of 15, she made her first U.S World Cup team. That would be the start of an incredible string of 15-year string of consecutive teams that she would be a member of. At only 17, she was selected as a member of the 1972 Olympic team in Sapporo, Japan. However, due to a dislocated hip, she was unable to participate. She remained determined and went on to win a bronze medal in the downhill competition at the 1976 Winter Olympics in Innsbruck, Austria, in 1976. There, she also served as the U.S. team's flag carrier during the opening ceremonies. She once again skied in the 1980 games in Lake Placid, New York, though she did not place. Amazingly, at the age of 28, she gave it one last hurrah and made the 1984 Olympic team in Sarajevo, but an injured right knee kept her out of the downhill competition.

Called the "Old American" by her European counterparts, Cindy was a member of the U.S. Ski Team from 1971 to 1985. She remains the only woman to ski on four U.S. Olympic teams. One of the most decorated skiers in U.S. history, she has won nine World Cup races and skied for the International Skiing Federation world championship team in 1974, 1978, 1982 and 1985. Among her numerous victories are two World Championship medals, including a silver in the combined at the 1980 Lake Placid Games and silver in the downhill at the 1982 World Championships. Her World Cup medals include a bronze in the combined in 1976, a silver in the downhill in 1979, and a silver in the giant slalom in 1983. Upon her retirement from the sport in 1985, she continued to contribute as the director of skiing for Vail Associates in Vail, Colorado.

CHUCK FOREMAN
The Vikings Go to the Super Bowl

The Vikings rebounded from a less-than-stellar 1972 season by finishing with 12 wins and only two losses in 1973 and eventually advanced to their second Super Bowl.

Led by scrambling Francis Tarkenton and by Rookie of the Year Chuck Foreman, the Vikings won nine straight to start the 1973 season. Minnesota sailed through the playoffs, beating Washington, 27-20, and then Dallas, 27-10, in the NFC Championship game. Tarkenton hooked up with John Gilliam on a 54-yard bomb in the championship game, stunning the Cowboys on their own turf. In their second Super Bowl appearance, the Vikings took on the mighty defending world champion Miami Dolphins on January 13, 1974, at Rice Stadium in Houston.

Much of the pre-game excitement and controversy the week before centered around the Vikings miserable practice facilities at Delmar Field in Houston. Birds had moved in, building a nest in the shower room, where most of the nozzles wouldn't work. The locker room had no lockers, just rusty nails on the wall.

"This is shabby treatment. This is the Super Bowl, not

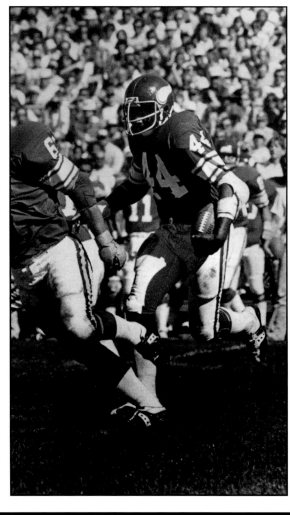

some pickup game," head coach Bud Grant told reporters at a press conferences. "The NFL sets up the practice facilities, and they had a year to do it right. Go look for yourselves, we don't have any lockers. Our seven coaches have to share one table for spreading out our clothes. These facilities definitely give the Dolphins the advantage." The defending Super Bowl Champion Dolphins, on the other hand, were working out at the Houston Oilers' plush practice facilities. Nonetheless, NFL commissioner Pete Rozelle fined Grant for his remarks.

By the early 1970s, the National Football League was a very powerful marketing machine, and their Super Bowl was the culmination of the 1973 season's events. Some Vikings, including Purple People Eater Gary Larson, found the whole Super Bowl hyperbole to be a bit much. In a pregame press conference, he remarked:

"I hope you don't think I'm a wise guy when I add that we've sweated a long time for this opportunity, and a whole bunch of people will be watching on TV. But there are 800 million Chinese who don't give a good god-damn about what happens in Houston this Sunday afternoon."

Maybe Gary was on to something, but all those Americans who did care about the game saw nothing more than a good old fashioned butt-kicking, as the Dolphins thrashed the Vikes and became the second team in NFL history to win back-to-back Super Bowls.

On paper, the game seemed to be a mismatch from the opening kick-off. You had the 23rd ranked Vikings run defense up against a relentless Miami ground attack. Miami wasted little time in exploiting Minnesota's weaknesses. Before the Vikings could manage a first down, the fish were up by the score of 14-0.

Following two time-consuming 62 and 56 yard drives, Miami fullback Larry Csonka plowed in first on a five-yard run, followed by a Jim Kiick one-yarder. Garo Yepremian added a 28-yard field goal to make it 17-0 at the half. In the third quarter, Csonka scored on a two-yard plunge to make it an uncatchable 24-0. Sir Francis kept it interesting, scoring on a four-yard run in the fourth, but that was all the Purple could do on that day, losing 24-7.

The 71,882 fans in attendance that day watched the Dolphin Csonka set a Super Bowl record by rushing for 145 yards. Scoring two touchdowns, he was awarded the MVP. Dolphins' quarterback Bob Griese had to throw only seven passes that day, completing six. Tarkenton, meanwhile, had put the ball in the air 28 times. He completed 18 of

them, then a Super Bowl record later tied by Ron Jaworski.

Foreman's reaction
"I don't have many good memories of that Super Bowl game against Miami," said Foreman. "There's not much to say except that they beat us on both ends of the ball. Of all the Super Bowls I've played in, that was the only one that I could justify losing in my mind. The Miami Dolphins had more talent and a better unit than we had. Personally, it was an incredibly exciting time for me being Rookie of the Year and playing in my first Super Bowl and all. Miami was the only team that I have ever played against that I could honestly say that they were better than us. It was just a tough loss after coming off the great season that we had."

From the Hurricanes to the Vikings
Chuck Foreman was raised in Frederick, Md., just outside Washington D.C. He played football, basketball, and baseball when he was growing up. Originally recruited as a defensive tackle, he attended the University of Miami in Florida. He made the switch to running back and broke all the freshman rushing records at the school.

After his final season with the Hurricanes, he went on to win the Senior Bowl MVP award. He remembered seeing Bud Grant on the sidelines scouting him at the Senior Bowl. The Vikings drafted the converted tackle in the first round of 1973. The transition to the pros was smooth for Foreman, winning the Rookie of the Year award in his first year, while rushing for 801 yards, catching 37 passes, and scoring four touchdowns.

Foreman was quoted in the Vikings book "The First Fifteen Years," as describing his unique running style: "I am sometimes surprised when I look at film of myself," said Foreman. "I just do what's natural out there and live by instinct. It's like when you're riding your bicycle and all of a sudden, a mad dog starts chasing you. There's a little bit of fear in your heart, and you've got to get away. I look at running as an art."

In 1975, Chuck set a new NFL record by hauling down 73 pass receptions. At the time, it was the most ever by a running back. He led the league in receiving in that year and became the NFC's leading point scorer. He also led the Vikings in rushing, receiving, and scoring.

Chuck had his best rushing year ever in 1976, racking up 1,155 yards, including a 200-yard game against the Philadelphia Eagles. Then, in 1978, Foreman, the hub of the Vikings offense for five seasons, suffered a knee injury which would ultimately lead to the premature end of an incredible career. He gained a career low 749 yards in 1978, becoming a backup to Ted Brown in 1979. Chuck was traded to New England in 1980, where he played one more season before finishing his career.

"Forty-Fourman"

Without a doubt, Chuck Foreman was the greatest running back in Vikings history. There hasn't been a dominant, explosive back since him to wear the purple. A brilliant passcatcher out of the backfield, his patented spin moves were what set him apart. From 1973 through 1979, Chuck set team records for yards rushing (5,879) and yards combined rushing and receiving (8,936). He led the Vikings in rushing for six consecutive seasons.

During that time he was considered to be one of the two or three elite running backs in the entire National Football League. With his trademark 360 degree spins and never-say-die attitude on the field, he was awesome. He could literally invent new moves on the fly, and create openings for himself to fit through. His offensive linemen appreciated him because he fought for every extra inch and always seemed to turn a sure-loss into some kind of gain. When he hit the open field, he could see and anticipate the corner backs' every move. With his high knee lifts and explosive power, he could create opportunities for himself that other backs simply couldn't. He was the Purple's finest.

A leader by example

One time, before Super Bowl XI, against the Raiders, Chuck asked the team captains for their permission to address the team. In what later become known simply as "The Talk," A passionate orator, Chuck let it all hang out in an attempt to get his teammates fired up for the big game. He made it clear that the old guard was getting past their prime and that this might be their last time at the big show. He said that everytime the Vikings got to the Super Bowl, they were calm and relaxed. He wanted them to show some emotion, scream, jump and get into it. "Let's go crazy. Let's get wild. Let's have fun. Let it hang out all the way from here to Pasadena." This was a radical move at the time, because players simply didn't say that kind of thing on a Bud Grant team. Players dared not even spike a ball in his presence, let alone "go crazy." But, that was the kind of guy Chuck was, intense, emotional and passionate.

Who was your hero when you were growing up?

"My father Francis was my hero. He was a great athlete."

What was it like to play in three Super Bowls?

"The games themselves were incredible to play in, but they weren't like they are today. Now they're like the greatest event in the history of the world. When you're standing out on that field at a Super Bowl game, you really realize just what you've accomplished. I was fortunate enough to be in three of those games. It was a great experience in my life, but certainly there was disappointment too, because, of course, we didn't win any of them."

What was your most memorable game as a Viking?

"I remember playing one against the Buffalo Bills when I scored four touchdowns to break a record, and I could have scored more had I not been hit in the eye with a snowball. This forced me to sit out the entire fourth quarter. I will always remember that game because I wound up losing the triple crown title [the NFL's rushing, receiving & scoring leader] by six measly rushing yards. I was really disappointed about

that."

On the fans in Minnesota:

"When I played, the fans were really a part of the success of the team, simply because we were accessible. You know, we went out there in that cold weather, and they would stay out there with us for hours. That was a big reason why our teams were so close to each other back then. There are a lot of great people here in Minnesota, and that's not to say there isn't racism or anything like that, because there is, but I'm saying overall, of all the places I've been, Minnesota is second to none."

What did it mean for you to be a Viking?

"I was always a big fan of the Purple People Eaters. I had to pinch myself when I was drafted by Minnesota. But before I came up here to join the Vikings, I actually did a lot of research on the NFL team and on the players. I wanted to know who played here and where they were from. I consider it to be a privilege to have been able to perform here."

Vikings tombstone:

"I would like to be remembered as a person that loved the game and played it 100 percent on every down. I respected the game as well as the people that I played with and against."

Was it tough for you to join the Patriots?

"It's just like what they do with thoroughbreds -- when they can't run anymore, they put them out to pasture. I really think I could have played a couple more years. But, that's just the nature of the game, and you know that at some point in time it's going to happen to everybody. Depression kind of set in because you realize it's coming to the end. We all know it's coming, but I think I could've played a couple more years."

On his son Jay, star linebacker at the University of Nebraska:

"I'm very proud of him, he is a unique individual. He's got great ability and a great work ethic, and he's going to be a great professional football player. One of his trainers at Nebraska recently paid me the highest compliment that a parent can get, by telling me that my son was one of the most beautiful people that he'd ever had the pleasure of being associated with. Jay is just a great kid."

Where are they now?

Chuck lives in the Twin Cities area, and is still an avid Vikings fan. He owns a memorabilia business and works for Sound Advice with Sports, a company that creates training tools for sports.

Tributes

"I think that Chuck was one of the finest running backs in the history of the NFL. At the peak of his career, he was one of the most highly skilled running backs that ever played the game of football. He was a great player."
-- **Jim Marshall**

"His talent is still unrecognized. He was one the best running backs ever. Chuck was so good the Vikings didn't realize how good he was. He was a great player, but as great as he was, I don't think the Vikings ever used his greatness to its fullest extent."
-- **Carl Eller**

"It was too bad Chuck didn't play the game a little longer. He was the best back in the league for five years. Running backs take a lot of wear and tear, and it was unfortunate that he got hurt."
-- **Bud Grant**

"Chuck was the best all-around running back that I ever played with. He was an amazing all-around athlete. He could block, tackle, run, catch, and score. Chuck Foreman could do everything."
-- **Ahmad Rashad**

"Chuck was just a great running back. He had the speed, talent, the moves, and he always came to play."
-- **Alan Page**

HERB BROOKS
The Gophers Win the
NCAA Championship

In 1974, the Gophers made history. Led by their second-year coach, Herb Brooks, they went on to win the first ever NCAA hockey championship. After finishing sixth in the WCHA the season before, the Gophers came full circle that season, proving to the world that Minnesota was indeed, the hockey hot-bed of America.

After starting 0-4-1, the Gophers put together a nine-game winning streak which included series sweeps of North Dakota, Michigan State, and St. Louis. Minnesota went on to lose only two of its final 16 home games at Williams Arena. They finished with a 14-9-5 record, good enough for second place in the WCHA, behind Michigan Tech.

The Gophers went on to beat two very tough Michigan and Denver teams in the WCHA playoffs, and suddenly they had found themselves on their way to Boston, where they faced the top-ranked, hometown Terriers of Boston University in the NCAA Finals. The Cinderella Gophers felt right at home in the Boston Garden, as they proceeded to knock off BU in a nail-biter, 5-4, to make it to the finals. There they faced their old WCHA nemesis, Michigan Tech, for the title.

The Gophers went back and forth with the Huskies throughout the first period, until John Sheridan scored late to give the maroon and gold a one-goal lead. John Perpich then beat the Tech goaltender to make the score two-zip in the second. The Huskies came back though, scoring at 3:24 of the same period, to get within one. It remained that way until the third, when John Harris and then Pat Phippen both scored 12 minutes apart to put the Gophers up for good. The Huskies added another one with under a minute to go, but it was too little, too late. With an impressive 39 shots-on-goal, the Gophers held on to win the title by the final score of 4-2. Coach Brooks had hit the jackpot, and Minnesota had its first NCAA hockey crown.

Brooks had led the Gophers to a 22-12-6 overall record, becoming the first team in 25 years to win the title with a team comprised exclusively of American players. And, he did it with only two years' worth of talent that he had recruited. For his efforts, Brooks was named WCHA Coach of the Year.

Team captain Brad Shelstad, a product of Minneapolis Southwest, was chosen as the tournament's MVP and was also selected as an All-WCHA selection. Les Auge and Hibbing's Mike Polich were named to the All-Tournament team. That season, centers Polich and Harris led the team in scoring. Polich went on to a successful career in the NHL, while Harris has emerged as a star in another sport, golf, where he won the 1993 U.S. Amateur Golf Championship and is a perennial member of golf's Ryder Cup team.

The 1974 team will perhaps be remembered most for their hustle, desire, and work ethic, all reflections of Brooks' hard-driving motivational style of coaching.

Moving from last place in the WCHA to first could not have been accomplished without unique leaders. "My first year, our two captains, Billy Butters and Jimmy Gambucci, were tremendous leaders that just did a great job of getting the program returned to a good, solid footing," said Brooks. "It was tremendously gratifying getting the school's first championship coming from where we did. The players weren't in awe of anything, and they were extremely strong mentally, plus they could really compete. They played well on the road, they played against the odds and overcame a lot that season. That first title was very special to me."

An east sider
Herbert Paul Brooks was born in St. Paul on August 5, 1937. He came from a hockey-crazy family. His father was a well known amateur player in the 1920s, and his brother, David, played for the Gophers in the early 1960s and also on the 1964 U.S. Olympic team. As a boy growing up on St. Paul's

tough East Side, a training ground for many future Minnesota hockey stars, he was a typical hockey playing rink-rat. He went on to star at St. Paul Johnson High School from 1952-1955. As a senior, the forward led Johnson to a 26-1-2 record en route to winning the state championship. In the title game, Brooks scored two goals in the 3-1 victory over their Mill City rivals, Minneapolis Southwest.

"Winning the state championship, that represented your neighborhood," said Brooks. "I would have to say that it was my biggest thrill ever. It was just the guys in the neighborhood, and that was special." Herb also earned three varsity letters as a first baseman on the baseball team as well.

The kid could flat-out fly
"I had an interview with the Air Force Academy, because I really wanted to be a fighter pilot," said Brooks. "Unfortunately, because I was slightly color blind, I washed out of the Academy. I also had a scholarship at Michigan, but my dad encouraged me to walk on at the U of M and try to play for Mariucci, so that was the route I took."

At Minnesota, Brooks became known for his blinding speed. "He was one of the fastest, if not the fastest, player in college hockey in that era," said his coach, John Mariucci. Brooks would learn a lot from "Maroosh," saying that he had more to do with shaping his ideas in hockey than any other individual. Brooks wore a Golden Gopher sweater from 1957-59, scoring 45 points over his three-year career. He graduated from the U in 1961 with a B.A. in Psychology.

Dreams come true
The next phase of Brooks' life involved his lifelong dream, the Olympics. After graduation, he began to build a successful career in the insurance business, but never fully got away from the game that continued to dominate his life -- hockey. Herb tried out for the 1960 Olympic team which was played in Squaw Valley. He eluded every cut except the final one, when he was the last player to be released. "My father said that they must have cut the right guy, because they won the gold medal," Herb said.

Brooks then spent nearly a decade playing for either Olympic or National teams. From 1961 to 1970, there were two Olympic teams and five national teams in all, more than any player in the history of United States hockey. He captained the 1965, 1967, 1968, and 1970 teams. "The Olympics were always my goal," said Brooks. "Playing in 1964 and 1968 was really a big thrill, and all things considered, it was one of the biggest highlights of my career."

Fastest game on ice
Herb went into coaching at this point, becoming an assistant under head coach Glen Sonmor at the U. At the same time, he pioneered Junior Hockey in the state as the first coach of the Minnesota Junior Stars in the Minnesota/Ontario Junior-A League. But in December of 1971, Sonmor left the U of M to become

TIMELINE

Hamline's Steve Lindgren wins the Division III Shot Put National Championship	The Gopher hockey team beats Michigan Tech, 4-2, for the NCAA Championship	Little Falls, Minnesota aviator Charles Lindbergh dies at the age of 72. "Lucky Lindy" flew the Spirit of St. Louis on the first solo transatlantic flight from New York to Paris in a time of 33.5 hours.	Minneapolis native Virgil Johnson is enshrined into the U.S. Hockey Hall of Fame	The state's largest rainbow trout is caught by Knife River's Ottway Stuberud on the Knife River: 17 lbs., 6 oz.	The Vikings lose to the Pittsburgh Steelers in Super Bowl IX, 16-6. The purple's only score came in the fourth quarter when Matt Blair blocked a Bobby Walden punt and Terry Brown recovered it in the end zone.	Brainerd International Speedway is born. It is the largest multi-purpose motor sports facility in North America. The three-mile course is the state's largest race track and hosts a variety of venues including motorcycles, superbike, sportscar, go-kart, funny cars and drag racing.

70

the G.M. and coach of the Minnesota Fighting Saints, in the World Hockey Association. Ken Yackel, Sr., one of the Gopher's greatest all-around athletes, was brought in to finish the season as an interim coach. In 1972, U of M athletic director Paul Giel named Brooks as the new head hockey coach. Brooks, the youngest college hockey coach in the country, inherited a program at it's lowest point, coming off a last place finish just the season before. "If it wasn't for Paul Giel giving me a break and hiring me, I don't know what would've become of my career," said Brooks.

The chant "Herbee, Herbee" was an all too familiar sound throughout the tenure of the man who would become Minnesota's greatest hockey coach. Brooks instilled a new brand of pride and tradition that next season, starting with his newly designed jerseys which proudly featured the Minnesota "M" on the front.

Brooks promised he would bring, "exciting, dynamic people into the program," and he kept his word. In only seven years, he had built a dynasty at Minnesota. More importantly, he did it all with Minnesota kids.

With his extensive knowledge and experience in European hockey, Herb became an advocate of the Russian style of play and in particular, the coaching style of Anatoli Tarasov. He would instill this philosophy in motivating his own players. From 1972-1979, Brooks won the only national championships in University of Minnesota hockey history. There were three in all: 1973, 1976, and 1979. His record may never be equaled.

While at Minnesota, Brooks won 175 games, lost only 100, and tied 20 for a .636 winning percentage. Under his regime, there were five All-Americans: Les Auge, Mike Polich, Tim Harrer, Neal Broten, and Steve Ulseth. Twenty-three of his protégés went on to play in the NHL.

"We went to the finals four of my seven years there, and we made a great run of it," said Brooks. "I think I put a lot of pressure on the players, and I had a lot of expectations of them. I didn't give them an 'out,' and I think I was always able to find the kids who were really competitive. The common denominator of all the guys who played throughout my seven years was that they were really competitive, very hungry, very focused, and mentally tough -- to go along with whatever talent they had. I think that really carried us."

Do you believe in miracles?
The next chapter of Brooks' life is the one that made him a household name, the "Miracle on Ice." After coaching the U.S. National team in the World Games in Moscow, in 1979, Herb took over as coach of the fabled 1980 U.S. Olympic Hockey team. Brooks guided the squad to their incredible upset of the heavily-favored Soviet Union team, setting the stage for the U.S. win against Finland in the gold medal game. That victory was one of the most memorable moments in U.S. sports history.

The big time
After a brief coaching stint in Davos, Switzerland, Herb's coaching success continued with the NHL's New York Rangers, where he gained 100 victories quicker than any other coach before him and, as a result, was named NHL Coach of the Year in 1982.

His Broadway stint with the Rangers lasted until 1985.

The small time
In an amazing move, Brooks came home and accepted the head coaching position at St. Cloud State University in 1987. He was the school's savior, leading them to a third place finish in the national small-college tournament, and more importantly, moving them to NCAA Division One status. He stayed for only a year, but with his clout, got the school a beautiful new arena and really got the Huskies' program turned around. "I've never met Herb Brooks, but I feel like I owe him everything, he's done so much for St. Cloud Hockey, it's incredible," said Bret Hedican, former Husky and current NHL All-Star.

Seeing Stars
Next stop in the Brooks' hockey adventure was Bloomington, to coach the Minnesota North Stars. It was another homecoming of sorts, his taking over the reigns from Lorne Henning and becoming the first Minnesota native to coach the NHL team. The season, however, didn't go well for Brooks. Unable to overcome an enormous number of injuries, the Stars finished in the Norris Division cellar. Citing philosophical differences with management, Brooks resigned and was replaced by Pierre Page that next season.

Brooks took some well deserved time away from coaching for a few years to get into private business. Then, in 1991, he first took over the New Jersey Devils minor league team in Utica, and was later promoted to be the head coach of the NHL team in 1992.

Herbie the Great
One of the greatest college hockey coaches ever, Brooks was enshrined in the U.S. Hockey, U of M, and East Side Hockey halls of fame. Among his numerous awards and achievements, he was named AP and ABC "Sports Athlete of the Year." Herbie is a legend in the world of sports and is very much a hockey icon in the U.S. Whether he's competing in the business world, on the ice, or even on the diamond of a world championship fast-pitch softball team, he takes the same attitude and intensity to whatever he does, and that's why he's so successful. He is a true Minnesota treasure.

Who was your hero when you were growing up?
"Olympic athletes were my heroes."

What did it mean to be a Gopher?
"Really, there weren't many options for an American kid or a Minnesota kid in college hockey back then. It was really tough. I always thought it was the toughest time of any Gopher era because of the Canadian kids who were coming down, the competition, and lack of NCAA rules back then. With that, it was very important to play for the University of Minnesota. It's not like it is today where there's a lot more hockey schools, and American kids have more opportunities. Playing for the Gophers then, when there were few opportunities, was real special."

Was it an honor to coach the Gophers?
"When I started at the University of Minnesota it wasn't my real goal to become the coach there. My real passion was to coach an Olympic team, and I knew that I would have to do well at the University to become an Olympic coach, so that was what I was always shooting for. I really enjoyed my seven years coaching at Minnesota, because we had some very good teams and some very good guys. But, my ultimate goal and passion was to coach an Olympic team."

Brooks' top career achievements:
1) Winning the state high school hockey title
2) The 1980 Olympics
3) Going from worst to first with the Gophers
4) Being voted the Sporting News - NHL Coach of the Year (because the coaches voted)

Minnesota hockey tombstone?
"The name on the front of the sweater is more important than the name on the back. They always forget about individuals, but they'll always remember the teams. That has always been the cornerstone of my philosophy."

Where are they now?
Herb and his wife Pat presently live in Shoreview. They have a son and a daughter, Dan and Kelly. Herb continues to do motivational speaking on team building and is also a scout for the Pittsburgh Penguins.

FRAN TARKENTON
The Unforgettable "Hail Mary"

Francis Asbury Tarkenton was one of the greatest quarterbacks ever to play in the National Football League. His story is a fascinating one, but the most bizarre chapter occurred on December 28, 1975. That was the day that will forever be known as the day the Cowboys got away with the infamous "Hail Mary pass."

After two straight Super Bowl losses in 1973 and 1974, the Vikings felt that they finally had their best team in 1975. They outscored their opponents that year by the margin of 377-180 and finished the regular season with a 12-2 record. Determined to bring home the Super Bowl championship that year, the Vikes headed into the NFC Divisional Playoffs against the dreaded Dallas Cowboys.

Pearson pushed off

After a scoreless first quarter, something pivotal happened in the second quarter that would play an important role in the outcome of the game. Dallas felt that they were jobbed by the refs when Cowboy safety Cliff Harris, who was waiting to receive a Neil Clabo punt on his own four-yard-line, opted to let the ball sail into the end zone for a touchback. However, the ball took a crazy bounce and Vikings linebacker, Fred

McNeil jumped on it. Harris didn't know what was going on, but the officials claimed it touched his leg on the bounce, meaning that it was a live ball for anyone to claim. Dallas argued to no avail, and Chuck Foreman leaped over the goal line for a touchdown one minute later, making it 7-0. After a missed 45-yard field goal attempt by Fred Cox, Dallas came back to tie it up on a Doug Dennison seven-yard run. In the fourth quarter, after a Dallas field goal, Vikings running back Brent McClanahan scored on a one-yard plunge to make it 14-10 Minnesota.

With time running out, another controversial play occurred. As the Cowboys drove through midfield, Staubach hit wide receiver, Drew Pearson on a key fourth-down play at the sideline. Pearson caught the ball at the 50-yard-line and appeared to be out of bounds, but the officials claimed that Vikings cornerback Nate Wright pushed Pearson in mid-air and forced him out. The Vikings claimed it would have been impossible for Pearson to have landed in-bounds, but the referee stood firm, and the drive continued.

With only 24 seconds left in the ball game, one of the most controversial plays in the history of professional football unfolded. Dallas quarterback Roger Staubach called play which sent Pearson running toward the end zone to catch a pass. After a bobbled snap, Staubach heaved the ball towards Pearson, who was shoulder to shoulder with defender Wright in a foot-race down the sidelines. The ball, wobbling in the wind and slightly under-thrown, descended near the Minnesota five-yard-line. There, Pearson slowed down, adjusted and pushed off of Wright to gain the advantage for catching the ball. The ball came down and miraculously lodged in between Pearson's elbow and hip, and he simply stepped into the end zone to score the game winning points.

More than 47,000 fans in the old Met sat in silence, shock, and disbelief. Everyone thought that there would be a penalty called, and there was, only on Minnesota's Wright. The Vikings players went berserk and then, in what some zealots later called "justifiable homicide" a drunk lunatic heaved a whiskey bottle from the stands and decked official Armen Terzian square in the noggin. Foreman ran to the aid of the bleeding ref and pleaded with the fans to remain calm. It was an ugly ending to an ugly game. The Cowboys had used up a lifetime of good fortune on a single play to beat the Vikings in the bitter cold Bloomington air.

For Tarkenton, things got much, much worse. Shortly after the game Fran learned that his father, Dallas, had died of a heart attack while watching the game on television. December 28, 1975, was the worst day in Francis Tarkenton's life.

"The touchdown pass was a prayer that was answered," said Vikings coach Bud Grant "From our side of the field, there is no question that Pearson shoved Nate Wright. It was as clear as day and night. He (Pearson) had nothing to lose. If they called a penalty on him, what had he lost? They would just line up and try another long pass. It was one chance in a hundred that he would get away with it, but it was the only chance he had."

"I had a clear view," said Tarkenton. "The man pushed his arm down and pushed Nate down. It definitely should have been offensive pass interference."

"It was very obvious," said Ron Yary, "that the officials were going to do all they could to make sure we didn't win this game."

"We all just stood on the sideline and watched Drew Pearson push Nate down," recalled Foreman. "That was probably the greatest football team that I ever played on. We were the best team in the NFL that year bar none. It was the toughest loss I ever experienced, and it happened on a blown call."

"I just threw it," said Staubach, "and prayed. I'll admit that we were very lucky on that play. But on the other hand, that touchdown we gave the Vikings in the second quarter had to be some kind of a fluke. If you take away that touchdown by the Vikings and our so-called lucky catch, we still would have won by a field goal and I think we deserved to."

Tom Landry, Cowboy head coach: "I knew our only chance was to throw one long and hope for a miracle."

"It was a lucky catch," remembered Pearson, "but it was the most important catch of my career."

After Fran's 15th season of pro football, the 35-year-old was named the league's MVP. He also made all-pro and was named Offensive Player of the Year. For the season, Tark won his first passing title, completing 273 aerials, then the third highest single season total in NFL history. He also threw for 2,994 yards and hooked up for a club record 25 touchdowns. Joining Fran on the all-pro team were: running back Chuck Foreman, who rushed for 1,070 yards and caught a league-high 73 passes for 22 touchdowns; safety Paul Krause, who picked-off 10 passes (he become the NFL's career interception leader that next season with 81, which still stands today); defensive back Bobby Bryant; running back John Gilliam; tackles Alan Page and Ron Yary; guard Ed White; and linebacker Jeff Siemon.

The greatest

Tarkenton was born the son of a Georgia preacher on February 3, 1940, in Richmond, Va. Fran attended high school in Athens, Ga., and excelled in football and basketball. He went on to star as both an Academic All-American and All-American quarterback at the University of Georgia, where he graduated with a Business degree in 1961.

St. Olaf vaulter Charles Novak wins the Division III Pole Vaulting National Championship	St. Thomas track and field star Mark Dienhart wins the Division III Shot Put National Championship. Today Dr. Dienhart is the University of Minnesota's Men's Athletics Director.	Billy Herman, a Minneapolis Miller in 1948, is inducted into the Baseball Hall of Fame	Vikings tackle Ron Yary is named as the NFL's Outstanding Blocker of the Year	The Gopher hockey team loses to Michigan Tech, 6-1, in the NCAA Finals	Gopher defenseman Les Auge is named to the All-American hockey team	Gopher center Mike Polich is named to the All-American hockey team	St. Paul native Tony Conroy is enshrined into the U.S. Hockey Hall of Fame

Tarkenton was selected in the third round of the NFL draft by the expansion Vikings in 1961. Eager to show his stuff, Fran made quite a statement in the season opener. George Halas' mighty Chicago Bears came to town. They were the oldest, toughest, and most respected team in the NFL at the time. Coach Norman Van Brocklin started the veteran quarterback George Shaw, but benched him after five minutes to offer up his new rookie as a sacrificial lamb.

"Everything the NFL had to offer in the way of experience and power was opposing me just a few feet away, and here I was, a kid of 21, fresh out of college, being required to lead an untried team into this battle where we'd have to out-think and outfight the old masters," said Fran. After only a few minutes on the field, Tarkenton threw his first touchdown pass. He scrambled around the field, tiring out the Bears as he threw two more in the third and added number four in the fourth. He even ran one in himself as the upstart Vikings shocked the NFL by beating the big, bad Bears, 37-13, and pulling off one of the greatest upsets in team history.

In 1966, after five stormy seasons with Dutch Van Brocklin's conservative coaching style, Francis was traded to the New York Giants. The final straw came near the end of the 1966 season when Van Brocklin benched Tarkenton before the Atlanta game, apparently out of spite because the game was televised in his native Georgia. Fran demanded to be traded and Vikings general manager Jim Finks pulled the trigger on a deal that sent him to the New York Giants for two first-round picks. The Giants desperately needed a marquee player much like their cross-town rival Jets had in Joe Namath.

Five years later, in 1972, coach Grant engineered the deal that brought Fran back to Minnesota. From 1973-1978, he led the team to an amazing 62-22-2 record and three Super Bowls.

In 1978, after 18 incredible seasons in the NFL, 13 of which were with Minnesota, Tark retired. Here are some of his amazing NFL records and final stats: most passing attempts (6,467), most completions (3,686), most passing yards (47,003), and most touchdown passes (342). And, for 15 consecutive seasons, he threw for more than 2,000 yards. He is a member of both the college and pro football halls of fame. After 18 years, his records were only recently broken by Miami Dolphins quarterback Dan Marino.

Sir Francis rewrote the Vikings record books. Here are his stats with the purple: all-time leader in passing attempts (4,569); completions (2,635); yards (33,098); touchdown passes (239); and rating (80.2). More impressively, he rushed for 2,543 yards, averaging 5.6 yards per scramble en route to scoring 22 touchdowns. Eleven times he threw for more than 2,000 yards, and 76 times he threw for 200-plus yards in a game.

The scrambler
"Perhaps the best way I can sum up my scrambling activity, and also press home my deepest philosophies about fighting to win, is this way: I was talking to a writer one time, and he wondered why I scrambled. He said, 'I guess there's no sense standing back there and getting clobbered.' You know, I had never thought about that aspect of it, and I quickly corrected him by

saying that there was only one reason to scramble - to win a ball game. The only thing I think about on a football field is winning."

The Georgia Peach
Fran was an a-typical quarterback and is dogged determination to keep trying in the face of failure, made him a fan favorite. Even though he was only 6-feet tall and weighed a buck-eighty, he was the model of consistency and durability, having never missed a game because of an injury. Back in the 1970s, the Vikings "golden era," he was every Minnesota kid's hero. Because he tried as hard as he did, sacrificed as much as he did, and, at times, carried the team on his back, he will be regarded as the best ever to wear the purple.

Turning negatives into positives
"Setbacks can drive a person to despair," said Tarkenton, "or they can energize growth and business success. The losses I experienced in three Super Bowls, in front of the largest TV audiences of their day, fueled me to business success beyond my wildest dreams."

On winning and losing
"I know that success is based not just on winning, but also on adversity and the initiative that comes from falling on your face," said Fran. "The most successful people I know have made the most mistakes. The biggest winners are also the biggest losers."

Where are they now?
Fran and his wife Linda reside in the Atlanta area. They have four children and three grandchildren. After hosting TV's "That's Incredible," Fran became an incredibly successful businessman. In the past 20 years, he started and built 12 businesses. A highly sought after motivational speaker, Fran is also a board member of several major companies including Coca-Cola Enterprises and Sterling Software. Presently, Fran owns the Fran Tarkenton Small Business Network, Tarkenton NETwork, and Tarkenton Net Ventures. Of his business interests, Fran says "I'm a capitalist without apology." If you want to see Fran today, just flip on the tube anytime after midnight, you'll probably find him selling something.

Tributes

"Fran was the greatest quarterback who ever played the game. There's no question about that. Just look at his statistics. In addition to that, he could run with the ball!"
-- Bud Grant

"He was our quarterback -- the guy that made the offense go. He was very bright and he understood the game forwards and backwards. Many times during the game he would create new plays in the huddle. In my opinion, he was one of the best quarterbacks to ever play the game."
-- Chuck Foreman

"I personally liked Fran. He was labeled as being selfish, but that was one of the qualities that I admired and respected most about him. I think that Fran knew most of all what he needed and wanted. Not only do I

respect him, but I have a great admiration for him for that. In that same sense, what was good for Fran was also good for the Vikings, and that's where I differ from a lot of people. I think that Fran was good for the team, and I think that he cared about his teams. He was just a great Viking player. In some respects, Fran was bigger than the Vikings, but we eventually we caught up to him."
-- Carl Eller

"Fran knew how to use all of his people. He could drop the ball off to his backs when the receivers were covered, and he knew how to use his tight ends. He knew how to manipulate all of his people to accomplish the goal of winning. I think of him as a highly skilled, mechanical, technician. He was a great quarterback."
-- Jim Marshall

"Fran was a good quarterback. To be honest, my recollection of Fran was probably greater playing against him, than as a teammate. It was always a great challenge to get to him, and he made you work for everything you got against him."
-- Alan Page

"He was a really smart quarterback. With Fran and I, it was like we both had ESP. I could make up routes on the fly, and it was like the ball would be right there. Fran Tarkenton was simply the best there was."
-- Ahmad Rashad

AHMAD RASHAD
The Vikings Head Back to the Super Bowl

In 1976, the Minnesota Vikings were crowned National Football Conference Champions again as they put together another incredible year, compiling an 11-2-1 regular season record. After defeating the Redskins and then the Rams in the playoffs, the Vikings seemed to be a team of destiny, ready to finally remove that Super Bowl monkey that had been on their backs for so long.

On January 9, 1977, they met the Oakland Raiders in Super Bowl XI. Head coach Bud Grant said that he felt his team was as prepared for that Oakland game as they could have been for any game he had coached, and quarterback Fran Tarkenton said, "There's an obsession with this team to win this game." Led by their outstanding new receiver, Ahmad Rashad, Minnesotans thought for sure that this time they would bring home the Lombardi Trophy.

The Vikings, attempted to seek redemption from the Super Bowl gods under the scrutiny of an estimated 81 million television viewers along with the 103,438 fans at the Rose Bowl in Pasadena. Minnesota got the first break, when Fred McNeill blocked a Ray Guy punt, and the Vikings recovered at the Raider three-yard line. But the momentum shifted quickly when Willie Hall pounced on a Brent McClanahan fumble.

Led by quarterback Ken Stabler, who completed 12 of 19 passes for 180 yards, and running back Clarence Davis, who gained 137 yards rushing, the Raiders quickly drove the length of the field to set up an Errol Mann 24-yard field goal. Before halftime they added a one-yard touchdown pass from Stabler to Dave Casper as well as a one-yard Pete Banaszak touchdown run. They were dominating the Vikings, holding them to a mere 86 total yards of offense for the first half, compared to their own 288 yards.

In the second half, after another Mann field goal, Sir Francis finally put Minnesota on the board, connecting with his rookie of the year wide receiver Sammy White on an eight-yard touchdown pass. However, two Raider interceptions led to another 13 points for the silver and black. One set up a Banaszak two-yard touchdown run, and the other was a 75-yard Willie Brown pick-off return. Minnesota rallied to get to within 18 points when substitute quarterback Bobby Lee hit Stu Voigt on a 13-yarder. But it was way too little too late, as the Raiders went on to beat the Vikes by 32-14. Oakland amassed a Super Bowl-record 429 yards, while Fred Biletnikoff earned MVP honors.

Nine years after getting spanked by the Packers in Super Bowl II, 33-14, the Raiders had won football's biggest prize. But their victory would be obscured by the shadow of Minnesota's Super Bowl futility -- a record four losses in eight years. It would mark the last time that the Vikings would get back to the big game.

To add insult to injury, head coach Madden said that his team had played tougher games in the conference playoffs. Afterward, Tarkenton was quoted as saying: "What we're trying to do is run through all the American Football League clubs to see if there's one we can beat."

"I still don't have good feelings about it," said Rashad. "It was one of those things where I thought that we changed everything that we did well during the season to try to do something different for one game, and when it didn't work it was just too late. In retrospect, I guess when you lose a game you don't have many good memories about it. For me, I figured that I had joined a team that had gone to four Super Bowls, so I figured that we'd be back three or four more times. The next thing you know, your career is over. There's something to be said about losing. It teaches you things, and everybody's got to lose at some point. It keeps you going."

From Tacoma to Minnesota
Ahmad Rashad grew up in Tacoma, Wash., and attended the University of Oregon on a basketball and football scholarship. "I felt like I could make a living playing football, and that's why I ended up playing the game instead of basketball," said Rashad. Formerly known as Bobby Moore, he was drafted number one by the Cardinals in 1972. Ahmad was traded to the Bills two years later in exchange for quarterback Dennis Shaw. After missing his second season in Buffalo due to a preseason injury, he was acquired by Minnesota in a 1976 trade for "Bench-Warmer Bob" Lurtsema and a player to be named later.

One of the Greatest Ever to Wear the Purple
Rashad ranks sixth on the Vikings all-time receiving list with 400 career receptions and 5,489 yards receiving. He had 13 100-yard receiving games from 1976-1982, and from 1978-1981 he was named to the Pro-Bowl. Perhaps his best season with the Vikings was in 1979, when he caught 80 balls for nine touchdowns and had 1,156 yards receiving. He still holds the NFL record for the longest non-scoring pass reception, when he hooked up with Cardinal quarterback Jim Hart on a 98-yarder in 1972.

He is a genuinely nice person, extremely intelligent, has a great sense of humor, is well liked, and is well respected in the world of sports and sports journalism. A superstar in the world of television, he is married to Phylicia Rashad, formerly "Claire Huxtable" of the Bill Cosby television show and is pals with Michael Jordan.

"If you can always try to be the best possible person you can be," said Rashad, "that's the only thing you can ask of yourself. In terms of all the other stuff like being a star -- that's not about me, and that has nothing to do with me personally."

Who was your hero when you were growing up?
"My hero growing up was Jackie Robinson, but my special football idol was Willie Gallimore of the Chicago Bears. He was the reason I wore No. 28."

What did it mean for you to be a Viking?
"Minnesota will always be my home because that's where I had the chance to blossom as a player. I had the perfect coach in Bud Grant, the perfect quarterback in Fran Tarkenton, and it was just an ideal situation for me. It was the first time that I had gotten someplace where I felt like I had a kinship with the players and was a part of the team. Anytime you play a sport, you want people to respect your performance. I feel like my years in Minnesota were great, and I was on a real run there. I can't remember ever having too many bad games. I played some pretty good Sundays in Minnesota."

What are your feelings about the state?
"The love affair went both ways I felt. I love Minnesota. I really enjoyed playing there, and I enjoyed the people. It really felt good to actually feel that love from the people because very few athletes get

TIMELINE						
The Gopher Hockey team beats Michigan Tech 6-4 for the NCAA Championship	Gopher Wrestler Evan Johnson wins the 190 lb. National Championship	The St. John's Football team wins the Division III Football National Championship	Mankato State Wrestler Jack Eustice wins the Division II 134 lb. National Championship	Mankato State runner Peter Pratt wins the Division II Triple Jump National Championship	The Denver Dynamos professional soccer team is purchased by a Minneapolis group and are turned into the Minnesota Kicks. In their inaugural season in Minnesota, playing at the Met, they won the Western Division title, and made it all the way to the Soccer Bowl, where they ultimately lost to the Toronto Metros by the score of 3-0.	The Hibbing Curling Club wins the State, National and World Men's Curling Championship. *(The US has only four World titles to its credit, so Roberts' win is an rare achievement.)* *Bruce Roberts - Skip Joe Roberts - Third Gary Kleffman - Second Jerry Scott - Lead*

a chance to do that in their careers." One of Rashad's fondest memories was reading an article in the Minneapolis Star Tribune, where a columnist wrote that along with Hubert Humphrey, Ahmad Rashad was a Minnesota "sacred cow."

"That was one of my most proud moments in life," said Rashad. "I love it here. We will always have a home in Minnesota. We still maintain a summer place in Lakeville."

On his buddy Bill Murray
"Bill Murray is a dear friend of mine, and one time we were returning a rental car to the airport after a golf weekend in Minnesota together. I would always tell Bill that 'Hey, Minnesota, man, that's my state, this is my spot, these people watched me play football in the cold, and they love me here.' The rental car guy came over as Bill got out of the car and immediately said: 'Bill Murray! Oh man, you're the greatest, I love your films.'

Then he saw me get out of the car and, in mid-sentence, stopped his tribute to Bill and ran over to my side of the car where he very passionately said: 'You are the legend.' The car rental guy said it from the heart, and it gave me all the credibility I needed to one-up Bill. He left Bill like a bad habit and just came right over to me," said Rashad. "It totally crushed Bill because he was just basking in it. To this day, because of that, Bill calls me and leaves me messages on my voice mail referring to me as 'the legend.'" (Murray has a fondness for the Twin Cities region also. He currently is a part-owner of the St. Paul Saints baseball team in the independent Northern League.)

What was your most memorable game?
"The Hail Mary catch against the Browns because it was incredible." In 1980, on a cold December day in Cleveland, Ahmad was on the receiving end of one of the greatest plays in the history of Minnesota sports. Down 23-9 with only seven minutes left to play in the game, the Vikings rallied to score 19 unanswered points, highlighted by quarterback Tommy Kramer's 46-yard pass to a backpedaling Ahmad Rashad on the last play of the game. Minnesota won, 28-23, to cinch the Central Division title.

On his tag-team partner and 1976 Rookie of the Year, Sammy White
"Sammy is a great guy, and he was the perfect complimentary receiver. He was super, and we really got along well. We would do whatever we needed to do for each other to get open. We had no jealousies towards each other, and we respected each of our own abilities."

Do you still cheer for the Vikings?
"I am a Minnesota Viking. When I look back on my career, I remember only playing for the Vikings. I know I played for St. Louis and Buffalo, but they don't count."

When were you the happiest?
"When I got traded to the Vikings. That was one the happiest moments for me because I was going to a team that had been to three Super Bowls. Being a receiver and knowing that I was going to play with Fran Tarkenton, what else could you want?"

What was your last game like?
"When I quit football after my last game, I never even went and cleared out my locker. When I drove away from the facility that day, it was like 'Hey man that's it, I'm gone...' I had prepared for my exit out of football, and I left the game on my terms. I said 'I'm going to quit,' and that means a lot, paying dividends the rest of my life. Plus, I felt like when I left, I left the fans wanting more rather than less. I had been All-Pro the year before, and it wasn't like my game was down at that point where people thought it was time for me to hang it up.

It's sad because you see so many guys today that had unfulfilled athletic careers and just won't let go. I had a life outside of football and was eager to begin the next phase of my life. Football wasn't everything to me. During the season, I used to come home after games and play tennis. Years later, Bud put all my pads and everything in a box and sent it to me. I have no idea where all that stuff is today."

Vikings tombstone:
"He was great every Sunday. I thought I was very consistent, and that's what I'm most proud of for my career in Minnesota. I was consistently good every week, and I don't think that I went through many ups and downs and all that kind of stuff. At the end of every year, the coaches would put together a 'mistake reel' of film that charted every play throughout the season. When you came back for training camp, they would go over it with you. One year I wasn't on the reel at all. That was a real pride thing with me, and I wanted to be consistently good every week."

What was it like to propose to your wife on national TV?
"The on-air proposal was just something that I just decided to do the night before. Luckily it worked out pretty well!"

Where are they now?
Ahmad, his wife Phylicia, and their children currently reside in New York City and Connecticut. Rashad hosts and serves as managing editor of the NBA show "Inside Stuff," and also anchors the Sunday football

pregame show "NFL Live" for NBC.

Tributes

"He was the Baryshnikov of wide receivers. I remember watching him run patterns, and he was just like a gazelle -- smooth and fast. He was a great addition to the Vikings and played a very important role on our last Super Bowl team. He is somebody that I admire and respect. He is a great player and a great person."
-- **Chuck Foreman**

"He found a home in Minnesota. He was one of the finest receivers I ever coached. He and Sammy White were a great pair together." -- **Bud Grant**

"Ahmad was a great receiver and made a lot of amazing plays for us. He could catch anything thrown to him. He was unbelievable." -- **Jim Marshall**

"Ahmad was a strong personality. I think Ahmad, like both Alan Page and Fran Tarkenton, had a sense of what was best for him and what he needed to do outside and beyond football. Those are great qualities, and I think are part of a sense of survival. Some players have it and some don't. It's a unique characteristic and a very good quality. He was a great talent."
-- **Carl Eller**

"Ahmad had great hands, great speed, and a great ability to get open. He was a great wide receiver."
-- **Alan Page**

"He sent me a couple nice telegrams when I broke his records with the Vikings, and that was definitely very nice. He is very likable, receptive, and helpful. He is a person that I look up to on and off the field, not only as a great player, but also as a great broadcaster. I have always wanted to follow him not only in the Vikings record book, but also what he has done nationally, as far as being successful in the broadcast arena."
-- **Cris Carter**

ROD CAREW
The Incredible Year of Rod Carew

In 1977 the biggest story in sports was Rodney Cline Carew. After switching over from second base to play first base, Rod had the greatest season of his incredible 19-year big league career. He nearly became the first hitter since Ted Williams to break baseball's magic .400 mark. Carew appeared on the cover of *Sports Illustrated* with the Splendid Splinter himself during that season. Rod's face also appeared on the cover of *Time* magazine with the headline, "Baseball's Best Hitter." He batted over .400 for the first half of the season, and his final .388 average was good enough to earn him his sixth batting title, while rapping out 239 hits, the most in the majors since Bill Terry hit 254 nearly 50 years earlier. He also scored 128 runs, hit 14 homers, and stole 23 bases. He struck out only 55 times in 616 at-bats. He had 38 doubles, 16 triples, and drove in 100 runs. At season's end the Twins' No. 29 had won the MVP award and for the 11th straight year was selected for the All-Star team, this time with the biggest number of fan votes ever recorded. He also received the treasured Roberto Clemente Award for distinguished service by a ballplayer to his community.

The Twins had one of their better seasons in 1977 and

were in first place in the West as late as August 16. Carew was joined by teammates Glenn Adams, Lyman Bostock, and Larry Hisle, who all hit over .300. Dave Goltz also became the Twins' first 20-game winner since 1973. The Twins boasted a .282 team batting average, the best in the big leagues, but faltered toward the end and finished in fourth place.

On the right track
The son of a Canal tugboat worker, Rod came into the world in a unique way. On October 1, 1945, in Gatun, Panama, Olga Carew went into labor on a speeding train. As luck would have it, a physician, Dr. Rodney Cline, just happened to be on that same train along with nurse Margaret Allen. They delivered Olga's baby right there on the train. The baby was a boy. A grateful Olga named her son Rodney Cline Carew, after that doctor, and nurse Allen became Rod's godmother.

As a boy Rod played baseball, basketball, volleyball, and soccer. He once swam in the width of the Panama Canal. But his favorite sport was baseball. He listened to major league games on his radio and dreamt of going to the United States and becoming a big leaguer.

"He was quiet and alone as a child," his mother was quoted as saying in the book "Rod Carew," written by Marshall Burchard. "He was always walking around with a bat and ball in his hand." Because his family was poor, the bat was really a broomstick and the ball was made up of a wad of rags wound in tape. As a little leaguer, Rod found that he could play better than the kids who were much older than him. At 13, he played in a league with players four years older than him.

Moving to the Big Apple
One day, his godmother Margaret Allen wrote a letter to his mother from New York City. She encouraged them to pack-up and move to New York to pursue a better life. So, in 1962, at the age of 16, Rod, his mother, brother, and sisters, moved to Harlem where his mother supported the family by working in a factory.

Speaking little English, young Rod had trouble fitting in at school. He was wary of the many drug dealers and thugs operating in his neighborhood. Rod spent his afternoons working in a grocery store to help support his family and, in doing so, dearly missed his passion, baseball. Then his luck changed when he tried out for a weekend sandlot baseball team called the Cavaliers, who played in the shadows of Yankee Stadium in the Bronx.

Discovered
He played shortstop and second base for the Cavaliers where he hit consistently and with power. During the course of one season, he batted .600. Word of Carew's skill soon

reached Herb Stein, a New York City transit detective, who also scouted young talent for the Minnesota Twins. Stein watched Rod play in several games and was impressed. "He was spraying hits all over the place," said Stein. "He had a pair of wrists that just exploded." Stein told Hal Keller, head of the Twins' farm system, to come see Carew play. That day, Rod went 6-7 with two singles, three doubles, and a grand-slam home run.

When Minnesota came to town to play the Yankees, team officials invited Carew inside for a pre-game try-out. After easily putting two balls into the Yankee Stadium seats, Twins manager Sam Mele looked around nervously to see if any of the hometown team had seen Rod in action. Then the cautious Mele ordered, "Get that kid out of here before somebody else sees him!"

From the Bronx to Minnesota
A month later, in June of 1964, Rod signed his first big-league contract with the Twins. Minnesota agreed to pay him an immediate bonus of $5,000, a minor league salary of $500 a month, and a future bonus of $7,500 when (and if) he made the major league roster. Although other big league teams had started to show some interest in him, Rod was anxious to sign with the Twins. He took the $5,000, gave some money to his mother, bought some new clothes, and put the rest in the bank.

He spent two years in the Twins farm system. First it was Melbourne, Fla., in the Instructional League. Then Class AA in Orlando. After spending the winter in the Marine Corps Reserves, Rod went to his second spring training workout with the Twins in 1966. The Twins sent him back down, this time to a team in North Carolina.

Twins owner Calvin Griffith decided that the 21-year-old Carew was ready for the big time, and, at the start of the 1967 season, he put promptly Rod into the Twins starting lineup. By the end of that season, he would be named Rookie of the Year and be selected to the All-Star Team.

Lesser known Carew tid-bits
There were some oddities to Carew's brilliant baseball career. For example, he treated his bats with extreme tender love and care, putting them in a hot closet next to the clubhouse sauna to "bake out the bad wood." He also washed his bats in alcohol to clean off the sticky pine tar, because he "loved to use a clean bat." Like a lot of ballplayers, Rod chewed tobacco during games. He said that a big plug of chew would stretch his facial muscles so he could squint more, and as a result, see the ball better. He used to drink Coca-Cola almost non-stop, sometimes gulping down more than a dozen glassfuls per game. Sometimes. he would ride his bicycle from his home to the ball park, a distance of some 15 miles. He loved to chase balls for the pitchers during batting practice, and once, during a game, he even fined himself when he quit running after giving

TIMELINE										
	Carlton runner Dale Kramer wins the Division III 5,000M Run National Championship	Gopher Wrestler Pat Neu wins the 134 lb. National Championship	Sports writer and journalist extraordinaire Hallsey Hall dies at the age of 77	St. Thomas' Robert Grim wins the Division III Discuss Throw National Championship	The Gopher Baseball team wins the Big Ten title	The Minnesota Kicks win the Western Division title	Gopher guard Ray Williams is named to the All-American basketball team	The Gopher Football team loses to Maryland in the Hall of Fame Bowl, 17-7 in Birmingham, Alabama.	Gopher center Mychal Thompson is named to the All-American basketball team	Gopher pitcher Dan Morgan is named to the All-American baseball team

up on a foul ball that blew fair. An amazing bunter, he used to impress his teammates by putting a handkerchief at various spots throughout the infield and dropping bunts onto it.

A Twins legend
Afraid that he was going to lose Carew to free agency, the penurious Griffith traded him to the California Angels on February 3, 1979, for outfielder Ken Landreaux and some prospects. And so it went that Carew would finish his career in California some eight years later.

"To me it was a business deal, and I understood what Calvin was doing," said Carew. "I appreciated Calvin's talking to me and giving me the opportunity to go someplace else that would pay the salary that the other players were getting because he knew that he couldn't afford to do it. Instead of allowing me to become a free agent, he let me pick the team that I wanted to go to. I was sad to leave Minnesota but happy to have new opportunities with the Angels."

No true Twins fan will ever forget the graceful power of Rod's smooth hitting style. Nor will anyone be able to forget the wonderful summer of 1977, when he made his unforgettable run at .400 and won the MVP. Carew was a career .328 hitter in 19 big league seasons and won seven AL batting titles (second only to Ty Cobb and Honus Wagner). He hit .300 or better for 15 consecutive seasons and finished with 3,053 hits, scored 1,434 runs, belted 92 homers, knocked in 1,015 RBIs, and stole 353 bases. He was named to 18 consecutive All-Star teams. He was elected to the Baseball Hall of Fame on the first ballot on January 8, 1991. His number was retired by the Twins on July 19, 1987. Carew was the greatest pure hitter of his era, a true wizard with the bat.

Who was your hero when you were growing up?
"Jackie Robinson, because he was the first African American to play in the big leagues."

What did it mean for you to be a Twin?
"I enjoyed the Twin Cities, and I really enjoyed the people. I came there as a young kid, still learning a lot about playing the game. In the years that I was there I really matured as a person and as a baseball player. I appreciated the Twins organization, Mr. Griffith, and the way the fans there treated me and responded to me."

What was your most memorable game?
"One of the greatest things that happened to me was during a day game against the White Sox in 1977 when I went four-for-five and broke .400. During that game I received six standing ovations. Their response by standing up every time I got a base hit, showing me that they cared and appreciated what I was doing."

When were you the happiest?
"I think it was after my first two seasons with the Twins. I was a little bit of a hot-headed kid. I played for Billy Martin, and he taught me how to stay on an even keel and not get upset at every little thing or every person that made a remark or comment about me. I started mellowing out when I met my wife, got married, and started having children. I found that coming home from road trips or ball games or just a bad day, it didn't really matter, because my daughters didn't

care that I was Rod Carew, the baseball player. For them, it was just dad coming home."

Do you still have ties to Minnesota?
"Certainly. We still have a lot of friends there, and my wife has a lot of family there. When we die, we expect to be buried there. Minnesota to us is still home. We have a lot of fond memories there. The people are what is important. I will always remember the way that they embraced us, even after I went to the Angels and came back to Minnesota in their uniform. They still kept me as one of their own."

Twins tombstone:
"I came to Minneapolis and played the game hard, gave people enjoyment, and they responded by showering me with love and respect."

Where are they now?
Sir Rodney is currently the batting coach for the Angels. Rod, his wife Marilyn, and their children reside in the Anaheim area. He remains a national hero in the country of Panama.

Tributes

"We were roommates for 10 years. Between the two of us I would tell people that our room was hitting over .700, even though his average was always higher than mine. Rod was a remarkable ballplayer, a great person, and a good friend." **-- Tony Oliva**

"He was one of the finest hitters I ever saw and the best bunter ever. He used to come out early to the park and practice his bunting. He could drop that ball down the third base line and, with the speed he had, nobody could throw him out. He was just outstanding and just a great, great hitter." **-- Harmon Killebrew**

"I followed Rod Carew's career when I was growing up, and I thought he had the best pair of wrists of anybody I ever saw. The way he could wait and put the ball out to left field was incredible. He was a very gifted hitter who studied the game, knew how to take advantage of pitchers and their weaknesses, and had a remarkable, outstanding major league baseball career." **-- Paul Molitor**

"In California, we had as close a relationship as any player and manager ever had. He knew how much I respected him and I felt like he felt the same way about me. It was a great privilege for me to manage Rod Carew. Watching him almost bat .400 was a season of the greatest hitting that I ever saw, and I played with Ted Williams. Watching him operate with the bat that year was incredible." **-- Gene Mauch**

"He was such a talented hitter, and I really enjoyed watching him do what he could do. He was a real magician with the bat. I have a warm relationship with him to this day." **-- Jim Kaat**

"Rod was a terrific player. The single thing I was always in awe about with Rod was that I really felt that

he could get a hit every single time he was at bat. He was such a good hitter. I used to just sit and watch him. I couldn't believe there was this Hall of Famer playing next to me. To watch him perform with a bat was just incredible. In a way, I was envious of him because he was able to do what he did with the bat with such apparent ease." **-- Tom Kelly**

"He was one of the toughest outs to get. I would have to say that he would be in the top five of the all-time best hitters. Aside from Carl Yasztremski, he was my toughest out in all of baseball. I felt that every time that he wanted to get a hit off me, he could. It was scary that Rod was so good." **-- Jack Morris**

"I remember when I got my first hit, it was against the Angels, and Rod was playing first base. I stood on base and said to him: 'How ya doin' Mr. Carew? I just want to tell you that I've been a big fan of yours, and it's my pleasure to meet you, man, because you're awesome, and I'm a rookie so I'm gonna shut up now and be quiet!' 'Please call me Rod,' he said to me. 'I know you're a rookie, and I just want to tell you to just keep playing, keep enjoying yourself, and keep playing the game the way you know how. And, the most important thing you should know, is to learn how to play when you're hurt, and you'll be just fine.' I will always remember that. Rod Carew is the very best there is." **-- Kirby Puckett**

Former UMD Football player Dan Devine wins the national championship as head coach of the Notre Dame Football team	Halfback Bruce Smith, the U of M's only Heisman Trophy winner (1941), had his number 54 retired. The Faribault native led the Gophers to a national championship in his senior year. The triple threat, led Minnesota in rushing, passing and punting. He went on to play in the NFL with the Packers and Rams, and is a member of several football and coaching Hall of Fames.

THE 1980 U.S. OLYMPIC HOCKEY TEAM: "THE MIRACLE ON ICE"

The 1980 United States Olympic Hockey Team will forever remain etched in our memories as one of the greatest sporting events of all-time. There have been numerous books written solely about the historic event. It put the sport, which at the time was perceived by some as a "hobby," and by others as merely a regional game found primarily in the North and East, into the national spotlight. It is, in some way I'm sure, partially responsible for the fact that the National Hockey League now has franchises in Florida, Texas, California, Arizona, Tennessee, Georgia and North Carolina. I'm sure that when they have the all-time greatest sporting events of the century in a couple of years, this one will be up near the top. And, be honest, whenever you see that replay of the players throwing their sticks up into the crowd, piling on the goalie, and crying to the sounds of Al Michaels saying, "Do you believe in miracles?", as they upset the heavily favored Soviets in the medal round, do you get goose-bumps? Yeah, me too!

A dozen home-boys
The coach of that fabled squad, Herb Brooks, who had just finished leading his Golden Gophers to the National Championship in 1979, had the responsibility of selecting the 20 players to represent the United States. 12 were native Minnesotans. Nine of them were players whom Brooks had coached as Gophers, they were: Roseau's Neal Broten, Grand Rapids' Bill Baker, White Bear Lake's Steve Janaszak, Rochester's Eric Strobel, Duluth's Phil Verchota, Minneapolis' Mike Ramsey, Babbitt's Buzz Schneider, St. Paul's Rob McClanahan and Richfield's Steve Christoff. The three other Minnesotans on the fantasy team were: Warroad's Dave Christian, who played at North Dakota, and Virginia's John Harrington, and Eveleth's Mark Pavelich, both of whom played at Minnesota Duluth.

"Having played international hockey for so many years, it gives me an awfully warm feeling to be selected as head coach for the 1980 Olympics," Brooks said. "I'm extremely honored and humbled. To be picked when there are so many outstanding amateur hockey coaches in the nation, well, let's just say it's something I never really expected to happen."

In early September, the team began as challenging an exhibition schedule as had ever been organized for an American Olympic Team. Beginning with an initial European tour in early September, the team played a 61-game pre-Olympic schedule against foreign, college and professional teams. The team finished the exhibition season with a 42-16-3 record. The only let-downs during the pre-Olympic schedule were four losses to NHL teams and to the Canadian Olympic team in the late Fall. The highlight of this period was winning the Lake Placid Invitational international tournament.

Entering the Olympic games, the team was a decided underdog, an evaluation that seemed to be confirmed by a 10-3 defeat at the hands of the Soviets in the final exhibition game in New York City. Facing Sweden in the opening game of the Olympics, Bill Baker scored with 27 seconds remaining in the third period to gain a 2-2 tie. The goal acted as a catalyst for the young U.S. team, which then upset Czechoslovakia 7-3. The inevitable letdown occurred against the less-highly regarded opponents Norway, Romania, and West Germany -- but were victorious.

Do you believe in miracles?...Yes!
This set the stage for the unexpected showdown in the medal round with the perennially powerful Soviets. The result was an historic 4-3 American victory produced by Mike Eruzione's goal midway in the third period. The gold medal was won two days later when the miracle Americans scored three goals in the third period to defeat Finland 4-2. It was pandemonium in Lake Placid, as the team piled on their goalie, Jim Craig.

Many of the players were visibly moved by what they had done, as evidenced during the singing of the National Anthem, where the entire team gathered on the top podium. Still wringing wet with their jersey's on, goal-tender Jim Craig, with an American Flag draped around him, sang the Star-Spangled Banner. The country went crazy over their newly found sense of national pride. Sports Illustrated named the team, collectively as "Sportsmen of the Year," Life Magazine declared it as the "Sports Achievement of the Decade," and ABC Sports Announcer, Jim McCay, went on to call the amazing achievement, "The greatest upset in the history of sports."

Mark Johnson, son of ex-Gopher, "Badger-Bob" Johnson, led the team in scoring in both the exhibition schedule and the Olympic Games. The line of Schneider-Pavelich-Harrington, all products of Minnesota's Iron Range, led the team's four lines in scoring with 17 goals and 20 assists in the seven Olympic tournament games. Brilliant goaltending by Jim Craig, who played all seven contests, was a big factor in the victory, as was the stellar play of defensemen Dave Christian, Ken Morrow, Mike Ramsey, Neal Broten and Bill Baker.

Instant super-stardom
A grateful nation, depressed by the Iranian hostage crisis, hailed the team as heroes. A visit to the White House followed, as well as appearances in cities across the land. Covers of Wheaties boxes, magazine covers, awards, honors, speaking engagements and a whole lot of hoopla would follow for all the players. In the heart of the cold-war, beating the Russians was a very big deal in this Country. Of particular importance to hockey development in the U.S. was the fact that most of the team went on to have very successful NHL careers. In 1997, the last one retired, Neal Broten.

The icy miracle was achieved by enormous ambition coupled with great passing, checking, speed, and sound puck-control. Shrewdly, Brooks refused to play the typical dump-and-chase style of hockey that was so prevalent in American hockey. "I didn't want the team throwing the puck away with no reason," said Brooks. "That's stupid. It's the same as punting on first down. The style I wanted combined the deter-mined checking of the North American game and the best features of the European game."

In late February of 1980, everything changed for Herb Brooks. The Olympics success merely added to the American notion that he was some kind of hockey miracle man. He became an instant celebrity, and in the process lived out a life-long dream. "They were really mentally tough and goal-oriented," said Brooks. "They came from all different walks of life, many having competed against one-another, but they came together and grew to be a real close team. I pushed this team really hard, I mean I really pushed them! But they had the ability to answer the bell. Our style of play was probably different than anything in North America. We adopted more of a hybrid style of play - a bit of the Canadian school and a little bit of the European School. The players took to it like ducks to water, and they really had a lot of fun playing it. We were a fast, creative team that played extremely disciplined without the puck. Throughout the Olympics, they had a great resiliency about them. I mean they came from behind six or seven times to win. They just kept on moving and working and digging. I think we were as good a conditioned team as there was in the world, outside maybe the Soviet Union. We got hot and lucky at the right times, and it was just an incredible experience for all of us."

Herb Brooks on the 12 Minnesota kids:
"I was really aloof from that team and I stayed away from them. There were a lot of Minnesota kids and I didn't want to be accused of any sort of favoritism. Some one said that I treated all my players the same - I treated them all like dogs!"

Herb Brooks on the state of the Olympics today:
"To me the Olympics are not about 'Dream Teams,' it's more about dreamers. And, it's not about medals, but the pursuit of medals. The Olympics are not about being number one, it's about sacrificing and trying to be number one. That's why I am real disappointed with the Olympic movement today. The 'Dream Teams' for me are 'ho-hum', business as usual for pro-sports. I think it's killed the hopes and dreams and inspirations of many young people that have hopes of playing in the NBA or NHL. I know that times change and I understand all those things. But I've always felt that our country didn't have to prove that we were better than the vehicle of the Olympic team. That's why the Olympics were always really special to me."

HERE'S WHAT A FEW OF THOSE MINNESOTA OLYMPIANS HAD TO SAY:

"What can you say about that team, eh? It was awesome. I can remember like yesterday calling my dad from Colorado Springs to tell him that I made the team. We were both so excited, it was just a great time in my life. We couldn't have done it though without Jim Craig, he was awesome. It's amazing, everyone still wants to talk about that game even today, I can't believe it! Twelve Minnesota guys on there, and to play with your buddies like that, it was great. At the time, I was one of the younger players on the team and I looked up to most of those guys. It was an amazing experience."
                                                                                                                        -- Neal Broten

"It's hard to put into words, you have to watch the tape over and over and sort of absorb it all. I guess we realized that we were on to something big, but just didn't realize at the time that it was going to be that big. Now whenever the 1980 team gets together for charity appearances, we tease Mike Eruzione all the time. None of us can believe it, the guy scores one goal his whole life, and he's more famous and makes more money than all of us!"
                                                                                                                        -- Mike Ramsey

"You can't describe it, it was amazing. Now the teams are under a lot of pressure because of the press, corporate sponsorships and the media. Hell, we didn't have all that crap to worry about. We had a great system, and an even better coach. If we would have had some older guys like they had on the 1992 team, they would've slowed us down. We were in 'Herbie shape,' and that just wasn't our makeup."
                                                                                                                        -- Bill Baker

"We had so many great players on the team, the talent was just incredible. It was an exciting time for all of us, and a proud time to be in hockey. It was so much fun to be around so many quality players, and to be a part of that group of winners."
                                                                                                                        -- Steve Christoff

HERE ARE SOME MORE "HERBIE" TRIBUTES & STORIES FROM SOME OF HIS PLAYERS AND COLLEAGUES

"He expected a lot from you. He was a big motivator and I really appreciated the fact that he knew the game of hockey so well. He expected a lot from his players and he got a lot from his players. He really never intimidated me, but I will say that he scared me a few times! Overall he's really just a big pussycat!"   **-- Neal Broten**

"We've been through a lot together. What he's done for me, I couldn't quantify it. He made me into an All-American, taught me so much about life, discipline and how to win. He would try and make you hate him enough by beating your rear-end off day after day. As a result, all of us as teammates bonded together and became better friends with each other. We would go to the arena for practice and get our butts whipped every day of the week. It was hell, I can remember falling down those stairs after practice because my legs could no longer stand Herbie's boot-camp practices. Our big joke was that we would get out of shape on the weekends, because we had games instead of practices!"
                                                                                                                        -- Bill Baker

"Herbie, to me, was a tremendous influence. His willingness to work with each guy on an individual basis, and help us learn more was incredible. He always had a little tid-bit about your ability that you could improve on. He had a personal touch for each guy, and wanted us to give our best. Herbie's a great coach, and it was a great experience to coach against him in the NHL as well."
                                                                                                                        -- Paul Holmgren

"I was fortunate to have played under Herb. If we lost under Herb, he'd buy us a beer, and if we won we skated our pants off. He knew how to motivate us, and he was a very positive coach. He would always stand behind you no matter what."
                                                                                                                        -- Reed Larson

"Herb was tough on me. One time in practice I got hit in the mouth, and lost all my front teeth. As I was laying there in pain, Herb skated over and said 'Get up you little wimp!' I responded by saying 'F— You!' as I spit seven bloody teeth out of my mouth at him. But, he had a fabulous vision, and he understood the game. He knew how to motivate people differently. He knows what makes people tick, and knows what buttons to push to motivate them. He didn't use the same techniques on everybody. Consequently because of that, people may have resented him. But ultimately in the end, they respected him."
                                                                                                                        -- Tom Vannelli

"Everyone was intimidated by Herb. He used to call me a 17-year-old prima-donna! He would breathe down your neck, and he skated us until we dropped, having us do "Herbies" forever. (A "Herbie" was an intense skating drill with players skating wind-sprints, a lot!) He would try to break us, but it all paid off in the end." **-- Mike Ramsey**

"He was the reason I went there, he was a great coach. He was tough, but always fair. It was the best thing in my career to have him as my coach. It was hard to get used to skating that hard, but we were in great shape. We skated when we won, and we skated when we lost. I learned so much from him and am very grateful for all he's done for me. But, it wasn't without our moments..." "I never used to wear a mouth guard and one time in a game at Wisconsin, Mark Johnson, my future teammate on the Olympic team, told on me to the ref while we were in a face-off. So, the ref gave me a 10-minute penalty, and there were only 10 minutes left in the game. When we got back to Minneapolis, Herbie made us skate laps after practice with big-huge mouth guards. We skated for a half-hour with Herbie lecturing us on wearing mouth guards the entire time. The next game I had gotten a 'Pro-Form' mouth guard and was all set to play. I checked a guy in the boards, and he hit me in the mouth knocking out all my front teeth. I went to the bench, and pulled out my bloody mouth guard with all my teeth still in it. I said to Herb 'Look at your damn mouth guard you made me wear, Ass-Hole!' The first time I ever wear a mouth guard, I lose all of them. So, after the second period, I got stitched-up, and I went back out to play, of course, without a mouth guard. So, I was in front of the net and a guy came by and butt-ended me in the mouth, knocking out, this time, all my bottom teeth. I just said the hell with it and gave up after that. Herbie could only laugh!"
                                                                                                                        -- Steve Christoff

"Herbie's practices? We used to say that if Herbie did this to a dog, the humane society would throw him in jail! But it taught us to keep pushing each other as teammates, and to be in shape for that third period so we could win. He always played mind games. When I was being recruited, Herb wanted me to go to Canada for a year of Juniors, in return for a half-scholarship at the 'U.' So, I told him that even though I needed the full ride because my parents needed to save money for my other family members that wanted to go to college, I would accept the half-scholarship. Herbie looked at me, smiled, and said, 'I'm proud of you for making the decision to come here even on a half-ride. I had a full scholarship waiting for you the entire time, but I wanted to see how badly you wanted to be a Gopher.'"   **-- Don Micheletti**

"I played with Herbie and worked with him as well. Herbie was very creative and has an excellent hockey mind. He's constantly interested in trying to devise new ways to make his teams better. He's very intense, and when he coaches, he puts his entire soul into it."
                                                                                                                        -- Lou Nanne

"When it comes to creative practice and game tactical ideas, adjustments to gain the upper hand during a game, and the plotting and execution of psychological ploys that raise players to go above and beyond their own parameters, there isn't a coach on the face of the earth as good as Brooks. If you measure coaching by 'how they play the game,' Brooks is the best; if you measure coaching by the simple bottom line, how can you fight it? Brooks wins, whether it's the WCHA, the NCAA, the Olympics or the NHL."
                                                                                                                        -- John Gilbert, Star Tribune Sports Writer

"When he had to pick the 1980 Olympic team, I remember Herbie calling all the high schools of the potential Olympians to find out their records on grades, if they got into trouble, did drugs, and what kind of people they were. When I asked him why the hell he was doing that, he said that he wanted to know what kind of player he was going to have when it comes down to the last two minutes of a game. He said he wanted to know which kids he should have on the ice come clutch time. Well, look who was on the ice during the Russian game — Pavelich, Christian and Baker. He knew all three of them. He had a vision, and a style. He has the greatest hockey mind in the country, and he is a student of the game."
                                                                                                                        -- Dave Brooks (Herb's brother)

JANET KARVONEN
The New York Mills Girls High School
Basketball Dynasty

1978

Janet Karvonen was one of the greatest athletes to ever hail from Minnesota and is the modern matriarch of women's basketball in our state. Back in the late 1970s, she single-handedly put the tiny town of New York Mills on the map. In 1978, she led her Eagles to their second straight Class A title, confirming a true basketball dynasty over her four-year high school career.

After an unbelievable 22-1 regular season record, the defending champions from "the Mills" went on to beat the Perham Yellowjackets, 78-58, at the Sauk Centre gym to win the Region 6A title. In that game, Karvonen, then a sophomore, scored 51 points, pulled down 16 rebounds, and was totally unstoppable. Next, it was off to the Twin Cities and the State High School Tournament for the Eagles, where they took on the Fertile-Beltrami Falcons in the first round. Behind Janet's 31 points, New York Mills crushed Fertile-Beltrami, 80-33.

Next up were the Minnesota Lake Lakers, and the Eagles waltzed to a 59-40 victory behind Karvonen's 21 points. At 6:43 of the first period, she made history when she hit a soft 15-footer to pass Morton's Mary Beth Bidinger and take over the all-time girls scoring record with 1,474 points. She was averaging around 30-points per game and she was only 15-years-old! It was back to the finals for the Eagles, where they would meet the undefeated Redwood Falls Cardinals, who had won the title two years earlier.

The Cards jumped out to a 14-9 lead after the first period, only to see the Mills score 16 straight points to start the second quarter and gain a 33-20 halftime lead. "I knew we were going to come back," said Janet. "Everyone on the team was hitting really well. I think that's the best we've played all year, in the second and third quarters." Led by 6'1" center Jenny Miller, who grabbed 21 boards, the Rutten sisters, and all-state point guard Kim Salathe (who would go on to become the school's head coach), the Eagles increased their lead to 52-36 after three periods. The Cardinals trimmed the lead to nine at one point, but the Eagles were too tough down the stretch. They went on to win the game, 64-55, earning their second title in as many years.

New York Mills coach Peggy Zimmerman's team outrebounded their opponents 46-20, and she set up a zone defense that forced the Cards to shoot from long range. "We knew how to stop them," said Karvonen, "and we did." Jean Hopfenspirger led the Cards with 19 points while her sister Joan added 10. The 7,000-plus fans were in awe of "Janet the Great," as the 6'0" forward scored a game high 24-points and added 10 rebounds. The team also set a tournament record, scoring 203 points.

It was a special time for New York Mills during those four years. Just like in the movie "Hoosiers," Janet recalled how the town "emptied out at tournament time," with many of the local farmers driving more than three hours back home from St. Paul every night to milk their cows. It was a big experience for everyone, including the girls themselves, who made the most of their time in the Cities by "watching planes take off and land at the airport and going to Southdale."

The little apple
Janet grew up in New York Mills, a small Finnish community of 800 people near Wadena, approximately 180 miles northwest of the Twin Cities. She was taller than most of her classmates for as long as she can remember, standing 5'9" in the sixth grade. Janet started playing sports at a young age, but was extremely well-rounded. It was no wonder that she would excel at basketball and tennis, seeing as she had a tennis and basketball court in her back yard. But growing up she also was an accomplished pianist, played the saxophone in the school band, and rode Arabian horses raised by her father. Janet also helped out at her father's funeral home, and she worked at his furniture store, as well.

Janet loved to play basketball, and her father often took her to Milwaukee to see the NBA Bucks play. She enjoyed watching shooters like Oscar Robertson, Pistol Pete Maravich, and Larry Bird.

Janet started to take the game very seriously, attending summer camps and, with a lot of hard work, made the varsity basketball team in 1976 as an eighth grader. That same year, girls basketball finally got the respect it deserved in the state, when it was officially recognized by the Minnesota State High School League, and given a tournament format that featured two classes: AA and A. New York Mills would compete in the Class-A bracket, even though there were schools with much larger enrollments in the same class.

In 1977, as a freshman, Janet led the Eagles past Mayer Lutheran High School by one point in the title game to win the state championship. It was an amazing feat for the small town, but the Eagles didn't stop there. They won it all the next year against Redwood Falls and just kept on rolling. In 1979, New York Mills would three-peat as state champs, this time beating Albany, 61-52. Karvonen scored 98 points for the tournament, a new record. As a senior, the Eagles again went to the state tournament to defend their title, only this time it would not have the same outcome. In 1980, New York Mills was upset by Austin Pacelli in the semifinals, 55-43. Although they rebounded to beat East Chain, 59-54, for third place honors, it signified the end of one of Minnesota sports' greatest dynasties. Karvonen set the single season scoring record her senior year with 845 points, averaging nearly 33 points per game.

When it was all said and done, Janet had completely rewritten the recordbooks. She had scored 3,129 points over her high school career, the most ever scored by either boys or girls in the history of Minnesota basketball. Norm Grow of Foley had previously held the all-time career scoring record with 2,852 points, back in the 1950's. To top it all off, she had earned the honor of being her class valedictorian.

Along with being named to the all-state team for her fourth consecutive year, Karvonen was named to the Parade All-American first-team and was named as the United States High School Player of the Year. She even got to appear on the Good Morning America TV show as a guest with O.J. Simpson.

It all happened like a blur for Janet, but she handled her newly-found celebrity with class, never letting it go to her head. "You have to understand that when I was 14, reporters were asking me what I thought of the ERA and Rudy Perpich - and I'd only just stopped playing with my Barbie dolls! I grew up fast, because I became very mature for my age."

(Janet held the career girls' scoring record for 17 years, until this past year, when Roseau's Meagan Taylor scored 3,300 points. The boys' record was broken in 1991 by Chisholm's Joel McDonald, who put in 3,292 points over his career. To this day, they are the only

Carlton runner Dale Kramer wins the Division III 5,000M Run National Championship	St. Cloud State gymnast John Fjellanger wins the Division II Horizontal Bar National Championship	Hamline's Mark Severson wins the Division III Discuss Throw National Championship	The Minnesota Kicks win the Central Division title	Minneapolis native Hub Nelson is enshrined into the U.S. Hockey Hall of Fame	The state's largest Northern Pike is caught by Mattson's (IL) Robert Quigley on Disappointment Lake: 18 lbs., 14 oz.	Hamline's Mark Severson wins the Division III Shot Put National Championship	UMD defenseman Curt Giles is named to the All-American hockey team	Gopher Gymnast Tim LaFleur wins the Nissen Award, presented to the nations top gymnast

three players in state history that belong to the prestigious 3,000-point fraternity.)

After sifting through more than 150 college offers, Karvonen opted for perennial women's basketball powerhouse, Old Dominion University. The media was out in force at the Karvonen home for the big signing, and her mom even served cookies and Kool-Aid.

Old Dominion had just won back-to-back national championships under one of the greatest female basketball players of all-time, Nancy Lieberman (Klein), who had just graduated. Lieberman, who made the Olympic team when she was 16 years old, was also a two-time Wade Trophy winner -- women's college basketball's Heisman equivalent. The pressure was on, as some felt that Janet was pegged to be her heir-apparent. In 1981, Karvonen led the Lady Monarchs all the way to the NCAA division one women's finals.

After two years at Old Dominion, Janet decided that the college wasn't right for her, and she left the school and enroll at ODU's biggest rival, Louisiana Tech University. She said it was a very difficult decision for her to leave, but one she felt good about. "I left Old Dominion as a starter and had to start over at Tech," she said. "I had to sit out a year, and it took that long before many of the Tech players accepted me." She eventually cracked the starting lineup and once again led the school to the women's Final Four in 1984, this time only to lose to USC.

Karvonen developed a great rapport with her coach at Tech, Leon Barmore. "I had a lot of respect for him. He was a great role model and a positive influence in my life." Life wasn't always a picture postcard there for her though. "I remember a game against UCLA," she said. "There was this guard I just couldn't handle. She blew by me at every turn and finally my coach called a timeout. He screamed at me to keep an eye on her and later took me out of the game." The UCLA player turned out to be a pretty good athlete in her day, Jackie Joyner-Kersee.

Janet graduated with a B.A. in Journalism from Louisiana Tech University in 1985 and came home to Minnesota. For a while, she worked as a reporter at a Duluth television station, KDLH, and later worked in the legislature for Minnesota Commerce Commissioner Mike Hatch. All the time, Karvonen was doing some soul-searching and somehow wanted to combine her love of basketball with her newly-found love of public speaking.

"I felt on a gut level that there was a need for female motivational speakers," Janet said. "There were voids that could be filled."

So, in 1988, Karvonen went into business for herself as a public speaker and basketball-camp director -- ironic for someone who had dropped out of her college speech class because she was "scared to death" of public speaking. She established her own educational and sports-oriented company called, Janet Karvonen, Inc. She even established a joint-venture relationship with Reebok and began one of the most successful dual careers in the local sports scene.

As a national public speaker and leadership workshop director, Janet appears in school, corporate, and civic engagements focusing on areas of drug-free choices, self-esteem, and motivation. She also runs the largest girls basketball camps in the Upper Midwest, appropriately called the Janet Karvonen Basketball Camp. In addition, she has become a household name serving as a television analyst for state high school basketball tournaments as well as Women's Big Ten Basketball games.

"I want to be a friend to youth, a great mother, and someone who leads the way and opens doors for more young women for them to discover their worth," she said. "I want to help girls in their teens as they struggle with sense of self, with issues such as suicide, eating disorders, alcohol and drug abuse, and teen pregnancy. In my speaking, I am able to make a difference, and that's been rewarding."

Simply the greatest

Karvonen was inducted into the National High School Hall of Fame in 1987, the Minnesota Sports Hall of Fame in 1989, and the Minnesota High School Hall of Fame in 1996. Today, Janet is recognized as one of the all-time great female basketball players. She has spent the better part of her life playing and promoting the game of basketball and has a significant role in giving the fledgling girls' tournament credibility in Minnesota. From the French-braided naive teenager that Minnesota fell in love with, to the mega-powerful, successful businesswoman today, she is a wonderful role-model for all young girls. Because of that, she has become one of the state's most widely sought after speakers.

Who was your hero when you were growing up?

"Ann Meyers from UCLA and my older brother John. He taught me how to shoot a jump shot, and I think I was probably one of the first girls to shoot a jump shot in the state. He was one the one that I patterned my game and attitude after in basketball."

What did it mean for you to be a pioneer?

"At the time, I really didn't think about it; you just enjoy what's happening. Obviously, I brought a lot of positive attention to a very small and relatively-unknown Minnesota community which, prior to girls basketball, was famous for being the home of Lund boats. When I look back now it's really surprising how many people remember my high school days. It was real special not only for the Eagles, but for the community of New York Mills as well."

On teaching young girls today and making a difference: "My philosophy is that we're developing young women and young women's skills in life. We're not just limiting it to girls basketball. We want to them feel good about themselves and send them home feeling more confident, ready to take on new challenges and start applying themselves. Academics are really the foundation, but athletics enhance who you are."

Minnesota sports tombstone?

"As someone who brought girls sports to a new level in Minnesota and who helped people across the state gain a greater appreciation for girls' talents and the importance of opportunities for girls in sports. Also, people knew that I could play, I had a jump shot, I had skills, and I was worthy of being appreciated. Girls basketball isn't a joke anymore. In the early days, it was pretty rough going, and I think it will be the same way for girls hockey now. Girls hockey is a much slower game, and it takes time to appreciate it, but more and more people will like and appreciate the sport as time goes by."

On women's professional basketball today: "I think it's a really exciting time for women in basketball right now. Girls growing up now can be drafted into the professional ranks and can have something tangible to look forward to. I think it's great."

Where are they now? Janet is married to Dr. Alan Montgomery and they live in Arden Hills with their sons, David and Matthew. It's business as usual for her educational and sports-oriented company, Janet Karvonen, Inc., and she continues to serve as a commentator for the boys and girls state basketball tournament on KMSP-TV.

Tribute
"Janet truly knows what the pursuit of excellence is all about. Her personality which uniquely combines femininity and toughness makes her a hit with groups of all kinds. She's a true winner." **-- Bill Musselman**

Led by centerfielder Shelly Medernach, who still holds 12 school records including batting average, RBIs, and runs, the Gopher women's softball team finishes third at the College World Series. It is the highest national finish in department history.

Mychal Thompson becomes the first Gopher Basketball player ever to be chosen first overall in the NBA draft. The Portland Trailblazers selected the forward but later traded him to the L.A. Lakers where he won two World Championships. Thompson remains the Gophers' all-time leading rebounder and second leading scorer. His #43 was later retired at Williams Arena.

Fresh from leading his Roseau High School Rams to the semifinals of the state high school hockey tournament, Neal Broten, considered to be the best prep hockey player in the nation, made it official. He would become a University of Minnesota Golden Gopher.

Some were skeptical as to how the smalltown kid would do in big-time college hockey under the demanding U coach Herb Brooks. But it only took Neal less than one season to establish himself as one of the Gophers greatest hockey players ever.

In 1979, as a freshman, Broten easily exceeded everyone's expectations when he broke John Mayasich's 25-year-old school assist record when he dished out 50 helpers to his teammates. In the process, he led the Gophers past North Dakota en route to winning their third NCAA championship. By the way, Broten also scored the game winning goal in the title game.

1979 started out well for the maroon and gold. It was smooth sailing in the early going of the season as the Gophers found themselves ranked number one in the country. They hit a slump in January, losing five of six, but rebounded winning six of eight in February. The final series of the season featured a tough North Dakota team coming to town in what would prove to be a WCHA championship showdown. The Gophers took the opener 5-2, but the Sioux rallied to take the title, in one of the best series ever witnessed at Williams Arena.

In the playoffs, the Gophers went on to sweep both Michigan Tech and then the University of Minnesota at Duluth at home. They then knocked off Bowling Green, winners of the CCHA, earning a trip to Detroit and the NCAA tournament.

In the first game of the Final Four tournament, led by Eric Strobel's hat trick, Minnesota held on to beat New Hampshire 4-3. It was on to the finals, where they would meet their old nemesis, North Dakota. Minnesota got out to an early lead on goals by Steve Christoff, John Meredith, and captain Bill Baker, to make it 3-1 after the first. The Sioux rallied in the second, narrowing the gap to 3-2. Then early in the final period, Broten the freshman sensation from Roseau, scored on a fabulous, sliding chip shot in what would prove to be the game winner. UND added another goal late, but the incredible goaltending of Gopher senior netminder, Steve Janaszak, proved to be the difference as the Gophers held on to win, 4-3, and the right to be again called national champs. This was the last of Minnesota's NCAA hockey championships. The drought continues to this day.

With 35 saves, Janaszak, fittingly, was voted the tournament's MVP. Three other Gophers also made the all-tournament team including freshman defenseman Mike Ramsey and forwards Steve Christoff and Eric Strobel. Additional honors would cascade down to a couple of other future Gopher legends as well. Billy Baker, who scored a then single season record of 54 points by a defenseman, was selected as an All-American, and Broten was named WCHA Rookie of the Year. As a team, the Gophers rewrote the record books that season, as they scored an amazing 239 goals in 44 games, led by Steve Christoff and Don Micheletti who both tallied 36 goals each. They also set a new record for most wins in a season with 32.

"I remember playing at the old Olympia Arena in Detroit," said Broten. "Just being in there and thinking about Gordy Howe and all those old Red Wings teams that had played there was really neat. North Dakota was our biggest rival back then, and beating them in the finals was a great win for us. That year was great, and I have a lot of great memories of my teammates from that season, it was pretty special."

Sportsman of the Year
The next chapter of Neal's life story proved to be the one that may well have linked his name to the sport of hockey forever. That off-season, Neal was selected to be a member of the much-celebrated 1980 U.S. Olympic Hockey Team in Lake Placid that shocked the world. Neal would play center and finish as the teams' fourth-leading scorer.

Hobey Baker winner
After the Olympics, Neal could've easily turned pro, having been drafted by the Minnesota North Stars. Instead he returned to the U of M to be reunited with his two former linemates from Roseau, his brother Aaron, and his high school pal Butsy Erickson, who had recently transferred to the U from Cornell.

"I needed to work on the weights and get a little stronger before I started pro hockey," Broten said. "Besides, the North Stars had a lot of centers at the start of the year, and I didn't think my chances of breaking in right away would be so good. And, I thought it would be fun to play with Aaron and Butsy again." New Gopher coach Brad Buetow quickly assembled the three to make up one of the most feared scoring lines in all of college hockey. Neal thus became the only member of the gold medal team to come back to collegiate competition.

The trio led the Gophers to the NCAA Championship game for the second time in three years, in 1981, ultimately losing to Wisconsin, 6-3, in the finals, which were held in Duluth. Neal went on to earn All-America honors as well as being selected as the first-ever recipient of the Hobey Baker Memorial Award, which recognized the nation's top collegiate player.

"I felt terrible winning the Hobey Baker over my brother Aaron. He deserved it more than I did," said Neal. "I mean he had 106 points and had a lot better year than I did. Aaron had always been in my shadows growing up, and he had a great year. He deserved the award way more than I did, and I still feel bad about it to this day."

Lord Stanley's Cup
That season marked the end of Broten's collegiate career. But for Minnesota hockey fans it would only be the beginning. Neal left the U just in time to join the Cinderella North Stars as they were heading into the Stanley Cup playoffs. The Stars had even traded center Glen Sharpley, freeing up Neal's lucky no. 7 jersey. The Stars made it all they way to the finals that year, before losing to the New York Islanders in five games.

"Glen Sonmor was a great coach, and he just let us play the game," said Broten. "It all happened so fast, I had only played three games for the Stars' when we went to the Stanley Cup Finals. I was so wet behind the ears, I didn't really know what was going on. Things happened so fast and the next thing I knew I was playing with guys like Bobby Smith, Steve Payne, Al MacAdam, and Freddy Barrett. It was a great experience and I will always remember that first run at the Cup."

Concordia Moorhead's Dave Bergstrom wins the Division III High Jump National Championship	St. Cloud State gymnast John Fjellanger wins the Division II Horizontal Bar National Championship	Hamline's Mark Severson wins the Division III Discuss Throw National Championship	St. Thomas runner Paul King wins the Division III 3,000M Steeplechase National Championship	Mankato State Wrestler Scott Madigan wins the Division II 150 lb. National Championship	UM Morris Wrestler Tom Beyer wins the 190 lb. Division III National Championship	Twins' second baseman John Castino is named as the American League's Rookie of the Year	Willie Mays, a Minncapolis Miller in 1951, is inducted into the Baseball Hall of Fame	Gopher defenseman Bill Baker is named to the All-American hockey team	UMD defenseman Curt Giles is named to the All-American hockey team

For 11 seasons Broten dazzled the Minnesota faithful as a member of the North Stars. He led them to their only other Stanley Cup finals appearance in 1991, before losing to Mario Lemieux and the Pittsburgh Penguins. He became the first U.S.-born player to score 100 points in a season when he tallied 105 in 1986. A perennial all-star, Broten led the Stars in scoring from 1982-1986, and holds team records for games played (861), points (793) and assists (544).

When the North Stars moved to Dallas, Broten played two seasons in Texas before being traded to the New Jersey Devils during the 1994-95 season. There, Broten became the final piece in the Devils' Stanley Cup puzzle. He ignited New Jersey's offense by scoring seven goals, including four game-winners, while dishing out 12 assists during their playoff run to become the first Gopher player ever to have his named inscribed on Lord Stanley's Cup, something he twice flirted with as a Star but could never quite reach. "I can remember sitting there in the locker room with him after they won it," said Neal's father Newell. "He looked at me and said, 'Dad, can you believe it after all these years?'" For his NHL career he has over 1,000 points.

The pride of Roseau
Neal Broten was born on November 19, 1959. To understand Neal, you have to go back to his hometown just south of the Canadian border. Roseau is a town of only some 3,000 people, yet the city has three hockey arenas. Roseau has sent a team to the State High School Hockey Tournament an unprecedented 26 times, en route to winning five championships in 10 title games. The tiny community has one of the richest hockey traditions of anywhere in the country, thanks to the three Broten brothers: Neal, Aaron, and Paul. They all played for the Roseau Rams, the Gophers, and all had successful NHL careers.

For the Broten brothers, it started at sun-up, when their parents would awaken before six on frigid winter mornings and drive them to hockey practice. "When he was a pee-wee, he was scoring five, six, seven goals a game," said Gary Hokanson, Broten's coach at Roseau. "You could see then that he was going to be something special. He was a little guy who could handle the stick and put it in the net like nothing I'd ever seen."

"Roseau is such a great town, with so much hockey tradition," said Neal. "We used to always watch Hockey Night in Canada on TV, and basically all we did was go to school and play hockey. Mom used to make us grilled cheese sandwiches after school, and then it was off to the rink. High school hockey was the biggest thing to do up there. We'd pack all 3,000 people in that arena, and the whole town would root us on. With so many people involved in hockey up there, it was a really special place to grow up."

For the kid coach Brooks called "The best player I ever coached at the U of M," the circle is complete. Three trips to the high school tournament, a Gopher title, a Hobey Baker, an Olympic Gold medal, two Stanley Cup runs with his native Stars, and finally winning a Cup of his own with New Jersey. Broten lived out a hockey dream as only John Mariucci might have dared to imagine it. Known and loved by every hockey aficionado in the state, Neal will forever be the measur-

ing stick, the hockey player against which all others will be judged. From his laser-guided passes, to his amazing sense of improvisation and remarkable peripheral vision, he is Minnesota hockey.

Who was your hero when you were growing up?
"The entire Montreal Canadians team. There wasn't really any one person, but I just idolized that team."

What did it mean for you to be a Gopher?
"It was a lot of pride for me. I enjoyed growing up and playing against the guys that you looked up to in high school hockey. The best guys went on to become Gophers, so having a chance to play with them as teammates was really neat. Getting a chance to play for a guy like Herb Brooks and being around those great fans was just incredible."

What did it mean for you to be a North Star? "It meant a lot to be playing for the home state team. It was pretty special for me to have been able to have played with all those great players in front of all the great Minnesota fans."

Most memorable game:
(In 1990, on the weekend when Roseau won the state high school hockey tournament, the North Stars had a "Broten Brothers Day," at a game against the Rangers at the Met. Neal and Aaron were both playing for the Stars, and Paul was playing for the Rangers.) "It was great supporting the Rams, the town, and to see them win the championship like that was incredible."

On the Stars' move to Dallas:
"It was tough for me to take. A lot of people took it pretty rough, and it was a real big deal. I remember this strange feeling and thinking that this can't be happening to me. You didn't really think it was going to happen until it happened, and then you're moving and driving down to Texas."

On the "Minnesota Connection" in the NHL:
"There's definitely a special bond with the Minnesota guys in the NHL, it's sort of a fraternity. I mean look at the 'Minnesota Line' in Philly with Podein, Otto, and Klatt - there's a hidden connection there."

Gopher North Star tombstone:
"I just want to be remembered as an unselfish team player that thought of his teammates before himself."

Where are they now?
Neal retired from the Dallas Stars in 1997. He, his wife Sally, and their two daughters Brook and Lara, currently reside in River Falls Wis., where they have a 75-acre horse farm. Neal is looking forward to his first summer off since he can remember, and is going to focus on deer hunting and golf.

Tributes
"We were playing against a tremendous North Dakota team. I think they had 13 guys that turned pro that next year. Broten scored a dramatic goal, sliding on his stomach and hitting a chip-shot over the goalie. It was incredible. I remember speaking at a Blue Line Club meeting the year before and saying that we were going to win it all that next season. It leaked out in the press and went across the country, putting a lot of pressure on our team. I kind of wish I wouldn't have said it now. But I just felt real strong about that team. I put a lot of pressure on those kids and I really raised the bar. But, because of their mental toughness and talent, we won the championship. Neal was a great player and played a big part on that team." -- **Herb Brooks**

"Neal is one of the most appreciative, humble, modest, and successful guys I have ever known. He has done so much for the U program and has been as unselfish with his time as any player that we have ever had here. It's refreshing to see a guy like Neal, he knows where his roots are and he is just a delightfully appreciative, and great guy." -- **Doug Woog**

"When I think of Neal, I think of him as a great player and a great teammate. He got as much pleasure from the success of his teammates as he did from his own success." -- **Bobby Smith**

"Neal is just a unique individual and a fabulous talent. He had the greatest career in hockey of any Minnesota born player. He had great skills and played so well consistently. He was just a wonderful guy to have on the team." -- **Lou Nanne**

| The Kicks win the Central Division Conference title | UMD center Mark Pavelich is named to the All-American hockey team | St. Paul native Bob Dill is enshrined into the U.S. Hockey Hall of Fame | The state's largest walleye is caught by Hermantown's Leroy Chiovitte at Seagull River at Saganaga Lake: 17 lbs., 8oz. | Twins second baseman John Castino wins the American League's Rookie of the Years Award | Gopher Football legend, Bronko Nagurski's number 72 was officially retired. The "Bronk" has long been considered to be the greatest and toughest football player of all-time. An All-American at three positions: tackle, end and fullback, in the late 1920's, he also led the Chicago Bears to three titles. He is a member of the NFL and College Hall of Fames. The International Falls High School honored their native son by renaming their schools' teams after him, the Broncos. |

KEVIN McHALE
The Gophers Make a Run for the NIT Title

Kevin McHale is without question the greatest basketball player ever to hail from the state of Minnesota. With his patented fade-away jumper and silky smooth touch, he was simply unstoppable in the low post. Kevin's legacy was a unique form of basketball artistry. From the jump-hooks he so loved to dish out, to his backhand flip-shots, or even his baseline reverse lay-ins, McHale was a true artist and the basketball court was his canvas. In 1980, McHale, then a senior, led the Golden Gophers to their first ever NIT title game against the University of Virginia.

Gold Country was cautiously optimistic about their hoops team at the start of the 1980 season. After all, the Gophers were coming off an ugly eighth-place finish in the Big Ten. They were a young team, but they were led by 6'10" forward, Kevin McHale.

"Kevin is one of the premier big men in the nation," said coach Jim Dutcher at the beginning of the season. "He has the ability to score inside or outside. We feel he is one of the most complete players in the country. He can rebound, score, block shots, and run well." McHale, the team captain, had taken the young group under his wing the year before when he found himself starting alongside of four freshmen -- forward Trent Tucker, center Gary Holmes, and guards Mark Hall and Darryl Mitchell.

The Gophers started off their non-conference schedule by reeling off four straight wins before losing to both Tennessee and Florida State. After beating Kansas State, Minnesota won the Pillsbury Classic tournament. Then, they dropped their conference opener, 71-67, at Michigan but rebounded two nights later with an impressive 93-80 win over the defending Big Ten and NCAA champs from Michigan State. It was up and down for the young Gophers as they lost several close games on the road after that. Included were three tough overtime losses against the Illini, Buckeyes, and Boilermakers, as well as a 73-63 defeat at the hands of Iowa for their only home loss. The U went on to beat Indiana, 55-47, as well as Ohio State, 74-70, Purdue by 67-61, Illinois by 79-75 and Michigan, 68-67.

All in all, it was a good season for the Gophers and a great senior season for McHale. Minnesota finished the regular season with a 17-10 record, tied for fourth place in the Big Ten with Iowa at 10-8. Although they didn't make the NCAA Tournament, the Gophers did, however, get an invitation to the 43rd annual post-season National Invitational Tournament. In the first round, at Williams Arena, the Gophers rolled over Bowling Green, 64-50, followed by that with wins over Mississippi and Southwestern Louisiana. Next, it was off to the NIT's version of the Final Four at Madison Square Garden.

In the semifinals, the Gophers avenged their overtime loss to fellow Big Ten rival Illinois in a nail-biter, 65-63, and, in so doing, set the stage for the championship game against 7'4" Ralph Sampson and the Virginia Cavaliers. The Gophers jumped out to a 21-12 lead in the first 10 minutes of the game behind the strong play of McHale, Tucker, and Randy Breuer. But, behind Sampson, who had 15 points and 15 rebounds, the Cavs took the lead into halftime.

It was a back and forth affair for both squads throughout the second half. Then with 1:31 to play, Sampson sank two free throws to put Virginia ahead for good, 54-53. Now with 1:06 remaining in the game, McHale's pass to Breuer was intercepted. With only 33 seconds on the clock, Minnesota fouled Virginia's Terry Gates. Gates missed the one-on-one, but the Cavaliers came up with the rebound. Jeff Lamp, a Cavalier guard, was fouled and proceeded to sink both shots and go up by three. With 11 seconds left, McHale, in desperation, drove for a dunk on Sampson and was fouled. He made both shots to get the Gophers within one point, but Minnesota was forced to foul immediately. Unfortunately for the Gophers, it was Lamp again who would go to the line. Lamp made both free throws to ice a 58-55 win for Virginia.

"We just got too cautious," muttered coach Dutcher, whose squad finished the year with an impressive 21-11 record. "We didn't push the ball down the floor and look for any fast breaks. And we got so conscious of getting the ball inside that we didn't take the outside shots we had." Mitchell, who scored a game-high 18-points, and Breuer made the all-tournament team.

"I remember the game very well," said McHale who scored eight points in the game. "We got all the way to the NIT finals and, unfortunately, we didn't play particularly well that night. I was sad on a lot of levels, besides losing the game, it was my last game as a Gopher. I felt a lot of anxiety at that moment because there were some big changes about to come my way."

McHale, who led the team in scoring and rebounding for the second straight year, was named to the All-Big Ten team. He was also voted as the teams MVP. From 1976-1980, McHale had averaged 16.7 points and 10 rebounds per game. He remains the Gophers' fifth leading scorer of all-time with 1,704 points, their second leading rebounder with 950 boards, and holds the career record for blocked shots with 235.

In 1995, McHale was honored as the top player in Gopher Basketball history, as the school celebrated its' 110th anniversary in the sport. His No. 44 was officially retired up into the rafters of Williams Arena that same year, joining Lou Hudson, Jim Brewer, and teammate Mychal Thompson, with whom Kevin played with on the fabled 1977 Gopher team that finished 24-3.

Hibbing Blue Jacket
Kevin McHale was born December 19, 1957, in Hibbing, Minn. His father was an iron ore miner on the great Mesabi Iron Range and encouraged Kevin to participate in and enjoy all sports. He attended Green Haven Elementary in Hibbing, where he played hockey, but, at Lincoln Junior High School, Kevin decided to switch his skates for a pair of sneakers. "I vividly recall that one night after we got done playing outdoor hockey, I went into the warming shack, and I couldn't feel my feet at all," said McHale. "I said to my brother John, 'That's enough!' I knew it was a heckuva lot warmer inside a gymnasium."

It was on Hibbing's hardcourts that McHale found his true niche. In high school, he led the Hibbing Blue Jackets to the Minnesota Class AA State Basketball Tournament title game against Bloomington Jefferson, where they ultimately lost to the Jaguars and their star, Steve Lingenfelter.

"The Minnesota State High School Basketball Tournament was a great experience and about as fun as it gets in sports," said Kevin. "Every kid from the Range dreams of playing in the state tournament. And, when you make it, you're playing there with teammates you've known your entire life. The entire experience was such a good time for me."

McHale had a great prep career at Hibbing High School where he twice was named all-city, all-conference, and all-state. After his senior year, he was named Minnesota's "Mr. Basketball." He started to get noticed as a junior, and several recruiters came up to the Mesabi Iron Range to check him out. One cold winter day, a coach from a southern university flew to Duluth and then drove for two hours north to Hibbing. When the headhunter arrived, he was frozen and his rental car was frosted over. Kevin patiently explained to the recruiter just how to operate the heater in the rented car and indicated to him how important a car heater is during the long northern Minnesota winter. Said McHale of the fiasco: "Imagine anyone who would want to go through all that just to see a big old white kid play basketball in northern Minnesota."

He eventually was offered a full-ride scholarship at the University of Minnesota, and the rest is history. After his illustrious career in Gold Country, he was selected third overall in the first round of the NBA draft by the Boston Celtics. Before he joined the team in 1980, he played on two U.S. gold medal-winning Pan-Am teams in Puerto Rico, and then in Mexico.

"Kevin McHale is the sort of young man I really enjoy working with," said Bobby Knight, who coached one of the Pan-Am teams. "He plays the game the way I believe it should be played. He gives his all. He's coachable. He's a team player. And within that framework, he displays a lot of ability. Kevin is my all-time favorite as far as an opposing player goes."

Celtic pride
On that note Kevin headed east to join one of the greatest teams in all of sports, the Celtics. He would help make up one of the most formidable front-lines in the history of the game, alongside of Larry Bird and Robert Parrish. He made an impact his first season, leading the team to the NBA title, en route to making the All-Rookie team. He led Boston to two more championships in both 1984 and 1986, as well as five Eastern Conference titles and eight Atlantic Division crowns. He was given the NBA's Sixth-Man Award both in 1984 and 1985, and among his seven trips to the All-Star game. He was selected to the All-NBA First Team in 1987. He was also named to the NBA All-Defensive First Team in 1986, 1987, and 1988. Over his incredible 13-year career he scored 17,335 points, while averaging 17.9 points, 7.3 rebounds, and 1.7 assists per game. He ranks 10th all-time in the NBA in career field goal percentage with .554. He also shot a remarkable 79.8 percent from the free-throw line. Twice he led the league in field-goal percentage, and he remains the only player in NBA history to shoot over 60 percent from the field and 80 percent from the line in the same season when he did it in 1987. In 1993 Kevin quietly retired from the game. The next stop for Celtics' No. 32 will be Springfield, Massachusetts, and the Basketball Hall of Fame.

"The Celtics played the game, I thought, the way it should be played," said McHale after his retirement. "They were absolutely the best days of my life." Perhaps Boston Globe writer Bob Ryan put it best: "The long-armed wonder from Minnesota's Mesabi Iron Range won his way into the hearts of Beantowners with his lunch-bucket approach to the game and his uncanny ability to play Tonto to Larry Bird's Lone Ranger."

"He's the best post-up player since Kareem," said teammate Parrish. "And no forward could guard him. No one." Danny Ainge, McHale's former teammate laughingly called him "the black hole," because once you got a pass to him inside, the ball was not coming back out. "He just struck fear in the hearts of the defenders," he said. "During the height of his career he was easily the best power forward playing the game, and I'd rate him in the top three of all time," said Bob Cousy, former Celtics great. "Kevin was a great college player but I think he turned out to be a better pro player. As a low-post player he's the best I've ever seen," said Larry Bird.

Coming home
Kevin came home to his beloved Minnesota in 1993 and began working with the Minnesota Timberwolves. For two years he worked as the assistant G.M. and also served as a TV analyst on Wolves' games. In May of 1995, he took over the team, becoming their general manager as well as vice president of basketball operations. One of his first moves with the Wolves was selecting high-school phenom Kevin Garnett with the fifth-overall pick in the 1995 NBA Draft. He wasted little time in retooling the entire Wolves roster and soon made his presence felt. In 1997, the team made their first-ever playoff appearance under McHale's former U teammate, head coach Phil "Flip" Saunders.

McHale's legacy will include many things. Of them, and possibly the most prominent, will be his mastery and reputation as the most unstoppable NBA low-post scorer of his era. He will also be remembered as the state of Minnesota's most celebrated basketball player. However, he is only the second most famous Hibbingite, behind singer, songwriter, and Hibbing High School graduate Bob Dylan. McHale once joked that he should be named as center on the all-Hibbing native team that had the late Governor Rudy Perpich and late baseball great Roger Maris at the forwards and Dylan and Laker and Knick star Dick Garmaker at the guards.

Who was your hero when you were growing up?
"My father was the biggest influence in my life."

What did it mean for you to be a Gopher?
"This was a great time in my life. I had a ton of fun going to school at the U and met so many good people. I still have a lot of great friends from my years there. We had such a good time playing ball. At that time I didn't even think about a future in the NBA. I was just happy to have fun and get an education. It was the whole atmosphere at the U that I just loved."

Why did you come back?
"Minnesota has always been home for me, and I'm really glad to be back in the state. It's very rewarding to be a part of the Minnesota Timberwolves, but there are parts of my job that I enjoy and others that I don't enjoy at all. For one, I don't get to do enough of the things that I came home for in the first place, like hunting and fishing. This job seems to get in the way of a lot of that. But, it is exciting work, and I am optimistic about the team's outlook for the future."

Gopher tombstone:
"I never felt like I was anything special. I always thought it was a special treat for me just to be able to play the game of basketball. I worked hard, but I was blessed with a lot of physical ability and height. Overall, I just had fun. I just loved playing sports, and it was the best thing that I ever got involved in. I just flat-out loved to play. I got to meet so many people, made so many friends, and got to travel all over the world. It is a great adventure, like a dream come true."

Where are they now?
Kevin and his wife Lynn, who were high school sweethearts, live in North Oaks. They have five children, Kristyn, Michael, Joseph, Alexandra, and Thomas.

Tributes
"Man! He prided himself on blocking my shots! In one game alone, he blocked five of them. He would say: 'I told you to get that !&*#$@ out of here Willie!' And he was telling me about it every step of the way out there too. It was a sort of Minnesota initiation thing all the way because he knew me, watched me, and he just wanted to let me know that it was all in fun. He was just a great player and I have a lot of respect for him."
                                                    -- Willie Burton

Dollar Bay native Frank Kahler, founder of the Minneapolis Millers, is enshrined into the U.S. Hockey Hall of Fame

Legendary North Star goaltender, Gump Worsley is inducted into the NHL Hall of Fame. Famous for his refusal to wear a facemask, the Gumper asked rhetorically: "Would it have been fair not to give the fans the chance to see my beautiful face?"

New Prague's Les Bolstad, a legendary Minnesota golfer, and Gopher Golf coach from 1947-1976, is inducted into the Collegiate Golf Coaches Hall of Fame. As a player he won every state championship during his career. Les won the U.S. Public Links title in 1926 as well as two Big Ten titles. The U of M Golf Course was renamed after him in his honor.

Gopher center Clayton Tonnemaker is inducted into the College Football Hall of Fame

Minneapolis' Gary Hoakanen wins the John Beargrease Sled Dog Race

Two hockey playing brothers from Bloomington, Brennan and Scott Olson, invent an off-season training tool that features a straight-lined roller skate. They name their invention - Rollerblades, and today the global sporting goods company based in Minnetonka generates hundreds of millions of dollars in annual revenues, and owns more than a 50% market share in the in-line skating industry.

1981

BOBBY SMITH
The Cinderella Stars Make a Run at the Cup

The 1981, the NHL North Stars gave Minnesota its' first taste of Lord Stanley's coveted Cup. Big-time hockey had made its way to the Twin Cities as the Cinderella Stars shocked the establishment during that enchanted season. Led by superstar center, Bobby Smith, who scored 93 points that year, Minnesota charged into the playoffs that spring, ready to take on the world.

The North Stars finished the regular season with an impressive 87 points that season, and no serious hockey enthusiast really gave the team much of a chance when they headed to the Boston Garden for the first round of the playoffs. After all, Minnesota was 0-for-Boston, having never beaten the Bruins in some 35 tries over the past 15 years. That all changed in game one though, when Steve Payne ended the drought with an overtime goal to win it 5-4. The Stars followed that up with a 9-6 victory the next night, and then finished off the Bruins 6-3 in game three at the Met Center for the series sweep.

"That had to be the biggest upset in Stars history," said legendary Stars broadcaster Al Shaver after the game.

With their newly found momentum, the Stars went on to beat the Buffalo Sabres four games to one. Next, it was on to Calgary. The Flames fell, four games to two. Minnesota had advanced to their first ever Stanley Cup Finals.

Obviously, the Stars were now in uncharted territory as they geared up for their next opponent, the powerful New York Islanders. Their adversary was no stranger to the hoopla surrounding the Stanley Cup.

"When we swept Boston to get the playoffs started, I knew it was going to be exciting," said Smith. "I can still remember standing on the bench as the conference finals game against Calgary was winding down, and Brad Palmer had just scored an insurance goal for us.

Just realizing that you had spent your whole life watching the Stanley Cup Finals and now you were going to be playing in them against a team like the Islanders, was tremendously exciting."

The Islanders' path to the finals went through Edmonton, and then Madison Square Garden, where they swept their cross-town rivals, the Rangers. Their roster was a regular who's who of hockey of the day. Every line featured legends such as Brian Trottier, Mike Bossy, Dennis Potvin, Butch Goring, and Billy Smith. The North Stars were led by hometown heroes Smith and Payne, as well as Al MacAdam, Freddy Barrett, Tim Young, Craig Hartsburg, Tom Younghans, Don Beaupre, Gilles Meloche, and two new rookies that had joined the team during the season. One was the exciting young Dino Ciccarelli, who had come on board early in the second half, and the other was a kid from Roseau, Minn., who was fresh out of the U of M, Neal Broten.

So close you could taste it
Game one of the Stanley Cup Finals kicked off in Long Island as the Stars, visibly nervous and scruffy-looking (from not having shaved in weeks) took the ice with aspirations of winning professional hockey's most coveted prize. Things got off to a bumpy start for Minnesota as New York jumped out to a quick 1-0 lead. The Stars then caught a break when Bob Bourne was assessed a major penalty for spearing. Unfortunately, the Islanders jumped right back and scored two unanswered shorthanded goals during the five-minute disadvantage, and the Stars were never able to regain their composure. A pair of third-period Islander goals on only three shots sealed an easy New York win.

Game two got off to a better start for Minnesota as young Ciccarelli scored a power-play goal to go ahead early. Then, precisely one minute later, Bossy tied things up for the Islanders, opening the flood gates for

goals by Potvin and Nystrom. But the Stars rallied and came back to tie it at three apiece in the second, off goals from Palmer and Payne. The defending champs got nervous, but their experience prevailed as Potvin, Ken Morrow, and Bossy each scored in an eight-minute stretch to mirror the result of the series opener.

Game three brought puck mania to the then so-called hockey capital of the world, Bloomington, Minn. The Met Center was the site of many tailgate bashes as the adoring North Star fans welcomed home their heroes from the Big Apple. The Stars jumped out to a 3-1 lead after the first, and the crowd went crazy. But Goring tallied twice in the second as the Islanders took a 4-3 lead into the final period. Again, the Stars rebounded, tying the game at the 1:11 mark of the third, only to see the Islanders regain the lead less than a minute later. With New York up by one, Goring put the final dagger in the collective hearts of Minnesota, scoring again for the hat-trick and the 7-5 victory.

Refusing to lie down and be swept by Islanders, Minnesota played brilliantly in game four. After exchanging goals through two, the Stars took a 3-2 lead on Payne's top-shelf slap-shot half-way through the third. Smith then sealed the deal by scoring late in the period to give the club a 4-2 win. Nineteen-year-old goalie Donny Beaupre, stood on his head in game four and turned away shot after shot to give Minnesota the edge against the potent Islanders, who were held to fewer than five goals only three times in 18 post-season games. The Stars thus lived to skate another day, sending the series back to the Islanders' home rink in Uniondale on Long Island.

Game five was decided early as the defending champions took care of business right out of the gate. Once again it was Goring who provided most of the dramatics. At 5:12 of the first period, a Minnesota clearing pass struck the referee and was picked up by Bourne, who fed Goring for the goal. Then, five minutes later, Goring, who would receive the Con Smythe Award, added another one as the Islanders crushed the Stars in front of a packed house of insane New Yorkers, 5-1. For the Islanders, the victory would be the second in what would be a string of four-straight Stanley Cups.

For the Stars, it was still a fairy tale season. No one expected them to do as well as they did, and it gave the organization a much needed shot in the arm. For their star Smith, it was just the beginning of an incredible career in the NHL that is still going strong.

The savior
Bobby grew up playing hockey in Ottawa. He played major junior hockey for the Ottawa 67s in the Ontario Hockey Association. In the 1978 he scored 69 goals and 123 as-sists for an amazing 192 regular season points and then tallied another 30 points in the playoffs alone. He topped the OHA in both assists and points, and won the Canadian Major Junior Player of the Year award. His stock rose as the young scoring machine was projected to be the number one player taken in that year's NHL draft.

TIMELINE

| Rush City's Dick Beardsley wins the first ever Grandma's Marathon and sets the course record which still stands today at 2 hours, 9 minutes and 37 seconds. He would go on to repeat as champion in 1982 as well. | UM Morris Wrestler Duane Koslowski wins the Division III Heavyweight National Championship | Gustavus Adolphus tennis doubles partners Shaun Miller & Jim Hearn wins the Division III National Championship | Hamline's Todd Wallert wins the Division III Shot Put National Championship | The Minnesota Kicks Soccer team folds | Gopher winger Steve Ulseth is named to the All-American hockey team | The Gopher Hockey team loses to Wisconsin 6-3, in the NCAA Finals which are held in Duluth | The Vikings abandon Midway Stadium as a practice facility and move into Winter Park in Eden Prairie, named after former Vikings and Lakers owner, Max Winter |

For the Stars, finishing dead last in the Smythe Division at the conclusion of the 1978 season may have been a blessing in disguise, for they were rewarded with the number one overall pick in the upcoming NHL draft. It was a tumultuous time for the organization. Against the background of several losing seasons, there were serious financial problems facing the struggling franchise. So the North Stars' management merged their franchise with the Gund brothers and their Cleveland Barons, who had once been the California Golden Seals.

The North Stars were saved from extinction by the merger. Now they needed to get the fans excited about hockey again in Minnesota. They needed a savior, and they got Bobby Smith. Lou Nanne, the long-time North Star who had moved from the ice up to the front office, was overjoyed to obtain the right to select the 20-year-old, 6'4" phenom from Ottawa.

Smith established a torrid scoring pace in Minnesota in his first year, scoring 30 goals and 44 assists en route to winning the Calder Trophy, as the NHL's top rookie. The Stars also improved by 23 points under the tutelage of veteran head coach Glen Sonmor. Bobby instantly became a fan favorite in his new home. He led the North Stars in scoring four of his first five years with the club. His finest sea-son with Minnesota came during the 1981-82 campaign when Smith achieved career highs in games played (80), goals (43), assists (71), and points (114).

In 1984, Smith was involved in one of the team's most talked-about trades ever, when be was dealt to the Montreal Canadians for Keith Acton, Mark Napier, and a third-round pick. Smith played seven seasons north of the border, recording 70-plus points in five of those years. In 1986, he led the Canadians to a Stanley Cup victory by scoring the game-winning goal in a 4-3 win over the Calgary Flames.

In 1991, Smith, then a 33-year-old veteran, returned to his beloved Minnesota to lead the Stars back the Stanley Cup Finals, this time against Badger Bob Johnson and the Pittsburgh Penguins. Unfortunately that series had all too familiar results, as Mario Lemieux and Jaromir Jagr beat the Stars in six games. Nevertheless, Smith's leadership and guidance on the ice and in the locker room to the younger players was non-quantifiable. He contributed eight goals and eight assists in the playoffs after a 46-point regular season, proving that he hadn't lost the edge that had always made him special in the minds of North Stars fans.

Next stop, the Hall of Fame
For 15 seasons Bobby ruled the red line. He played in 1,077 games with the North Stars and Canadians, scoring an amazing 1,036 points. And after 13 playoff seasons and 184 games, Smith retired with 64 goals and 96 assists for 160 points, ranking him 12th on the NHL's all-time playoff point leaders list. He also played in four NHL All-Star Games in 1981,1982, 1989, and 1990. From 1981 to 1990, Smith also served as the vice president of the NHL Players' Association.

After retiring from hockey in 1993, Smith fulfilled a lifelong dream and went back to college at the U of M. He received his B.S. in Business and then went on to obtain an MBA at the Curt Carlson School of Business

Management. That experience would pay quick dividends, because, in 1996, he became the Phoenix Coyotes' first executive vice president of hockey operations.

Bobby was one of the greatest hockey players to ever lace up the skates representing a Minnesota team. He had incredible instincts, an amazingly accurate shot, and a great passing touch. He was the ultimate competitor and team player, always putting his teammates first. The North Stars, sadly, were transferred to Dallas from the Twin Cities by owner Norm Green in 1993. Bobby retired after that season, ending two wonderful chapters of Minnesota hockey.

Who was your idol when you were growing up? "Growing up in Canada in the 1960s, we pulled for Toronto in our house, but I really enjoyed watching Jean Beliveau, the captain of the Canadians."

What did it mean for you to be a North Star? "I felt as if I was playing for one of the best organizations in the NHL, and I really enjoyed my career here. I was always extremely proud of being a North Star and was proud of how our fans in the state represented our franchise to the NHL. I always realized how fortunate I was getting to play on such a good organization in the best league in the world, and I never took it for granted."

On being traded to Montreal
"I was really very excited about going to the Canadians. I realized that it would be an excellent opportunity and would lead to a very exciting time for me. I won a Stanley Cup in 1986 with them and without question, that is the biggest highlight of my career. On the other hand, it was very difficult to leave Minnesota. It was the place where I wanted to live. Although it was a very good move for my career, it was sad to leave Minnesota."

On returning to the North Stars
"I thought it was great for me to finish my career in Minnesota. I had played 12 years in the league at that point and was pretty excited about the opportunity to play for a team coached by Bob Gainey and managed by Bob Clarke. There was a huge interest in hockey in the Twin Cities at that point, and it was very exciting for the players. We had a lot of success that year and going back to the Stanley Cup Finals was a real thrill for me."

On watching the team move to Dallas
"It was a very sad day for the NHL and certainly for hockey in the Twin Cities and the state of Minnesota."

On being a Minnesotan
"I feel like a Minnesotan and am pleased to be featured in your book as a Minnesota sports hero. When I came here from Canada, I immediately felt comfortable in the Twin Cities and instantly knew that this was a place that I wanted to live for a long, long time. We love it here and that's why my family still maintains a home here."

North Star tombstone:
"I would like to be remembered as a guy who always competed to the best of his ability, and became as good a hockey player as he could have become. And, as a guy who played his best hockey in the playoffs, when it was the most important as well as when it was the most difficult to play your best."

Where are they now?
Bobby and his wife Elizabeth along with their three children, Ryan, Megan, and Daniel, reside in both Scottsdale, Ariz., and Eden Prairie, Minn. Currently Bobby serves as the NHL's Phoenix Coyotes' vice president of hockey operations.

Tributes
"Bobby was an excellent talent. He had a great reach and had tremendous offensive skills. He has a real deep desire to be the best."   **-- Lou Nanne**

"He was one of the classiest guys that we ever had here in professional sports. He always had his head screwed on straight, knew the direction that he was headed in, and didn't take any short cuts along the way. That's why he is in the position he is in today. He is just a classy, classy guy."   **-- Doug Woog**

"Bobby was a great teammate and a great player. We went through a lot together, and I have a lot of respect for him as a player and as a person." **-- Neal Broten**

Winona's Tracy Caulkins wins the Sullivan Award. At age 15, she is the youngest ever winner. She also wins the 1982 Sportswoman of the year. She won her first national title at the age of 14.

Duluth's Tommy Williams, a former Boston Bruins great, is enshrined into the U.S. Hockey Hall of Fame

Former Laker guard Slater Martin is inducted into the Basketball Hall of Fame

Minnesota native Tom Hoover wins his fifth annual Crown Auto Funny Car Championship at Brainerd International Speedway

On November 18th, the Dome deflates due to a blizzard that dumps 10-inches of snow in Minneapolis

Gopher diver Chris Curry, the U of M's first woman athlete to receive an athletic scholarship based on athletic ability, wins the AIAW National 3-Meter diving title. Curry went on to receive the Big Ten's Medal of Honor for her athletic and academic achievements.

TRENT TUCKER
The Gophers Win the Big Ten Title

1982 was a dream season for the University of Minnesota's basketball Gophers. Led by All-American guard Trent Tucker, Minnesota finished 14-4 in the conference, good enough to win their first Big Ten title in 10 years and their only one under coach Jim Dutcher. For Dutcher, the 1981-82 squad was his third team in seven years to win 20 or more games in a season. And for the first time, his squad earned an NCAA post season tournament bid.

The Gophers certainly had a lot of talent on their team that season. In addition to Tucker, the team featured seven-footer Randy Breuer, Darryl Mitchell, Mark Hall, Gary Holmes, Jim Peterson, and Tommy Davis. The Gophers won their first five non-conference games, including victories over San Francisco State, Dayton, Loyola, Drake, and an impressive 76-54 win at Marquette. Minnesota tasted it's first defeat on December 21, when Kansas State beat them 62-52.

The Gophers returned home to the friendly confines of Williams Arena where they first crushed Army, 79-37, and then the Arizona Wildcats, 91-62, en route to capturing their eighth consecutive Pillsbury Classic holiday basketball title.

In their final non-conference game, the brilliant Tucker led the way with 22 points, as Dutcher's contingent easily handled Cal State Long Beach 75-67. With an impressive 8-1 record, the stage was set for the start of the 1982 Big Ten Conference race.

Unfortunately, the Gophers lost the opener to a very tough Ohio State team, 49-47, in Columbus. Minnesota bounced back two nights later, however, with a 64-58 victory against Michigan State at East Lansing. Next stop was Williams Arena and the hated and feared rivals to the south, the Iowa Hawks.

More than 17,000 zealous fans jammed the barn that Thursday night to watch the Gophers upend the Hawkeyes. Behind Randy Breuer's 22 points, Minnesota did just that, winning the game 61-56. Two nights later, Tucker stepped up to pour in 21 points as his team triumphed 67-58 over Michigan.

Minnesota continued to build their confidence throughout the season, and Tucker and Breuer were shouldering much of the load. The fans were turning rabid as the Gophers started to show signs that they were for real. That next week, they simply outplayed the Badgers in Madison, winning in a blowout by 78-57. Their next opponent, Illinois, would give them trouble all season. The Illini came to town on January 23 and knocked Minnesota off their high pedestal by 64-57. The loss could have been a turning point for the team, but they would have little time to dwell on it as they traveled to Evanston, Ill., and Bloomington, Ind., the following week. But, in what was starting to become a trend for the squad, they rebounded from the Illinois loss by beating the Northwestern Wildcats, 61-53, and Bobby Knight's Indiana Hoosiers 69-62.

They followed this up with a 73-50 drubbing of the Purdue Boilermakers at home, but stumbled against Knight's Hoosiers at Williams Arena, losing a squeaker 58-55. Unfazed and determined, the Gophers sucked it in and won three in a row against the Badgers, Boilermakers, and Wildcats to set up the much anticipated rematch with the Illini in Champaign. In a game that was closer than the final score would reflect, Minnesota once again fell to Illinois, 77-65.

It was crunch time for the Gophers as they headed into the final two-week stretch of the season. The Gophers, of course, were still very much in contention for the coveted Big Ten title. First, Minnesota invaded Michigan where they hadn't beaten the Wolverines since 1963. That 0-16 record fell in a big way on that day, as Minnesota prevailed by 60-51. With their confidence higher than ever, the Gophers then traveled to Iowa City and do battle with the Big Ten front runners, in the biggest Big Ten game of the year. The impli-

cations were enormous as Iowa led Minnesota in the conference standings.

The game was back and forth throughout the entire contest. It seemed that every time Minnesota struggled to gain the lead, the Hawkeyes found a way to pull ahead. It was a thriller that went down to the wire, and the two teams went to overtime. Then another overtime and amazingly, one more. Finally, in the third exhausting overtime, Darryl Mitchell sank two free throws with no time showing on the clock for a stunning 57-55 Minnesota triumph.

"That triple overtime game against Iowa was probably the most memorable game I ever played in. It was unbelievable," said team captain Tucker. "It was a really tough situation in a very hostile environment, but we got a total team effort to win it. I'll always remember Breuer's big blocked shot to save us to get us back into it, and then Darryl Mitchell's two free throws to seal it. The whole thing was just incredible!"

Big Ten champs at last
The Gophers, now deadlocked with Iowa for the Big Ten lead, returned home to host Michigan State the following Thursday. In front of a packed mob of excited fans, the Gophers did not disappoint. Despite only shooting a paltry 35 percent from the floor, they upended the Spartans, 54-51, in another nail-biter. Mitchell led the way with 16, Breuer added 14, while Tucker put in 13. In an interesting side-bar, Illinois beat the Hawkeyes to put Minnesota in the driver's seat on the championship road. On the final regular season game of the year, Breuer lit it up by scoring a career high 32 points, as the Gophers beat Ohio State, 87-75, to win the 1982 Big Ten championship.

"For me, it was seeing all my expectations and goals come true," said Tucker. "I came to Minnesota in 1978 as a part of the biggest and most celebrated recruiting class in the history of the program. So the pressure was there from day one, and we were expected to someday win a championship. Now, it was year four, and we had matured to a level where we could win it all. To hear the final horn go off and to see the jubilation of the fans, coaches, and players was just great."

"It was a tight race all season long, but we held on to win it. It was amazing," added Breuer, who led the team in scoring, rebounding, and blocks. "It was tremendously gratifying because we were the team that was predicted to win it all from the beginning. We had a lot of seniors on the team, but it was a tough fought battle all season long. You couldn't relax for one game because the season was tight all the way."

Although head coach Dutcher had twice been to the NIT, he had never been to the NCAA's post-season tournament with the Gophers. This was before the days of the currently-popular 64-team format, so the seedings were different back then. But with their top-10 national ranking, the Golden Gophers were eager to show the world that they were indeed a team to be taken seriously.

TIMELINE

Hamline runner Dennis Hensch wins the Division III Long Jump National Championship	UM Morris Wrestler Duane Koslowski wins the Division III Heavyweight National Championship	The Gustavus Adolphus men's tennis team wins the Division III National Championship	Rush City's Dick Beardsley wins his second Grandma's Marathon	Hamline's Mark Manders wins the Division III Discuss Throw National Championship	Minneapolis' Dave Eckstrom wins the Twin Cities Marathon Wheelchair Division	Hamline's Mike Manders wins the Division III Shot Put National Championship	Gustavus Adolphus doubles tennis partners Shaun Miller & Rich Skanse win the Division III National Championship	Gustavus Adolphus tennis singles player Shaun Miller wins the Division III National Championship	The St. Thomas Womens Country Team wins the Division III National Championship

Minnesota was slotted to head south, to Alabama, where they would do battle in the Mideast Region. The Gophers would have to overcome the ghosts of Gopher-past right out of the gate. After all, the Gopher basketball team was staying at the Sheraton Hotel in Birmingham, the same hotel that the Gopher Football team stayed at when they were beaten by Maryland in the Hall of Fame Bowl only five years earlier.

Fortunately, the Gophers received a first-round bye. The team then geared up to take on Tennessee-Chattanooga. Nearly every TV set in Minnesota was tuned in to watch the Gophers squeak by UTC, 62-61, in a thriller. The Sheraton Hotel jinx was over. In fact, the Gophers were now the lone representatives of the Big Ten in the tournament. The Buckeyes lost to James Madison, 55-43, in the Eastern Regional's first round, the Hoosiers were pummeled by Alabama-Birmingham in the Mideast Region's second round, and poor, poor Iowa lost a triple-overtime heartbreaker to Idaho, 69-67, in the second round of the West Region.

Next up for the U was Denny Crum's Louisville Cardinals. In another close game, the Gophers played well, but simply couldn't stay with the Cards as Louisville won it down the stretch, 67-61. It was a disappointing loss and a sad ending for a fabulous season for the Gophers, who finished with an impressive 23-6 overall record.

Post-season honors were highlighted by the naming of Tucker to the All-American team. Fifteen years later, he remains the last Gopher to earn such honors. Tucker went on to be drafted in the first round by the New York Knicks, who took him sixth overall. Breuer and Mitchell were also named to the 1982 All-Big Ten team. Breuer, a native of Lake City, was selected in the first round of the NBA draft by the Milwaukee Bucks and later played for the Minnesota Timberwolves. In a testament to Gopher basketball success, Hall, Holmes, Peterson, and Davis also went on to be drafted into the NBA.

Tucker was one of the greatest pure shooters ever to have come out of Minnesota. His jump shot was legendary, and one could only imagine what he would have done if they had a three-point shot back then. He will always be remembered not only for being an incredible basketball player who led the school to a Big Ten title, but also because he is a genuinely nice person who always played team basketball. The common denominator found most often when describing "Tuck," was that everyone thought he was a great guy.

From Flint to Minneapolis

Trent Tucker grew up in Flint, Mich., absorbing everything he could about sports. He played basketball and baseball at Flint Northwestern High School, just north of Detroit. There, the 6'5" guard averaged 29 points and 12 rebounds per game, good enough to be named a high school All-American. Out of high school he was heavily recruited throughout the Big Ten, especially by the home state Wolverines at the University of Michigan. Tucker had always been a big-time Michigan Football fan. But, luckily for Gold Country, he was recruited by Jesse Evans, an assistant coach with the Gophers who was his junior high school basketball coach. And, as luck would have it, when Trent came to Minnesota on a recruiting trip, he watched the

Gophers upset his Wolverines at Memorial Stadium, and from that point on he knew that he wanted to be a Gopher.

Tucker wore the maroon and gold from 1978-1982. He went through a lot during his tenure in Gold Country, including learning the game from a couple of pretty fair teammates, Mychal Thompson and Kevin McHale. For his career, he remains seventh all-time in scoring with 1,445 points, 12th all-time in assists with 219 and fifth all-time in steals with 153. He averaged 12.5 points and 3.4 rebounds per game over his four-year career, while shooting 50 percent from the field and nearly 80 percent from the charity stripe.

After his brilliant career at the U, Tucker went on to play 11 seasons in the NBA, nine of them with the New York Knicks, but also with Michael Jordan and the Chicago Bulls, where he won a championship ring in 1993. He retired from active competition after that season. For his career in the NBA, Tucker averaged 8.2 points, 2 assists and 2 rebounds per game. He tallied 6,236 career points, of which 1,725 were three-pointers.

Who was your hero when you were growing up? "My mother Verta and my father Jimmy."

What did it mean for you to be a Gopher? "As a freshman, I didn't understand what it really meant to be a Gopher because I was too young to understand. But as I progressed and got older, the significance of being a Gopher and what it meant to the community became apparent to me. It was an unbelievable experience and something I will always treasure. I looked upon my teammates just like we were a family. You'd go through the ups and downs with your teammates and when the last game was played, all you have is memories. I miss those moments of guys pulling together, trying to overcome all the adversity, and then finding a way to win as a team. Aside from furthering my education, the University of Minnesota also afforded me the opportunity to fulfill my lifelong childhood dream of playing in the NBA. Knowing that all that hard work had paid off was very gratifying to me."

Gopher tombstone? "Trent Tucker was a guy who came out and gave everything he had every night and played the game the way it was supposed to be played."

Where are the pure shooters in the NBA today? "Michael Jordan could be the reason why guys can't shoot basketballs anymore. He transcended the game to a level where no one else can reach. Most kids today want to put the ball between their legs, dribble behind their back, and dunk the ball. Although dunking brings big excitement from the crowd, it won't get them very far in basketball. Kids don't focus enough on the fundamentals like the jump shot, it is a lost art in the NBA game, but it's also a huge part of basketball. I run basketball camps, and the first thing I tell kids is that if they can make jump shots, then they have a chance to play at any level."

About the patented Tucker jumper: "I was born to shoot a basketball, like some guys are born to hit a baseball. I had the knack from day one. I had the proper technique and the proper balance as a player to shoot the jump shot. I was a natural shooter, and I honed the skills that I was given."

Where are they now? Trent is single and currently resides in Minneapolis. Tucker has come home to Minnesota where he is currently working as a television analyst for the Timberwolves.

Tributes

"Trent is such a nice guy. He is someone you would look up to and follow. He was a heck of a competitor. We played against each other a few times in the NBA, but I had already developed a tremendous amount of respect for him back when I was in college. Off the court he was the nicest guy around, but on the court, whoaaa!"
-- Willie Burton

"He is a great guy and was a great basketball player. He also had a great family. I remember his parents and brothers coming up to Minnesota to watch us quite often when we were playing, and I thought that was really neat. I enjoyed playing with him a lot, and, boy, we had a great time."
-- Randy Breuer

The North Stars win their first-ever Norris Division championship	Gopher catcher Greg Olson is named to the All-American baseball team	Gopher gymnast Robin Heubner is named to the All-American team for her second time. The former two-time Big Ten all-around competition champion also holds several school records.	Gopher diver Chris Curry wins the women's 3-Meter Diving title at the AIAW Swimming & Diving Championships	Actor Paul Newman wins the Pepsi Trans-Am race at Brainerd International Speedway -- his first pro victory	The Twin Cities Marathon was founded. Organizers realized that a marathon between downtown Minneapolis and downtown St. Paul, combining the spectacular autumn beauty of both cities, would be a much greater attraction than two marathons on both sides of the Mississippi River competing against each other. That year, the TCM attracted more than 4,500 entrants, which was a record for a "first-time" race. The first race had 3,511 finishers. (The 1996 event had 5,478 finishers.)	Gopher runner Cathie Twomey sets the women's world record in the 20K.

VERNE GAGNE

Verne Gagne was born in Corcoran, Minnesota, and grew up in Hamell during the Depression, attending a one-room school house. A tremendous athlete, he grew up loving sports. "At the age of 10 I knew that I wanted to be a football player and a wrestler," said Gagne. Later he transferred to Wayzata High School for one year, ultimately graduating from Robbinsdale High School in 1943. There he earned all-state honors in football, and, even though he weighed only 185 pounds, he also won the state heavyweight wrestling championship.

During the early 1940s, because of World War II taking so many young men, the University needed football players. So, Gagne was recruited by Bernie Bierman to play for the Gophers. But his main sport quickly became wrestling. After winning the Big Ten heavyweight wrestling title in 1944 as a freshman, he went into the Marine Corps. There, Gagne played football for the El Toro Marine team in 1944 and 1945. He returned to the University of Minnesota to continue playing football. As an end, he played in the 1949 College All-Star Game. As a wrestler, Verne became arguably the greatest grappler to ever come out of Minnesota. He won the Big Ten heavyweight championship four times and won two NCAA national championships as both a heavyweight and as a 191-pounder. The two-time All-American also wrestled on the 1948 Olympic team.

After college he was drafted as a defensive end by the Papa Bear, George Halas, and the Chicago Bears. But, because Halas wanted him to give up a year of eligibility and sign a contract as a junior, Gagne passed and that next season signed with Curly Lambeau's Green Bay Packers. Verne played for the Pack throughout the 1949-50 pre-season, but just before the first regular season game, coach Lambeau informed him that because the Bears still owned his rights and wouldn't release him, he couldn't play for the Packers. Gagne said "to heck with football" and went into the sport that would make him one of the most recognizable athletes of his day, professional wrestling.

Verne spent a life-time participating and promoting the sport that he loved, a sport that was born in Minneapolis, "All Star Wrestling." Verne was a local celebrity and became a local hero to a lot of people around the country. He was a daily feature in all the old newspapers and became synonymous with the sport. "In pro wrestling back then, there were a lot of great wrestlers like myself, who came out of major universities and wanted to continue in the sport," said Gagne. "Sure there were famous guys we wrestled, like Gorgeous George back in the late 40's and early 50's, but back then it was more like collegiate wrestling. Today there are no 'wrestlers' in wrestling."

"We did a TV show called "All Star Wrestling" that we broadcasted from the old Calhoun Beach Hotel, starting in 1950 and going all the way until 1992, never missing a week. The program was syndicated all over the United States, in the far east and all over the world. During the 60's, 70's and 80's it was the highest rated television show in Twin Cities, period. With a 26-share rating, we beat every sit-com, the Vikings, the Twins, everybody. We had no idea that it would grow as big as it did. We even drew the biggest crowd ever at Madison Square Garden. I was traveling the country and making more money than Joe DiMaggio and Mickey Mantle."

The grand grappler retired in 1981 but had more than a few come-backs with his son, and tag-team partner, Greg Gagne. Verne was an entertainer and one of the most successful one's at that. I've long contested that 90 percent of all people occasionally watch professional wrestling, and the other 10 percent lie. Maybe it's because it's on 14 different channels 24 hours a day. For whatever the reason, it intrigues and entertains us. Verne was always one of the "good guys," and that's why everyone rooted for him. He was a pioneer of a sport that, although it has evolved in a direction that he wouldn't have chosen, is still a major power today. Love it or hate it, the television numbers don't lie - it's here to stay. If anyone could rescue the sport it would have to be Gagne. Hey Verne, how about one more come-back?

On wrestling today: "Today it's entertainment, it's not wrestling. Now wrestling is horrible! It's atrocious! It's a show! It's only entertainment! They're not really wrestling, they aren't hitting each other, they're not putting on holds to make somebody give up, they're just running through a routine."

On being a promoter: "I learned that wrestling was foremost, but you have to have some show to promote it. You had to relax the rules, have a 20-count, a boxing ring, and create some entertainment. If you just had a mat on the floor it would eliminate a lot of the excitement."

On the aspect of sport vs. entertainment: "People don't realize it, but for the television show through the 60's and 70's, we tried to hold the line as much as we could as far as keeping it a sport. When the ratings got so big and it became so popular, television just kind of took it over."

On Ted Turner: "Wrestling made Ted Turner's station! When Turner got his first station in Atlanta, wrestling was his highest rated program. So he doesn't care how wrestling is run, obviously, but it's always going to be on there as long as he's got something to say about it. Wrestling did so much for him, and he never forgot it -- and I can appreciate him doing what he is doing. But now he's let people run it that don't know how to run it."

Who was your idol or hero growing up? "Bronko Nagurski -- as a wrestler. The football people don't really publicize that, but he wrestled for much longer and made much more money than when he played football."

What did it mean for you to be a Gopher: "It was pretty exciting back in those days. When we were growing up as kids and listening to the Gopher Football team winning the national championships in the 30's and 40's, every kid wanted to play football for the Gophers. I never dreamt that I would have a chance to go to college. I was very fortunate."

Most memorable Gopher match: "In 1947 I lost in the national finals to a kid from Oklahoma named Dick Hutton, who won on a referee's decision. I met him again in 1949 for the National Title and that time I beat him."

Gopher tombstone: "Down for the count, but I've still got one shoulder up."

Where are they now: Currently Verne and his wife, Mary, reside in Eden Prairie. They have four children and five grandchildren. He still is a great supporter of amateur wrestling in the state and contributes wherever he can to give back to the sport that gave him so much.

MINNESOTA SPORTS TID-BITS

BABE WINKELMAN

Babe Winkelman is undoubtedly Minnesota's most famous outdoorsman. He found a way to be a very successful entrepreneur doing what he loves to do most -- hunting, fishing, and enjoying the outdoors. Babe grew up on a small family farm near the tiny town of Duelm, in central Minnesota, tromping around, kneeling in the mud, fishing, hunting, and observing wildlife. He began fishing at the age of six, along tiny Stoney Brook which ran through his family's farm. During the 1960s, every possible moment was spent at the family cabin on Hay Lake near Brainerd, where he taught himself a "pattern" approach to fishing that he continues to teach others today.

In the early 1970s, Babe spent several years as a guide and fished in competitive tournaments. He co-founded the Minnesota Bass Federation, serving as its president in the early years, and also co-founded the Masters Walleye Circuit. Around that same time, after helping build a successful construction business with his father and brothers, Babe listened to his true calling and took a huge risk by starting Babe Winkelman Productions. It would be a company bearing his name and his personality. Its mission: To teach others how to be successful when fishing and hunting while always remaining respectful of the natural world. "I would have been comfortable and made a good living for the rest of my life in the construction business," said Babe. "But it's not what I wanted to do."

Twenty-five years later, Babe Winkelman is a world-renowned fisherman and hunter. He is also a highly successful businessman. Since 1975 he has been a professional, full-time fisherman, and since 1980, he has been on television promoting the sports he loves. He is the host of two very successful television programs seen throughout North America on both broadcast and cable stations, Outdoor Fishing and Outdoor Secrets.

His most memorable trip, in fact, was a deer hunt to Idaho a few years back. "I love the challenge of hunting a critter on his terrain," Babe says, "and spending the time it takes to understand him. We passed up about 350 deer and never pulled the trigger in seven days of hunting. I was after a specific deer and never found him. I don't go hunting just for the sake of dispatching an animal, and for a lot of reasons that was a great hunt."

Babe Winkelman Productions produces video titles, "Comprehensive Guide" book series, instructional audio cassette courses, thousands of newspaper and magazine articles, and several dozen major television commercials for companies as big as Chevrolet trucks. The company has won scores of awards, and Babe himself has been individually honored with two prestigious Cindy awards for on-camera charisma. A truly motivational speaker and dynamic on-air personality, he has also served as corporate spokesman for a host of major corporations including: Chevrolet, S.C. Johnson & Son, Cobra Electronics, Remington Arms, Leatherman Tool, and Ray-O-Vac. (In the case of Ray-O-Vac, Babe is in very elite company: Arnold Palmer and Michael Jordan are the firm's other spokesmen.) He is also a member of the Fresh Water Fishing Hall of Fame, and in 1992 he was inducted into the prestigious Sports Legends Hall of Fame (alongside the world's best athletes in baseball, football, boxing, etc.) by the Touchdown Club of Columbus, Ohio - the only outdoors figure to be so honored before or since.

For Babe, the biggest reward is hearing from his countless enthusiastic viewers who find success and satisfaction and become better caretakers of the land. "We know we've turned tens of thousands of people on to fishing and hunting, because we've got their letters," said Babe. "We've helped millions of anglers not only understand how to catch more fish, but to understand more about nature and develop their appreciation for the environment. And now, with Outdoor Secrets, we're doing the same thing with hunting."

Currently Babe, his wife, Kristeen, and their five girls live in Brainerd. It's business as usual for Babe and his amazing production company in Nisswa, Minnesota.

JILL TRENARY

Charm, grace, beauty, and talent all fit Minnesota's greatest figure skater to a tee. Born on August 1, 1968, the Minnetonka High School graduate grew up figure skating on our icy lakes and ponds.

During a very successful amateur skating career, Jill won her first U.S. National Championship in 1987, upsetting World Champion Debi Thomas.

A year later, she qualified for the Olympic Team and finished fourth at the winter games in Calgary. She earned her second National Championship in 1989 in Baltimore and that same year won a Bronze medal at the World Championships. In 1990, Jill won her third U.S. National Championship, and, later the same year, she won the World Championship at Halifax, Nova Scotia, by defeating the reigning champion Midori Ito. She added a U.S. Open Championship in 1992.

Since her incredible amateur career, Jill has toured professionally with the "Tour of World and Olympic Champions," Torvill and Dean's "Face the Music and Dance" Tour, and the "Skate the Nation" Tour.

In recent years, Jill has begun television commentary and broadcast commentary for NBC and Fox. Currently she is skating with the "Discover Stars on Ice" Tour. She maintains homes in Colorado Springs, Colorado, and London, England, with her husband, Christopher Dean.

BUD GRANT
The Viking Coaching Legend Retires

In 1983, Bud Grant, possibly the greatest athlete ever to play and coach in the history of Minnesota sports, retired as the head coach of the Vikings. The gray-haired, crew-cutted warrior's exit from the game signified an end of one of the greatest era's of all time.

The early 1980s was a tumultuous time for the Vikings. Much of the teams' infrastructure, personnel and personality was about to change. The Purple People Eaters were all gone, and in 1982, the Vikings lost much of their mystique when they moved indoors to the Metrodome, something Bud never really liked. 0 The cold weather had always given Minnesota a psychological advantage. "We knew you could play with numb fingers and frozen feet, which gave us an edge," said Ahmad Rashad. "A lot of times I caught passes without ever feeling the ball, just this heavy thump against my frozen hands." Bud never allowed his players to use heaters on the sidelines or even wear gloves or turtlenecks under the jerseys. He wanted them to stay focused and theorized that if his players were thinking about getting warm then they weren't thinking about football. "The Vikings always ran out for the warm-ups with this big facade, like we weren't cold," said Rashad in his book of the same name. "Of

course, we were freezing. But the other teams didn't know that, not for sure. They would be looking at us out of the corners of their eyes, thinking 'How come these guys look so warm?' They must be some bad dudes."

"The things that bothered me about going into the dome is that it took some of the coaching out of it," said Grant. Outside I could use the elements to my advantage. Things like the: wind, sun, rain, snow or a even a frozen field."

At the end of the 1983 season, the Vikings had finished with an 8-8 record, good enough to place fourth in the NFC Central. Shortly after that season, Bud announced his resignation as the team's head coach. Not only was the entire state of Minnesota shocked by his announcement, but so too was the entire world of football. Bud simply decided it was time to get out. He wanted to spend more time with his family and enjoy more of the outdoors in the summer and fall, hunting and fishing.

"In my mind, timing is the most important thing. I decided this was the time to quit. There wasn't any pressure on me. There are a lot of things I want to do while I still have my health."

Grant was happy to be getting out on his terms, and he could now enjoy life from the stands, rather than the sidelines. He was replaced by assistant, Les Steckel, who had a drill sergeant's mentality and, unlike Bud, ran preseason training like boot camp. But, after sitting by and watching the team he had built for so many years crumble before his eyes, it hurt Grant. He became moved by the sudden decline in the Vikings' public image during the disastrous season. Steckel had racked-up an embarrassing 3-13 record, something that was hard for Grant to watch.

On December 18, 1984, 327 days after calling it quits, and after owner Max Winter and G.M. Mike Lynn begged him to resuscitate some life back into their franchise after its' disastrous season, Grant unretired. With Lou Holtz packing the Dome for Gopher games, Lynn needed a sure thing. "It's unusual, but we're in an unusual business and you have to have the opportunity to be unusual," said Bud. "I think I'm old enough now to claim a little senility." Grant's team rebounded in 1985 by going 7-9 and finishing third in the Central Division. Bud wanted to rehabilitate his team and get it back on track. He succeeded.

So, on January 6, 1986, only 384 days after his return, Bud shocked the world one more time by announcing his re-retirement for the second time in as many years. "I've been in professional sports for 36 years," said the 58-year-old Grant. "I think I'd like to enjoy the

fruits of those endeavors." His replacement this time was long-time assistant coach and friend, Jerry Burns. Determined to hang em' up for good, he turned down other offers to coach in the NFL.

From Superior upbringings

Harry "Bud" Grant was born on May 20, 1927, and raised in Superior, Wisconsin. His father Harry, was the Superior Fire Chief. He grew up playing sports and became a tremendous prep athlete. After playing football, baseball and basketball at Superior's Central High School, Bud joined the Navy in 1945 and was stationed at the Great Lakes Military Base outside Chicago. Bud continued his athletic prowess as Great Lakes played Big Ten teams under head football coach Paul Brown and head basketball coach Weeb Ewbank, both hall of famers. In 1946, Bud was discharged and enrolled at the U of M.

There, even without a scholarship (because he was in the service, the G.I. bill paid for his tuition), he would excel in three sports, earning nine letters from 1946-1949. He was a two-time All-Big Ten end on the grid-iron, starred as a forward and was the team MVP on the basketball team, and also played centerfield and pitched for the baseball team, where he led the team in hitting as a freshman. Under Bernie Bierman, Bud played with Gopher greats such as Leo Nomellini, Clayton Tonnemaker, Gordie Soltau, Billy Bye, Jim Malosky and Vern Gagne. To earn spending money in the summers throughout college, Grant became creative. Since he could pitch three days a week and bat clean-up, he played baseball for several small towns around Minnesota and Wisconsin and made approximately $250 a week.

In 1950, Bud joined George Mikan and Jim Pollard as the newest member of the mighty Minneapolis Lakers dynasty. When he had finished his tenure at the U of M, he was considered the most versatile athlete ever to compete there. That was affirmed when he beat out Bronko Nagurski and Bruce Smith to be named as the "top athlete at the University of Minnesota for the first 50 years of the century."

In joining the Lakers, Bud also became the NBA's first "hardship case," meaning he could leave college early and play professionally. Lakers G.M., Sid Hartman petitioned the league and made it happen for him. As a Laker, Grant averaged 2.6 points per game in each of the two years he played for the Lakers, both of which were NBA championship teams.

From the hardcourt to the gridiron

Anxious to try something different, Bud joined the NFL's Philadelphia Eagles, who had made him their number one draft pick. In 1952, after switching from linebacker - where he led the team in sacks, to wide receiver, he finished second in the league in receiving and was voted to the Pro Bowl. After two years in Philly, he decided to take a 30 percent pay-raise and head north of the border to play for the Winnipeg Blue Bombers of the Canadian Football League. In so doing, Bud became the first player in NFL history to

TIMELINE									
Hamline swimmer Beth Peterson wins the 100 yd Butterfly National Championship	Duluth's Marcia Bevard wins the Twin Cities Marathon - Wheelchair Division	Augsburg wrestler Bob Adams wins the 134 lb. Division III National Championship	Minneapolis native Sid Gillman, former coach of the Rams and Chargers, is inducted into the Pro Football Hall of Fame	St. John's runner Brian Smith wins the Division III 5,000M Run National Championship	The Minnesota Strikers Professional Soccer team moves to town from Fort Lauderdale	St. Thomas runner Debra Thometz wins the Division III 10,000M National Championship	Hamline's Mark Manders wins the Division III Discuss Throw National Championship	Hamline's Mike Manders wins the Division III Shot Put National Championship	St. Thomas runner Rose Mcilrath wins the Division III 1,500M National Championship

play out the option on his contract. He missed hunting and fishing, something he could readily do in Canada.

There, he played both ways, starting at corner and at wide receiver. He led the league in receiving for three straight years and also set a record by intercepting five passes during a single game. Then in 1957, after only four years in the league, and at the prime of his career, the front-office offered the 29-year-old the teams' head-coaching position. He accepted and proceeded to lead the Blue Bombers to six Grey Cups over the next 10 years, winning four of them.

Bud heads south, to balmy Minnesota
On March 11th, 1967, Grant came home again, this time to take over the Vikings. "I enjoyed Winnipeg very much, but coming to Minnesota was coming home for me," said Grant. It was a position that former Lakers owner, Max Winter, who now ran the Vikings, had originally offered to him, but had declined, in 1960. He took over from Norm Van Brocklin, and although he only won three games in his first season, that next year he led the Purple to the division title. The year after that, in 1969, they made it to the Super Bowl, and Bud was named the league's Coach of the Year. That was the beginning of one of the greatest coaching sagas in all of sports. Bud could flat out coach, and his players not only respected him, but they also liked him. Bud treated them like men, didn't work them too hard in practice, and his players always knew they could count on that post-season playoff check.

The greatest Minnesota coach of all time
Grant, who was a head coach for 28 years, won a total of 290 regular season and post-season games, 122 as coach of the Winnipeg Blue Bombers of the CFL from 1957-66 and 168 as coach of the Vikings from 1967-83 and 1985. At Minnesota, his teams made the play-offs 12 times, and won 15 championships: 11 Central Division (1968-71, 1973-78, and 1980), one NFL (1969) and three NFC (1973, 1974 and 1976). In 1994 Bud was inducted into the Hall of Fame. With it, he became the first person ever to be elected to both the NFL and the Canadian Football League Hall of Fames. "It's something that they can't take away from you," said Bud, who was introduced at the event by his best friend, Sid Hartman. "Usually in sports there is a new champion crowned every year, but this is forever."

Who was your idol or hero growing up? "I grew up during the war and our heroes were war heroes. Men like Richard Bong, an ace fighter pilot that shot down 40 Japanese planes flying P-38's over the Pacific. Many of my friends were going i to the service and being wounded or killed. So, there wasn't a lot of time for heroes, other than war heroes back then, we had more important things to worry about in life."

What did it mean for you to be a Gopher? "It kind of grows on you a little bit. It wasn't anything that I felt particularly strong about when I got there, but now it means a lot. Back then, the Gophers were the only game in town, and we always played before a packed house. It was a tough time, with no scholarships and little money, but we had a lot of fun."

On the four Super Bowls: "The reason they call it the Super Bowl is because it's only one game. It's winner-take-all for the two best teams. You have to

live with it, and that's just the way it is. It's nothing that really haunts me. I mean my life would be exactly the same today whether we won or lost those games. It's an accomplishment, not a failure to get to the Super Bowl. In order to survive in this business and not go crazy, you can't go back and replay games, second guess yourself and ask 'what-ifs?'. I was always looking ahead, and I can honestly tell you I've never looked at a Super Bowl film. They're over, you have to move on, or otherwise you are living in the past." He did however acknowledge that if they had won a couple of them, there might be a few more Vikings in the Hall of Fame today, guys like Paul Krause, Ron Yary, Jim Marshall, Carl Eller and Mick Tinglehoff.

Minnesota sports tombstone: "There were people that could run faster, jump higher, throw harder and shoot better than me, but I don't think anybody competed any harder than I did. I felt that I always had an advantage over my opponents because I never got tired. The longer we played, the stronger I got. Then I could beat you. And I applied that same theory to coaching. That was the type of player who I was always looking to get to play for me. Also, one thing that most coaches can't say, is that I've never been fired. I've always left whatever I was doing on my own accord, and I am proud of that. Every dollar I have ever made was from professional sports. I've had no other business or profession, and the only investments that I've got are six kids with college education's. Other than that, I don't have much."

Where are they now? Bud and his wife Pat presently live in Bloomington. They have six children: Kathy, Laurie, Peter, Mike, Bruce and Dan, and 11 grandchildren. Although he still has an office at the Vikings headquarters, he is officially retired from football and spends much of his time either with his family or in the great outdoors. He has also championed the cause against commercial fishing with nets and spears on Minnesota lakes.

Tributes

"Bud should go down as one of the most intelligent coaches in the game. He understood how to deal with men. He had a unique sense about him that he could get the best out of everyone of his players. He was a great organizer, he put together the team, ran a tight ship, and he brought true discipline to the team. He knew how to harness the talent and the energy that we as players had. I feel very respectful towards him for understanding that and not trying to change that part of what we had. He was not an egotist. He was a winner." **-- Jim Marshall**

"I came to know, understand, and appreciate Bud much later in life. My affection for Bud has actually grown more since I left football. He was not a person to get close to his players, yet he cared deeply for his players. He had a great charisma, knowledge, and skill of the game. I appreciate his strengths and qualities much more now." **-- Carl Eller**

"He commanded respect as well as anyone I've ever known, and he did it without yelling or intimidating or chewing people out. He never put himself up as an offensive or defensive genius. But everybody knew that he was the leader. He just wasn't overbearing. He's a very wise man." **-- Fran Tarkenton**

"One thing about Bud, he didn't tell you what you wanted to hear, he told you what you needed to know... and that's a big difference." **-- Chuck Foreman**

"Bud was the greatest professional coach that I have ever been around. He treated you like a man. He never wasted words. Bud was one of these guys that used to say: 'You practice, you prepare, you play, you go home, you have dinner.' He was a no-nonsense guy. And just a great person." **-- Ahmad Rashad**

"I played football the old fashioned way, and I believe I was a great student of Bud Grant. He didn't coach a lot about X's and O's, but rather with an attitude. There was a deep fire in Bud that you never saw. He was as good a coach to work with as I've ever seen." **-- Joe Kapp**

"He was very tenacious, a great defender, and he could shoot from the outside. He was always assigned to guard the opposing team's best scorer. One of his great talents was his ability to throw me the ball into the pivot. I loved him!" **-- George Mikan**

Since their first official game back in 1931, the University of Minnesota's Duluth campus has established a hockey tradition that is synonymous with the American brand of hockey. For many, hockey is a religion in northeastern Minnesota, and the UMD Bulldogs have gained a tremendously loyal following.

There have been a lot of Bulldog hockey stars over the years: Tom Kurvers, Bill Watson, Brett Hull, Norm MacIver, Curt Giles, Derek Plante, Chris Marinucci, Jim Johnson, Chad Erickson, Tom Milani, Mark Pavelich, Murray Keogan, Chico Resch, Dave Langevin, Walt Ledingham, Ron Busniuk, Dennis Vaske, Bob Mason, Dan Lempe, Jim Toninato, Brett Hayer, Pat Boutette, and Keith "Huffer" Christianson.

In 1984, the Dogs finished with an impressive 29-12-2 overall record, the best in school history, while going 19-5-2 in the WCHA, good enough to win their first-ever conference title in the 20 years in the league. Led by All-Americans Tom Kurvers and Bill Watson, UMD came as close as a team can possibly come to winning a national championship, in what many say was the greatest game ever played in college hockey.

UMD coach Mike Sertich's team, fresh of their first-ever showing in the NCAA playoffs against Providence the year before, started out their magical season with receiving a lesson in humility by getting spanked by the U.S. Olympic team, 12-0. Winger John Harrington of Virginia, and goaltender Bob Mason of International Falls were both former Bulldogs who played on that 1984 squad.

UMD settled down after that and kicked off the WCHA season by sweeping Colorado College. From there, the Bulldogs won eight of nine and finished the regular season losing only four of their final 16 games. They swept Wisconsin at the season's end to win their first McNaughton Cup, signifying the conference title.

Forced to host a "home" series at Williams Arena in Minneapolis due to a scheduling conflict with the Duluth Arena, the Dogs slaughtered North Dakota, 8-1 and 12-6, before near-capacity crowds in the WCHA championship series to advance to the NCAA quarter-finals at home against Clarkson College. They split with Clarkson, and earned themselves a trip to Lake Placid for the right to take on North Dakota again, this time in the Final Four. In an overtime thriller, the Dogs beat back the rejuvenated Fighting Sioux, 2-1.

Their opponents in the championship game were the champions of the CCHA, Bowling Green, who had knocked off Michigan State in the semifinals.

It was a tale of two teams and two different playing styles. Bowling Green, whose lineup was dominated by Canadians, had only four Americans on the squad. Duluth on the other hand, comprised mostly of home-grown Minnesotans, had only four Canadians. The sellout crowd of nearly 8,000 people had no idea that they were about to be a part of inter-collegiate hockey history when the opening puck dropped.

For the first time in two games, UMD fell behind as Bowling Green defenseman Garry Galley crashed into Bulldog goalie Rick Kosti, and went "top-shelf" on a backhander at 5:58 of the first. The Dogs came back, as they had done so often that season, when Aurora's Bob Lakso stole the puck in the Bowling Green zone, and slipped a pass to Chisholm's Mark Baron, who flipped the biscuit under the crossbar to tie it at one apiece.

Then, after being stymied on their first three powerplay attempts, Hoyt Lakes' Matt Christensen directed a face-off to the left point and Watson proceeded to tip in a Kurvers blast to go up by one.

In the third, Lakso, who would be named to the all-tournament team, spurted between two Falcon defensemen and fired a low wrister to

beat Falcon goaltender Gary Kruzich on the short side. Things were looking pretty good for UMD as they went up 3-1. It didn't last long, as Falcon forward Jamie Wansbrough, pressured by Bulldog defenseman Jim Johnson, went five-hole on Kosti. (That's hockey terminology for a shot between the goalie's legs.) UMD answered back at 11:55 on a hard wrister by International Falls' Tom Herzig.

As it went back and forth throughout the third, Bowling Green scored once again at 12:42. Kosti stopped a blue line blast by Falcon, Mike Pikul, but got caught up in traffic in front of the net as he tried to recover.

Forward Peter Wilson put in the garbage goal to make it 4-3, Duluth. Then with 1:37 to go, Bowling Green tied it up on a fluke goal. With their goalie pulled, the Falcons dumped a long, off-target shot into the zone from beyond the red line that many people felt was off-side. Oddly, the puck bounced off the end boards and past Kosti, who had stepped behind the net to control a puck which would never arrive. The puck hit a crack in the dasher board, deflected to the net, hit the left post and stopped in the crease. With Kosti way out of position, John Samanski, who had sprinted down the slot, tapped in a "freebie" to tie it up.

"I've seen it happen, but I've heard of it happening. However, it never happened to me" said the goaltender on the tough-luck bounce. "It happened so fast that I didn't know what to do. I felt helpless."

The teams went to OT. In fact, it would be four over-times! Save after save, both goalies battled to stay alive. In the blur of the overtimes, Kruzich and Kosti, both freshmen goalies, played out of their heads. Kruzich stopped three UMD breakaways while Kosti stopped 19 shots in the final 37 minutes. Time stood still. It was unbelievable. Both teams were visibly fatigued and seemed to be skating only on adrenaline.

Finally, at 7:11 of the fourth overtime, it ended. And with it broke the collective hearts of UMD hockey fans forever.

Falcon forward Dan Kane sped into the Bulldog end from the neutral zone and, from the high slot, threaded a pass to Gino Cavellini, who broke in all alone on Kosti. Cavallini took the puck from left to right, and put a back-hander in to make college hockey history.

Kosti, who tied a tournament record with 55 saves, really had no chance on the game-winning goal. Kane made the perfect pass, and Cavallini made the perfect shot. That was it. As soon as the puck hit the back of the net, Kosti skated straight to his bench, where he was met by his teary-eyed teammates, who sat motion-less in disbelief.

The Bulldogs and Falcons had skated for 97 minutes and 11 seconds at Olympic Arena, in a game that took nearly four hours, while taking part in the longest and most memorable game in college hockey history. The

TIMELINE

| Osseo's James Martinez, a Gopher wrestler, wins a bronze medal in the L.A. Olympics | St. Paul's Stephen Erickson wins an Olympic gold medal in Star Class Sailing | Bemidji State beats Merrimack College for the Division III hockey National Championship | Wayzata's Greg Lemond wins the Tour De France and earns Sports Illustrated's Sportsman of the Year honors | St. Thomas runner Nick Mancui wins the Division III 10,000M Run National Championship | St. Thomas University wins the National Division III Indoor Track Championship | St. Thomas University wins the National Division III Women's Cross Country Championship | Augsburg Wrestler Steve Gliva wins the 118 lbs. National Championship | St. Olaf hurler Todd Nash wins the Division III Triple Jump National Championship | Gopher Women's tennis player Claudia Brisk wins the Big Ten Player of the Year Award |

historic arena in Lake Placid that housed the famed "Miracle on Ice" Olympic team four years earlier, had now played host to the "Marathon on Ice."

"The thing I remember most about the overtimes was being really tired and gasping for air during the whistles," said team captain Kurvers. "I think we only played four defensemen for most of the game. After a while, you didn't take any chances. You just played your position and tried not to make a mistake. The whole over-time was confusing. I hardly remember any of it. I was hugely disappointed at the loss, but it was an incredible game."

"Just to be going into overtime was a huge letdown, and we didn't feel that we had to be there," said Watson. "It's one thing to score late to get into over-time, and it's another thing to squander the lead to get into overtime. The excitement level was incredible. The overtimes went on and on and on, and it just became a situation of survival and mind over matter as to just how much you wanted to win. It was tough playing on the much bigger Olympic ice surface too. It was probably my toughest loss ever as a player."

"We've just got to be proud of what we've done," said future Minnesota North Star Johnson after the game. "This was the biggest game of my life and these guys played their hearts out."

UMD turned the corner that night in the world of college hockey. No longer were they just the second-best team in Minnesota. Bulldog hockey had arrived in the big time. In an ironic twist, UMD returned to the Final Four again the following year. This time, led by a young freshman named Brett Hull (son of Bobby), they lost a three-overtime heart-breaker 6-5, to R.P.I. in Detroit. They rebounded to finish third in the nation by winning the consolation game 7-6 over Boston College, in, you guessed it, overtime.

Over those two fantasy seasons, two Bulldogs: Kurvers and Watson, each stood out to capture college hockey's highest honor, the Hobey Baker Award.

Tom Kurvers was born on September 14, 1962, and grew up skating in the shadows of the Met Center in Bloomington. In 1980, his Bloomington Jefferson Jaguars were knocked off in the Minnesota State High School Hockey Tournament by Grand Rapids, who was led by future North Star goalie, John Casey.

Kurvers wore Bulldog maroon and gold from 1980-1984 and during that time he scored 43 goals and added 149 assists for 192 total points. All three stats are still all-time records for a defenseman. His 149 helpers are also number two all-time. For his efforts he was named a first-team All-American in 1984. He went on to play for seven teams over 11 seasons in the NHL where he scored 93 goals and added 328 assists for 421 career points. He retired in 1995.

Who was your hero when you were growing up?
Kurvers: "I was a huge fan of all Minnesota sports, and I loved the Vikings, Twins, and Stars. I looked up to all the teams and never really had one idol."

What did it mean for you to be a UMD Bulldog?
Kurvers: "After not seeing a college game in the last 12 years, I finally got to see the Bulldogs play. Just

remembering how much I had missed college hockey was awesome. I love the connection that I feel towards Duluth. There's a pride and bond there because of all the success that we had."

Bulldog tombstone - Kurvers: "He was one of the best hockey players to come out of Minnesota. Obviously not the best, but I am honored when my name gets tossed around with a Mike Ramsey, Reed Larson, Neal Broten, or Phil Housley - not as a comparison, but just in the group. It means so much to me to be thought of in the same breath as those guys, who I have a lot of respect for."

Where are they now?
Tom Kurvers and his family live in the Twin Cities. Currently he is back in college, getting his MBA in sports management at St. Thomas University. When he graduates, he hopes to go into coaching.

Tribute
"As a teammate, he really evolved into a great leader. When our class came in, I think it helped Tommy a lot that we could take a little bit of the burden off of his shoulders. Our friendship grew more and more as the team kept on winning. He is a great guy and a tremendous hockey player." -- **Bill Watson**

• • • • • •

Bill Watson was born on March 30, 1964, and grew up playing hockey in Powerview Manitoba. He went on to star on back-to-back national junior hockey championship teams in Prince Albert, Sask. He came to UMD in 1982, and by the time he had left, the right-winger scored 89 goals and added 121 assists for 210 total points. He still holds the record for most assists in one season with 60. He remains fifth on the all-time list for most goals scored and is seventh all-time for assists. For his efforts he was twice named as a first-team All-American in 1984 and 1985. He went on to play with the NHL's Chicago Blackhawks for five seasons before retiring in 1990 because of a shoulder injury. There, he scored 23 goals and added 36 assists for 59 career points. From there Bill came home to pursue his passion, coaching, and he served as head coach of Duluth's St. Scholastica hockey team.

Who was your hero when you were growing up?
Watson: "Phil Esposito. He was the greatest."

As a Canadian, how do you view the U of M's policy of only taking the Minnesota kids? - Watson:
"It is unique in college hockey. I think it's absolutely great, and it creates such a strong tradition at Minnesota. Being a Canadian I get asked that question a lot, and I always felt that it was one of the neatest traditions in sports. I have two sons that are Minnesota-born, and I would love it if they had an opportunity to play hockey at the U. I don't ever see why they would have to get away from that tradition."

What did it mean for you to be a UMD Bulldog?
Watson: "There is such great hockey pride and tradition there. Duluth has always had a reputation of pro-

ducing great players. We have had not only great individuals, but we had some great teams as well. We went out there every night under the lights and play hard to win. Great players make a great program."

Bulldog tombstone - Watson: "My career was more than the Hobey Baker Award and the individual trophies. It meant a great deal to play in Duluth. It was very tough for me that we didn't win that national championship. As close as we came, we probably should have won back-to-back national championships. I felt that I was on a team that was probably as good as any team that college hockey as ever seen - and that was probably the biggest honor that I could ever have bestowed upon me."

Where are they now?
Currently, Bill Watson resides in Michigan with his wife and family where he is an assistant hockey coach at Western Michigan University in the CCHA.

Tribute
"Billy Watson was our best player. Even the year that I won the Hobey Baker, he was our MVP and go-to guy. If he had played another year at UMD, he could have possibly scored the most points ever for a college player. I've always said that if we were playing a pond hockey game and could draft anybody in the universe to be my teammate, Bill Watson would be the one - he was that good of a hockey player." -- **Tom Kurvers**

There have been a few memorable T-formation quarterbacks at the University of Minnesota, but none of them was as versatile a performer as was Rickey Foggie. Foggie could pass, run, scramble, and wreak havoc on opposing defenses. When his tenure was over in Gold Country, there were quite a few pages in the record books that had to be rewritten.

In 1985, Foggie, then a sophomore, led the Golden Gophers to their first and only post-season victory since the Rose Bowl in 1962. With Foggie at the helm, Minnesota defeated Clemson in the Independence Bowl in Shreveport, La.

The 1985 season started out well for the Gophers. Under second-year coach Lou Holtz, who had transferred to Minnesota from Arkansas, the maroon and gold kicked off the season with a 28-14 win over Wichita State. Foggie carried the team on his back as he rushed for three touchdowns on 140 yards rushing while throwing for another 157.

From there, the Gophers crushed Montana, 62-17, as Foggie again played masterfully. In that game he ran for three more touchdowns while throwing for another.

After losing a heartbreaker to top-ranked Oklahoma, 13-7, the team rebounded by pouncing all over Purdue, 45-15. In that game Foggie threw for 212 yards and a TD, while rushing for 47 yards and another touchdown. The Gophs went on to beat Northwestern in week five, 21-10, behind nearly 300 yards of total offense from Foggie. From there, they beat Indiana, 22-7, in a game that featured Valdez Baylor rushing for a career high 141 yards and a TD.

Minnesota then lost two nail-biters -- to Ohio State, 23-19, and Michigan State, 31-26. Foggie scored the only two touchdowns in the Buckeye game, and then sat out the Spartan game with a groin pull. In week nine, the Gophers won over Wisconsin, 27-18, in a game that was highlighted by an 89-yard record-setting TD bomb from Foggie to Mel A. Anderson. The Gophers finished out the season with a huge downer, getting pummeled by Michigan, 48-7, and Big Ten champion Iowa, 31-9. The crushing defeats meant that the team finished only fifth in the Big Ten with a 4-4 record. But, overall they were 6-5, good enough for a bowl game trip, something that hadn't happened at the University of Minnesota since the 1977 Hall of Fame Bowl.

It was off to Shreveport for Minnesota where the team would meet the Clemson Tigers in the 10th annual Independence Bowl. Nearly 43,000 fans, many of whom made the trip from the Gopher State, crowded into Independence Stadium to watch the big game. Taking over as head coach of the team was former assistant coach John Gutekunst. This turn of events occurred because, after the season, Holtz decided to exercise a special clause in his contract entitling him to step down to take the head coaching position at Notre Dame.

In the Independence Bowl, on the first play from scrimmage, Clemson QB Rodney Williams hit wide receiver Ray Williams in the flat. Williams, upon being tattooed by Gopher defender Doug Mueller, coughed up the ball at the Tiger 39. Minnesota started to drive, and tailback Ed Penn's 25-yard run got the Gophers down to the Clemson five-yard line. But after a holding call, they could only muster a field goal attempt. Chip Lohmiller came in, but was wide-right on a 22-yarder, keeping the score at double-bagels. But two plays later, Clemson again fumbled on their own 26-yard-line. This time, Lohmiller drilled a 22-yarder through the uprights to put the maroon and gold up by 3-0.

In the second quarter, after forcing the Tigers to punt, the Gophers put together an impressive drive that started with two David Puk nine-yard scampers up the middle. Foggie then hit tight end Craig Otto on another nine-yarder to get to their own 43, followed by 15 and 20-yard runs by Baylor. Finally, on third-and-four, at the Tiger nine, Foggie hit Anderson on a nine-yard scoring strike, and the Gophers went up 10-0. Clemson rallied back in the third on two Jeff Treadwell field goals to make it 10-6. Then, behind the running of Clemson tailback Kenny Flowers, the Tigers drove and scored on a Jennings touchdown catch to take a three-point lead, 13-10.

The valiant Gophers came back, this time in the fourth quarter behind their leader Foggie. His running and passing sparked an 85-yard drive that was capped by another Lohmiller "chip-shot" field goal to tie the game at 13 apiece.

After the Gophers got the ball back, Foggie came out in the shotgun formation. They started out the drive on a 10-yard pass to Anderson, followed by a 16-yard Baylor run to the Clemson 36. Then Foggie hit flanker Gary Couch on a 14-yarder, quickly followed by a Baylor run that gave him 12 more of his team-high 98 yards. So, with the Gophers at the seven, fullback Puk rumbled down to the one. That was all Baylor needed to launch himself into the end zone as Minnesota took a seven-point lead.

But the Gophers weren't out of the hot water yet. Faced with a fourth-and-six at their own 39, Clemson pulled off a fake punt to stay alive. Then on fourth and 12, Williams completed a 21-yarder to Jennings to reach the Gopher 31. So, with 90 seconds left in the game, the Tigers tried a trick play. Williams tossed a long, backward pass to wide receiver Ray Williams, who then turned around and lofted a pass of his own to tight end Jim Riggs near the goal line. But, defensive back Donovan Small just got a finger on the ball, deflecting it out of bounds and preserving the win for the Gophers.

"When they first threw that ball out wide," said Small, who was named the defensive player of the game. "I was going to come up to try to tackle the guy. I thought it was a screen pass. But just out of the corner of my eye I saw this Clemson guy running really hard downfield. I wondered why that guy was running so hard, so I decided I'd better try to catch up to him."

"I have fond memories of that game because I always wanted to attend Clemson," said Foggie, who threw for 123 yards and a touchdown in the game. "But the Clemson coach told my high school coach that I was too slow to run their offense. So there was a definite revenge factor there for me personally. I knew a lot of the guys that played for Clemson, and to go out and play well and to beat those guys was just really satisfying for me. Minnesota hadn't been to a bowl game for a while, so to win it was a really special experience for everyone."

For the season, Foggie, accounted for 1,821 yards in total offense and was named to the All-Big Ten team. Baylor led the team in rushing with 680 yards while kicker Lohmiller led the team in scoring with 75 points. Linebacker Peter Najarian, who described the win as the "greatest feeling I've ever had," was the

TIMELINE

St. Thomas runner Erik Rosenkranz wins the Division III Decathalon National Championship	St. Johns runner Jim Gathje wins the Division III 3,000M Steeplechase National Championship	Macalaster runner Julia Kirtland wins both the 3,000M and 5,000M Division III Indoor Track National Championships	St. Thomas runner Lisa Koeltgen wins both the Indoor and Outdoor Division III 1,500M Indoor Track National Championships	St. Thomas runner Nick Mancui wins the Division III 10,000M Run National Championship	St. Thomas University wins the Men's Division III Indoor Track National Championship	Hoyt Wilhelm, a Minneapolis Miller from 1950-51, is inducted into the Baseball Hall of Fame	Gopher winger Pat Micheletti is named to the All-American hockey team	Baseball's All Star Game is played at the Metrodome, as the American League beats the National League, 6-1	Canterbury Downs horse track opens in Shakopee and that next season nearly $135 million is wagered at the track

Golden Gophers' top tackler with 133 total hits. He remains the schools all-time leader in the category.

The fog rolls in

Rickey Foggie was born on July 1, 1966, in Waterloo, S.C. He grew up as one of nine siblings in a family that loved playing sports. At Laurens High School, he was an all-conference and all-state performer in both football and basketball, and, in his senior year, he led his high school football team to the South Carolina state championship.

After being heavily recruited in both sports, Foggie came on board at Minnesota in 1983, following the disastrous 1-10 Gopher season under Joe Salem. As a freshman, he led the team in both rushing and passing and showed great promise by redefining the conventional rules of the quarterback position. For his career he remains the university's all-time leader in total offense, with 7,312 yards. He is still number seven all-time in rushing with 2,150 yards, and ranks number two all-time behind only Marquel Fleetwood in career yards passing, with 5,162 yards.

From 1984-1987 he scored 160 points, putting him eighth all-time in that category. He also holds the record for most touchdown passes with 34 and is third in rushing touchdowns, with 25. Throughout his career he completed 311 passes, good enough for fourth all-time, while amassing an amazing 16.8 yard average gain per completion, tops in school history. Considered a threat everytime he touched the ball, he became only the third quarterback in college football history to run over 2,000 yards and pass for more than 4,000 yards.

When Rickey finished his tenure at Minnesota, he headed north of the border to play in the Canadian Football League, first with the British Columbia Lions, then the Toronto Argonauts, and lastly the Edmonton Eskimos. From there he headed to Memphis when the CFL expanded to the United States. Then Rickey had a homecoming of sorts when he came home to Minnesota to play with the new Fighting Pike of the Arena Football League. In 1996, after only one season in the Target Center, the Pike folded. Foggie headed east and began his 10th year of professional football with the New Jersey Red Dogs of the same arena league.

With his amazing ability to run the option attack like no other before him, Rickey will go down as one of the best Gopher quarterbacks ever. He electrified the fans in Minnesota and was pivotal in turning a shattered football program around. When he left Gold Country, the Gophers had not only gone to two bowl games, but Foggie had returned the program to a semblance of its old glory.

Who was your hero when you were growing up?
"My Older brother Perry, because he was the best."

Why did you decide to enroll at the U of M?
"It came down to Minnesota or North Carolina for me, and I chose to get away from home. Minnesota was especially appealing because coach Holtz gave the opportunity to play quarterback in the same option-style system that I ran in high school. It was tough for me to be away from my family that first year, but I know now that I made the right choice."

What did it mean for you to be a Gopher?
"Once I learned the great tradition of the school and its winning success, it all kind of sunk in. Coach Holtz brought back a lot of the tradition. To be able to play in front of sellout crowds for our first two years was great. I felt that we brought a college football atmosphere back to the U of M. The fans were great, and it always meant a lot to me that they supported me the way that they did. Maroon and gold is something that I will never be able to get out of my system, and I am always proud to say that I am a Gopher."

On the Fighting Pike: (Minnesota's short-lived Professional Arena League Football team)
"I felt like I had a good reception from the fans, and it was great to be able to come back to the Twin Cities. We had a lot of fun that year, but it was unfortunate that we didn't get to win any games at home. I was disappointed that my Pike experience wasn't a successful situation, but I was glad to get back into the atmosphere of having the Twin Cities fans come out and watch me perform again."

On Lou Holtz:
"Lou's got to be one of the top five greatest college coaches of all time, without question. Everywhere Holtz has been, he's won. He turned our U football program around and got people in the stands. He was able to recruit good athletes to come in and make us competitive again. His greatest asset was to be able to recruit and to motivate his players to go out and win at all costs. I just wish he would've stayed at Minnesota longer, because there's no telling where the program would be today if he had."

On John Gutekuntz:
"This was a big change for us, but, because Gutie was already on the staff, we were familiar with him, and we kind of knew what to expect. But, going from Lou Holtz, who was a fiery, up-tempo guy, to Gutie, who was a more laid-back kind of coach, was a big change. Gutie wasn't the motivator that Coach Holtz was, but he knew the X's and O's of the game, and he was a good guy."

On the Metrodome:
"I loved it. You never had to worry about the wind or the weather, so it was great. If it weren't for that dome, I would never have come to Minneapolis in the first place. There was no way that I was going to play in 100-below-zero weather, man!"

On black quarterbacks in the NFL:
"It's just bias for some reason, and that's not a hidden fact. The NFL feels that because black quarterbacks are such good athletes, they should be playing other positions like receiver and cornerback. But why not quarterback?"

Gopher tombstone:
"I would hope to be remembered as a guy who went out and just had fun playing the game, was part of rebuilding a program that had been down for a couple of years, and helped bring the excitement and

respectability back to Gopher football."

Where are they now?
Rickey and his wife Andrea live in Charlotte, N.C., and have four children: Jazzmin, Rickey, Diamond, Trey. He is the starting quarterback for the New Jersey Red Dogs in the Professional Arena League. Rickey also is working on finishing his last 10 credits of his Business Management degree at the U of M.

Tribute

"Rickey is a really good guy. I remember that when I was a freshman, he was so nice to me and really helped me through a lot. Throughout all the pressure of the games, he was good at keeping things fun and light. He even used to give me little gifts before games and, when he wasn't joking around with me in the huddles, he was giving me tips on how to improve my game. I appreciated it, and we still keep in touch today."

-- Darrell Thompson

TIMELINE

| Baseball's All Star Game is played at the Metrodome | UMD goalie Rick Kosti is named to the All-American hockey team | UMD defenseman Norm Maciver is named to the All-American hockey team | Minneapolis native Harold Trumble, former head of the Amateur Hockey Association, is enshrined into the U.S. Hockey Hall of Fame | Freeport's Janice Ettle wins the Twin Cities Marathon in a time of 2:35:47 | Grand Marais' John Patten wins the John Beargrease Sled Dog Race | Hibbing native Louis Robert Blake is enshrined into the U.S. Hockey Hall of Fame |

The University of Minnesota Golden Gopher Football program has a long and epic history dotted with peaks and valleys. Minnesota has always been known to represent the "three yards and a cloud of dust" mentality of Big Ten football, which was anchored by a sound running game. There have been so many great running backs through the years in Gold Country including legends such as Bronko Nagurski, Bruce Smith, Paul Giel, Pug Lund, Bill Daley, Marion Barber, Rick Upchurch, Bob McNamara, and Chris Darkins. But none of them could run like Darrell Thompson of Rochester, who rewrote the record books during his tenure at the U. In 1986, Darrell, as a true freshman, led the maroon and gold to the Liberty Bowl in Memphis, where they lost a heart-breaker to the Tennessee Volunteers.

In 1986, the Gophers were anxious to show the world that their Independence Bowl victory over Clemson the year before was no fluke. It was John Gutekunst's first full season as head coach at the University of Minnesota, having taken over the reigns from Lou Holtz, who went on to coach at Notre Dame. (Holtz had a "Notre Dame Clause" in his contract that gave him the green light to jump ship if he was given the

opportunity to do so. Holtz retired from Notre Dame in 1996 after his 11th season, ostensibly because he didn't want to break Knute Rockne's "sacred" all-time winning record.)

The season got underway for the 1986 Golden Gophers against Bowling Green, and, in Darrell's first collegiate game, he rushed for 205 yards and scored four touchdowns en route to a 31-7 victory. Thompson was for real. But, from there the season hit a few bumps in the road, including a giant pothole in the shape of the University of Oklahoma Sooners, who crushed the Gophs by 63-0. The men of gold followed that up with a 20-24 loss to tiny Pacific, despite two more touchdowns by Thompson. From there the Gophers went on a roll, beating Purdue 36-9, Northwestern 44-23 (led by Darrell's 176 yards rushing and two touchdowns), and Indiana in a squeaker 19-17 (where Darrell ran for another 191 yards).

Minnesota ran into some more trouble in week seven, when they got shutout by the Ohio State Buckeyes, 33-0, and then lost to the Michigan State by 52-23. But the Gophers rebounded in week nine, as they had done all season long, this time defeating the Wisconsin Badgers. 27-20, to retain Paul Bunyan's Axe. In that game, freshman sensation Thompson rushed for 117 yards and became the first Gopher frosh to run for 1,000 yards. Next up, number-two ranked Michigan, who had beaten Minnesota the past eight times, keeping possession of the Little Brown Jug for as many seasons.

The Michigan game was one of the greatest ever for the University of Minnesota. After back and forth scoring the entire game, it all came down to the wire. Michigan coach Bo Schembechler opted to go for the tie instead of a two-pointer to win, with a little over two minutes left. With the game all tied-up at 17, Minnesota drove the ball down the field. Then with 47 seconds left, quarterback Rickey Foggie took off from the Michigan 48 and ran for 31 yards to the Michigan 17. The stage was set for kicker Chip Lohmiller, and the "Chipper" came through in a big way, nailing a 30-yarder as time ran out to give the Gophers a 20-17 victory as well as the coveted Jug.

"I knew once we got it inside the 40, Chip could put It through," said Foggie. "He's got a great leg."

"Give me Liberty..."

Although they finished the season by losing to Iowa, 30-27, the Gophers still earned a birth in the Liberty Bowl, where they would face Tennessee, right in the Vols' backyard of Memphis. The game got underway with the Volunteers jumping ahead 14-0 on two Jeff Francis touchdown passes. The first came to Joey Clinkscales in the left flat as he beat

both cornerback Matt Martinez and safety Steve Franklin and scooted into the end zone for an 18-yard touchdown. After a second quarter Foggie fumble at midfield, Francis dumped a screen pass to fullback William Howard on the ensuing drive to make it 14-0. The Gophers came close twice in the half - once to the Tennessee six where Foggie came up short on a sneak, and then again when Thompson fumbled on the Volunteer 33. Minnesota's only points came on a Lohmiller 27-yard field goal that ended a 70-yard drive at the end of the half.

When the third quarter opened, Foggie appeared to be a man with a mission. The junior quarterback led Minnesota on a 10-play, 88-yard drive that was capped by his own 27-yard run followed by an 11-yard touchdown quarterback-keeper. Then, Thompson added a two-point conversion to make the score 14-11. Still in the third, behind 38 of Thompson's game-high 136 yards, the Gophers started a long march down to the Tennessee 14. But, a holding call nullified their touchdown hopes, and Minnesota settled for another field goal by Lohmiller.

With the score tied at 14 apiece in the fourth, the Vols cruised upfield on a 67-yard drive that was capped by Clinkscales' second TD catch of the game less than two minutes later. With Tennessee up, 21-14, the Gophers tried to rally. Their next drive was stalled on their own 49-yard line, and after an exchange of punts, Minnesota got the ball back at midfield largely because of two great plays by freshman linebacker Jon Leverenz. He first forced a two-yard loss on a first-down play, and then broke up a key third-down pass. So, with Foggie and Thompson poised for the upset, they tried one last drive to win it all. Unfortunately, the seven-play drive ended near midfield when Foggie's fourth-down pass to Ron Goetz fell incomplete. Tennessee took over with 16 seconds left and simply ran out the clock to win the Liberty Bowl. Minnesota out-gained Tennessee in the game 374-324, but, in the end, the final score read 21-14 Vols.

In the season, the Gophers finished at 6-5 and tied for third in the Big Ten with a 5-3 record. It was the best conference finish for the team since 1973 when they went 6-2. All in all it was a great season for the U. Darrell set a new U of M single season rushing mark with 1,240 yards, led the conference in rushing, and along with earning All-Big Ten honors, he was named the team's MVP.

"It was a big deal because you grow up watching the bowl games on TV, and when you finally get to play in one, it is a very special event," said Thompson. "I mean, only the year before I was playing for Rochester John Marshall High School, and now here I was starting at running back in the Liberty Bowl, it was an exciting time."

Foggie set a new University of Minnesota career total yardage record by reaching the 5,118 mark. Lohmiller set a new Gopher field goal record with a 62-yarder against Iowa, and was named to the All-Big Ten team. Bruce Holmes, a senior linebacker, who led the team with 118 tackles also made the All-Big Ten team.

"Daaaa-rrrr-ellll!" "Daaaa-rrrr-ellll!"
Darrell Thompson was born on December 23, 1967, and grew up playing several different sports in Rochester. He grew up with parents that encouraged their children to play a lot of sports and to be well-rounded athletes. After all, his dad played basketball at Clark College in Atlanta and his mom was a three-sport star at Alcorn State University in Mississippi. Thompson's younger brother and sister also went on to earn scholarships playing volleyball.

At Rochester John Marshall High School, Thompson was a three-sport star. Along with being a forward on the basketball team, Darrell also earned all-state honors in track. There he ran the 100, 200, and 400 meters, and even anchored the 1985 state championship mile relay team. But his main sport was football. His senior year he rushed for over 1,000 yards, scored 102 points and averaged an amazing 9.7 yards per carry. Not only was he all-state in football, he was also an All-American. In fact, Darrell was the state's most highly recruited football player ever, and was wooed by nearly every major college in the country.

For his career at the University of Minnesota, Darrell rushed for 4,654 yards on 936 attempts, and scored 40 touchdowns, making him the school's all-time career rushing, attempts, and touchdowns leader. He also scored 262 total points, placing second on the all-time scoring list behind only teammate Lohmiller. From 1986-1989, his team-mates voted him the teams' MVP. He is the only running back in Big Ten history to go over 1,000-yards as a freshman and a sophomore. In 1987, he became the first player ever to gain more than 200 yards in a game against Michigan. In that same game he dazzled the sellout Metrodome crowd as well as the national TV audience with a 98-yard touchdown run, the longest run from scrimmage in Big Ten history. He also threw two passes for the Gophers, both good for touchdowns. His linemen loved him because of his work ethic, and in return Darrell showed his appreciation by presenting them with trophies for making holes for him in the line.

After a phenomenal senior season, Darrell was drafted in the first round by the Green Bay Packers. He went on to play for five seasons with the Pack, before hanging up the spikes in 1995. Because he was hampered by injuries throughout much of his pro career and was often forced to play out of his natural position, he was never able to truly showcase his talents in the NFL.

The best ever
Statistically speaking, Darrell was the greatest running back that has ever at the University of Minnesota. With his 6'1", 220-pound, frame combined with his 4.4 speed and acceleration, Thompson was an elusive yet punishing running back. "Darrell can get into another gear at any time," said former Gopher head coach John Gutekunst. "It's phenomenal. He has quickness and shiftiness laterally. He can step out of things, change direction, and get back to full speed in a hurry." One of the only things tougher than trying to tackle Darrell Thompson was trying to get him to talk about his amazing accomplishments. "I don't see it as that big a deal," said Darrell on his gridiron talents. "I

can run a football, but some other guy can hook up a stereo. God gave everybody their own thing." Darrell was not only an incredible athlete, but is also one of the most cordial people in the state. He was definitely the big man on campus, but when you got to know him, it became readily apparent that he was just a modest guy from Rochester who happened to be darn good at carrying a pigskin.

Who was your hero when you were growing up? "I loved watching Walter Payton and Earl Campbell. They were the best."

What did it mean for you to be a Gopher? "I took a lot of pride in it. I really enjoyed playing for the U, and I'd like to see more kids from Minnesota experiencing the same pleasure that I had there. Athletes can carve out a real nice niche in the community here."

Why did you select the U of M? "At the time I didn't think that pro football was a very realistic expectation, so I figured that I would rather end up working in Minneapolis when I was through playing at the U. When I was being recruited, I went to schools like Nebraska, Wisconsin, and Iowa, but I didn't think that I would want to live in those towns after my football career was over. They were great football towns, but Minneapolis is a great city to live in. I see a lot of Big Ten football players from all over the country living here now because it's just a great place to live."

On being the Packers' first-round pick: "I was really happy, and I was blessed. It was something that I never thought was even that realistic, but when it happened it was special. We were a pretty close knit family, and it was neat that they could all drive up to Green Bay from Rochester to see my games."

On leaving the NFL: "I played for five years with Green Bay, but eventually the game just beats the fun out of you. It gets to the point where all you are doing in the off-season is rehabilitating injuries, stretching, massage, acupuncture, and deep-tissue therapy.

Also, it was really hard for me to play out of position all the time. I just didn't feel like I was given an opportunity to really do what the Packers drafted me to do. I mean, they drafted me to run the football, and then they asked me to play fullback and learn how to block. Because I never blocked much in college, naturally I was only going to be an average fullback in the NFL. It just got to be too much for me at the end, and, eventually, like anything else, the team is always looking for someone to replace you."

Today are you a Packer fan or a Viking fan? "Both, but if they played each other I'd have to pull for the Pack -- they were my team!"

On Minnesota fans: "We have great fans here in Minnesota, but I wish they were more like the Packer fans in that those people support their team win or lose."

Gopher tombstone: "I'd want to be remembered as a guy who played hard, loved to compete, and was someone that commanded respect from his teammates."

Where are they now? Darrell, his wife Stephanie, and their two baby girls live in the Twin Cities. Thompson has been retired from the game for a couple of years now, and currently works in Minneapolis where he manages youth programs and charitable foundations. "I tell kids today that they can play in the pros if they work really hard at it - but I tell them to be realistic," said Thompson. "Since there's only a one-in-10,000 chance of making it in the pros, I tell them that they need to study and make other plans in life so that they can be successful even if they don't make it."

Tribute

"He was a great guy and a great talent. We are still good friends today and stay in contact with each other. Darrell's physical build was just incredible. He was such a good runner, and I remember that I as a true-freshman he came in and rushed for over 1,000 yards. It took a lot of pressure off of me to have Darrell as a threat in the backfield so we could run that option. We had a lot of good times out there together, and I know that we really complimented each other well."
-- Rickey Foggie

KENT HRBEK
The Twins Win the World Series

Across the land, accomplished baseball pundits predicted another season of mediocrity for the 1987 Minnesota Twins, probably no better than fourth place in the AL West. This time, the pundits were dead wrong.

The Twins took baseball by storm in 1987, featuring a lineup that was comprised of Minnesota's own "Fab-Four," the quartet of Herbie, Kirby, the G-Man, and Bruno.

They acquired Dan Gladden, and closer Jeff Reardon. Frank Viola began to show great consistency as a starter along with pitching partner the crafty veteran Bert Blyleven, who, believe it or not, was with the Twins the last time they were in the American League Championship Series. The Twins finished the regular season with a modest 85-77 record, but it was good enough to win the West.

After being stiffed for All-Star Game selection, Hrbek took out his anger on opposing teams for the rest of the season. Herbie ended the season with a career-high 34 home runs, and added 90 RBI's en route to a .285 batting average. Hrbek was a major reason why the

Twins were able to win their first divisional title since 1970.

Their first opponent was the Detroit Tigers. The Twins took the first two in Minnesota and went on to win two of the final three in Detroit, stunning the Tigers. Herbie's pal Gaetti was named the ALCS MVP. In the World Series, the Twins' opponent was the legendary St. Louis Cardinals.

The first two games weren't even close. In game one, the Twins blasted St. Louis 10-1 in a game highlighted by Dan Gladden's grand slam. The second game was another cakewalk, an 8-4 victory. (Editor's addition:) Just when it looked like a series sweep for Minnesota, the Cards came back and took the next three games in St. Louis. One victory for the Cardinals at the Metrodome, and St. Louis would be world champions.

Just like in the backyard...
Game Six was a childhood dream come true for Kent Hrbek. With the Twins up 6-5 Herbie would make history that night, as he stepped up to the plate in the sixth, with two outs and the bases juiced. Herbie then proceeded to hit a 439-foot grand salami over the center field wall, and into a sea of white homer hankies. The series was evened at three games apiece. As he circled the bases with his fists pumping and his mouth wide open, he remembered playing out that same play 100 times before in his back yard.

Said teammate Roy Smalley after game six: "Before Kent went up to bat I looked at Frank Viola and said, 'You watch... This is too set up. This is too much like a storybook. It's too perfect.'"

"It is something I will never feel again," said Herbie after game six. "People talk about thrills in baseball. Just making the big leagues was a thrill. Hitting a home run at Yankee Stadium in my first game in the big leagues was a thrill. Hitting a grand slam in the World Series in your home state, that is indescribable."

Game seven had all the drama you could ask for. Three Twins were thrown out at home plate. Greg Gagne drove in the winning run on an infield hit. Frankie V. pitched eight beautiful innings, giving up only two early. And, fittingly, Jeff Reardon came in for the ninth, getting the final out on McGee's ground ball to Gary Gaetti. When the G-Man threw the ball across the diamond to Herbie at first, the Twins had won the game 4-2, earning the title of baseball's World Champions.

At the series finale, the Minnesota fans had actually grown quite fond of the parachute-topped edifice better known as the "Homerdome," a true testament to its' inex-

plicable magic it had provided the Twins. Frank Viola would earn Series MVP honors, and for Herbie, there would be ticker-tape parades, presidential meetings, and even Late Night with David Letterman.

"I just step back and think of the guys that I played with back then," said Hrbek. Great guys, like Viola, Gaetti, Brunansky, Laudner, and Bush. We grew up in the big leagues together, we lost in the big leagues together, and then, in 1987, we were the best in the world together. I can still remember sitting on the clubhouse floor after the game. Everybody thought we all were drunk as pigs, but we weren't, we were all just mentally and physically spent. It was something that we had all worked so hard for, and had so much fun doing, that when it was over we just soaked it all in and enjoyed it."

"That team was the closest-knit group of guys I've ever been around," added Kirby Puckett. "It was unbelievable. I mean win or lose, every night you could find at least a dozen of us eating together at a restaurant. We hung together, and we won together. I still remember, after we won Game Seven, a bunch of us were just sitting there on the floor in the clubhouse, drinking champagne, and staring at each other like, 'What did we just do?'

I've had a lot of people ask me since then, 'How did it feel?' And you know what? I can't tell them. It's some-thing you have to experience for yourself to get it. It was something only the people in that room could understand."

Growing up in the shadows of the Met
Kent Hrbek was born on May 21, 1960, and grew up a stone's throw from Metropolitan Stadium in Bloomington. He grew up following the Twins and playing baseball. Herbie went to Bloomington-Kennedy High School where he batted .480 his senior year, while playing great defense. "He was an excellent fielder," Buster Radebach, his high school coach would say. "He was a student of the game and he studied it." It was in American Legion ball where Hrbek started to get noticed. His coach, Red Haddox, recalled that fans were simply in awe of his massive home runs.

"He could handle the glove and could run for a big man," said former Twins owner Calvin Griffith who went to see one of Kent's Legion games. "I could see that his stroke alone was sufficient to gamble on him." So, in the 17th round of the 1978 draft, Herbie became a Twin, accepting a $30,000 offer.

After a brief stint in Visalia, where he was voted the MVP of the California League, he got the call to come up to the show. He finished second to Cal Ripken in the Rookie of the Year voting, and was the lone rookie on the All-Star team that year. "My sister has probably sent in 10,000 votes on her own!" Kent said in regards to the All-Star balloting. He made the cover of Sports Illustrated with the title: "Best of the Worst," and appeared on the ABC-TV's Good Morning

TIMELINE

St. Thomas runner Jeff Hyman wins the Division III 3,000M Steeplechase National Championship	Macalaster runner Julia Kirtland wins both the Division III 3,000M and 5,000M - Indoor Track National Championships	Augsburg's Melanie Herrera wins the Division III Shot Put National Championship	Carleton runner Shelley Scherer wins the Division III women's Cross Country National Championship	The St. Thomas University women's Country Team wins the Division III National Championship	After beating the Saints and 49ers, the Vikings lose to the Washington Redskins, 17-10, in the NFC Championship Game	Ray Dandridge, a Minneapolis Miller from 1949-52, is inducted into the Baseball Hall of Fame	North Star Bill Masterton's number 19 is retired into the rafters of the Met Center	Little Falls native Jim Langer, a former Viking center, is inducted into the Pro Football Hall of Fame

He was most appreciated by his teammates and the fans for his upper-deck power and agility. He also will be remembered as one of the best fielders ever to play first base. A .282 lifetime hitter over his 14-year career, Hrbek finished second in the 1984 MVP race when he hit .311. He is among club leaders in nearly every offensive category: 2nd in home-runs (293), 2nd in RBI's (1,086), 4th in hits (1,749), 4th in runs (903), 5th in total bases (2,976), 2nd in walks (838), 3rd in total games (1,747), 5th in at-bats (6,192) and 3rd in doubles (312). He retired in 1994 and his number 14 was formally retired on August 13, 1995.

Who was your hero when you were growing up?
"Tony Oliva was my hero, and I always idolized him. My mom even sewed a big #6 on the back of my T-Ball jersey, so I could wear his number."

What did it mean for you to be a Twin?
"I thought being a Twin was just about the greatest thing in the world. Being from Minnesota, and being just a huge sports fan, I have always rooted for our teams, whether it was the Twins, Vikings, North Stars, Timberwolves, or Gophers - I just wanted our teams to win. I don't think there is anybody that wanted to win a ball game more than Kent Hrbek, and there probably never will be!"

Were you really considering signing with the Tigers or Red Sox?
"Sure I thought about going somewhere else to play when I started getting some offers, and my wife and I sat downstairs and talked about it. But I didn't see any reason to go anywhere else. I just couldn't justify it with all of our family and friends here, and we realized that we had it all right here. What the hell was the use of packing up and going someplace else? I love the area and I enjoy the people here. Now, of course you can't make it sound like that when you're negotiating your contract, because you need some kind of pull to let them think you might go to another team! The Tigers would have to have given me the moon in order for me to move. I love it here."

On Minnesotans:
"I just think the people up here are great. I don't know, and people might think I'm a dink for saying this, but I think East Coast people could care less about family, and the West Coast people, they don't even know if they have a family! When you can walk into a mom & pop restaurant in the middle of Iowa while you're out pheasant hunting, and everybody knows everybody, and they all care about each other, that to me is home."

What's the biggest fish you ever caught?
"Down in Spring Lake one time, I pulled in a 40-pound carp using a chunk of oatmeal, and I'm damn proud of it too!"

Twins tombstone:
"I had a great time playing. I liked to put on a show and have a good time and make people think that I wasn't so much different than they were, because I was a major league baseball player. People always thought that I had too much fun on the field, but having a good time was the only way I played well. I'd like to think that I was a fun-loving guy who felt like 'Hey, don't look at me badly because I could drink a beer and I was a major league baseball player.' There

are too many guys now that thought they were so much better than others because they were major league baseball players, and I could never stand that! Let me tell you, you're not better than me because you can hit a 90 mph fastball, and because you make $6 million a year! Don't think that your sh-- doesn't stink, because it does!"

On retirement:
"I just want to be Kent Hrbek, have a family, and be able to stop at Super America and pump my gas without worrying about signing this or that. I want to be able to walk around with my fly down, or with spit dribbling off my chin, because I'm human, and everybody else has done that before. I don't want to be Kent Hrbek, the Minnesota Twin, I just want to be 'Joe Blow,' because that's who I am."

Where are they now?
Kent, his wife Jeanie, and their daughter Heidi, currently live in Bloomington. "Those two are what's making retirement wonderful, and one of the big reasons why I'm not playing baseball anymore," said Herbie.

Tributes

"He was awesome man. He was the best first baseman that I ever played with. He was one of the best teammates that I ever had. He was a great person, fun to be around and he made every day special coming to the ball park. I always felt that he should have won several gold gloves and been on more all star teams. He's like me, just care free and just wanted to play. He loved what he did and he played hard every day. He got hurt a lot at the end, I think he separated that shoulder like three or four times, but they were all tough injuries during the call of duty. You knew that whenever you had Herbie and me in the same clubhouse, it was going to be loud and something would always be going on. Herbie always made me laugh, and he didn't even have to try."
-- Kirby Puckett

"Kent is a fun-loving guy and he always played and conducted himself that way whether he was on or off the field. He was such a talented hitter and player, and he enjoyed playing the game. He probably wanted to win more than any other player I have managed. He had such a desire and will to win. He was a home grown athlete who was just a great player."
-- Tom Kelly

"He was a guy that I truly don't think I got to know very well. He was a lot more of a fun-loving guy than I thought he was as an opposing player. I can only describe him as a good guy and a good person. He never really had anything bad to say about people, he was a positive, funny guy. He was a great competitor."
-- Jack Morris

"He grew up with me. I coached him all the way through the minor leagues and into the big leagues, he was a wonderful player and a great person."
-- Tony Oliva

"I said for about five years that Hrbek was the best fielding first baseman that I have ever seen, and I played with Keith Hernandez, and I saw Don Mattingly up close for several years as well. I think that when he was healthy, he was as good as anyone in the game. He was a throw back to my era. All he wanted to do was play baseball and go home and hunt and fish and have fun. He really enjoyed the game and he played it well."
-- Jim Kaat

The Millerettes

Stew Thornley, a local baseball historian and author, has written a couple of pieces about baseball in Minnesota during the golden years. One is about our women's baseball team called the Millerettes, and the other is about the rivalry between the Minneapolis Millers and St. Paul Saints. They are reprinted with his permission here.

Of the Minnesota professional sports teams that have virtually been written out of history -- the Twin City Skippers, St. Paul Lights, Minnesota Buckskins -- the least remembered of all the franchises that ever represented the state may be the Minneapolis Millerettes. In 1944 the Millerettes competed, along with the Rockford Peaches, South Bend Blue Sox, Racine Belles, Milwaukee Chicks, and Kenosha Comets, in the All-American Girls Professional Baseball League (AAGPBL). The founder, organizer, recruiter, and promoter of the AAGPBL was Chicago Cubs owner Philip K. Wrigley, who was trying to do nothing more than hedge his bets with the creation of the league. With the immediate future of men's baseball in doubt because of World War II, Wrigley saw girl's baseball as a way to keep ball parks in use in the event the major leagues were forced to halt operations. "If we can put Rosie the Riveter in the factory," reasoned P. K., "why can't we put girls on the baseball diamond?"

The game the girls and women played in their initial season of 1943 was a baseball-softball hybrid. As the years passed, however, the ball got smaller and the diamond larger, and pitching evolved from underhand to sidearm to full overhand. The players, recruited from throughout the United States and Canada, ranged from girls as young as 15 to women in their early 20s. Besides being the organization's founder, Phil Wrigley also carefully created the image of the league. Special short-skirted uniforms with satin shorts were designed by Mrs. Wrigley. And the regimens of spring training included a charm school, featuring a visit from guest instructor Helena Rubinstein to teach the ladies how to dress, walk, and talk, as well as, most importantly, "how to attract the right kind of man."

Traveling teams of female ballplayers can be traced back to the 19th century. While no evidence supports the charges, these barnstormers were accused of practicing "a profession considerably older than baseball." Wrigley wanted to make sure no such aspersion would ever be cast upon his players and assigned each team a chaperon responsible for the conduct, care, and appearance of her players.

Regardless of the image Wrigley strived to produce, there was no hiding that these girls and women were superb athletes. Many were national champions and record-holders in basketball, softball, field hockey, speedskating, and many other sports. Minneapolis Tribune sportswriter Halsey Hall summed it up as he described the opening of the Minneapolis Millerettes' season in 1944: "Common courtesy and sweet little niceties accorded ladies go by the boards next weekend at Nicollet Park."

The Millerettes were managed by Claude Jonnard, a former pitcher for the New York Giants and Toledo Mud Hens. (Others who managed in the AAGPBL include Hall of Famers Max Carey, Jimmy Foxx, and Dave "Beauty" Bancroft.) The Millerettes were led by right fielder Helen Callaghan, who hit .287 with three home runs in 111 games. (She would lead the league in hitting the following year.) Baseball ran in the Callaghan family. Callaghan's sister, Margaret, was also a star in the league, and Helen's son, Casey Candaele, has played with the Montreal Expos and Houston Astros in recent years.

Callaghan wasn't the only Millerette who would have a relative in the major leagues. The Minneapolis pitching rotation included Annabelle Lee, the aunt of Bill "Spaceman" Lee, who pitched with the Expos and Boston Red Sox in the 1970s and 1980s. In fact, the Spaceman credits Aunt Annabelle with teaching him how to pitch (but adds that some of his other habits -- including sprinkling marijuana on his pancakes in place of syrup -- were learned elsewhere). Center field at Nicollet Park was played by Faye Dancer, a crowd-pleaser who could frequently been seen turning somersaults in the outfield between pitches.

The 1944 season was divided into halves with the winners of each half meeting in a post-season tournament to determine the league champion. The Millerettes opened the season at home Saturday, May 27, against the Rockford Peaches. Even though the Millerettes blew a 3-0 lead and lost, 5-4, Halsey Hall reported that a crowd of "several hundred" marveled at the throwing arm of shortstop LaVonne "Pepper" Paire and the "ground-covering, fly-catching genius" of Dancer.

League historian Sharon Roepke characterized the play in the league as "Few home runs; lots of squeeze plays." She could have added, "Lots of stolen bases." On July 1, Rockford stole 18 bases off the Millerettes, whose catcher, Edna Frank, threw out only one runner. (Racine's Sophie "The Trophy" Kurys stole 166 bases in 1944; two years later she was successful in 201 of 203 stolen base attempts.) Runs were always at a premium in the AAGPBL. In a June 16 game against Racine, Millerettes' hurler Dottie Wiltse held the Belles hitless for the first 10 2/3 innings. She completed a six-hitter in 15 innings, but was a 3-2 loser as she watched her teammates strand 22 runners on base. (Wiltse posted a 1.88 earned-run average in 1944 and, despite the lack of support she often received from her mates, finished the season with a won-lost record of 20-16.)

The Millerettes played respectable baseball in the season's early weeks, but a slump that followed dropped them to the cellar, where they stayed, and they closed out the first half of the season with a dismal record of 23-36. Things didn't get any better in the second half. Few fans were turning out to Nicollet Park to see the Millerettes, and the other teams began complaining of the long road trips to Minneapolis to play before such small crowds. As a result, in late July the remainder of the Millerettes' home games were switched to other cities and the team, which became known as the Orphans, was forced to play the rest of the season on the road.

The team moved to Fort Wayne in 1945. Roepke and colleague Danielle Barber blame the Millerettes' lack of support in Minneapolis on a "hostile press."

"The media was antagonistic in Minneapolis compared to other cities, where the outcome of the games received banner headlines," claims Barber.

The AAGPBL lasted for a dozen years, longer than several men's major leagues, but according to Roepke, "It's been written out of history." Its anonymity can be seen in the case of Jean Havlish, a St. Paul native who was inducted into the Minnesota Sports Hall of Fame in 1988 for her accomplishments as a bowler. Havlish played in the AAGPBL with the Fort Wayne Daisies in 1954, but no mention is made of her involvement in baseball on her Hall of Fame plaque that hangs in the Hubert Humphrey Metrodome.

It is the mission of Roepke, Barber, and others to change this. Roepke has been active in promoting reunions among the former members of the league, who now have organized a players' association. In 1988, a temporary display of women in baseball opened at the Baseball Hall of Fame in Cooperstown, NY. Roepke and the players association are continuing to lobby officials in Cooperstown for a permanent exhibit.

Note: Since Thornley wrote this piece in 1988, a permanent display to women's baseball has been established in Cooperstown. The AAGPBL was also featured in the movie, "A League of Their Own."

"Pay Days"
Millers vs. Saints

Before the Twins came to town in 1961, Minnesotans enjoyed the century-long rivalry between the St. Paul Saints and Minneapolis Millers. Over that time the Millers won 4,800 games and the Saints 4,719, with each team winning nine American Association pennants. Stew Thornley takes us back to a better time.

"Even during the Depression, we could always count on a good crowd when the Saints and Millers played each other," recalled Oscar Roettger, a pitcher and first baseman for the St. Paul Saints in the 1920s and 1930s. 'Pay days,' - that's what those games were." The diamond rivalry between Minneapolis and St. Paul was in its golden years during Roettger's playing days, but its roots were part of the post-Civil War baseball boom in America. Minnesota veterans returning home from Bull Run, Shiloh, and Gettysburg waged their own War between the cities, a battle fought with less lethal weapons -- bats and balls instead of muskets and bayonets -- but one that lacked a cease-fire for nearly a hundred years.

From the town teams of the 1860s and 1870s, the professional nines of the latter 1800s, and finally the great Saints and Millers clubs of the 20th century, they fought-player vs. player, fan vs. fan, sometimes player vs. fan. The newspapers joined the struggle, firing their artillery at enemy camps across the Mississippi River. In the 1890s, when both cities were represented in the Western League, the *Minneapolis Tribune* leveled a charge of "dirty ball" against its neighbors to the east, the Saints, who were owned and managed at that time by Charles Comiskey. "Manager Comiskey," reported the *Tribune,* "will be served with a formal notice that the Minneapolis club will not play today's game unless guaranteed that there will be no spiking of Minneapolis players, no interference on the part of the crowd, no throwing of rocks, no throwing of dust and dirt in the eyes of the Minneapolis players, and a few other tricks which the game yesterday was featurized by."

The Western League changed its name to the American League and changed its status from a minor to a major league in 1901 - sans Minneapolis and St. Paul. The following year, however, the Millers and Saints became charter members of the American Association. And by the time they hung up their spikes and shin guards for the final time, they had created a legacy for the incoming Twins to follow. Through their 59 years in the league, the Millers compiled the best winning percentage of all Association teams; the Saints followed a close second. In addition, the two teams shared the Association record with nine pennants each.

The year 1915 saw the hottest race between the Saints and Millers. Minneapolis's early-season hopes rested on a southpaw from Hackensack, New Jersey, Harry Harper. In May, the young phenom no-hit St. Paul, but two months later the Saints didn't even need their bats to pound Harper and the Millers, as the wild lefty walked 20 batters (in only eight innings), a performance that remains an Association record to this day. Harper was gone from the Minneapolis roster by the end of July, but the Millers hung on, edging out the Saints on the season's final weekend to cop the flag by a game-and-a-half.

But no matter where they stood in the standings, the Millers and Saints ignited the passions of the partisans with their 22 inter-city games each year. Interest peaked each season with the holiday doubleheaders at Lexington Park in St. Paul and Nicollet Park in Minneapolis: a morning game at one park followed by a streetcar ride across the river for the afternoon game in the other was the Twin Cities' primary entertainment on Decoration Day, the Fourth of July, and Labor Day.

Ab Wright of the Millers saved his biggest 1940 fireworks for the morning game on Independence Day. En route to winning the American Association Triple Crown that season, Wright belted four home runs and a triple against the Saints for 19 total bases, a league record never equaled.

And the explosions heard on the Fourth of July in 1929 were from a Nicollet Park brawl between the rivals, described by one writer as "the most vicious affair ever witnessed at Nicollet" and one that "required fully a dozen policemen to quell the disturbance." Millers' reserve infielder Sammy Bohne came out of the coaching box to land some of the hardest punches, and the next day's the headline over Halsey Hall's story in the *Minneapolis Journal* read, "Sammy Bohne Doesn't Play, But Gets More Hits Than Those Who Do."

Hostilities even extended into the stands at times. In 1959 Minneapolis manager Gene Mauch scaled the railing at Midway Stadium in St. Paul to confront a fan whose remarks Mauch deemed "a bit too personal." In 1911, Millers' skipper Joe Cantillon took a bat with him to silence a heckler in the box seats at Lexington Park.

But despite the occasional bad blood, Oscar Roettger -- the main recipient of Sammy Bohne's fists in that 1929 fracas -- remembers that both teams were good friends off the field, often barnstorming across the state together after the season to "have some fun and get a little pheasant hunting done." Howie Schultz, a Saints' first baseman in the 1940s, concurs and adds, "Fans were more involved in the rivalry than the players were.

As for the players, a number of them wore the colors of both cities during their careers, among them Mauch, Angelo Giuliani, Bill McKechnie, and Johnny Goryl, but the most notable man to work both sides of the river was Mike Kelley. Kelley helped found the American Association in 1902 and managed the Saints to pennants two of their first three years in the league; he also played first base in an infield that included Hall-of-Famer Miller Huggins. Kelley defected to Minneapolis in 1906 for a managerial fling that was as stormy as it was brief, but he later returned to skipper the Saints to three more league championships.

In 1924, Mike made the move again. Lured by an offer to become part-owner of the club, Kelley came back for another shot at managing the Millers. He eventually bought out the other owners and established a re-tooling factory for aging major leaguers in Minneapolis. Combining these players with youngsters on their way up, Kelley built the powerful Miller teams of the 1930s that included fence-crackers Wright, Joe Hauser, Buzz Arlett, Spencer Harris, Fabian Gaffice, and Ted Williams and an ancient but crafty pitching staff of Rosy Ryan, Jess Petty, and Rube Benton. Kelley also became famous for his Dalmatians that roamed the bullpen during games and menaced opposing right fielders chasing batted balls into that area.

The last of the independent owners in the league, Kelley finally sold out to the New York Giants in 1946. By this time, the Saints were a Brooklyn Dodger farm club, adding a local flavor to the Big Apple rivalry and giving Twin Citians the chance to watch Duke Snider and Roy Campanella play for the Saints and Willie Mays, Monte Irvin, and Hoyt Wilhelm perform for the Millers.

The battlefields on which they skirmished -- Robert Street Grounds, Aurora Park, Lexington Park, and Midway Stadium in St. Paul; Athletic Park, Minnehaha Park, Nicollet Park, and Metropolitan Stadium in Minneapolis and suburban Bloomington, -- produced their share of decorated veterans. Five members of Baseball's Hall of Fame once played for the Saints, while Minneapolis produced 14 players and one manager who are now enshrined in Cooperstown.

What started as a Sunday afternoon diversion in the 1860s -- reflecting the larger struggle between two emerging metropolises to become the dominant city in the state -- rapidly escalated and increased in intensity until it reached its Appomattox in 1961. On April 11th of that year the Minnesota Twins played their first game, finally forming a union among area baseball fans. The baseball battle between East and West had ended. The Pay Days were history.

In 1988, all of Minnesota was still dizzy and hungover from the World Series hoopla that swept through the state during that magical season a year earlier. So, that next year, people were more interested than ever to see if the club could repeat as American League and world champs. Fans turned out at the Metrodome in droves.

The 1988 season saw the Twins finishing with a quite respectable 91-71 record (a better percentage than the year before) en route to a second place finish in the AL West. In fact, it was the Twins' first 90-win season since 1970. Minnesota battled Tony LaRussa's Oakland team for the better part of the season, but in the end the Athletics were too tough and won the AL crown.

As a group, the Twins placed second in the major leagues with a collective .274 batting average. Kirby Puckett had another monster year, batting .356 while leading the league in hits with 234. The "G-Man," Gary Gaetti, hit .301, Kent Hrbek hit .312, and previously-unheralded pitcher Alan Anderson won 16 games while producing the league's lowest ERA at 2.45.

As for their skipper, the remarkable Tom Kelly, he reaped the benefits of leading his ballclub to the 1987 World Series and was honored by managing the 1988 All-Star game. He was joined at the All-Star festivities in Cincinnati by Puckett, Tim Laudner, Gaetti, Jeff Reardon, and Frank Viola. Frankie V. was the starting and winning pitcher for the AL as they beat the NL, 2-1.

Viola's heroics weren't confined to the 1988 All-Star Game. He picked up right where he left off in 1987, when he won the World Series MVP, and brought some more hardware to Minnesota, winning the coveted Cy Young award as the leagues best pitcher. 1988 was a dream season for Viola as he led the league with 24 wins, posted a 2.64 ERA, and struck-out 193 batters. He also set the Twins record for the all-time best winning percentage that season at .774.

To top it all off, the Twins became the first American League team ever to draw three million fans, as 3,030,672 people passed through the Metrodome turnstiles to watch the reigning world champs defend their title. The team was riding the wave from the clubs' first-ever World Series title, and the expectations of the fans had grown. The faithful wanted to see up-close a part of the history, that for many of them, had unfolded before their eyes only on the television.

The man ultimately responsible for the success of the team was manager Kelly. The Twins skipper never made a lot of noise in the dugout, yet was able to lead his team all the way to the promised land occupied by baseball's world champions.

Kelly's soft-spoken, 'lead-by-example' attitude filtered throughout the club-house and became infectious with all of his players. Tom has carried with him the reputation of being a fan favorite, a media darling, and all-around good guy. Perhaps the biggest compliment paid to him is that he is referred to as a players' manager. His career has been a long and winding one, with its roots in Minnesota.

Minnesota born

Jay Thomas Kelly was born on August 15, 1950, in Graceville, Minn. His family ultimately moved east, and Tom grew up in New Jersey. Baseball had always played a role in his life because his father, Joe, was a Northern League pitcher during the 1940s and later played in the New York Giants system. Tom went on to become an outstanding ballplayer at St. Mary's High School in South Amboy, N.J. He went on to attend Mesa Community College in Mesa, Ariz., and also Monmouth College in West Long Branch, N.J.

T.K. fulfilled a boyhood dream in 1968 when the fledgling Seattle Pilots selected him in the

fifth round of the Major League Baseball free agent draft. So, he reported to Newark to play in the minor leagues. In his first year he hit an impressive .317, led the league in stolen bases and became a league all-star. From there it was off to Clinton and Jacksonville, until 1971, when he was signed as a free agent by the Twins. After spending a year in Charlotte, he began a four-year stint in Tacoma, the Twins triple-A club.

Then, in 1975, Kelly got the call he had been waiting for his entire career - he was going to the show. On May 19, he got his first major league hit when he singled off Detroit's Joe Coleman. It wasn't a very long stint in the bigs, 127 at bats in 49 games to be exact. But it was something he had dreamed of during his entire career as an active ballplayer. So, for a career minor leaguer, those 1975 Twins games were pretty special to him. He ended up with 23 hits, while driving in 11 batters, scoring another 11 runs and batting a buck-eighty-one. Kelly's lone dinger of his career came off Tigers pitcher Vern Ruhle.

"It's something you always dreamed about, to play at the major league level," said Kelly. "As a minor leaguer, you were always working towards that goal. I got the opportunity, but I wasn't good enough to stick around. At least, I did have a chance which was great for me, and it is something I will always remember."

After a season at triple-A Rochester, Kelly caught another break. This time he found his calling as he would spend the next three years in Tacoma and Toledo as player and as a manager. In 1979 and 1980, he managed a Twins' farm team in Visalia, where he led the club to two consecutive divisional titles. He was also named the California League Manager of the Year for two years in a row. He then was promoted by the Twins to Orlando where he was named manager of the year after guiding his team to the league championship.

In 1983, he got another call to the majors, this time as the new Twins' third base coach, becoming the first Minnesotan to ever become a member of the Twins' managerial staff. In 1986, T.K. took over the Twins' managerial duties from a faltering Ray Miller.

His big chance

In 1987, Kelly became only the fifth manager in baseball history to win a pennant as a rookie when the Twins beat the Cardinals in the World Series. For his efforts the 37-year-old was named American League Manager of the Year. It was a tremendous victory for all of Minnesota and T.K. was given much of the credit. And deservedly so, for it was he who supplied the glue to hold the players together.

Kelly's heroes won their second World Series over the Atlanta Braves four years later. Tom thus became first Twins manager ever to lead his club to two divisional titles (and subsequent world championships) and the third manager ever in baseball history to have won two World Series and never lost one. In 1991, Kelly again was named American League Manager of the Year,

TIMELINE

| Watertown's Dennis Koslowski wins a bronze medal on the Olympic wrestling team | Minneapolis' Robert Seguso wins a gold medal on the Olympic doubles tennis team | Laker center Clyde Lovellette is inducted into the Basketball Hall of Fame. | Stewartville's Bart Bardwell wins his third consecutive Twin Cities Marathon - Wheelchair Division | Carleton runner Anna Princas wins the Division III 3,000M Indoor Track National Championship | Augsburg's Carolyn Ross wins the Division III 400M Dash and 400M Hurdles Indoor Track National Championship | The Concordia Moorhead women's Basketball team wins the Division III National Championship | Augsburg wrestler John Beatty wins the Division III 134 lbs. National Championship | Bemidji State's Liz Mulvihill wins the Division III Indoor Track Shot Put National Championship | The Mankato State Men's Country Team wins the Division III National Championship |

was also named WCCO Radio's 1991 Distinguished Good Neighbor, an award given annually to someone who brings honor to the state of Minnesota. In 1992, managed the American League All-Star team in San Diego. (It was the AL over the NL in a 13-6 rout.) Fittingly, Kirby Puckett was the All-Star Game MVP.

The iron man

As T.K. finishes his 12th season as the Twins manager, he has quietly become entrenched as baseball's longest-tenured manager. He is also the all-time winningest manager in Minnesota history, having won his 800th game in 1997. TK won two World Series in a span of five years. This may not sound impressive until one realizes that the Chicago Cubs have not won a single World Series since 1908, or the Red Sox since 1918. Kelly will no doubt go down in history as the greatest Twins manager.

Who was your hero when you were growing up?

"Willie Mays. I grew up watching the Giants at the Polo Grounds in New York, and I just thought he could do it all."

What does it mean for you to be a member of the Twins organization?

"In 1975, I was just so happy to be in the big leagues that it didn't mean much to me right away. But now that I have been in the organization for 20-some years, I think it's very special, and I put more credence to it now than I did then. The Minnesota Twins have been good to me and my family. I feel like a part of the organization, maybe not an intricate part, but a piece. I feel like it's more of an honor now. We try to convey that point to the players, that it is an honor to wear the Twins' uniform. We think it's important that they represent the uniform as well as they represent themselves and their families."

On the 1987 World Series:

"Being it was my first full year as a manager, it was a very special thing. It was a new experience for me getting into the playoffs and into the World Series. Typically, we are somewhat afraid and apprehensive about new experiences because we don't know what to expect. There was a lot of cautious optimism surrounding the whole experience. The playoffs were a little more nerve-racking than the Big Dance, but, all in all, it was an incredible experience."

On the 1991 World Series:

"By 1991, we knew what to expect, so I think I enjoyed that one a little bit more because I knew what was going on. I wasn't as nervous this go around as I was in 1987. I frequently use the phrase 'storybook-like' to describe the games that series, because each game was like turning a page in a book to find out what was going to happen. Having the games come down to the ninth inning and the last at-bat was incredible. We were very fortunate to win, because either team could have easily won. What was really rewarding was the fact that we went from last place in 1990 to first place in 1991. It was also very special to me because we proved that smaller market teams could still win it all."

Twins tombstone:

"He was someone who worked hard to get where he got, all the time knowing that good things can happen to someone who works hard."

His longevity as Twins manager

"It just shows that I have had a lot of good players here over the years, and good players make managers look good. You have to remember that any manager is only as good as his players, and I've been very fortunate. I think it's the result of a good Twins minor league system, good scouting, and good coaching. It's not just one person, and there are a lot of people involved. The game itself can beat you up. All the time I spent playing and managing in the minor leagues with the bus rides, the traveling, and the wear and tear was tough. I am 46 years old, but I am starting to feel the 'longevity' of the game maybe a little more than the average 46-year old -- it's catching up to me. But I am grateful to be where I am, and I do think it is an honor to be the manager of the Minnesota Twins."

Where are they now?

Tom and his wife Sharon currently live in Maplewood and they have two children, Sharon and Tom. His managerial contract is signed through the year 2000.

Tributes

"We played together for a season, and we had a very good relationship. I liked him then, and I like him today. I like the way that he goes about getting his players ready to play. He's a player's manager, and all of the players that have played for him, speak very highly of him. He allows his players to enjoy playing the game, and I think that is important. Tom goes about handling all the personalities on the team in a very professional and fun way, and that's why he is successful." -- **Rod Carew**

"T.K. will always be my favorite manager. He's such a great guy. He was like my mother at the ballpark. He knew how I was feeling when I walked in the door just by looking at me. I just think he is an awesome manager, and I just love the guy. It's very hard to get to know him because he is a different person on and off the field. He is a great baseball man and he knows it so well. He is so far ahead of the game, I mean as soon as the first pitch is thrown, he's thinking down the road to the eighth inning. He knew that we played our best

by being loose and having fun, so he let us play that way. I mean what can you say, he's got the longest tenure of any manager in the majors." -- **Kent Hrbek**

"I consider Tom to be the most fair manager that I ever played for. He let everybody know that there were no superstars on our team, and I think that the players respected that." -- **Jack Morris**

"We go way back. I played for T.K. back when I was in the instructional leagues, and we always got along well. All he ever asked of me was that I gave a 100 percent, and I've always listened to whatever he has to say." -- **Kirby Puckett**

"Even before I came here I had the greatest respect for Tom Kelly. The way that his teams would perform in last-place seasons, or in championship seasons was remarkably consistent, and that definitely relates to the manager's control and leadership. It says a lot about how he can handle teams in this era of players, who maybe don't have the respect that the major league baseball deserves. Coming to the Twins, he surpassed my expectations as a manager in the manner of how he handles teams, rosters, and the ups and downs of a typical season." -- **Paul Molitor**

"He is a great person. He wants you to work hard, and he knows a lot about baseball. I don't have enough good words for Tom Kelly, he is a great man." -- **Tony Oliva**

"I have the utmost respect for him, and I think he is the best manager in the game. I think the way he molded that 1987 team was incredible." -- **Jim Kaat**

Doug Woog has become a coaching icon in Minnesota sports. He is the Minnesota equivalent to the Notre Dame football coach. He has achieved an incredible amount of success in Gold Country, and more importantly he has done it all with Minnesota kids. This alone may be the single greatest tradition in all of college sports, yet it is something that is constantly used against him as the reason why his teams have never won the NCAA championship. Always the bridesmaid, never the bride.

Woog's teams have come so close, having gone to an amazing six NCAA Final Fours, but has come home empty-handed every time. One thing is certain, he will never come as close to winning a title as he did in 1989, against Harvard at the Civic Center in St. Paul.

The Gophers were coming off of their first WCHA championship under Woog and were expected to finish even better than the last year's Final Four loss to Maine. Things looked promising for the team at the start of the season. Dave Snuggerud and Tom Chorske who would lead the team in scoring had returned from the Olympics, the reigning Hobey Baker Award recipient, Robb Stauber, was in goal, and returning leader-

ship could be found in players such as: Randy Skarda, Todd Richards, Lance Pitlick, Luke Johnson, Jason Miller, Ken Gernander, Dean Williamson, the Hankinson brothers, Larry Olimb, Sean Fabian, Grant Bischoff, Jon Anderson, and David Espe. In addition, there were two highly regarded freshmen, Tom Pederson and Travis Richards.

The Gophers opened the season winning 12 of their first 14 games which included sweeps over Wisconsin, Denver, North Dakota, and Colorado College. The team was awesome that year, losing back-to-back games only once. They went on to win the WCHA crown by a seven-point margin over Michigan Tech, making it back-to-back McNaughton Cups for the first time in the history of Gopher hockey. With an impressive 34-11-3 overall record (26-6-2 in conference play), they went on to meet Colorado College in the first round of the WCHA Playoffs, sweeping the Tigers 5-4 and 7-1. Then, at the WCHA version of the Final Four at St. Paul's Civic Center, Denver and Wisconsin both upset the Gophers, each winning by one-goal margins.

Minnesota then swept the Badgers in the ensuing NCAA playoffs, also in the Civic Center, by matching 4-2 scores to set up a rematch with their old adversaries from the East - Maine, in the NCAA Final Four. Revenge was sweet for the maroon and gold, as they crushed the Black Bears 7-4, behind Jon Anderson's hat trick.

Skarda hit the pipe
So, the stage was set. The Gophers, on their home-ice, would face Harvard for all the marbles in the NCAA hockey championship game. Minnesota jumped out to a 1-0 lead when Jon Anderson went downstairs, stick-side off a sweet Benny Hankinson pass at 6:24 in the first. Then Harvard's Ted Donato and Lane MacDonald each scored in the second to go ahead by one. Bloomington's Jason Miller evened it up at two when he scored his fourth goal in three games, off a Lance Pitlick rebound. In the third both teams exchanged power-plays until Ted Donato tallied again to put the Crimson back on top. But, like so many times before that season, the Gophers came back. This time on a Pete Hankinson shot to make it three-apiece. The teams went into overtime.

Just as the fourth period got underway, Randy Skarda skated down the ice, made a move and took a slapper at Harvard goalie Chuckie Hughes. All you could hear was a dull plunk. That could've only meant one thing: "Skarda hit the pipe. Half an inch and we're champions," said Woog. Then, at 4:16 of sudden-death, Harvard's Ed Krayer got a gift. After Stauber stopped a missile that took him out of position, Krayer picked up the rebound that landed on his stick and slid a back-hander

under the sprawled goalie, right into the collective heart of Minnesota hockey fans.

Stauber, who stood on his head the entire game, stopping 24 shots and earning every bit of his Hobey Baker award from the year before, sat motionless on the ice in utter disbelief. As the nearly 16,000 Minnesota fans sat silent, shock set in as they pondered just how close they had come to winning it all. Many in the large crowd thought that the 4-3 decision might have been the best college hockey game that they had ever viewed.

"I don't like to think about it," said Stauber, who led the WCHA in goaltending. "I remember the shot, and I reached for the rebound but missed it. There were so many things in that game I would've done differently. Sometimes in big pressure games you tend to be more reserved and play more conservatively than you'd like to. But, that was a great year, and we had nothing to be ashamed of that season at all."

Randy Skarda had come within one inch of getting that 900-pound gorilla off Doug Woog's back on that fabled day in April. "It was probably the most crushing defeat of my life," said Skarda. "Kenny Gernander set me up, and I hit the inside of the pipe. After the game I couldn't leave my house for two weeks, I was devastated."

As for the Wooger, the thought of coming that close was something he will never forget. "We had the advantage of being at home in St. Paul that year, and the disadvantage of not getting to bed the night before until 3:00am because of all the fans," said Coach Woog. "I remember Hankinson scoring late and tying it up for us as we came back, and I can still see Randy Skarda making a rush on their goalie and the sound of hitting the pipe. That one pipe changed the history of Gopher hockey forever. It delayed the inevitable that we will win a national championship. There is always something that puts humility into the pot, and that's the one you gotta answer every week - 'When will we win the big one?'"

The Wooger
Doug Woog grew up playing hockey in St. Paul. Before graduating in 1962 from South St. Paul High School, he earned all-state hockey honors for an amazing three consecutive years. He also starred in football and was a good student. From there Doug fulfilled a life-long dream by accepting a scholarship to play for the U of M and learn the game from one of the all-time great coaches, John Mariucci.

Woog went on to a fabulous career in Gold Country, earning All-American honors his junior season after leading the team in scoring. He was named captain for his senior season en route to leading the team to a 16-12-0 record, and a second place finish in the WCHA. For his efforts he was named the team's MVP. From 1964-1966 the center scored 48 goals, 53 assists for 101 career points. Doug graduated with honors from the "U" in 1967 having earned a Bachelor of Science degree in Education.

From there Woog went on to play for the 1967 U.S. National Team and was a candidate for the 1968 U.S. Olympic team. It was off to the real world for the Wooger as he began teaching geography while coaching foot-ball and hockey at Hopkins West Junior High School. Then in the fall of 1968, he took a job at his high school alma mater, where he became the head soccer coach as well as an assistant on both the hockey and baseball teams. While coaching at South St. Paul, his soccer program won six conference titles and twice finished as runner-up's for the state championship.

From 1971 through 1977 he branched out to coach the St. Paul Vulcans and the Minnesota Junior Stars, who he led to two U.S. Junior National titles. During that time, in 1973, Doug fulfilled another dream when he earned his Master's Degree in guidance and counseling from St. Thomas University.

In 1978 Wooger was selected to lead the West team in the U.S. Olympic Festival in Colorado Springs, where his team won the gold medal. That same year he had another homecoming of sorts, once again returning to South St. Paul to take over as the head hockey coach. Over the course of the next seven years, including a leave of absence in 1984 to serve as an assistant coach on the 1984 Olympic team, Woog's Packer teams won two conference titles while advancing to the state tournament four times. In 1985, Woog was named as the head coach of the U.S. National Junior team. That's when he got his big break.

That summer, Woog was formally named as the head coach of the University of Minnesota, replacing Brad Buetow. In his first season, Woog led the Maroon and Gold to a new school record of 35 wins and a trip to the final four. Every year Woog fields one of the top college hockey pro-grams in the nation as he continues to take Minnesota's Pride On Ice to an even higher level. The Golden Gopher accomplishments under Woog's tenure are amazing: He has been to the NCAA playoffs in each of his 12 seasons (13 straight overall), has had seven 30-win seasons, six NCAA Final Four appearances, four WCHA titles, a career .698 winning percentage, and the list simply goes on and on.

Doug has been involved with amateur hockey, his community, as well as local charities at all levels throughout his career. He continues to rack-up the "W's" in his quest to bring home the hardware to Minnesota. He is a great coach, a wonderful person, and a tremendous friend to Minnesota hockey.

Who was your hero when you were growing up?
"As a kid I looked up to guys like Rocket Richard, Jean Believeau, Terry Sawchuck, Gump Worsely, and Glen Hall."

What did it mean for you to be a Gopher?
"It was a life-long dream come true for me to be able to play for the Gophers. The fact that we had scholarships was just a means to an end. Back then there weren't that many opportunities for us after college as far as hockey was concerned, with only six NHL teams and all. So, we played for the love of the game and were happy to get to school to be able to make a living. Yeah, being a Gopher was pretty special."

On coaching:
"To see how it has grown and prospered and how the people of Minnesota have grasped on to hockey is unbelievable. People realize that Gopher Hockey is associated with quality, and to be the coach of that is a real honor. There's a pedigree and an aura for kids to play Gopher hockey. Starting with Herbie in the 70's, our program has been consistent and we have had a lot of wins. This program was doing fine as far as their ability to win before I got here, and it didn't need me to come over.

"What I have given the program is a level of respectability in terms of how I communicate to the public. I think I gave some consistency to the educational value of the sport and brought some credibility to the program in terms of the media and television. It has also become very profitable for the University in terms of dollars, and our program alone generates television revenues that probably exceed the entire WCHA put together. The new rink was a statement to the people and to thank them for their support to the program."

Only Minnesota kids:
"I'm committed to going with the Minnesota kid, and I'm going to stick to it as long as I'm here as coach. We're providing opportunities for Minnesota kids to get professional jobs, and we've got more kids than any other school in the country playing professionally. I'm proud of the fact that kids in Minnesota grow up dreaming about being Gophers, and they have great role models to look up to and watch.

But, it's tougher these days with Duluth, St. Cloud, and now Mankato all competing for Minnesota kids. A kid might rather play on the first line somewhere else rather than to play on our third or fourth. That's how we're recruited against, but I wouldn't change a thing."

Gopher tombstone:
"I want to be thought of as someone that won with dignity and performed with dignity."

Where are they now?
Doug and his wife, Janice, currently reside in South St. Paul. They have three children: Amy, Steve, and Dan - who played for his dad at the U over the past few seasons. Doug will begin his 13th season as Gopher coach in 1997-1998.

Tributes

"I coached Doug on the Gopher freshman team, and he was a great player. Doug has been a very successful coach at the "U" and he's a guy that's really committed to the program. He's got his own feelings on how he wants to develop it with Minnesota kids, but he's been successful for the most part and he's had a wonderful run. He's just got to win the championship to accomplish everything else."   **-- Lou Nanne**

"Wooger is such a great guy. It's tough to be a coach, but you couldn't ask for a better guy. He's so knowledgeable about hockey, and he knows everything. He'll win the big one soon enough."
-- Robb Stauber

"Look at any team in Minnesota. There's not one team that can come close to his winning percentage, he's awesome! I think he does a great job, and he'll shut 'em up someday soon."
-- Trent Klatt, former Gopher and current Philadelphia Flyer

"They don't have to win the title to be successful. I would say there are American born players out there who could help him. I wouldn't say don't go out and get them to have them contribute, but I think we can be competitive with the Minnesota kids. It takes 20 players, and a hot goalie to win it. Woog will get it done."
-- John Mayasich

"I played for Doug with the Vulcans. He was a terrific coach as well as a tremendous player. For a small guy, he could be really intimidating. I enjoyed playing for him, and I think he's done a great job with his teams."
-- Paul Holmgren, former Gopher and NHL coach

One still pictures Kevin Lynch dribbling down the court, and, with time running out, putting up a desperation three-point shot to win it all, sending the University of Minnesota basketball to the NCAA Final Four.

It was not to be. The basketball clanged off the rim, ending the game, as well as one of the greatest seasons ever for the Gopher hoopsters. Minnesota would finish that season with a respectable 23-9 record, making it all the way to the "Elite Eight" before losing the heartbreaker to Georgia Tech at the Super Dome in New Orleans.

The Gophers had arrived big-time and were eager to show the world that their previous season's NCAA "Sweet 16" run was no fluke. Led by Senior-sensation, Willie Burton, coach Clem Haskins' squad captured the hearts and imagination of the state of Minnesota that season, finally putting the Gophers back on track and into the national spotlight.

After losing the season opener on a buzzer-beater, 66-64, to the Bearcats of Cincinnati, Minnesota reeled off nine straight wins, highlighted by victories over

Kansas State and Iowa State, to kick off the Big Ten schedule with a 9-1 non-conference record.

The Gophers' Big Ten opener was at home against Illinois and their star, Kendall Gill. Led by Melvin Newbern who poured in 27, Willie Burton who added 21, and Kevin Lynch who tallied 17, the maroon and gold easily beat the Illini 91-74, who had been ranked fourth in the country.

After losing a pair of tough ones on the road to Purdue and the reigning national champs from Michigan, Haskins' Gophers came home to beat Northwestern and Ohio State. The outlook appeared good for the team, and they enjoyed an unprecedented string of five consecutive nationally televised contests. Unfortunately, the first of these was a brutal 77-75 defeat in the land of cheese, as the Wisconsin Badgers knocked off the Golden Gophers in Madison. Minnesota rebounded, though, with an 84-72 thumping of the Hawkeyes back at the friendly confines of Williams Arena.

Then, in one of the most significant games of the season, the Gopher seniors accomplished something that had eluded them during their entire collegiate careers in Gold Country. Led by Burton's 22 points, they blew-out the Indiana Hoosiers by the unconscionable score of 108-89 on Super Bowl Sunday. It was the most points ever scored against a Bobby Knight-coached team.

At the halfway point of the season, the Gophers continued on cruise control, downing Michigan State 79-74. After losing to Illinois, Minnesota came home to the old barn where they knocked off Purdue in one of the season's best games. Newbern was the hero du jour, nailing a turn-around jumper in the final seconds to seal a 73-72 victory for the nearly 17,000 Gopher faithful in attendance.

Next, Burton began to dominate. He poured in 25 points and grabbed 10 rebounds in a loss to Michigan. After winning four straight, which included a victory over hapless Northwestern, a cliff-hanger win over Wisconsin, a blow-out defeat of Iowa, and a sweep over Indiana, the Gophers lost an overtime heartbreaker at home to eventual Big Ten champion Michigan State. The shot at the buzzer caromed off the rim in that emotional home finale. The five Gopher seniors - Burton, Richard Coffey, Connell Lewis, Newbern, and Jim Shikenjanski took a farewell lap around Williams Arena, and Willie whooped it up by getting up on a chair for his final curtain call.

On to the Big Dance
After losing to Ohio State in the season finale, the Gophers were invited to the NCAA

tournament. "It was awesome because everything that coach Haskins had said and told us began to really come true," said Burton. "The hard work, running in the mornings, being put down all the time by the fans at the other schools, it was tough, but it all came together, and we were a force to be reckoned with."

It was off to Richmond, Va., for the NCAA Southeast Regional's no. 6 seeded Gophers, for a date with University of Texas at El Paso. The Gophs knocked off the men of UTEP, 64-61, in an overtime thriller, behind 18 points from Lynch and 11 rebounds from Coffey.

Now it was Northern Iowa's turn to feel the wrath of the Gophers. Willie B. was on fire, scoring a career-high 36 points while grabbing 12 boards, as the Gophers outlasted the Panthers from Cedar Falls, Iowa, by 81-78. Newbern tied a U of M record with nine assists that game, and for the second year in a row, Minnesota was going to the Sweet 16.

For Minnesota, it was on to the Crescent City of New Orleans and the Southeast Region semifinals. There, the Gophers met highly-touted and heavily-favored Syracuse. Led by future NBA stars Billy Owens and Derrick Coleman, the Gophers knew they would have their hands full.

"My club has come a long way," Haskins said. "They have shown great improvement and they remember getting to the Sweet 16 a year ago only to get whipped by Duke. They haven't forgotten that. And they'll carry that memory into the Syracuse game."

The Gophers, down by four at half-time, came back and hit an amazing 79 percent of their shots from the field in the second half, while holding the Orangemen to a shooting percentage of 37 percent. Newbern led the way with 20 points, the ex-paratrooper Coffey snatched 12 boards, and even Big Bob Martin of Apple Valley, Minn., got into the act, scoring 10 off the bench. Minnesota went on to win the game 82-75.

Next in the Southeast Region was Georgia Tech, led by the "Lethal Weapon 3" of Dennis Scott, Brian Oliver, and Kenny Anderson. Tech had knocked off Michigan State to make it to the Elite Eight, stepping stone to the Final Four.

For Minnesota, making the Elite Eight was special. No U basketball team had ever ventured this far in the NCAA tournament. Now the Gophers found themselves a mere one game away from the Final Four.
"I finally realized, in my heart, that if we lost, we would never play together again as a team," said Burton before the Georgia Tech game.

"We didn't want it to be over, so we went out there with destruction on our minds. We just didn't want the ride to end."

Willie led the Minnesota attack, and the Gophers jumped out to a 12-point lead, but the Yellow Jackets closed the gap and trailed by only 49-47 at halftime. Tech played it equally tough in the second half. The lead went back and forth until the final seconds when Burton drained a three-pointer to make it 93-91 Georgia Tech. The Gophers fouled, and after a missed Yellow Jacket free-throw, the Gophers inbounded the ball to Lynch, who raced down the court. With the clock running out, he launched a three-pointer from just outside the arch to win it all and send the Gophers to the NCAA's promised land. At the buzzer, a collective groan could be heard from Minnesota fans as the ball bounced harmlessly off the front of the rim.

In reference to that final shot by Lynch, Burton, who finished with 35 points, said: "It almost went in. It really bothers me because it was a good shot, and he barely missed it. Personally, I think that the last shot was just too much pressure for him to take. I mean at the time he was open, going top speed, and he had a look at the hoop, but it was a lot of pressure to deal with. When Kevin missed, I was so bummed out because I didn't want it all to end like that. I remember that, after the game, I stopped and looked hard at everyone. I took a picture of everybody together in my mind for one last time."

"They shot 25 more foul shots than we did, and they won by two," said Willie when asked about the blatantly lopsided refereeing during that game. "I had 35 points and never took a foul shot the entire game. Maybe it was because those refs were from the ACC, Georgia Tech's home conference. We just couldn't get a break that night, and it was frustrating because the referees just wouldn't blow their whistles for us."

Several thousand Gopher fans showed up at the Twin Cities International Airport following the Georgia Tech loss to show their appreciation for an unbelievably entertaining and exciting season.

The final game held a lot of significance for the five Gopher seniors. Their legacy will live on at the U as the team that completed one of the greatest turnaround's in Minnesota sports history. When they were freshmen and sophomores, the five were part of teams that lost 21 straight Big Ten games. They had joined a ravaged and ragged Gopher program, and, as seniors, stepped down from active intercollegiate play as saviors, giving Gold Country fans two magical back-to-back trips to the Big Dance.

A Gopher hoops legend
Burton finished the 1990 regular season with an amazing 616 points, and, in the post-season, went on to average 24.4 points per game while grabbing nearly eight rebounds per contest. For his efforts that season he was named to the All-Big Ten Team, received honorable mention All-American honors, and for the third straight year, was voted the Gopher MVP. Willie finished his Gopher career averaging 19.3 points per game with 6.4 rebounds. He is ninth in career rebounding (705), sixth in career blocks, (79) and is third on the all-time scoring list, behind Mychal Thompson and Voshon Lenard.

After his memorable career with Minnesota he went on to become a first-round NBA lottery pick, where he was selected ninth overall by the Miami Heat. He would later find himself playing for the Philadelphia 76'ers, where he scored a career high 50 points in

1995. His quick first step and fine post-up ability drew the admiration of NBA aficionados everywhere.

From the Motor City
Born on May 26, 1968, Willie grew up in inner city Detroit playing baseball, basketball, football, and track. He was proficient in both athletics and academics in high school where he graduated with a 3.6 GPA. His prep athletic credentials also were impressive. As a senior, he averaged 22 points and 12 rebounds per game. He earned three letters in basketball and two in baseball. In basketball, he was a two-year All-State selection as well as an All- Detroit selection.

Who was your hero when you were growing up? "Terry Cummings. I wore number 34 because of him. He had a complete game, and I liked that."

Why did you come to Minnesota?
"The reason I went to the University of Minnesota was because it had more to offer after basketball. I took a recruiting visit to the Twin Cities and just fell in love with the region. I thought it was a beautiful place, the people got along, I loved the mix of the cultures that were there, and it was just a dream place as far as where I would like to live once my basketball days were over. I knew in my heart that it was the place that I wanted to be. I signed a letter of intent for coach Jim Dutcher one month before the program's troubles in Madison. But, through it all, I never said I would leave because my goal was to be a Gopher and to live in Minnesota. Coach Haskins and I started out together and we just started the basketball program over. All of us seniors came in together when Clem took it over, and that's why we were so close to each other. We went through a lot of scrutiny after all that happened, but when it was all over we showed the world we could go a long way."

What did it mean for you to be a Gopher?
"Playing at the University of Minnesota was the most meaningful thing in my life. The time I spent on campus was the best four years of my life. My teammates and I were like brothers who all genuinely cared about each other. I loved it there. I lived in Centennial Hall for all four years that I was there, and it was great. I still proudly wear a University of Minnesota baseball cap because I've earned the right to wear it always. I can't put into words what the University of Minnesota meant to me. The experience was just awesome."

About those Minnesota fans:
"My relationship with the Gopher fans was incredible. I think I bonded with them because they genuinely cared, even when I had to wear that goofy mask! (During the 1990 season, Willie broke his nose and had to wear a protective mask during games.) When I came to Minnesota, in my freshman year, we were getting clobbered, but the fans still came and filled up Williams Arena. I will never forget that, and neither did my teammates. That was the reason we went out and we played the way we played. From the moment we beat Iowa my junior year, that's what started it all.

They were the first ranked team that we had ever beaten, and that's when we became the giant killers of the Big Ten. Coach Haskins always emphasized 'the fans, the fans, the fans.' When we were losing and down, the fans were always loyal and there for us. He wanted us to give them a show, something to look forward to. Clem always said, 'We may not win them all, but we will play hard.' I recently came back to Williams Arena and went out to half-court with no one else in the building, and, you know, I could still hear the fans."

Gopher tombstone:
"I want to be remembered as being a good person with a good heart. Someone who genuinely appreciated the game, the fans, and the everyday people of the Twin Cities. You could say that I was one of the nicest guys in the world until the game started, and then I had a hockey player's mentality. I didn't want the spotlight, I just wanted to play."

Where are they now?
Willie and his wife, Carla, have two children, Natasha and Jaron. He is a NBA free agent, recovering from a torn calf muscle that has kept him out of the game. Burton has five classes left to finish his degree at the University of Minnesota. He's looking forward to someday retiring from active play and residing in Minnesota. He says he is excited about finally getting to go through commencement ceremonies at his alma mater.

The Gopher Men's Gymnastics team finishes as runner-up's in the NCAA Finals hosted at Williams Arena	Gopher second baseman Brian Raabe is named to the All-American baseball team	Gopher catcher Dan Wilson is named to the All-American baseball team	UMD goalie Chad Erickson is named to the All-American hockey team	Eveleth native Connie Pleban, former Olympian and National Team member, is enshrined into the U.S. Hockey Hall of Fame	The Twin Cities hosts the U.S. Olympic Festival	Wayzata's Greg Lemond wins his third Tour de France Bicycle race	The Gund brothers sell the North Stars to a group that ultimately sells the team to Norm Green	Eveleth native Willard Ikola, a former goaltender great, is enshrined into the U.S. Hockey Hall of Fame. The former Olympian coached the Edina Hornets to an amazing 600-140-38 record, making him the state's all-time leader.

JACK MORRIS
The Worst to First Twins
Win Another Pennant

In 1990, the Minnesota Twins finished dead last place in the American League West. That fact alone is not important. However, when referring to the classic "worst to first" season of 1991, then 1990 is significant in the sense that it represents the "worst" part of the cliché. The 1991 Twins were a full-circle success story that will forever be remembered for Jack Morris' game seven heroics.

Early in the 1991 season, many Twins fans had a good feeling about a new bunch of players. Some predicted an inkling of destiny when the Twins tore through the American League that summer, reeling off 16 wins in a row en route to winning the West. They then went on to easily win the ALCS, beating the Toronto Blue Jays four games to one, to earn a trip to the World Series. There, the Twins faced another cellar-dwelling team from 1990, the resurrected Atlanta Braves, who had beaten the Pittsburgh Pirates 4-3 in the National League Championship Series.

The World Series got off to a great start for Minnesota. The Twins won games one and two in front of the Metrodome faithful 5-2 and 3-2, respectively. Game two was highlighted by Kent Hrbek's now famous all-star wrestling tag of Atlanta's Ron Gant on first base. The series then shifted south, to "Hot-Lanta" where the Braves won all three of the next games, highlighted by a 14-run shellacking of the Twins in game five.

Up three games to two, the Braves returned to the Dome to try and wrap it up. Kirby Puckett thought differently though and played the game of his life that night. Kirby robbed Gant of a homer over the plexiglas and then, in the eleventh, he hit the greatest home run in the history of Minnesota sports to win the game 4-3 and even the series at three apiece.

Game seven

The locker room was surprisingly calm before the world championship game. The clubhouse television sets were all tuned to football games when the players arrived. Manager Tom Kelly had named Jack Morris his starter in the most important baseball game of 1991. Atlanda manager Bobby Cox countered with John Smoltz, a Detroit native who grew up worshipping the ex-Tiger Morris, for the final game.

The game was a back and forth pitching duel that went scoreless into the top of the eighth. The inning would prove to be one of the most tense of the series. With Lonnie Smith on first, Terry Pendleton hit a liner to the gap. Then, Smith, who was running on the pitch, mysteriously eased up and slowed down as he was rounding second. Replays showed that Twins second baseman, Chuck Knoblauch, put on a fabulous deke, faked that he was going to catch the ball coming in from the outfield. Little did Smith know however, that the ball was, in reality, still rolling around in the outfield at the time. By this time he could only advance to third. Gant then hit a squibber to Hrbek for an easy out, followed by Sid Bream who hit into a 3-2-3 double play to end the inning. Jack leaped into the air flailing his fist up to the sky as the Twins had dodged a huge bullet.

Through the tenth, the Twins and Braves matched donuts on the scoreboard. It had become only the second game seven in World Series history to reach extra innings. Kelly would later say: "There was no thought of changing pitchers. Morris could rest in November; the outcome of October was his to decide."

Dan Gladden led off the last of the 10th with a single that he somehow managed to stretch into a double. Knoblauch, who would be named Rookie of the Year, had just one sacrifice bunt all season. He got his second by moving Gladden to third. The Twins were 90 feet from their second title ever. After intentionally walking Kirby and Herbie to load the bases, Gene Larkin now stood at home plate for the at-bat that every kid has dreamt about in his backyard. Larkin took the first pitch

and then hit a fly ball to left-center. Atlanta leftfielder, Brian Hunter, who was playing in, could only look on helplessly. The ball flew over his head. The rest is history. Fittingly, Morris was the first to grab Gladden as he touched the plate. Two mobs of players, one at home and the other at first, eventually merged in the center of the diamond in a sea of chaos. The hated Atlanta Braves had been tomahawk-chopped by the Minnesota Twins.

October 27, 1991, was an historic date. It marked the end of one of the greatest World Series ever played. With five games decided by a single run, it was, in a word, incredible. In front of 55,118 rabid fans at the teflon tent, Morris had pitched a seven-hit, 10-inning, 1-0 shutout gem. Jack won two pivotal games for his Twins in the World Series, and they were the most important -- the first and the last. His performance in game seven will go down in baseball lore as possibly the greatest ever. His two wins coupled with an amazing 1.17 ERA, easily earned him the Series MVP.

"Of course, Don Larsen's perfect game was incredible, but with regards to Morris' pitching performance in game seven of the 1991 World Series, I don't think there has ever been a better pitching performance under pressure, ever," said former Twins pitching great Jim Kaat.

"I wasn't really aware of what was going on historically when I was in that game, because my focus was strictly on getting out the Atlanta Braves and making sure that the fans at the stadium and everyone else watching would not go away disappointed," said Morris. "I've only watched the replay of game seven a few times because I get kind of choked up. I've recognized and realized that as soon as the game was over that it was probably my best day ever. Nothing else would compare in my career, and I recognize that I could never do any better than that, so I should just take it and appreciate it."

The Vikings?

When Jack was asked just what was going through his mind when he took the mound in that 10th inning, here's what he had to say: "I don't mean this in any derogatory way, but Fran Tarkenton had a big influence in that game. I remember growing up in Minnesota and watching the Vikings lose their third Super Bowl. I know that it is unfair for me to say that Fran was the reason they lost, because obviously it's a team sport. But you know, I think there were so many people that were disappointed in the Vikings, and particularly in Tarkenton, because he was the leader. The quarterback and the pitcher are considered to be the team leaders, and they are the people with the most influence on the outcome of a game. As I sat there, and the game progressed, I just couldn't help but think of the Vikings and those Super Bowl losses. During that seventh game, I looked up in the Metrodome crowd and saw all these people, just exhausted from screaming and cheering, but going absolutely berserk, wanting a winner so bad, and a sort of calmness came over me.

Augsburg College win the Division III wrestling National Championship	St. Thomas' Ben Bautch wins the Division III 35 lb throw Indoor Track National Championship	Augsburg wrestler Chester Grauberger wins the Division III Heavyweight National Championship	UMD runner Jodi Swenson wins the Division III High Jump Indoor Track National Championship	Concordia Moorhead hurler Kristin Kuehl wins the Division III Discus National Championship	St. Thomas runner Leonard Jones wins the Division III Long Jump Indoor Track National Championship	Twins general manager Andy MacPhail is named as Major League Baseball's Executive of the Year	Gophers Wrestler Marty Morgan wins the NCAA's 177 lb. National Championship	Deephaven's David Wheaton makes it to the U.S. Open Tennis semi-finals before losing to Boris Becker	The St. Thomas University Women's Basketball team wins the Division III National Championship

It was like something was driving me from that point on, and I just refused to let the fans of Minnesota go home disappointed. I knew that we were going to win, if it took all night long. We weren't going to be losers, we weren't going to be the Vikings."

Morris then shocked the Minnesota fans in December of 1991 when he announced his plans to sign with Toronto. Although the Jays offered him a lot more money that the Twins did, the fans were upset nevertheless. Many remembered the tears he had shed when he came home to sign with the Twins and him saying he finally found happiness back in Minnesota.

Local boy does good
Growing up in St. Paul, Jack then went on to college at Brigham Young University. He was drafted by the Detroit Tigers, and went on to become the baseball's winningest pitcher in the 1980s. He was the only pitcher to have won 14 or more games in each year of the decade. Three times he won 20 or more games in a season and twice he led the AL in wins. Although some were critical of his perennially high ERA, Jack would shrug and say that he was paid to win games, and that his contract did not stipulate that the margin of victory be by a shutout or by a score of 6-5.

Morris retired after the 1994 season from the majors with 254 total victories and 175 complete games. Among the most reliable pitchers in history, he holds the AL record with 515 straight starts, once going more than 10 seasons missing only one scheduled start. An excellent all-around athlete who was often used as a pinch runner, he holds the major league career record for put-outs by a pitcher, with 387.

He threw a no-hitter in 1984, and took three different teams - the Tigers, Twins, and Blue Jays, to the World Series. He would later play a brief stint for his hometown St. Paul Saints of the Northern League, eventually retiring from the game for good in 1996.

Who was your hero when you were growing up in St. Paul?
"Like a lot of kids growing up in the Cities, I followed the Twins. My heroes were guys like Harmon Killebrew, Tony Oliva, and Bob Allison."

What did it mean for you to be a Twin?
"Every ballplayer whether they signed out of high school or college probably has some kind of dream of playing with their hometown team. And I was no different. After being drafted by Detroit and playing there through the years, I thought I might finish my career there. But as the political football of baseball goes, you gotta do what you gotta do, and when the opportunity arose to come play for Minnesota, it was like a dream come true. The 1991 season was a fairy tale."

On leaving
"As players, we don't always recognize what points of light come across our paths until after they're gone. I never had any intention of leaving Minnesota when I was here, I never wanted to, but I understand what happened. Mr. Pohlad had to save his money for a guy named Kirby Puckett. He lost several great players and really the nucleus of a ball-club, because of the fan appeal of one player. I'm not blaming anybody, Kirby did what he had to do, and he was justified in doing it.

Carl Pohlad did what he had to do, and all of us players who left the Twins did what we had to do as well. It was just unfortunate that we couldn't have kept it together - because I wanted nothing more than to win it all again with that same group of guys."

Who was the toughest hitter you ever faced?
"Carl Yastrzemski - he was awesome!"

On the Minnesota fans
"Minnesotans are tough fans for this simple reason that they will always support a winner, but if you don't win, they don't show up any more. My theory is that the Minnesota summers are pretty special to people here after being cooped up all winter long. There are so many things to do here in the summer and so little time to do them. If the Twins aren't winning, why go to the ballpark?"

Twins tombstone:
"I think people need to know that I loved the game of baseball. I really appreciate and respect the game and had fun playing it. I realize that I am rough around the edges. I've never really been well versed enough to be smooth and sensitive to everybody, because I was so driven in one direction - and that was to win. I blocked out a lot of distractions. It was the price of winning. In the process I turned off a few people. I just want people to know that I gave it all I had, and winning was most important to me. I think that when you are a perfectionist like myself, the only way you're justified in your effort is to win. It creates a huge burden on you - and you become your own worst enemy as well as your own worst critic."

Where Are They Now?
Jack is currently single, and has two sons from a former marriage. He lives in Stillwater and owns a large grain farm in Montana. He even drives a combine!

Tributes

"Jack was a very competitive player. He was very intense about his job and was very workman-like as a pitcher. He knew how to win games and took the ball every four or five games. He was a great pitcher."
-- **Tom Kelly**

"His game seven performance was the most jacked up I have ever seen a pitcher pitch in a ballgame, and I don't think there will ever be another game pitched like it. To me that was the single most gutsy performance by a pitcher that I have ever seen.
-- **Kent Hrbek**

"Tiger Jack was probably one of the most intense people that I have ever been around. He was a warrior and gave you everything he had. Whatever he had going, he would use to get it done, and that's the mark of a great pitcher. He protected us as well. I mean if another pitcher threw at us, he would throw at their players - and that is the way the game is supposed to be played. He took the ball no matter what and wouldn't miss a start, and I respected him greatly for that."
-- **Kirby Puckett**

"He was a hard-nosed ball player and I respected the way he went about his work. He was a tough, mean competitor, like a Bob Gibson. I remember when you got a hit off of him, he would talk to you on the bases, telling you it was luck, and to wait for the next one!"
-- **Dave Winfield**

"Jack and I grew up competing against each other in St. Paul. To finally become teammates together in Toronto was special. Jack was always known as the best athlete in St. Paul when I was a kid. He had the best arm of all the city pitchers, and was a tremendous basketball player as well. He instilled fear in many hitters at the high school and American Legion levels. Jack was a fierce competitor and was the guy that you wanted to give the ball to in the big games. In 1991 he was amazing."
-- **Paul Molitor**

| St. Thomas runner Trish Tinucci wins the Division III 400M Hurdles National Championship | St. Cloud's Janice Ettle wins her second Grandma's Marathon | Payne Stewart wins the U.S. Open over Scott Simpson at Chaska's Hazeltine National Golf Course | Gopher shortstop Brent Gates is named to the All-American baseball team | Twins' second baseman Chuck Knoblauch is named as the American League's Rookie of the Year | Eveleth native John Matchefts is enshrined into the U.S. Hockey Hall of Fame | Gustavus tennis doubles partners Dave Jussila & Ryan Skanse win the Division III National Championship | Unbridled, owned by Bloomington's Frances Genter, wins the Kentucky Derby (sired Derby winner Unbridled's Song, as well) | After beating Chicago, St. Louis and Edmonton, the North Stars lose the Stanley Cup to Pittsburgh, four games to two. | Jan Stenerud, a Vikings kicker from 1984-85, is inducted into the Pro Football Hall of Fame |

KIRBY PUCKETT
The Puck Inks a Deal that Makes Him a Twin for Life

There was a circus-like atmosphere prevalent when Kirby Puckett signed his new Twins contract during a live, made-for-TV extravaganza. There had been Kirby sightings in Boston, New York, and even one in Des Moines. Would he stick around and finish his illustrious career with Minnesota?

Kirby ended the anxious anticipation by inking a five-year, $30-million contract on December 4, 1992. Kirby had become the highest paid player in baseball, for a few hours at least, until Barry Bonds signed his deal with the San Francisco Giants.

Humble beginnings
Kirby Puckett was born March 14, 1961, in Chicago. He grew up in the Robert Taylor Homes, a public housing project on Chicago's tough South Side, just down the road from the White Sox's Comiskey Park. Kirby's dad, William, was a postal worker, and his mom, Catherine, stayed at home in their 14th floor apartment to take care of Puckett's nine brothers and sisters. Kirby usually came home from school, did his homework, then went out to play ball.

"It was a long haul, coming from where I came from,"

said Kirby. "I can remember as a kid I broke up so many lamps and windows up in my room hitting the ball around -- even with a wadded up sock ball. I was just playing baseball, just doing what I loved to do."

In 1973, his family moved out of the projects and into a better neighborhood outside of the city. Kirby would begin school at Calumet High School where he would emerge as a star third baseman. Kirby found it hard to get noticed by any major league scouts or college recruiters.

"Not too many scouts came to the ghetto to see me play." said the Puck. "We didn't even have a field, so we just played in a forest preserve that didn't have any fences or anything." Kirby persevered through it all and graduated in the top 20 percent of his class.

That summer, Kirby took an assembly line job working at the Ford Motor Plant on 130th street in Chicago. "There were only two buses a day that went out there," said Puckett, "so if you missed one, you were done for. It took 90 days to get into the [autoworkers] union, and I remember I was there for something like 89 days, and then they laid me off."

Kirby's luck would change though. At a Kansas City Royals free agent try-out camp, amongst several hundred hopeful kids, Bradley University coach, Dewey Kalmer, offered him a scholarship. Puckett did well at Bradley, even making the all-conference team. Then, one year later, in 1982, tragedy struck when his father died of a heart attack.

Kirby wanted to be closer to home and his family, so he left Bradley and enrolled at Triton Community College in River Grove, Ill. Puckett came into his own there, finally getting the attention of some scouts. But most of them just weren't impressed. They thought he was too short to play to be a big league prospect. Then his luck changed again. Jim Rantz, the Twins' director of minor leagues, took a chance on the fireplug-shaped ballplayer.

"He stood out," Rantz said. "It wasn't because he had a home run, a double, stole two bases, threw a guy out at home, and had a shaved head, either. What stood out was the enthusiasm he had for the game on a miserably hot night, when everybody was dog tired. That was the thing you noticed!"

Once he was in Organized Baseball, Kirby tore up the minor leagues. There was Elizabethton, Visalia and finally Toledo. Virtually everywhere he went, he won the league's Player of the Year award. The Twins began to realize that they had themselves a diamond in the rough.

What a ride to the show
While playing for Toledo in Old Orchard Beach, Me., he got the call. Cal Ermer, the Mud Hens manager, called him in to tell him the good news and that he had to get on a plane to Los Angeles right away.

"I was called up, and I was so nervous," said Kirby. "The plane was five hours late and by the time I finally got to the airport, there was nobody there to meet me. I had no idea how far the stadium was, and I only had $10 to my name. So when I got in a cab and told the driver that I needed to get to Anaheim for my first game, the driver gave me a funny look. By the time we got there, the fare was $60. So, I left all my stuff in the cab, and he waited for me to run in and get some money. I ran in and got my meal money from the Twins, telling them it was $85, so I could tip the driver $25 bucks. I still wish I had remembered to get the taxi driver's name because I was really grateful to him."

Kirby didn't disappoint the Twins. On May 8, 1984, Puck became the sixth player in AL history to get four hits in his major league debut. He had arrived.

Puckett's career was a storied one. There were two World Series and two ticker-tape parades down the streets of Minneapolis. There was game six in the 1987 "Cinderella-Series," against the Cardinals, when he got four hits and scored four runs to carry the Twins. And there was the "Worst-to-First Series" of 1991, when, in that game six, Kirby had one of the greatest games of his life. In that contest, Puck robbed Braves outfielder Ron Gant of a home run on a Ringling Brothers-like grab off the plexiglass, and then, to top it all off, in the 11th inning, with the game tied at three, Kirby stepped up and hit a shot off Atlanta's Charlie Liebrandt that was the greatest home run in Twins history.

His bat didn't always make for heroics though. There was the Tony Oliva-inspired home-run epiphany during spring training in 1986, when, during batting practice in Orlando, Puck hit 10 consecutive balls over the fence, and after each hit, heard a strange sound. "Little did I know that they had some kind of auto show going on next door," said Puckett. "A motorcycle cop drove out onto the field where he told Kirby, "Swing at one more pitch, and I'll put you in jail!" Kirby's monster flyballs had been breaking car windshields.

He was incredible. Only Willie Keeler had more hits in his first 10 years in the big leagues (2,065) than Puckett (2,040). In 12 seasons and 7,244 at bats with Minnesota, Kirby finished with a career batting average of .318, which included 2,304 hits, 1,071 runs, 1,085 RBIs, and 207 homers. He won a league MVP, played in 10 All-Star games, was named an All-Star game MVP, finished with a .989 percent fielding percentage, and earned six Gold Gloves. He was also awarded the treasured 1996 Roberto Clemente Man of the Year Award by Major League Baseball for his outstanding community service.

TIMELINE

Minnetonka's Janice Klecker wins her second consecutive Twin Cities Marathon	The Metrodome hosts Superbowl XXVI as the Redskins beat the Buffalo Bills	The NCAA Basketball Final Four is held at the Metrodome and Duke beats Michigan for the National Championship	St. Paul's Amy Peterson wins an Olympic Short Track Speedskating silver medal in the 3,000M Relay	Watertown's Dennis Koslowski wins a silver medal on the Olympic wrestling team	Garden Grove's Janet Mulholland wins a bronze medal on the Olympic Volleyball team	Mankato State hurler Charles Zheng wins the Division II Pole Vault Indoor Track National Championship	Mankato State runner Dale Bahr wins the Division II 800 Meter Run Indoor Track National Championship	Gustavus Adolphus tennis player Jon Lindquist wins the Individual Division III National Championship	Augsburg Wrestler Gary Kroells wins the Division III 158 lb. National Championship

112

A career cut short

Tragically, in 1996, Kirby's career was ended due to irreversible retina damage in his right eye. Amazingly, his last trip to the disabled list was also his first. "I knew that baseball wasn't going to last forever," said Kirby. "It was great living in a fairy tale for 12 years, and I enjoyed every minute of it. I just thank God that I got the chance to live out the dream I had since I was five years old. Isn't that the way life's supposed to be?"

Puckett went on to add that he finds it remarkable that anyone could feel sorry for a man who, in 1997, despite not being able to play, is in the final year of a $6-million contract. He grants himself but one regret, he would have liked to have reached 3,000 hits.

His trademark smile, goatee, and bald head, are only some of the reasons why Kirby is the most popular athlete in Minnesota history. His boyish enthusiasm for baseball is his greatest trait and his positive attitude not only inspired his teammates but the fans as well. From his patented after-the-hit "bat-flip," to his in-depth explanations on his hitting style, which included: "I'm just trying to get my hacks man..." and "I'm just seeing the ball good man..."

Maybe it has to do with his cartoon-like physique, or possibly it's his funny-to-say name which was highlighted on his appearance on the David Letterman television show, where he read the "Top 10 Ways to Mispronounce Kirby Puckett" (Number Seven: Turkey Bucket). There were two Wheaties boxes and even "Kirby Puckett Pancakes."

"Man, those pancakes were good," said Kirby, "just add milk and eggs, and you're ready to go."

Perhaps former Twins general manager Andy MacPhail put it best when he said: "If Kirby Puckett had played his career in New York or Los Angeles, they would be building statues of him today."

Who was your hero when you were growing up?
"I had three. They were Ernie Banks, Billy Williams, and Willie Mays."

What did it mean for you to be a Twin?
"My first love was always baseball, and it still is baseball. I've lived a dream, man, and being a Twin means everything to me."

Twins Tombstone:
"I was a gamer, and I came to play every day. I never took the game for granted. Not for one day. I had a smile on my face, but when I stepped between the white lines, I tried to hurt you because that was my job, man. I took my job very seriously because I knew that people paid their hard earned money to come see me play, and I wanted to give them the best possible show that I could every time I steeped onto a baseball field. I always did the little things that could give my team the edge, and that's why my teammates loved me."

"No matter what, with the game on the line, I wanted to be the man. I thrived on that, and that's what made me the player that I was. I never thought of myself as a superstar or anything like that, I'm just Kirby. My mom used to always tell me what goes up has to always come down, and sooner or later, all those people that you treated badly on the way up, you see again on the way down. I've remembered those words."

Where are they now?
Kirby his wife Tonya, and their two children, Catherine and Kirby Jr., currently live in the Twin Cities area. Presently Kirby serves as the Twins' executive vice president of baseball and serves on the team's board of directors. He is still very active in the community and hosts a celebrity billiards tournament every year for charity.

Tributes

"I loved to play against this guy because he would be your friend just before the game, but when you got on the field he would do everything he could to try to stop you. That's what I liked about him. That and because he had fun doing it. I could see the positive affect that he had on other players who he had played with over the years. For him to have to prematurely retire was such a strong disappointment for me, knowing that I wouldn't have the chance to play with him. He was just a great player and is a tremendous person."
-- **Paul Molitor**

"He is one of the most energetic, giving, influential playmakers that I ever played with. He was a dynamite player, who was ready to go every day. He was always up and always a positive influence. I think it hurt me more when he couldn't play than when I couldn't play any more. He was one of my best friends in the game, and I really enjoyed working with him. I understand now why he was able to carry that franchise over all these years."
-- **Dave Winfield**

"I have played with a lot of great guys and a lot of great players over the years, but never have I played with anybody more popular than Kirby. Pitching against him you always felt a sense of accomplishment if you got him out because he wanted to hit you every time. Just by his actions he could show the whole world his love and appreciation for the people and the game of baseball."
-- **Jack Morris**

"He's in a class by himself. He added more charisma on and off the field, to the game than any player, maybe ever. He is such an outgoing and friendly person, and always had time to say hello to everybody he had contact with, and I think that is a very special quality. He was a terrific player, worked very hard and had a lot of good things happen for him. He has a magical quality about him that will always be remembered."
-- **Tom Kelly**

"He loved to play the game. I watched him hit for 12 years from the on-deck circle, and I don't care what they threw at him, he could hit everything. He was definitely the best hitter I ever saw in baseball. I got him into fishing, and I think he's now cleaning out the lake, not of fish, but of weeds. He's pretty green under the gills out there. He still has a lot of Chicago in him! Kirby is a great friend, and what more can I say about a player who was the greatest there ever was?"
-- **Kent Hrbek**

"Kirby and I have developed a very good friendship over the years. That's one of the reasons that when my daughter was being buried a year ago in Minneapolis, I asked Kirby to be one of the pallbearers. That's how close I feel to him. He's made a name for himself on and off the field, and he does so much for the community. He is such a happy-go-lucky, fun-loving guy, and he went out and enjoyed playing the game of baseball. Kirby is the type of individual who never forgot who he was or where he came from. He never thought he was better than anyone else because he was a baseball player and an athlete."
-- **Rod Carew**

"He is just a great person, and it was a real pleasure and a gift from him for me to be his coach. He would always come to the ballpark ready to work, smiling all the time. He is great, just great. I don't have enough words to describe Kirby because he is so special to me."
-- **Tony Oliva**

TOM LEHMAN

Tom Lehman was born on March 7, 1959, in Austin, Minnesota, but grew up in Alexandria. There, Tom starred on the high school football and golf teams. He was heavily recruited to play college football at his father's alma mater, St. John's University. His father, Jim, who also played for the Baltimore Colts, was a star halfback for the Johnnies and led the country in scoring under head coach John Gagliardi. "Tom was a great high school quarterback at Alexandria and was originally supposed to come to St. Johns to play football for us," said Gagliardi. "I always kid him and tell him that my great contribution to sports is that I didn't try to rush up there to talk him out of his golf scholarship at the University of Minnesota. I was all set to give him a big speech on 'What the heck kind of future could there be in golf?' I think he went on to an okay career though, what do you think?"

Tom came to Gold Country in 1979 and immediately made an impact. From 1979 to 1981 he was named to the All-Big Ten and All-American teams. In 1981 Tom won the Minnesota Amateur title and soon was considered to be one of the top ten amateurs in the country. He graduated from the University of Minnesota with a B.S. degree in accounting in 1982 and turned pro that same year. Lehman spent the next several "nomadic" years struggling on foreign and mini tours. He couldn't seem to catch that big break that he needed to make the jump to the PGA Tour. It was a trying period in Lehman's life, but through it all he always maintained his firm belief in God, and believed that he would give him the strength to succeed. "I've been in every situation imaginable -- broke, "cardless," even homeless once or twice," said Lehman.

In 1990, Tom came to a crossroads in his career. Looking for more stability in his life, he applied to become the head golf coach at the University of Minnesota. Then, at the last minute he withdrew his name from the running and decided to make one last go of it on the tour. One of the factors in his decision to not pursue the position was that he wasn't too big on a certain aspect of the job description that included having to coordinate cross country ski rentals on the golf course during the off-season. That's when he finally settled down and found his rhythm out on the links. Soon he started to rise in the rankings.

In 1991, ranked 581st on the tour, Tom finished on top of the Hogan (now Nike) Tour money list. Two years later he finished third in the Masters and won his first professional victory, the Casio World Open in Japan. Then, in 1994 he finished second in the Masters, while earning his first ever PGA Tour victory at the Memorial. The next year he continued to make huge strides when he won the Colonial, by shooting a tournament record 20-under par, and then finished third in the U.S. Open. For his efforts he was selected as a member of the U.S. Ryder Cup team.

Tom had officially arrived as a bona fide star in the world of golf at this point, and in 1996 he had the season that most tour professionals can only dream about. In that amazing year he captured the prestigious Claret Jug (by winning the British Open at Royal Lytham and St. Anne's) and the Tour Championship, had 13 top-ten finishes -- including a tie for second in the US Open, won the money title with $1,780,159 in earnings, won the Vardon Trophy with a 69.32 scoring average, and was named the PGA Player of the Year. He also was named as a member of the President's Cup Team.

Then, early in the 1997 season, after finishing fourth in the MCI Classic, he passed Greg Norman to become the world's number one ranked golfer. Norman had held the title for a record 96 weeks. He had jumped an incredible 581 spots to become the world's best golfer! He also won the Loch Lemond that year, was runner-up at the Mercedes Championship and once again finished third in the U.S. Open.

On religion, life, and the tour: Along with Corey Pavin and Steve Jones, Lehman is a proud member of the PGA Tour's "God squad." "Whatever you do, you do the best you can for the glory of God. He is in control of your best. I would have been a failure if I had God-given talent and didn't work hard at making the most of it. But if I ever lost my card now, I wouldn't consider it a failure. It would just mean that golf is not part of my future any more." He went on to add: "Religion is about who you are. What you believe makes up your character and establishes your integrity, your word. Your word means everything -- it's the foundation of every decision you make in life."

Tom is not a bible-thumper. Rather, he is a person who has a strong faith, works hard, is very determined, and believes in family values and success. He is very humble, and when he's at home he just wants to be Tom, the dad and husband. So modest is he that he doesn't even care about displaying his trophies and awards. "I just want to be Tom, not a PGA player, not a British Open champion. I get so much pleasure coming home and playing $10 Nassau's with my buddies. I'm just one of the guys. I wish I could do more of it."

What did it mean for you to be a Gopher? "Choosing the University of Minnesota over Houston or some other southern school was a great decision for me. It allowed me the chance to compete right away against some of the best talent in the country. Contrary to what many people say, you don't have to go to college in the South to be successful in golf; you have to go somewhere where you will get the opportunity to compete all the time against quality opponents. The University of Minnesota program provided a great opportunity for me, and it continues to do so today for many young aspiring golfers."

Golf in Lehman's terms: "I play golf to be good. Everyone has different motivations for playing -- some want to win tournaments, some want to make as much cash as they can. I play because I want to be the best. If you look back at the truly great players, money has never been an object. You play golf and the money will come."

On pressure: "My swing gets better when pressure is more intense. I tend to tune in on one shot at a time and rely on my faith in having hit that shot before."

Inspired by? "Michael Jordan -- he comes to play every night."

Future outlook: "The most exciting part for me now is that I have not yet reached my physical potential. I can still putt and chip a little better, become a better sand player and hit straighter drives -- more refinements than anything else."

The greatest Minnesota golfer ever: With over $5 million in tour earnings, Tom has etched his name into the sport's record books. He continues to outperform the best pros on the tour and is playing better today than at any time in his career. He has strategically aligned himself with his brother Jim's company, Signature Sports, in Minneapolis to secure several major marketing ventures, including Levi's, (Dockers), Northwest Airlines, Taylor Made, Titleist, Norstan and Power Bars. His four tour wins and great attitude towards the game have inspired Minnesotans to become one of the top per capita states for total number of golfers -- a statistic even more impressive given the fact that we can only play for half the year up here!

Where are they now? Today the 38-year-old resides in Scottsdale, Arizona with his wife Melissa and their three children: Rachael, Holly, and Tom, Jr. He met Melissa on a blind date that was set-up by fellow PGA member Loren Roberts. Tom continues to give his time to causes and charitable organizations. In 1995 he founded the Dayton's Challenge, a charity golf tournament held at Minneapolis Golf Club that draws some of the biggest names in golf. Tom won the event in its inaugural year. He has also begun designing golf courses and is overseeing the construction of Troy Burne Golf Course, about four miles south of River Falls, Wisconsin. He will also help design courses in Alexandria as well as a joint-venture with Arnold Palmer to design a Tournament Players Club course in Blaine. "I'm treating this work the same way I want people to look at my golf game," said Lehman when asked about Troy Burne. "I want my game to be respected, and that's the way I want the people who will play here to feel about this course." It's business as usual for the number-two world ranked Lehman, as he prepares for even further success in the upcoming 1998 season.

MINNESOTA SPORTS TID-BITS

SOME OF MINNESOTA'S PROFESSIONAL TEAMS
THAT HAVE COME AND GONE OVER THE YEARS

Minnesota Grizzlies - Pro wrestling team
Minneapolis Lakers - NBA basketball team
Minnesota Marines - NFL football team in the early 1920s
Minnesota Red Jackets - NFL football team in the late 1920s and early 1930s (1930)
Minnesota Fighting Saints - WHA hockey team in the early to mid 1970s
The "New" St. Paul Fighting Saints - WHA hockey team that merged with the Cleveland Crusaders in 1976
Minnesota Kicks - NASL pro soccer team in late 1970s and early 1980s
Minnesota Strikers - NASL pro soccer team in mid 1980s
Minnesota Muskies - ABA pro basketball team (1967-68)
Minnesota Pipers - ABA pro basketball team (1968-69)
Minnesota Strikers - MISL pro soccer team in mid 1980s
Minnesota Arctic Blast - Indoor roller hockey team in the Roller Hockey International
St. Paul Saints - Professional Basketball League of America - late 1940s
St. Paul Saints - pro baseball team
St. Paul Lights - NPBL pro basketball team in 1950 - folded after two months
Minneapolis Bruins - CHL pro hockey team in early 1960s
Minnesota Goofys - pro softball team (played at Midway Stadium)
Minnesota Norsemen - pro softball team (played at Midway Stadium)
Minnesota North Stars - NHL hockey team from 1967-1993
Rochester Flyers - CBA pro basketball team in late 1980s
Rochester Mustangs - Pro hockey team - US Amateur League
Duluth Kelleys - NFL pro football team in mid 1920s
Duluth Eskimos - NFL pro football team in late 1920s
Twin City Skippers - pro bowling team in the early 1960s
Minnesota Buckskins - a World Team Tennis franchise in 1974
Minnesota Moose - an IHL hockey team from 1994-1996
Minneapolis Millers - pro baseball team
Minneapolis Millers - IHL pro hockey team 1959-1963
Minneapolis Millers - AAL hockey team from 1940s-late 1950s
St. Paul Saints - IHL pro hockey team 1959-1963
Minneapolis Monarchs - women's pro volleyball team in the late 1980s
Minneapolis Lumberjacks - pro football team, (Mid-American League) 1997
Minneapolis Loons - pro baseball team, 1994-95
Minnesota Penguins - Pro Tennis Team
Minnesota Fillies - Women's pro basketball team

DON ROBERTS
A GUSTAVUS ADOLPHUS HOCKEY ICON

For the past 33 years Don Roberts has been a fixture behind the bench of the Gustavus Adolphus College Hockey team. In 1997 Don called it quits, leaving the game as the winningest hockey coach in NCAA Division III history. Not bad for a guy who never even played hockey before! In fact, he had to learn the rules from his players and from reading instructional books.

The Appleton native was a high school football, track, and basketball player and was recruited to play football for the Gusties in 1952, where he went on to earn All-Conference honors. Don stayed on at his alma mater to coach the wrestling team. Then, in 1964, the school decided to add a hockey program and Roberts was named as the team's first coach. One of Roberts' first players, Chuck Linnerooth, who would go on to become the first hockey player inducted into the NAIA Hall of Fame, reminisced about those first few years: "Don didn't know a thing about hockey," said Linnerooth. "Sometimes, during a game, the ref would blow the whistle for icing or offside and Don would turn to us and ask, 'What was that whistle for?'" Don picked up the game quickly, though, and wound up becoming the patriarch of Division III hockey coaching.

From 1964-1997 Don's career record in St. Peter was 532-278-25. The first coach to ever win 500 games, his teams won 13 Minnesota Intercollegiate Athletic Conference titles, played in three national championship finals, and missed postseason play only three times. The eight-time MIAC Coach of the Year was named as both the NAIA and American Hockey Coaches Association Coach of the Year in 1975. In 1993, he received the AHCA's John MacInnes Award for his lifetime commitment to the sport of hockey.

Upon his retirement from the game in 1997, Don reflected: "The winning and the losing, that's something we all do as coaches. Starting the youth hockey program in St. Peter and building the indoor rink (Lund Arena) at Gustavus are among the most rewarding things I've done. I'll always remember the great friendships I've made and all the traveling I've done because of hockey."

DAVE WINFIELD
Winnie Hits Number 3,000

1993 was the year that Minnesota saw the return of one of their greatest native sons. Dave Winfield, probably the greatest all-around athlete to ever come out of the Gopher State, came home to get the 3,000th hit of his illustrious career.

Fresh off his World Series run north of the border in Toronto, Winnie was the lone bright-spot on an otherwise mediocre Twins year. The highlight of the season occurred on September 16t, 1993, when the Dave hit number 3,000 off Oakland's venerable relief pitcher Dennis Eckersley, becoming only the 19th player in major league history to achieve that mark.

"It was great," said Winfield. "I was so glad to come home and to have been able to accomplish such a major milestone in front of my home crowd in the Metrodome. That was definitely a special event for me in my career, and it's something that I will always remember."

St. Paul roots
Winfield grew up in St. Paul where he graduated from St. Paul Central High School. After a phenomenal high school career, he could have chosen to go to college anywhere he wanted. Luckily for us, he went to the U of M in Minneapolis, where he would go on to become a two-sport star. He originally came to the U on a baseball scholarship to play for Gopher coach Dick Siebert. He was eventually "discovered" by Gopher basketball coach Bill Musselman while playing in an intramural basketball league on campus. The Gopher varsity basketball team needed some tough competition to practice against, and since Winfield's intramural team, the "Soulful Strutters" were campus champs, a scrimmage was arranged. Upon seeing Winfield's incredible athleticism, Musselman immediately made Dave a two-sport star at the U.

His Gopher sports career was nothing short of incredible. Winfield was a three-time All-Big Ten pitcher

and was a career .353 hitter. In 1973, upon the Gophers winning the Big Ten title, Winfield was selected as an All-American as well as the MVP of the College World Series. Winfield played outfield, pitched, and led the Gophers his senior year with a .390 batting average. As a pitcher, his 19-4 career record afforded him a winning percentage .826. He finished with 229 career strikeouts, second only to Paul Giel's 243, and his single season record of 109 strikeout's stood for nearly 25 years.

Dave credits much of his collegiate success on a summer he spent in Alaska where he played for the "Gold Panners," in a college-only league against extremely tough competition. The University of Minnesota baseball program has since honored the former great by giving the Dave Winfield Pitcher of the Year Award, to the team's top annual hurler.

As a basketball star at Minnesota, Winfield played a pivotal role on the notorious "Iron-Five" squad that won for the Gophers the first Big Ten championship in 53 years. As a result of the suspensions from the infamous Ohio State brawl, Dave was immediately thrust into the starting lineup.

"For me, I was a baseball player first," said Winfield. "But I loved playing basketball for the Gophers as well, and I was lucky enough to play both sports. I really liked all the guys on the basketball squad, and we had a lot of good competitors on that team. Mentally and physically I thought I was ready, and each game I thought I got better. It was here and now, and we just had a good time. That's why we were successful."

Drafted in three professional sports
Upon graduating from the U, Winfield found himself with several post-graduate options. He is one of the few persons in the history of sports to be drafted in all three professional major sports. He was taken in base-

ball by the San Diego Padres, in basketball by the NBA's Atlanta Hawks as well as the ABA's Utah Stars, and in football by the Minnesota Vikings.

The Vikings? "In football, they drafted me strictly as an athlete," said Winfield. "I was six-foot-six and 230 with good hands, speed, and strength. The Vikings officials figured they could make me into a tight end. Who knows? It would have been great to have caught some of those Fran Tarkenton passes! There's no question that I made the right choice though, and I would have had a short career playing football."

Not surprisingly, Winfield chose baseball, going directly to the big-leagues to join the Padres, where he batted .277 his first year. In 1979, he became the first Padre voted to the All-Star Game starting lineup. The next year, he signed with the New York Yankees and became the richest man in sports. He stayed with the Bronx Bombers until being traded to the California Angels in 1990. He signed with the Toronto Blue Jays in 1991 and won a World Series with that club in 1992. In 1993, he came home to join the Twins, but eventually left to pursue another pennant late in the 1994 season when he went to the Cleveland Indians.

Spanning nearly a quarter of a century, two countries, two leagues, and six cities, Winfield has done it all. The 12-time all-star won seven Gold Gloves and six Silver Bat awards. Winfield has amassed more hits than Babe Ruth, more home runs than Joe DiMaggio, and more RBIs than both Mickey Mantle or Reggie Jackson. He is one of only five players with over 3,000 hits, 450 homers, and 200 stolen bases. An all-star and fan-favorite who played hard well into his forties, Winnie will always be remembered as one of the game's great ones.

Off the field, his accomplishments are equally impressive: He is on the board of President Bill Clinton's National Service Program. He was a Williams Scholar at the U of M. He received the first Branch Rickey Community Service Award, and he was given baseball's coveted Roberto Clemente Award. Now Dave devotes much of his time to what might be considered to be his crown jewel of achievements, the Winfield Foundation.

Dave was the first active athlete to create a non-profit operating foundation, and for more than 20 years, the Winfield Foundation has been a reflection of his commitment to children. Winnie has always been a very popular athlete and role model and has given of himself long before it became fashionable. His foundation's message to kids isn't "be a superstar" but rather "be the best that you can be." His generous monetary gifts, contributions of time, creativity, and commitment are immeasurable. He has traveled coast to coast to conduct drug-prevention assemblies and sem-inars. His organization has generated and distributed millions of dollars, and worked with four presidential administrations, government, organizations, corporations, media, celebrities, and everyday people to bring forth grassroots programs that have touched countless

TIMELINE									
The Gopher Basketball team beats Georgetown University for the N.I.T. Championship In New York's Madison Square Garden	The Augsburg University Wrestling team wins the Division III National Championship	Bemidji State beats Mercyhurst College for the Division III Hockey National Championship	Augsburg wrestler Gary Kroells wins the 158 lb. National Championship	Augsburg wrestler Joe Hoialmen wins the 134 lb. National Championship	Edina's John Harris wins golf's National Amateur Championship	St. Thomas runner Kelly Copps wins the Division III 10,000M National Championship	UMD hurler Kerrick Johnson wins the Division II Discuss National Championship	Augsburg wrestler Nick Fornicoia wins the 118 lb. National Championship	St. Thomas' Pat Ahern wins the Discuss and the 35lb throw Indoor Track National Championships

thousands on a one-to-one basis.

"I always looked at baseball three ways," said Winfield. "It was a game, a science, and a business. I used it as a springboard to do the other things that I am doing in life such as the Dave Winfield Foundation. I met a lot of people, traveled the world, and have done a lot of great things. I have become a role model, if you will, for a lot of young people. I think I have become someone that people listen to and they respected the way I went about my work, and I am proud of that. It seemed that the better I played, the more I was able to accomplish."

Who was your hero when you were growing up?
"I loved the Twins. At first I looked up to guys like Zoilo Versalles & Harmon Killebrew, and, later on, it was Tony Oliva and Rod Carew."

What did it mean for you to be a Gopher?
"For some reason I just always knew that I was going to be a Gopher. Out of high school, I was recruited by other schools, but my best opportunity was right here. Growing up here, it was just taken for granted that we were going to go a college, and it was just a natural progression going to the University of Minnesota. It is a very fine school -- academically as well as athletically. The U was great for me, and it was the Big Ten with top-level NCAA competition. Minnesota is where my roots are, and I've always acknowledged that."

What did it mean for you to be a Twin?
"It was a real pleasure to play for the Minnesota Twins. Minnesota is a place that I really wanted to play at during some point in time over my baseball career. I just didn't know if it would ever happen, but luckily it worked out. It was easy playing and working in Minnesota, and I was really glad that I got a chance to do it. There were a lot of people here who I liked and respected in the game; guys like Kirby Puckett who is one of my best friends."

What about the Ohio State brawl?
"Believe me when I tell you that people still remember that fight. Throughout my baseball career, I heard about the incident from the first day to the last. It was incredible."

Twins / Gopher tombstone:
"That he was one of the few guys that could have done whatever sport he had chosen. Maybe I could've been a multi-sport athlete before the other guys did it, but I chose not to, and I have no regrets about it. I just wanted to be the best at what I did -- as good as I could be -- for as long as possible. I just enjoyed the heck out of sports."

Where are they now?
Dave, his wife Tonya and their children, Lauren, David, and Arielle, reside in both Florida and California. He currently supervises the Dave Winfield Foundation.

Tributes

"When I was in 8th grade, Dave was a senior in high school. I saw him play, but I never had a chance to play with him. I think in a lot of ways, I owe him a lot, because as a member of the Gophers when he was drafted, he opened some eyes about Minnesota baseball. That gave kids like myself a lot more opportunities to get some exposure. The parallels of our careers are somewhat remarkable in that we grew up on the same playgrounds, played for the same Legion team, competed at the same University, and we both had to go north of the border and wait until the latter stages of our careers to win a World Series championship. For two guys who grew up five blocks apart in St. Paul to end up both accumulating 3,000 hits with their hometown teams is pretty remarkable, I think. I marveled at Dave's play for many years. He was a tremendous, tremendous athlete. I consider him to be a good friend, and whenever we see each other, we always reminisce about our past and growing up in St. Paul."

-- Paul Molitor

"Dave is one of the most extraordinary athletes that I have ever been around in my life. He is one of the hardest working people, and one of the most sincere athletes that I have ever seen. For 20 years, the first thing that I checked every day during baseball season was Dave's box score wherever he was playing. We are good friends, and I think the world of Dave. I have so much respect for him, because he was on a Gopher baseball scholarship and didn't have to play basketball. What he sacrificed knowing that he had a career in baseball was incredible. I mean that he could have gotten injured.

I have never seen anybody play harder than Dave Winfield. He had the most incredible endurance and was the best rebounder I have ever seen. When he was 28, he told me he was going to play baseball until he was 45, and I think he finally retired at 44. He took great care of himself, and his combination of speed and strength was just awesome."

-- Bill Musselman

"When I was a rookie, Winnie took me under his wing. I'll never forget going to New York City and talking to him. I remember saying 'Hello Mr. Winfield,' and I remember him saying to me, 'I've heard a lot about you, rook.' I was just in awe. He's like 6-6 and so intimidating. Then he sent me a note in the clubhouse inviting me to dinner with him that night after the game. I remember just talking to him. He was so nice to me. That was really special to me."

-- Kirby Puckett

"It was fun playing with him toward the end there. I know that, playing against him, I was scared to death of him. He could hit a baseball as hard as anyone ever has. I was always afraid that he was going to kill somebody out there when he hit the ball. I remember one time when he hit a line-drive bullet right between shortstop Lenny Faedo's legs, and poor Lenny didn't even have time to get his glove down on the ball. For a big, huge, opposing figure-of-a-guy like he is, he's very gentle at heart and is really a super-nice, sweet guy."

-- Kent Hrbek

"He was just a super athlete and a classy human being. He was very, very athletic, and the things he could do at his age were remarkable. He conducted himself and carried himself with such class. He has such a wonderful attitude and so much professionalism. I really enjoyed having him here as a Twin. His 3,000th hit was another new experience for me. We were trying to get him to get it at home by spacing out his at-bats, and when it finally happened, it was a thrill for all of us."

-- Tom Kelly

"He is truly an amazing athlete and, as our captain, he was a strong team leader. I don't know of any sport he can't excel at. I remember when David asked for a half-hour off from baseball practice to compete with his buddies in an intramural track meet. He had never before high jumped, and all he did was place first, going 6-foot 6-inches while still in his baseball uniform. He may be the finest all-around athlete I have coached, or for that matter to ever compete for Minnesota. To top it all off he was also a fine student."

-- Dick Siebert

"Dave is a first-class gentleman. He has so much professionalism and was just a great athlete. He used his great athleticism to turn himself into a Hall of Fame hitter.

-- Jim Kaat

Gopher diver Pat Bogart wins the NCAA's Platform Diving National Championship	Gopher track & field star Martin Eriksson wins the NCAA's Indoor pole-vaulting National Championship	Austin's Lee Janzen wins the U.S. Open Golf Tournament	Gopher second baseman Mark Merila is named to the All-American baseball team	The North Stars are uprooted and moved to Dallas, where they become the Dallas Stars	UMD defenseman Brett Hauer is named to the All-American hockey team	UMD center Derek Plante is named to the All-American hockey team	The Hibbing Curling Club Women's team wins the U.S. Women's Curling Association National Bonspiel Championship. Georgean Glumack - Last Rocks Susan Vesel - Skip Gail Murray - Second JoAnne Baratto - Lead

CRIS CARTER
CC Breaks the NFL's Single Season Receptions Record

In 1994, the Minnesota Vikings finished with a respectable 10-6 record, good enough to stay ahead of the Packers, Lions, Bucs, and Bears to win the NFC Central Division. The team's hopes of getting past the first round of the playoffs, something head coach Denny Green has yet to do, were dashed when the Purple was spanked by the Bears, 35-18, at the Metrodome.

The bright spot that season was the spectacular play of Vikings wide receiver, Cris Carter. In 1994, CC had the biggest season of any wide receiver in the history of the National Football League, snagging a then league-record 122 balls, shattering Sterling Sharpe's record of 112 catches set with Green Bay the year earlier. Carter set a team record for receiving yards in a season with 1,256, breaking former team-mate Anthony Carter's record of 1,225 yards in 1988. The 1,256 yards receiving were fourth best in the NFC and seventh in the NFL. He averaged 10.3 yards per catch while finding the end zone seven times.

With the addition of his tag-team partner Jake Reed's 85 catches, the duo set an NFL record for receptions by a receiving tandem with 207, breaking the previous

record held by Houston's Haywood Jeffires and Drew Hill with 190 receptions in 1991. Both tandems had the luxury of quarterback Warren Moon throwing them the ball.

Carter led the Vikings that season, at times carrying them on his back. On September 9, CC had the first three-touchdown performance of his career, when he caught three in the first half against the Dolphins. Later that season, on October 2, he single-handedly took care of the Phoenix Cardinals when he caught 14 passes for 167 yards. Those 14 grabs were the second most in team history behind Rickey Young's 15 against the Patriots in 1979. Then on December 1, against the Bears, Carter had two touchdown catches, including the game-winner in overtime on a 65-yard bomb, thus earning NFC offensive Player of the Week honors. He scored the first ever two-point conversion in team history on September 18 against the Bears, and he also led the team in 100-yard receiving games that year with five.

Carter became the first Vikings player in history to have three seasons with 70-or-more receptions, and at season's end, had caught at least one pass in 54 consecutive games, including the playoffs. For his efforts, No. 80 was selected to the Pro Bowl for the second straight sea-son, his first as a starter, as well as earning All-Pro and All-NFC recognition.

"It was nice to break the NFL record, but, for me, I wasn't all that wrapped up in it," said the 6-foot, 3-inch, 210-pounder. "It was a great year for us as a team, and winning the NFC Central was a great accomplishment for everyone. It was especially great to have Warren Moon with us as well. It was Warren's first year and we were experimenting and getting used to one another on the field. We put together 244 balls, which is still a record for back-to-back seasons. Our timing and cohesiveness was just great. Warren was just a phenomenal quarterback."

Cristopher D. Carter was born in Troy, Ohio, on November 25, 1965. He graduated from Middletown High School in 1983, where he caught 80 passes for over 2,000 yards, and earned Parade All-American honors as a senior. He also excelled as a basketball player, scoring over 1,600 points during his prep career. His older brother Butch went on to play for seven years in the NBA and is now an assistant coach with the Milwaukee Bucks.

Heavily recruited out of high school, Cris chose to go to Ohio State, where he earned first-team All-American honors in 1986. When it was all said and done, Carter would finish as the Buckeyes' all-time leader in receptions with 168, and touchdown catches with 27. CC also ranks as number two in

Buckeye history with 2,725 yards receiving. In the process he set 1986 OSU single-season marks for touch-down catches, with 11, and receiving yards, with 1,127. He also set a Rose Bowl record by gaining 172 receiving yards as a freshman.

Cris went on to the big-time when he was selected in the fourth round of the 1987 supplemental draft by the Philadelphia Eagles. On November 11, perhaps as an omen of things to come, he caught his first-ever NFL pass, for a 22-yarder against the Cardinals, for a touchdown.

Then in September of 1990, after three productive years in Philly, in what was considered to be one of the more "not so intelligent" mileposts of controversial head coach Buddy Ryan's career, Carter was released by the Eagles. Ryan claimed irreconcilable differences. CC was immediately claimed off the waiver wire by the Vikings. Philadelphia's blunder was Minnesota's gain. Now the Purple had two Carters, Cris and long-time Viking great, Anthony, to form one of the most lethal receiving tandems in the league. Cris got some sweet revenge against his old mates on November 15 that year when he nabbed six receptions for 151 yards, including a 78-yarder for a TD.

"I was really excited about the possibility of playing in Minnesota because I knew about the tremendous tradition that the Vikings had built over the years," said Carter. "But I was most excited about the opportunity to play with Anthony Carter."

In 1991, Cris led the Vikings in receptions with 72 and added 962 receiving yards with five touchdowns. That next year, he knew he had made it to the big time when he was selected as a member of John Madden's notorious "All-Madden" team. CC once again led the club in receptions, receiving yards and TD's, despite missing the final four games of the season with a fractured collar bone.

1993 would be a break-out year for Carter, as he would finally be recognized as one of the NFL's elite players. After setting then career highs for catches with 86 and receiving yards with 1,071, he was rewarded with an all-expense paid trip to Honolulu to play in his first Pro Bowl. Then of course, he would set the receptions record in 1994, making him a "fantasy-football must pick." Since his incredible year in 1994, he has gone on to be considered one of the game's aristocracy, in the company of Jerry Rice, Carl Pickens, and Herman Moore.

Showing that 1994 wasn't a fluke, CC went on to catch another incredible 122 balls for the second consecutive year in 95, giving him the most catches ever in the NFL over a two-year span. He also became the second player in NFL history to have back-to-back 100-catch seasons, along with Sterling Sharpe who did it two years earlier in 1992 and 1993. Carter went on to set team single-season records for touchdown receptions with 17, which also tied for the NFL lead, and receiving yards with 1,371. Carter's 17 six-pointers broke

TIMELINE

Twins pitcher Scott Erickson throws a no-hitter in a 6-0 win over Milwaukee	St. Paul's Amy Peterson wins two bronze medals in the 500M and 3,000M Relay in Olympic Short Track Speedskating	The Bemidji State Hockey team beats Alabama Huntsville for the Division II National Championship	The states largest lake sturgeon is caught by Hinckley's Kim Bergston in the KettleRiver: 94 Lbs., 4 oz.	St. Thomas' Leonard Jones wins the Division III High Jump and Long Jump Indoor Track National Championships	Concordia's Renee Erickson wins the Division III Javelin National Championship	Gopher second baseman Mark Merila is named to the All-American baseball team	UMD winger Chris Marinucci is named to the All-American hockey team	Roseville's Randy Bartz, arguably the state's greatest ever speed skater, wins an Olympic silver medal on the 5,000M Relay Short Track Speedskating team

118

Jerry Reichow's long-standing 34-year-old Viking team record of 11. Cris had become the first Vikings player in history to have four seasons with 70-or-more receptions. To put that stat into perspective, no other player in Vikings history has had more than two seasons with 70-or-more grabs. His other records include becoming the first player in the history of the NFL to have two or more touchdown receptions in four straight games. He also set a club record for consecutive games with a touchdown catch with five straight, led the team in 100-yards plus receiving games with five, and tied for fourth in the NFL by scoring an amazing 102 points. He would go to his third consecutive Pro Bowl, and more importantly to him, Carter was once again All-Madden.

"I think that season I accomplished even more than in 1994 by catching 122 again, as well as catching 17 touchdowns," said Carter. "That might be the best year that I have ever had as a pro."

There was some speculation at the end of that season as to why the Vikings didn't get Cris the ball in the last quarter of the last regular season game so he could break the record of 122 receptions from the season before. His record was broken the next year by Detroit's Moore, and many felt that Carter should have been passed the ball at any cost during that game so he could defend his record.

"It would've been nice to tie the record, but it was still a great year," said Carter, "regardless of how it turned out at the end."

In 1996, Carter made his fourth Pro Bowl team in his eighth season with the Vikes. Perhaps his biggest accomplishment that season came during the off-season, when he was ordained as a minister. He owns virtually all the Vikings receiving records and is still going strong. Among his records, Cris is first in receptions with more than 600, first in touchdown catches with more than 60 and recently surpassed Anthony Carter in receiving yards with more than 7,000.

On his current outlook for the Vikes, he says, "There is no other time in my career that I can remember being as happy as I am right now. I like the direction my life is going in, as well as my family and also my professional career." After the first game of the 1997 season, Carter, who caught two TDs, set another team record by catching at least one touchdown pass in six straight games.

Who was your hero when you were growing up?
"Lynn Swann. Pittsburgh was relatively close to us when I was growing up, and I used to follow their teams. I admired Swann's gracefulness. I think that was what separated him from any other player, and, in the big games, he always seemed to make the spectacular plays."

What does it mean for you to be known as a Viking recordbreaker? "It's really nice because those records are pretty substantial, and the players who played before me were phenomenal. That gives the records a lot of credence and value in my mind. It's always nice to be compared to great people of the past and also with people who are still playing in the league. Growing up and watching Ahmad (Rashad) and Sammy (White) catch passes in those blustery

days at old Metropolitan Stadium, to me is unbelievable. It's nice to have been able to have seen some of their incredible careers, along with guys like Anthony Carter, and know that I was be able to pass them up. This means a lot to me."

Vikings tombstone:
"I would like to be known as a strong competitor and for my ability to compete. I think that would be the thing that would make me the most proud."

Which catch do you remember the most?
"Against Atlanta in 1991. I was running a corner flag pattern, and the defender had the better position on the ball. Wade Wilson threw it, and I was on the other side of the defender, but I was somehow able to put one hand on his back, keep my balance, dive over the other side of him, and catch it with my right hand. I landed on the five-yard-line and rolled into the end zone for a touchdown. That by far was my best catch ever. Besides the ability to compete in the man-on-man battles, I would like also to be remembered for some of the more remarkable catches that I have made as a Viking."

What do you think of Minnesota's football fans? "I really enjoy the fans in Minnesota. They're great, and I love playing before them. It seems that they have warmed up to me as my performances have gotten better. I feel that they have shown their appreciation toward me and have always been very respectful of me. It has always given me a sense of confidence in my ability, knowing that, during tough situations, the fans are behind me. Because a lot of times in certain situations, they know that I'm going to get the ball, and it's nice knowing they are behind me. In Minnesota, the fans really know their sports, and they know the history of their sports heroes."

Would you make Minnesota your home?
"I'm not a big fan of the Minnesota weather, and I only live here during the season, but I can definitely see the appealing aspects of guys wanting to live here as far as the quality of life goes. When my family and I are here, we definitely love it, and we have become very comfortable in our second home. I really wouldn't want to play anywhere else besides Minnesota. The people are very cordial, and it's a pleasure for my family and I to be with Minnesotans."

Do you favor playing inside a dome?
"I like the temperature and the consistency with regards to the wind. I've gotten used to the dead spots in the ceiling and on the turf and being able to see the ball out of the lights. I like how the fans are so close in the end zones, so I really like playing in the Metrodome. I'm not so sure that I would be so fond of playing outside in Minneapolis in December."

Who are the toughest defensive backs?
"Deion Sanders and Albert Lewis."

What about your partner in crime, Jake Reed?
"Jake is great. He's very quiet and kind of to himself,

but he has really grown as a player and as a person. He is a great receiver and athlete."

What do you think of the salary cap?
"It's one of the more upsetting things as far as my career is going right now. The cap really isn't a cap when you give guys huge signing bonuses, and it's frustrating not being able to get some of the big name free agents in Minnesota like some of the large-market teams do. It makes it really tough for the Vikings to win."

What are you going to do when your career ends?
"I definitely hope to pursue a career in broadcasting after football!"

Where are they now?
Cris is currently the star receiver on the 1997 Vikings. He lives in Boca Raton, Fla., during the off-season with his wife Melanie, and children Duron and Monterae. Carter frequently speaks to schools about drug awareness and is actively involved in the Big Brother-Big Sister program. He joined with fellow player, William White of the Chiefs to establish the Carter-White Charitable Foundation, which sponsors numerous activities, such as non-profit football camps for underprivileged children and assists underprivileged high school students preparing for college entrance examinations by financing preparatory courses.

KEVIN GARNETT
The Timberwolves Draft
a High School Phenom

In 1995, the Minnesota Timberwolves astonished the basketball establishment when they became the first NBA team in more than 20 years to draft a player directly out of high school. With the fifth overall pick of the first round, the Wolves' Kevin McHale gambled on the raw talent of 19-year-old Kevin Garnett. Less than a month removed from his senior prom, Garnett, the most highly recruited high school player of maybe all-time became Minnesota's lottery prize. The Wolves, who were entering their seventh sad year of mediocrity, had always seemed to be just one ping-pong ball away from drafting a superstar. Minnesota simply had nothing to lose by drafting a high schooler.

To fully understand why this gamble was so big, and why the story was equally as big, one has to go back to the franchise's infancy and look at the evolution of mishaps and draft-bungles that put the team in a position to take such a risk.

After a 29-year hiatus, the NBA returned to the Gopher State in 1989 with the granting of an expansion franchise to Harvey Ratner and Marvin Wolfenson. It was a big deal having a new professional team in town, and basketball fans came out in droves to see the fledgling Minnesota Timberwolves. The Timberwolves built their new franchise around their first two draft picks Pooh Rich-ardson of UCLA and Villanova's Doug West. Led by former Gopher coach, Bill Musselman, the Wolves played their first two seasons in the Metrodome, and at the end of their inaugural season, they had set a new all-time NBA attendance record with well over a million customers walking through the Metrodome turnstiles. Unfortunately, that was the only worthwhile record the franchise set. From 1989-1995, the Wolves won only 126 games and lost 366. By 1995, the honeymoon had clearly worn off, and the fans were growing weary of being the league's doormat. Minnesota's sporting public wanted a winner and were growing inpatient. NBA expansion teams were notorious for slow starts

and growing pains, but, by that time, the three other expansion franchises that came into the league around the same time that the Wolves did had all made the playoffs, and Orlando even made it to the finals.

The Timberwolves had experienced more than their share of tough luck, but much of the blame had to be put on poor drafting and inadequate management. Along with two ownership groups and an aborted move to New Orleans, the head coaching position had been a regular revolving door. After Musselman came Jimmy Rodgers, then former Wolves guard Sidney Lowe, followed by Bill Blair who was succeed by present coach Phil "Flip" Saunders. The Wolves had chosen six consecutive lottery picks -- Richardson, Felton Spencer, Luc Longley, Christian Laettner, Isaiah Rider, and Donyell Marshall. By the time young Garnett came on board, only Laettner and Rider remained, and both were shipped elsewhere shortly after. So, in an attempt to create the perfect team chemistry, the Wolves weeded out the bad apples and hedged all their bets by rebuilding their team around Kevin Garnett.

A basketball prodigy

Kevin was born on May 19, 1976, and grew up in Mauldin, S.C., just outside Greenville, as a die-hard Lakers fan. A four-time all-state player, Kevin was named Mr. Basketball for the state of South Carolina as a junior in 1994. For his senior year, the young phenom moved to Chicago, where at Farragut Academy, he was once again selected as Mr. Basketball, this time in the state of Illinois. As a senior he averaged 25.2 points, 17.9 rebounds, 6.7 assists, and 6.5 blocks per game. For his efforts, he was tabbed the National High School Player of the Year by USA Today and also earned All-America first team honors. He capped off his prep career by being named the MVP of the 1995 McDonald's All-Star Game. It was there where he dominated the country's best college prospects, and gained the reputation of being an NBA "sure thing."

Kevin was wooed by nearly every Division I college in the country. Early reports had him going to either Michigan or North Carolina. But, because he hadn't achieved the necessary college-admittance test scores and because the big money was there, he bypassed it all and made himself available for the NBA draft.

Hoop Dreams

Drafting a 19-year-old was no easy task. The nay-sayers were out in force, and if the Wolves wanted to keep up any fan base at all, Garnett would have to deliver come up big. The Minnesota fans were skeptical because few had ever seen the lad play, but that added even more to his mystique. Garnett also carried some baggage with him that would raise some questions. The move from South Carolina his senior year to Chicago came in large part as a result of an incident in which he and several friends were charged with assaulting a student. His police record was later cleared, though, because he participated in a pretrial diversion program for first-time offenders.

There were genuine concerns about his maturity, social skills, stamina, sense of responsibility, friends, and even his diet. He was more than a typical NBA "project," and he needed a lot of T.L.C. As one reporter put it, "People in Minnesota hear the word project, and they break out in a Luc Longley-sized rash."

There had only really been four players that had successfully made the transition from high school directly to the NBA -- Moses Malone in 1974, Darryl Dawkins and Bill Willoughby in 1975, and Shawn Kemp in 1989 (who did play briefly at the collegiate level). At the same time, Sports Illustrated fed the media frenzy by featuring him on their cover with the headline: "Ready or Not."

The 6'11" beanpole was a terrific all-around talent, maybe the best athlete in the draft, the magazine reported. Described as a cross between Reggie Miller and a kinder, gentler version of Alonzo Mourning, he could run, leap like crazy, block shots, monster-dunk, handle the ball like a guard, and shoot 20-footers with ease. He represented the most elusive of all commodities for the league's bottom-feeders, and that was hope. Some members of the media hyped him as a "savior," and the "next Michael Jordan."

Would he dominate and revolutionize the game of pro basketball? Or would he join a long line of NBA casualties crushed by fame, too much money, and the groupies? To be sure, there are countless young men who play pro hockey and baseball at even younger ages. But this was different -- this was the NBA.

"Is he a franchise player?" retorted former Timberwolves head coach Bill Blair at a press conference. "I can't say that but this kid does some things that excite you. From a maturity level? No way he can be ready. He's not ready for the airplanes, the four games in six days, and for the free time he's now possessing. Those things we have to help him with."

Concordia's Aaron Banks wins the Division III Shot Put Indoor Track National Championship	The Augsburg College Wrestling team wins the Division III National Championship	The Bemidji State Hockey team beats Mercyhurst College for the Division III National Championship	St. Cloud State Wrestler Gene Hanemann wins the Division III 158 lb. National Championship	Augsburg Wrestler Jesse Armbruster wins the 126 lb. National Championship	Mankato State runner Jon Keillor wins the Division III 3,000 Meter Steeplechase National Championship	St. Thomas runner Kelly Copps wins the Division III 5,000M and 10,000M National Championships	Gopher diver Pat Bogart wins the NCAA's One Meter Diving National Championship	Twins' outfielder Marty Cordova is named as the American League's Rookie of the Year	Concordia's Renee Erickson wins the Division III Javelin National Championship

You just hope he's so interested in basketball, you hope he wants to be the best player in the league."

Reaction around the basketball world was mixed. "He's a genetic freak," said Detroit head coach Doug Collins. "All the great ones are." Said McHale: "Garnett is a basketball junkie. He's the kind of guy we'll have to chase off the court, rather than worry he's not spending enough time on it." University of Minnesota Gopher basketball coach Clem Haskins added: "You won't find athletes with more raw talent than Garnett. He has great upside with great enthusiasm for the game." Former Seattle general manager Bob Whitsitt, who drafted Shawn Kemp said: "The team that takes Garnett has to commit its entire organization. Ownership, coaches, other players, everyone has to realize this is a 24-hour-a-day process. You have to be willing to spend the years, not the days, the years, to make this work." Russ Granik, the NBA's deputy commissioner, even put in his two cents worth: "If it were up to us, we'd prefer not to see someone come into the league at that tender age, but the courts say otherwise."

Da Kid

On June 28, 1995, in Toronto's SkyDome, the Wolves, after patiently watching Joe Smith, Jerry Stackhouse, Antonio McDyess, and Rasheed Wallace go in the first four picks, selected Garnett. As McHale presented him with his new No. 21 jersey (ending any speculation that it was going to be retired due to the brilliant performance of its previous owner Stacey King) Garnett just smiled proudly. "Mr. McHale can give me a lot of good advice," said Garnett at the press conference. "Mr. McHale had a lot of success... in his day and age." McHale, now smiling, said: "I wish you'd left out that age part!"

"I'm not gonna rush nothing," said Garnett. "I'm not going to do anything I know I can't do. I can't wait to get in the gym with Mr. McHale, and learn some of those dazzling moves he has." He went on to add: "The one thing that bothers me is everybody thinking I just got into this without thinking it over. I thought about it a lot, and I think I'm ready."

Safety nets

Knowing that it was going to be a full-time job, developing and grooming the young player into his new surroundings, the Timberwolves took some steps to protect their investment. General manager Flip Saunders called the steps "safety nets," and laid out the groundwork to ease his transition. One proposal was to have Garnett live with a family during his rookie season. He said that his mother, Shirley, was going to move to the Twin Cities to support him for his rookie sea-son, but would not live with him. When asked if he would be receptive to living with a surrogate family, Garnett said: "Anything that helps me develop as a person."

The Wolves got scared when they heard Garnett's response to being asked whether he was looking forward to playing with the notorious Isaiah Rider, who had gotten into his fair share of trouble with the Wolves over the years. "I really look up to J.R. and respect him as a player," he said. When Coach Blair was asked about the comment he replied: "We're gonna get him another role model."

The Wolves were building for the future and, in 1995,

big things were happening at the Target Center. Shortly after the season got underway, coach Bill Blair was replaced by general manager Saunders. Later in the season, Christian Laettner was dealt to the Atlanta Hawks. Laettner had complained about the treatment the rookie was receiving. And, at seasons' end, Rider and all his baggage were sent packing to the Portland Trailblazers. The team finished 26-56 that season, good enough for fifth in the Midwest Division. The rookie Garnett averaged a modest 10.4 points, 6.3 rebounds and 1.8 assists per game. He also broke Felton Spencer's club record for blocked shots in a season finishing with 131. He was also named to the NBA all-rookie second team.

With Laettner and Rider gone, the Wolves started to turn more heads in the NBA. In 1996, the team drafted ace Georgia Tech point guard Stephon Marbury, who labeled as the "perfect compliment" to Garnett. When the season started, the Wolves also started to receive some solid dividends from forward Tom Gugliotta, who had come to Minnesota the season before as a result of a trade with Golden State for Donyell Marshall.

In 1996-97, Garnett started to blossom as the league's most coveted young player. He averaged 17 points, 8 rebounds, 2 blocks, and 3 assists per game in his sophomore campaign. More importantly, the team dazzled the fans by winning 41 games and making it all the way to NBA playoffs before being swept by Sir Charles Barkley, Hakeem Olajuwon, and the mighty Houston Rockets.

Heir Jordan?

There is no question that Kevin is an remarkable NBA player. Following his sophomore season, a poll of league coaches and general manager asked who they thought was going to be the star player of the next decade. Garnett was their overwhelming choice. From his "poster-dunks" to his animal-like cleansing of the boards, the 6'11" forward (who is actually taller than 7'0" but doesn't want to be known as a seven-footer) is the complete package. The most identifiable traits of the young superstar are his infectious smile and his genuine boyish enthusiasm for the game. Fans seem to live vicariously through Kevin on the court, and sometimes even his teammates seem to be in awe of him. Garnett is, in a word, awesome.

Where are they now?

Kevin is presently single and resides in the Twin Cities area. In October of 1997, Kevin signed a six-year contract extension with the Wolves worth an amazing $125 million, or nearly $21 million per season. The Wolves ownership has clearly sent a signal to the fans of Minnesota that K.G. is the future, and that they are willing to spend some pretty big bucks to be a contender in the league. The contract came after months of arguing back and forth between Garnett's agent, Eric Fleisher, and Wolves owner, Glen Taylor. Garnett originally turned down a $103.5 million offer, which struck an emotional chord with sports fans across the country. Luckily for Minnesotans, Kevin will remain a T-Wolf for a long time. What's scary is to think

about the fact that when his long-term contract is up, he will only be in his mid-twenties. Maybe we'll be looking at the first $200 million man?

On signing the largest multi-year contract in pro sports history:
"I'm happy to be here and I'm happy it's over. I was going to play like K.G. whether I was playing for a dollar or for $3 *quadrillion*. It wasn't a money issue."

Tributes

"Kevin Garnett is a great kid. He is a tremendous, tremendous young man. I really like him, and I think he is going to go down as one of the all-time really great NBA players. He just has a love of the game and he plays it with such a sense of enjoyment. He is truly a unique kid, and I think we're really fortunate here in Minnesota to have him. With a lot of hard work, he can be one of the best players in the league, if not the best."
-- Kevin McHale

"He's the best. He's got tremendous basketball skills. For me to have an association with Kevin Garnett is a real pleasure. It's fun to be around him because he brings this great charisma and energy to the game, and he's a future NBA star. When the league talked about being in trouble when the Michaels and Magics left the game, players like Grant Hill, and Penny Hardaway stepped in. You watch, the kid from the Timberwolves is going to be right there with them." **-- Trent Tucker**

| Stillwater's Tami Oothoudt wins her seventh Twin Cities Marathon - Wheelchair Division | Augsburg Wrestler Tom Layte wins the Division III 150 lb. National Championship | Mankato State Wrestler Tony Kenning wins the Division III 123 lb. National Championship | Gopher center Brian Bonin is named to the All-American hockey team | Gopher defenseman Mike Crowley is named to the All-American hockey team | Gopher catcher Shane Gunderson is named to the All-American baseball team | Gopher Basketball star Voshon Lenard graduates from the U of M as the Gophers' all-time leading scorer, with 2,103 points. The three-time team MVP is the only player in school history ever to surpass the 2,000-point plateau. | Former Gopher quarterback Tony Dungy is named as the head coach of the Tampa Bay Bucs. Dungy was the team MVP in 1975 and 1976 and remains on several all-time offensive categories at the U. He played for the NFL's Steelers and 49ers and was an assistant coach with the Gophers, Vikings, Steelers and Chiefs. The Steelers made him the youngest defensive coordinator in NFL history, at the age of 28. |

TIMELINE

PAUL MOLITOR
Molly Comes Home
and Hits Number 3,000

On December 5, 1995, Paul Molitor came back to Minnesota. He fulfilled a lifelong, childhood dream by getting the opportunity to play for the Twins. In 1996, he led the Twins with an outstanding .341 average and led the league in hits with 225. Then, on September 16, 1996, in a road game against the Kansas City Royals with Jose Rosado on the mound, Molly made history. With the entire state of Minnesota waiting in anxious anticipation for the big event to finally happen, Paul became the 21st player in major-league history to get 3,000 hits, as well as being the first player ever to get it on a triple. In an otherwise ho-hum Twins season, Paul Molitor had made baseball fun again.

"I definitely tried to put it on the very back burner last year," Said Molitor on the 3,000th hit. "You don't go about assuming that you're going to get 211 hits in a year when you're going to turn 40 years old. When that ball got into the gap and I got to third, it finally sunk in. I found out afterwards that no one had ever hit a triple on their 3,000th hit, and that made it kind of special too, because it adds to the uniqueness of joining what is already a pretty small group of people. It's my most memorable game in baseball and just having

it happen to me as a member of the Minnesota Twins was amazing."

One of eight children, Paul was born in St. Paul on August 22, 1956. He grew up a Twins fan, and loved to play baseball as a kid. A natural athlete, his talents became apparent as a high schooler for the Cretin Raiders in St. Paul. "I first thought of Molitor as having the potential to become a professional when he was in the ninth grade," said Bill Peterson, his high school and American Legion team coach. "He was always an exceptional player and had a very strong arm."

In his senior year at Cretin High School, Molitor missed the entire regular season with mononucleosis.

"He wasn't even supposed to practice," Peterson recalled, "but he begged and begged to hit. He must have had a month's worth of energy stored because he put on a hitting exhibition like I've never seen."

Molly rejoined the Raiders for the playoffs and led his team to the Central Catholic High School title. So, it was off to the Minnesota State Tournament, where in the championship game, Paul pounded a 380-foot grand slam home run, en route to helping Cretin repeat as state champs. Paul would garner All-State honors that year in baseball as well as in basketball.

At this point, Molitor had drawn the interest of both college and major league scouts, who had their eyes on Minnesota. In 1973, when the San Diego Padres drafted fellow St. Paulite Dave Winfield, it had spurned fresh interest in northern baseball. After Winfield, major league baseball scouts paid closer attention to the quality of players who had been developed in the arctic reaches of the U.S., so Molly was noticed throughout his high school career.

Paul was getting mixed reviews from the major league scouts, particularly those representing the Minnesota Twins. They thought he was too small and would have a difficult time in organized ball. However, the St. Louis Cardinals decided to take a chance on the young shortstop and selected him in the 25th round of the entry draft. The Cards offered him a $4,000 contract, which was just the kick in the rear he needed to opt for a free university education instead.

In 1975, Paul was offered a scholarship by Dick "Chief" Siebert, the Gopher baseball coach, who had an special eye for talent. Siebert would later say that Paul had the best base-running instincts of any player he ever saw in amateur or professional baseball, and that he was, without a doubt, the best major league prospect he'd ever seen. The Chief apparently had seen something the Twins

scouts overlooked.

"During tryouts Molitor just stood heads above everyone else from the first day he walked on campus," said John Anderson, former Gopher baseball student manager and current U head coach. Molly was a quiet, lead-by-example type of player, who would always play aggressive and go after the ball. The co-captain would lead the Gophers to a Big Ten title in 1977.

As Paul and his teammates prepared for the 1977 College World Series, he heard the substantial news that he had been drafted by the Milwaukee Brewers. He was the third overall player chosen in the draft, after the White Sox took Harold Baines and the Expos Bill Gullickson. The Twins, who had made it clear that they were now interested in drafting him, had missed their chance at the young slugger. "It took me a little while to get down to the ground," said Paul after hearing the news. College baseball's hottest prospect, and newest cheesehead, signed with the Brewers for $85,000.

By the time Paul had become a Brewer rookie after his junior season at the U, he had established himself as one of the greatest all-around baseball players in Gopher history. He had become the Gophers' career leader in runs-scored, hits, RBI's, triples, home-runs, total bases, and stolen bases. In his three seasons, he set five single-season records and seven college-career records.

The Gopher shortstop's best year was his sophomore season in which he batted a career-best .376, earning himself first-team All-American honors for the second straight season. He would finish his college baseball with an impressive career batting average of .350.

"I thought he had more ability than any player I have ever coached, and I coached Dave Winfield, so Paul's accomplishment is a pretty tall order," said coach Siebert of Molitor's career as a Gopher.

From Minneapolis to Milwaukee
The 20-year-old Molitor was sent to Milwaukee's Class-A farm team in Iowa to play with the Burlington Bees. It soon became apparent that Molly was the best player in the Midwest League. He could have gone up to Triple-A after only three weeks with Burlington, but he asked to stay with the Bees to help them win the league championship. He did, leading the Bees to the Midwest League title and, in the process, won the batting title with a .348 average. From then on, there were no more minor-league stops for Paul. It was off the "show." Winfield had gone directly to the big leagues from the campus of the University of Minnesota; it took Molly 64 Midwest League games to get there.

Robin Yount was the Brewers everyday shortstop. Even though he was less than a year older than Molitor, he was already a seasoned pro, having gone straight to the majors in 1974. Drafted as the shortstop of the future, Molly was quoted years later on his

	TIMELINE									
	Anoka's Brandon Paulson wins a silver medal on the Olympic wrestling team	Minneapolis' Briana Scurry wins a gold medal on the Olympic soccer team	Duluth's Kris Benson wins a bronze medal on the Olympic Baseball team	St. Paul's Thomas Malchow wins a silver medal on the Olympic swimming team in the 200M Butterfly	Minneapolis' William Carlucci wins a bronze medal on the Olympic Lightweight-Four Rowing team	Concordia's Aaron Banks wins the Division III Shot Put National Indoor Track National Championship	Gopher diver Pat Bogart wins the NCAA's One Meter Diving National Championship	Concordia's Renee Erickson wins the Division III Javelin National Championship	Mankato State wrestler Tony Kenning wins the Division II 123 lbs. National Championship	Allen Hartley wins the NHRA Champion Auto Nationals at Brainerd International Speedway. The total four-day attendance is over 100,000

memories of that first visit to County Stadium: "I remember Sal Bando coming over and throwing Robin an outfielder's glove and saying to him, 'Well, I guess this will be your last year at shortstop, kid...'. "All I wanted was to get out of there!"

Profoundly modest, Molitor doesn't care about personal accolades, rather he has always preferred to be a team player. He is an explosive athlete with an ability to attack with the sudden element of surprise, whether at bat or on the bases. He is a hitting machine, able to swing so late, stretching time until that optimum instant for contact seems to have passed. His eyes can evaluate a pitch, calculate its curve, its spin, its velocity, and then measure it, to precisely drive the ball exactly where he wants it to go, all in about the same time it would take the average person to blink. That is his signature, and his knowledge of the physics of the game allows him to get better with age.

Paul played 15 seasons with the Brewers, making it to the World Series in 1982 before losing to the Cardinals in the so-called "Suds Series." He gave Joe DiMaggio's consecutive hits record a run for the money in 1987.

Molitor left Milwaukee to go north of the border in 1993 where he led the Blue Jays to the World Series championship and was named MVP of the Series. Following this accomplishment, many felt that Paul could have run for the position of Prime Minister in Canada, and they weren't kidding. The career .300-plus hitter, and eight-time all-star, is now at home with the Twins, where he is as good a hitter now at the ripe-old age of 41, as he was at the ripe-old age of say...30. Explanations for his longevity include a regiment of common sense, zen, and staying in great shape, combined with a daily focused routine of discipline and thoroughness.

Who was your hero when you were growing up?
"Harmon Killebrew. He was the one player that I tried to emulate when I was playing out in the backyard. He was the best."

What did it mean for you to be a Gopher?
"Growing up in the St. Paul, as I did, I knew that the Gophers had a tremendous baseball tradition. I remember in high school, following the Gopher baseball team and, in particular watching Dave Winfield lead the club to the College World Series, before they ended up losing some heart-breakers down in Omaha. When Coach Siebert offered me a scholarship to be a Gopher, I realized how much pride the program had in presenting the state's baseball abilities. Back then, it was a very rare occasion when the Chief would recruit outside the state to bring in players, so almost everyone in uniform was home-grown. I think that when you played for his teams, you realized that it wasn't just the U, but the type of baseball that Minnesota kids played, that was being represented. It carried a lot of significance for me, and it meant a great deal for me to be a Gopher."

What does it mean for you to be a Twin?
"In the 20 years I have played in the majors, I have always had a certain attachment to the Twins, because of my roots are in Minnesota. I followed them and was always aware of how the team was doing, even when I was a Brewer and a Blue Jay. I have always been a

Twins fan, and I wasn't really sure that I would ever have a chance to play for them. I had always thought that I would be a lifetime Brewer, and then after Toronto, I expected that would be my last contract."

"So, when the opportunity finally came up where I was available, and they had an interest, I couldn't pass up the opportunity to finally be a Twin in spite of a lot of interest from elsewhere and probably more money from some other teams. To have a chance to return home and to kind of complete the cycle, so to speak, was something that goes back to that dream as a kid. Now, to have it happen so far down the road was a little bit ironic, but also a real nice way to end my career. I am very content now and am excited about finishing up my career at home."

Safe at home
"I think at least for Dave Winfield, Jack Morris, Terry Steinbach, and I, after growing up and playing high school baseball here, we had a certain pride about being from Minnesota that maybe people from other parts of the country might not easily understand. This has to do with the lifestyle and priorities of family - it's a midwestern thing. I'm not sure that just that on it's own would've been enough to entice us back, but when you factor the current status of the team under manager Tom Kelly, it became even more appealing. Combine that with the chance to return home to friends and family, and then to play for the team we followed as youngsters was just an irresistible package for me."

Who was the toughest pitcher you ever faced?
"Nolan Ryan, when he was with the Angels. He was more than dominating. He was as tough to face as it gets."

Twins and Gopher tombstone:
"I hope that people will have seen in the way that I played that I had a certain passion and, yet, respect for the game. Whatever I have accomplished, I have tried to do with humility and when I failed, I tried to maintain a certain level of consistency about my demeanor. I think that's important because in a lot of ways sports reflects life. How you handle your ups and downs says a lot about your character. That's what I hope has left an impression, and particularly on young people."

Where are they now?
Paul is currently an active member of the Minnesota Twins. He and his wife Linda, and their daughter Blaire live in Edina.

Tributes

"I grew up with Paul in St. Paul. We played Babe Ruth ball, city ball, and American Legion ball against each other. Finally we played with each other in Toronto and won a pennant together. Paul is a great, great player. He is one of the greatest hitters I have ever seen and easily in the top five of all time. I've never seen a guy

with better hands than Paul. He is truly a hitting machine."
   -- **Jack Morris**

"He is such a classy and professional individual. He plays the game at a higher level than anybody that I've ever seen. Pauly was on a mission last year to get that 3,000th hit out of the way, and it was quite an experience that capped off a fabulous season for him."
   -- **Tom Kelly**

"I played against Paul in the Suds-Series of 1982 and have gotten to know him over the years. He is a solid individual and one guy that I appreciate very much. He seems to know everyone, calls them by their first names, and has the time for them. He has great respect for the game, and as a result of that, I have great respect for him."
   -- **Jim Kaat**

"We always had that local tie together and felt that since we were both Minnesota boys, we should like each other. He is a super-nice guy, and I would have to say that if Kirby Puckett is the best right-handed hitter ever, Paul would have to be right behind him."
   -- **Kent Hrbek**

There have been numerous exciting basketball seasons at the University of Minnesota, but nothing like the one they had this year in Gold Country.

The Gopher basketball team had their most memorable season ever in 1997, finishing with an amazing 31-4 record en route to winning the team's first Big Ten title in 15 years. Led by conference MVP, Bobby Jackson, and Big Ten and NCAA Coach of The Year, Clem Haskins, the Gophers made it all the way to their first-ever Final Four and were ranked as high as number two in the nation for much of the season.

There was no question that the leader of this great team was Bobby Jackson. The 6'1" guard from North Carolina was joined in the backcourt by Eric Harris, who had honed his skills playing against Minnesota Timberwolves' rookie guard Stephon Marbury in his native New York City. The small forward and center had both been long-time regulars at Coach Haskins' summer basketball camps since they were kids, Sam Jacobson from Park High School in Cottage Grove, and Minneapolis Roosevelt's John Thomas. Power forward Courtney James rounded out the front five.

The group gelled early under coach Haskins' system, but were often substituted for. Throughout the season, nine Gophers averaged double-figure minutes. "The only reason we have five starters is because five players have to start," said point guard Eric Harris.

Excitement continued to build throughout the season as the team rolled through the Big Ten with an amazing 16-2 record, highlighted by perhaps their biggest game of the year, a 96-91 over-time victory at Indiana. In that game, Jacobson nailed a three-pointer as the Gophers rallied from seven points down in the final minute and then beat the Hoosiers in overtime. It was one of many come-from-behind wins for the team.

The Big Ten champion Gophers were rewarded with a number one seed in the NCAA Midwest Region. Thousands of the Gopher faithful followed them, first to Kansas City where they knocked off Temple at Kemper Arena to get into the NCAA's "Sweet 16," and then on to San Antonio. There, they stunned some so-called college basketball experts by first defeating Clemson in a double over-time thriller to make the "Elite Eight" and then coming from behind to beat a tough UCLA team. Next stop was the Final Four in Indianapolis to take on the defending national champs from Kentucky. No other Gopher hoop team had ever ventured this far.

In reality, there was nothing Cinderella about this team. The Gophers had won the Big Ten outright and deservedly earned a number one seed in the tournament. Number-one seeds are given that designation for a reason. What was unexpected was the support of the fans. Nearly 10,000 turned out for a rally in Indianapolis before the big game.

A Tale of two halves
Things didn't start out so hot for the Gophers against Kentucky's Wildcats in the RCA Dome. In the first 20 minutes, a tense squad in maroon and gold turned the ball over 15 times, and the stalwart bench that usually delivered the goods was nowhere to be found. Further, Kentucky's relentless defense was clearly presenting problems for Minnesota.

Then with 14:31 remaining in the second half and Kentucky leading 47-43, James went down the lane and scored on a monster dunk. Everybody in the dome, including North Carolina and Arizona fans who by now were rooting for the underdog Gophers, went berserk. The deafening roar of the crowd was drowned out, however, by the sound of the referee's whistle, as he negated the basket and called a charging foul on James. Coach Clem was apoplectic and his suit coat went flying. Then, before the Armani jacket could hit the floor, the referee slapped Clem with a "T." It was one turning point in a game that had many. The resultant six-point swing put the Wildcats up by 51-43.

The Gophers came back as they had done all season long. First, Jacobson floated in mid-air to hit a jumper. Then, Jackson proceeded to hit a lean-in, a double-pump lay-up, and then popped in a three-pointer. The RCA Dome exploded in noise as the Gophers were finally fighting their way back from pesky turnovers and fouls to take the lead, 52-51, with 10:45 to play. With nine minutes left, the game was tied at 54-all.

Then it got ugly for the maroon and gold. The Wildcats, led by All-American Ron Mercer, reeled off 14 of the next 17 points. The fat lady warmed up her vocal chords. Unable to play at Kentucky coach Rick Pitino's torrid pace, the Gophers ran out of gas down the stretch and lost the game 78-69. In the end, Minnesota, the escape artists of college hoops, had succumbed to great coaching, a blown charge call, and a terrific Kentucky defense. The previously mistake-free Gophers had yielded to the relentless Kentucky press that caused them to turn over the ball to the Wildcats 26 times.

The Golden Gophers gave us all some great memories during the 1996-97 season and renewed our pride in Minnesota basketball. Jackson, who finished the game with 23 points, had a once-in-a-lifetime season. For his efforts in the tournament, he was named Mid-west Regional MVP and was named to the All-Final-Four team.

"Words can't describe how great that season was for me," said Bobby. "We worked really hard to get where we went, even when it seemed everybody doubted us. We just wanted to play hard and show everybody what we were about. I had never been in a Final Four situation, and it felt so good to accomplish that much. The Gopher fans played a major part in our success, and I would like to thank them for being there for us."

Kentucky played a lot of great teams that season, but nobody pounded them like the Gophers did at the RCA Dome. "We beat a team that was as physically and mentally tough as any I've coached against since I've been at Kentucky," coach Pitino said. "They got up in our pants, they took us out of our offense, and they were very tough-minded. I have tremendous admiration for Minnesota."

The basketball season of 1996-97 was one Gopher supporters will not soon forget. The team had a storybook year that kept building every week of the season. Now the bar has been raised for Gopher basketball.

From North Carolina to Minneapolis via Nebraska
Bobby Jackson was born on March 13, 1973, in Salisbury, N.C. He grew up in basketball country, playing and dreaming of playing college ball. Jackson went on to average 22 points per game over his junior and senior seasons at Salisbury High School, earning all-conference and all-state honors in those same two seasons. From there, Bobby went to Western Nebraska Junior College in Scottsbluff, Neb., where he garnered second team All-American honors in 1995.

TIMELINE

Minneapolis' Dave Peterson, a pioneer of Minnesota hockey and the coach of the 1988 and 1992 Olympic teams, dies	Wayzata's Tim Herron wins the Texas Open PGA Golf Tournament	Twins pitcher Brad Radke sets a team record by winning 12 straight starts	The Timberwolves make their first-ever playoff appearnce but are swept by the Houston Rockets	The Minneapolis North boys High School basketball dynasty keeps rolling after winning three state championships	Edina's John Harris wins the U.S. Amateur Golf Championship and is named to yet another U.S. Walker Cup team	Hasting's Larry La Coursiere, a lightweight boxer, loses to reigning champion Julio Ceasar Chavez	Tommy Kendall wins his second Sprint PCS Grand Prix of Minnesota Trans Am race through downtown Minneapolis	Former Augsburg College football and basketball star Lute Olson wins the NCAA Basketball National Championship as head coach of the University of Arizona Wildcats. (He also coached at the University of Iowa	

Jackson then transferred to Minnesota for the 1996 season, and although he was only here for two seasons, he made the most of his time here. With his patented long white socks, he finished his illustrious tenure in Gold Country with a career scoring average of 14.4 points per game, 5.5 rebounds per game, and 3.5 assists per game. Not only was Jackson named the Big Ten MVP, he was also the conference's Defensive Player of the Year. He also earned second team All-America honors.

Bobby can just flat out play. During the NCAA tournament, he was a man among boys. He is an amazing scorer, who can light it up at any time during the course of a game. He possesses unbelievable speed, quickness, and an explosive first step. With his fantastic court vision and unselfish passing abilities, he will undoubtedly make a tremendous NBA player.

Who was your idol when you were growing up?
"Growing up in North Carolina, my idol had to be Michael Jordan."

What did it mean for you to be a Gopher?
"Coming out of junior college, I could've gone to Wake Forest, Cincinnati, or Minnesota. I chose Minnesota because of their team concept. I was looking for an opportunity to come in and help my team out right away and make an impact. I wanted to come in and win a conference championship, and that's exactly what we did last year. Being a Gopher really means a lot to me. There are only a certain amount of people that get to wear the maroon and gold, and I am just happy that Coach Haskins let me be a part of it all."

Gopher tombstone:
"I would hope to be remembered as a guy that went out and played hard every day, and always smiled and had fun every time he stepped on the court."

Where are they now?
Bobby graduated in the summer of 1997 and received a degree in sports management. He was a first-round draft pick of the NBA Seattle Supersonics, but was immediately traded to the Denver Nuggets.

• • • • • •

Clem the gem
Clem Haskins is a players' coach who practices what he preaches. "Play hard" and "winning with integrity and respect - both on and off the court," have become the catch-phrase hallmarks of his attitude and coaching philosophy. He has earned the respect of his players, the fans, and even Minnesota residents who know little about basketball because he is perceived as a good coach and more importantly, he is a good person.

Clem grew up playing basketball as one of 11 children on a farm in Campbellsville, Kentucky. He went on to a stellar prep career at Taylor County High School, where he led his team to the state tournament. From there, Haskins went on to star at Western Kentucky University, becoming one of the most dominant players ever to play in the Ohio Valley Conference. Twice leading the conference in scoring, the All-American was the only player in league history to be chosen Player of the Year for three consecutive seasons. He led the Hilltoppers to two conference titles and two consecutive appearances in the NCAA Tournament.

Clem received his bachelor of science degree in 1967 and earned his master of arts degree in 1971.

In 1967, the Chicago Bulls selected Haskins with the third overall pick in the NBA draft. He went on to play nine solid seasons in the league with the Bulls, Suns, and Bullets. He returned to his alma mater; Western Kentucky, first as an assistant coach under Gene Keady and then as head coach in 1980. After six stellar seasons with the Hilltoppers, which included 101 victories, several NCAA tournament bids, and a Rookie Coach of the Year honor, Haskins was named head coach at Minnesota in 1986.

Clem took over the U program in trouble. Before his arrival in Gold Country, three Gophers had been involved in an incident in Madison, Wis., that led to rape charges, although the players were acquitted. Nonetheless, coach Jim Dutcher had abruptly resigned, and a total rebuilding effort was in order for the program. In his first season, Clem went 2-16 in the Big Ten, but, three years later, the same group of Haskins' freshman came within a Kevin Lynch three-pointer of going to the Final Four as seniors. This incredible turnaround signaled the establishment of one of the best college basketball programs in the country. "The school thought it had hired a Band-Aid, but found out it had a surgeon," said Clem's wife, Yevette.

Clem has won 201 games in his 10 years as the head coach at Minnesota. Under Haskins, the Gophers have gone on to post-season play eight of the last nine years. In 1993, his Gophers won the National Invitational Tournament. His list of accomplishments and achievements is long: he was an assistant coach for the 1996 U.S. Olympic Team (which he described as "the highlight of my coaching career"); he led the North squad to the gold medal at the 1991 U.S. Olympic Festival in Los Angeles; and he won another gold medal in 1994 when he led the U.S. Junior team in the Pan-Am games in Argentina.

Clem has been named to the Kentucky, Western Kentucky and Kentucky High School Athletic Association Hall of Fames. He is also the chair of the

Big Ten basketball coaches. In 1997, he received numerous NCAA Coach of the Year honors, as well as receiving the Big Ten Coach of the Year award.

Who was your hero when you were growing up?
"I've always tried to emulate my father, and I hope that I've followed his example. He was a tough, six-foot guy who, with only a fourth-grade education, raised five sons and six daughters. He made it during a time that was awfully hard for any man, particularly a black man to raise a family of that size. He's the smartest and toughest individual I've ever-known. If I could follow his example, then I'd consider myself very happy."

On Gopher fans: "Golden Gopher fans are without a doubt the best college basketball fans in the country. Their enthusiasm helps us carry our game to another level. The people of this state love Golden Gopher basketball. That's one of the reasons I fell in love with Minnesota, and that's why I'm committed to finishing my career here. They say that the basketball Gophers have the 'toughest ticket' in town, and we want to keep it that way. We want to continue to provide our fans with a good show every night by playing aggressive and exciting basketball. If we continue to do that, our fans will support us. They are loyal, loyal fans. They are second to none."

Where are they now?
It's business as usual for Clem as he starts his next decade of coaching in Gold Country. He and his wife Yevette live in Minnetonka and have three children: Clemette, Lori, and Brent. He also recently finished an autobiography entitled "Breaking Barriers."

Tributes
"Clem Haskins is a great guy and a great motivator. Because he was a great player, we know that he's been through the same situations that we have. He knows a lot about the game and he's just the perfect role model." **-- Bobby Jackson**

"Clem is a teacher. He was born to teach and pass on the things that he knows. He was a real father figure to us players. He was our coach, father, disciplinarian, and friend." **-- Willie Burton**

Gopher swimmer Gretchen Hegener wins the 100-Yard Breaststroke National Championship and sets a new American record	Jim Moynagh, of Hopkins wins Irwin Jacobs' $1 million Forrestwood Open Bass Fishing Tournament on Lake Minnetonka	Ila Borders makes history when she pitches in a game against the Duluth Dukes, thus becoming the first woman ever to play in the Northern League	Former Gopher pitcher Denny Neagle wins 20 games for the Atlanta Braves	The NHRA/NSSR Snowmobile Drag Nationals are held at Brainerd International Raceway. ESPN covers the event live, as more than 110,000 spectators watch the festivities. The NHRA Top Fuel and Funny Car events were supposed to be the main event, but the sleds stole the show.	"Haydays," an annual Summertime snowmobile race extravaganza held in Lino Lakes, draws more than 50,000 spectators	Vikings kicker Eddie Murray sets the NFL's all-time consecutive PAT record with 235 straight extra-points

Afterword by
KENT HRBEK

As a child growing up, literally, in the shadows of Bloomington's Metropolitan Stadium, Kent Hrbek often fell asleep to the sounds of cheering Twins and Vikings fans. It's no wonder then, that he grew up as a die-hard Minnesota sports fan. From his days of rounding the bases on the T-ball field with his big number six jersey, in honor of his hero, Tony Oliva, to "touching em' all" in the Dome, Kent became one of Minnesota's greatest home-grown baseball players. Who better to write about the state of the state and our next 50 years of Minnesota sports, than our own native son, Herbie.

It's kind of weird, but I've come full-circle in my life. I started out as a huge Minnesota sports fan, playing and loving sports, and just wanting to be around the ballpark. Then, I was fortunate to have become an athlete who was considered as an idol to a lot of people and had a successful career in my home town. Now, today, I'm a huge Minnesota sports fan again. It's hard to believe that it's been four years since I hung it up. I guess you don't realize that you're a fan again until you go back to the ballpark and see your mug hanging from a banner out in right field.

Sports is a really important thing for a lot of people in Minnesota. And, with regard to the fans and athletes of Minnesota, I think we've always been known as a state of underdogs. I don't care if it was the North Stars, the Twins, the Vikings, the Timberwolves, or the Gophers, we've never been favored to win anything. I know that no one expected us to win the World Series in 1987 and 1991, and when we did it, it just made it all that much more special.

Minnesota fans are great. Not only are they knowledgeable about our local sports teams, but they stick by them. But, that doesn't mean that they're not fickle. They definitely need a winner for them to show up at the ballpark, I found that out first-hand! I think it's hard today for a lot of people to follow a team that's not winning. It's tough for a fan to go sit in a ballpark during the summer after the hard winters up here. When the sun shines, people want to enjoy the outdoors while they can. They appreciate it and feel that they've earned it. It seems that everyone has a cabin on a lake somewhere that they can go to, and if they don't, they probably have a relative who does. But when they are in those cabins, hunting and fishing, you can bet that they have their TVs and radios on - and are tuned in to a ball game.

I think that a lot of the sentiment against sports that is going on today has to do with money and free-agency. It's a big issue nowadays and it makes it kind of scary to think about what's in store for small markets like us. Back when I was a kid, we followed the Twins and Vikings season after season and got to know them it seemed, as if they were family. Today, with free agency, the fans feel burned when players that they rooted for leave to go somewhere else. And, it's hard for teams to keep a strong nucleus together for any length of time to be successful. So, it's tough for the fans to make an emotional investment in a team and its players when they know that it might change the next year.

I also think that sports have become a competitive business where people nowadays can follow not only the local players but their heroes from all over the country. When I was a kid, we hardly ever saw Mickey Mantle play on TV. But today, kids can see stars like Ken Griffey Jr. every other night. So, the media has made it easier for people to still be close to their heroes without actually going out to the ballpark. And, I think that has hurt the attendance, which affects the economics of the sport. Because of the big salaries in the game today, professional sports has moved from being a family affair to a corporate one. And that's too bad. The evolution of sports has turned a simple game into more about selling tickets, advertising, naming stadiums, and big corporations. But, if franchises want to survive, that's what has to happen I guess. Everyone seems to be upset at the players and the salaries today, but it's hard to fault them if the owners are willing to give them the money.

Unfortunately the Garnett contract situation blew everything up this year. I don't know, is it anyone's business? I mean it never used to be. I never had any idea what the heck Tony Oliva or Rod Carew's salaries were every year. I just loved them for what they did on the field and the joy they brought me when they hit one over the fence. I could give a crap what the heck they did off the field or how much money they made. But, today that's all different. Who knows what's in store for the next 50 years? It will definitely be very interesting. It's scary to think that football and baseball might be a thing of the past here in the near future, and thank goodness we got hockey back. I don't know, it's a tough call. A lot of people would rather see our tax dollars go toward education, which I would have to agree is a very valid argument.

But I think everything goes hand in hand, and by that I mean that in order to have kids doing well in school, they need positive role models and idols to follow, and who better than sports heroes. As a kid, the only opportunities that I had were all somehow related to sports - little league baseball, football, hockey, soccer, basketball, and what have you. Kids need sports because it's a positive influence in their lives that builds teamwork, a positive attitude, and self esteem. I think it goes right along with education, because they learn a lot of things out there that they wouldn't otherwise learn in the classroom.

This book is about heroes, and it's too bad that Ross couldn't go into the countless other unsung heroes on all the teams that weren't always in the limelight, because they were just as important. I think too that as a kid grows up and gets older and wiser, they realize that their childhood heroes were just athletes, and it was their moms and dads who were the real heroes, making them the people that they are. I'm optimistic about our future, and am glad that we can celebrate out past. I think that the concept for this book was really neat, and it was an idea that was long overdue. I really enjoyed reading about our rich sports heritage that we have here. It was a fun read and it brought back a lot of great memories of when I was a kid, and I think that's what sports is all about - great memories.

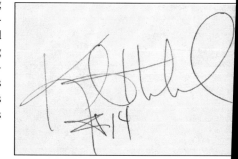

List of Works Cited

1. * Ross Bernstein: Interviews from over 100 Minnesota sports personalities and celebrities
2. "Hubert H. Humphrey Metrodome Souvenir Book": by Calvin Griffith, Jim Klobuchar, Halsey Hall, Muriel Humphrey Brown, Charles O. Johnson, Patrick Reusse, Joe Soucheray - compiled by Dave Mona. MSP Publications, Inc.
3. "Rashad," by Ahmad Rashad with Peter Bodo: Viking Press, 1988
4. "Gold Glory": by Richard Rainbolt: Ralph Turtinen Publishing, 1972
5. "Basketball Stars," by Nick Dolin, Chris Dolin & David Check: Black Dog and Leventhal Publishes, 1997
6. "The 100 Greatest Pitchers of All Time": Barnes & Noble Press
7. "The Harmon Killebrew Story": by Hal Butler: Juliann Messner Publishing
8. Star Tribune Article by Curt Brown - March 11, 1993 (An Investment of 26 Years Yields Nothing But Memories)
9. Minnesota Almanacs - various throughout 1970s
10. "The Official National Hockey League 75th Anniversary Commemorative Book": by Dan Diamond, NHL Publications, 1991.
11. "A Thinking Man's Guide to Pro Hockey": by Eskenazi, Gerald, E. P. Dutton, 1972.
12. "The Hockey Encyclopedia": by Fischler, Stan, and Shirley Fischler, Macmillan, 1983.
13. "NHL The World of Professional Hockey": by Jay Greenberg, On Frarik, and Gary Ronberg, Rutledge Press, 1981.
14. "The Pictorial History of Hockey" by Joseph Romain, and Dan Diamond, Gallery Books, 1987.
15. "The Sporting News Hockey Guide & Register": Sporting News Publishing Co., 1984-85, 1986-87, 1989-90.
16. "Season Review": ESPN Sports Almanac by Jerry Trecker, Total Sports Publications, 1983.
17. "NFL Football" (The Official Fans Guide) by Ron Smith, Collins Publishers, NFL Properties, 1995
18. "Unstoppable": The Story of George Mikan, the First NBA Superstar: by George Mikan and Joseph Oberle, published by Masters Press, Indianapolis, 1997.
19. "The Kid From Cuba" by James Terzian, Doubleday Press
20. "Twenty Five Seasons": The First Quarter Century With the Minnesota Twins by Dave Mona and Dave Jarzyna: Mona Publications
21. "Rod Carew": by Marshall Burchard: Longman Canada, Ltd., 1978
22. "Sid!" The Sports Legends, the Inside Scoops, and the Close Personal Friends: by Sid Hartman and Patrick Reusse - Voyager Press, 1997
23. "Good Timing": The Paul Molitor story, by Stuart Broomer: ECW Press
24. The Winfield Foundation publication
25. Sports Illustrated: article on the Minnesota Twins, May 22, 1997
26. "Kirby Puckett": by Bob Italia: Abdo and Daughters, 1992
27. "Season of Dreams": by Tom Kelly and Ted Robinson: Voyageur Press
28. "Kent Hrbek": by Jerry Carpenter & Steve Dimeglio: Abdo and Daughters, 1988
29. Star Tribune article: Kirby Puckett Weekend, May 23, 1997
30. Star Tribune article: 1987 Twins, Aug. 8, 1997
31. Star Tribune article: "Broten Lived Out a Dream" by Dan Barriero: Oct.16, 1996
32. The U.S. Hockey Hall of Fame Handbook
33. Pioneer Press: Dick Siebert article: "A molder of Champions," by Charley Walters
34. Pioneer Press: Dick Siebert article: "Siebert Built "U" Baseball," by Charley Hallman
35. Sun Times: Kevin McHale article: "He's Just Warming Up," by Phil Hersh
36. University of Minnesota Sports News: Chuck Mencel article: "Making His Mark Through Effort and Intelligence," by Len Levine
37. Press: Dick Siebert article: "From the Majors to Minnesota," by Jim Ramsburg
38. High Minnesota State High School Hockey Tournament Media Guide, 1997
39. "Tony-O," the Trials and Triumphs of Tony Oliva, by Tony Oliva with Bob Fowler: Hawthorne Books
40. "One Goal - A Chronicle of the 1980 US Olympic Hockey Team": by John Powers and Art Kaminsky: Harper Row, 1984
41. The US Olympic Hockey Guide -1996
42. "Players of Cooperstown": Publishing International
43. "Tarkenton": by Jim Klobuchar and Fran Tarkenton: Harper Publishing, 1976
44. "Winfield" - A Player's Life, by Dave Winfield with Tom Parker: WW Nortan, 1988
45. "Gagliardi of St John's": The Coach, the Man, the Legend: by Don Riley and John Gagliardi: R. Turtinen Publishing
46. Saint Johns University Football Media Guide, 1996
47. Star Tribune: North Stars article by Curt Brown - March 11, 1993
48. Star Tribune: North Stars article "An Investment of 26 Years Yields Nothing But Memories" - 1981
49. "Frank Viola": by Jerry Carpenter And Steve Dimeglio: Abdo and Daughters, 1988
50. Links Magazine - "Heroes of American Golf" March 1995, by Pamela Emory
51. Sports Illustrated: "Ready or Not" artcicle on Kevin Garnett, June 25, 1995
52. Dayton's Challenge Official Souvenir Program, 1997: (Tom Lehman article, by Ken Cohen)
53. North Stars Media Guides (various 1970s - 1990s)
54. "Before the Dome" - Baseball in Minnesota when the Grass was Real, by David Anderson: Nodin Press, 1993
55. Twins Magazine: "Home for Good" - Terry Steinbach article by Jim Bohem, July 1997
56. Twins Magazine: "Baseball Pioneers" article by Mark Engebretson, July 1997
57. Sports Illustrated Article oin Terry Steinbach, "Cold Sweet Home" (1-27-97)
58. Dog World: January 1997, "The Magic And Mystique" - by Roger Pinckney
59. John Beargrease Sled Dog Marathon Race Program - 1996
60. College Hockey Magazine: "Don Roberts Bids Farewell to Gustavus Adolphus," by Jim ueda - Free Lance Writer for the Mankato Free Press
61. Mpls.St. Pul Magazine, Aug. 1997 "North to the Pole" - Ann Bancroft Article
62. "Greg Lemond's Complete Book of Cycling," by Greg Lemond and Kent Gordis: G.P. utnam Publishing, 1987
63. "On to Nicollet," by Stew Thornley, Nodin Press, 1988
64. "Basketball's Original Dynasty," The History of the Lakers, by Stew Thornley, Nodin Press, 89
65. "The Christian Story": Christian Brothers, Inc. Press Release Information
66. "Gopher Hockey by the Hockey Gopher," by Ross Bernstein
67. "Minnesota Trivia," by Laurel Winter: Rutledge Hill Press, 1990
68. "Minnesota Awesome Almanac," by Jean Blashfield: B&B Publishing, 1993
69. The University of Minnesota Duluth Hockey Media Guide, 1997
70. "Gopher Sketchbook," by Al Papas, Jr.: Nodin Press, 1990
71. "NCAA Championships": The Official 1996 National Collegiate Championships R Records, by the National Collegiate Athletics Association
72. The Phoenix Coyotes Media Guide: 1997
73. "Kirby Puckett, I Love This Game": by Kirby Puckett: Harper Collins, 1993
74. The U.S. Olympic Committee, Olympian Report
75. The In-Fisherman Press Release: 1997
76. Canturbury Park Media Guide: 1997
77. Minnesota Daily: article on Tom Lehman, Jan. 19, 1995
78. Brainerd International Speedway Media Guide: 1997
79. Will Steger internet article: "Solo from the Pole"
80. Ann Bancroft biographical notes, Rhonda Grider Promotions
81. The Star Tribune Minnesota Sports Hall of Fame insert publication
82. Star Tribune: article on Grandma's Marathon: 6/97
83. Star Tribune: article on Kirby Puckett: May 23, 1997
84. Article: "Nicollet Park, Home of the Millers," by Dave Mona
85. "Lexington Park: Campy, The Duke, The Babe, and Oh, That Coliseum!," By Patrick Reusse
86. Babe Winkelman biography information, press release
87. The In Fisherman, press release
88. Star Tribune: articles on Gopher Baseball, June 15-17, 1956
89. Fran Tarkenton press releases: Washington Speakers Bureau
90. "Hockey": The Illustrated History, by Dan Diamond
91. Sports Illustrated: North Stars article, May 25, 1981
92. Sports Illustrated: North Stars article, June 1, 1981
93. "One Hundred Years of Hockey": by Brian McFarlane
94. "The Official NHL Stanley Cup Centenial ," by Dan Diamond
95. Minnesota Twins - 1978 Yearbook
96. "Can You Name That Team?" by David Biesel
97. Tribune: Various artiles from Janet Karvonen, March 16-22, 1978
98. Pioneer Press: Various artiles from Janet Karvonen, March 16-22, 1978
99. Janet Karvonen Basketball Camp Brochure
100. Tribune: Vikings article, Jan. 13, 1976
101. Sports Illustrated, Fran Tarkenton article, Jan 5, 1976
102. Tribune: Tarkenton article , Dec 29, 1975
103. Star Tribune: Bud Grant article, Jan 7, 1986
104. Star Tribune: Bud Grant article, Jan 28, 1984
105. Tribune: Kevin McHale article, March 20, 1980
106. Tribune: Chuck Mencel article, Feb 21, 1955
107. Star Tribune: Rickey Foggie article, Dec 22, 1985
108. Tribune: Mariucci article, March 13-14, 1984
109. University of Minnesota "Gopher" Year Books: 1954, 1955, 1956
110. Star Tribune: Gopher Hockey article, April 1-2, 1989
111. Links Letter: Patty Berg article, Feb. 1997
112. Country Club Golfer: July 1977, Feb. 1980
113. Golf Course Management: Dec. 1985, March 1986
114. The Senior Golfer: June 1988
115. The Memorial: May 1988
116. Fairway: Patty Berg article and interview 1989
117. Minnesota Golfer: Spring 1993
118. Links: March 1995
119. Duluth News Tribune and Herald: UMD Hockey artcle, March 25, 1984
120. The Sporting News: UMD Hockey article - April 2, 1984
121. Sports Illustrated: Rod Carew Cover Story article, July 16, 1977
122. "The Autumn Warrior," by Mikie Wilkinson, 1992
123. Ivory Tower: John Mariucci article - "The Coach Behind the Comeback," by Peter Vanderpoel, 1953
124. Ambassador Magazine: "Leveling the Playing Field" - Alan Page article, by Curt Brown, July, 1996
125. Minnesota Monthly Magazine: "Bent but Not Broken" - Alan page article, by Paul Levy, August 1996
126. Star Tribune: article on Alan Page - "Mindworks" by Misti Snow, May 25, 1993
127. Minneapolis Star: "Twice Down for Nine Count - St. John's Rallied" - Dec. 16, 1963
128. St. Cloud Times: John Gagliardi article - Nov. 4, 1963
129. Minneapolis Tribune: Gagliardi article - Nov. 29, 1963
130. "The Vikings: The First Fifteen Years," Minnesota Vikings Publications
131. "Obsession: Bill Musselman's Relentless Quest to Beat the Best "- by Heller: Bonus Books
132. Twins Yearbook: 30th Anniversary Edition - 1991
133. Article: "Year by Year with the Minnesota Twins": by Bill Morlock and Rick Little
134. Article: "How the Vikings Came to Be": by Jim Klobuchar
135. "Hockey Chicago Style: The History of the Blackhawks," by Paul Greenland: Sagamore Publishing
136. "No Time for Losing," by Fran Tarkenton: Revell Publishing, 1967
137. "Purple Hearts and Golden Memories," by Jim Klobuchar: Quality Sports Publications, 1995
138. Sports Illustrated Vikings artcicle: "In on a Win and a Prayer," - Jan. 5, 1976
139. Sports Illustrated Twins artcicle: "The Best of the Worst," - Aug. 30, 1982
140. Sports Illustrated: Vikings article: Jan. 13, 1976
141. Minnesota Department of Natural Resources: Fisheries - "Largest fish records"
142. Twin Cities Marathon Race Program, 1997
143. Grandmas Marathon Race Program, 1997
144. Jill Trenary biography press release: IMG
145. "Minnesota Vikings"- Professional Team Histories
146. "Minnesota Timberwolves" - Professional Sports Teams Histories
147. "Minnesota Twins" - Professional Sports Teams Histories
148. "Dallas Stars" - Professional Team Histories
149. The Minnesota Vikings Media Guides (various)
150. The Minnesota Twins Media Guides (various)
151. The Minnesota North Stars Media Guides (various)
152. The Minnesota Timberwolves Media Guides (various)
153. The Minnesota Kicks Media Guides (various)
154. The Minnesota Strikers Media Guides (various)
155. University of Minnesota Men's Athletics Media Guides: Football, Basketball, Hockey, Baseball, Track & Field, Golf, Swimming & Diving, Wrestling, gymnastics and Tennis
156. University of Minnesota Women's Athletics Media Guides: Basketball, Volleyball, Track & Field, Golf, Swimming & Diving, soccer, gymnastics, softball and Tennis